Kenya
a country study

Foreign Area Studies
The American University
Edited by
Harold D. Nelson
Research completed
June 1983

On the cover: Zebras, a familiar example of Kenya's abundant wildlife

Third Edition, 1983; First Printing, 1984

Library of Congress Cataloging in Publication Data
Main entry under title:

Kenya, a country study.

(Area handbook series) (DA pam ; 550-56)
"Research completed June 1983."
Rev. ed. of: Area handbook for Kenya / coauthors, Irving Kaplan [with] Margarita K. Dobert . . . [et al.].
2nd ed. 1976.
Bibliography: p.
Includes index.
1. Kenya. I. Nelson, Harold D. II. Kaplan, Irving, 1923-
Area handbook for Kenya. III. American University (Washington, D.C.). Foreign Area Studies.

IV. Series. V. Series: Da pam ; 550-56.
DT433.522.K46 1984 967.6′2 84-6420

Headquarters, Department of the Army
DA Pam 550-56

For sale by the Superintendent of Documents, U.S. Government Printing Office
Washington, D.C. 20402

Foreword

This volume is one of a continuing series of books prepared by Foreign Area Studies, The American University, under the Country Studies/Area Handbook Program. The last page of this book provides a listing of other published studies. Each book in the series deals with a particular foreign country, describing and analyzing its economic, national security, political, and social systems and institutions and examining the interrelationships of those systems and institutions and the ways that they are shaped by cultural factors. Each study is written by a multidisciplinary team of social scientists. The authors seek to provide a basic insight and understanding of the society under observation, striving for a dynamic rather than a static portrayal of it. The study focuses on historical antecedents and on the cultural, political, and socioeconomic characteristics that contribute to cohesion and cleavage within the society. Particular attention is given to the origins and traditions of the people who make up the society, their dominant beliefs and values, their community of interests and the issues on which they are divided, the nature and extent of their involvement with the national institutions, and their attitudes toward each other and toward the social system and political order within which they live.

The contents of the book represent the views, opinions, and findings of Foreign Area Studies and should not be construed as an official Department of the Army position, policy, or decision, unless so designated by other official documentation. The authors have sought to adhere to accepted standards of scholarly objectivity. Such corrections, additions, and suggestions for factual or other changes that readers may have will be welcomed for use in future new editions.

William Evans-Smith
Director, Foreign Area Studies
The American University
Washington, D.C. 20016

Acknowledgments

The authors are grateful to those individuals in various governmental, international, and academic organizations who gave of their time, data, special knowledge, and authoritative perspective on Kenya. Gratitude is also extended to members of the Foreign Area Studies support staff who contributed directly to the preparation of this book. These persons include Kathryn R. Stafford, Dorothy M. Lohmann, and Andrea T. Merrill, who edited the manuscript, and Harriett R. Blood, who prepared the graphics with the assistance of Farah Ahannavard. The authors appreciate as well the assistance provided by Gilda V. Nimer, librarian; Ernest A. Will, publications manager; Eloise W. Brandt and Wayne W. Olsen, administrative assistants; and Margaret Quinn and John Dupont, who typed the manuscript.

The aesthetic touches that enhance the book's appearance are the work of Marty Ittner, whose illustrations appear on the title pages of the chapters, and Farah Ahannavard, who illustrated the cover. The inclusion of photographs has been made possible in part by the generosity of various individuals and public and private agencies. The authors acknowledge their indebtedness especially to those persons who contributed original material not previously published.

Contents

List of Figures

Preface

This study replaces the *Area Handbook for Kenya*, which was completed in late 1975. During the nearly 12 years of independence since 1963, the country had been able to maintain a substantial degree of political stability, a relatively open society, and a high rate of economic growth. Some of its old problems persisted, however, and several new ones had been generated. In the period since 1975 a number of developments have reflected increasing political tensions and economic difficulties. The death in 1978 of the country's first president, veteran leader Jomo Kenyatta, and the variety of politico-economic problems that have ensued warrant a fresh look at Kenyan society and its role in world affairs.

Like its predecessor, *Kenya: A Country Study* seeks to provide a compact and objective exposition of dominant social, economic, political, and national security aspects and to give the reader an idea of the forces involved at this time in the country's history. In presenting this new study, the authors have relied primarily on official reports of governmental and international organizations, journals, newspapers, and materials reflecting recent field research by scholarly authorities. Detailed information on many aspects of the society was not always readily available, however, and gaps in the data, as well as varied interpretations of certain matters, existed among some of the sources consulted. Where appropriate, such gaps and differences have been noted in the text. Should readers require greater detail on core area topics, the authors have noted the availability of amplifying materials in bibliographic statements at the end of each chapter. Full references to these and other sources used or considered are included in the detailed Bibliography.

Place-names generally have been spelled in accordance with those established by the United States Board on Geographic Names in its current *Official Standard Names Gazetteer* of March 1978. The gazetteer was prepared with the cooperation of the Survey of Kenya and Kenya's Standing Committee on Geographical Names. In the handling of African ethnic names and languages, the authors of *Kenya: A Country Study* have omitted the class prefixes characteristic of those languages that occasionally appear in other contemporary publications. Thus Kamba, rather than Akamba, has been used as the term for that ethnic group and Swahili rather than Kiswahili for the language spoken by many Kenyans.

An effort has been made to limit the use of foreign and technical words and phrases. When this has not been appropriate, such terms have been defined briefly where they first appear in any chapter or reference has been made to the Glossary, which is included at the back of the book for the reader's convenience.

Although Kenya's monetary system does not include a pound note, the government's statistics are frequently expressed in Kenya pounds (K£ equals KSh20). That practice has also been followed in this study.

All measurements are presented in the metric system. A conversion table will assist those readers who may not be familiar with metric equivalents (see table 1, Appendix).

Country Profile

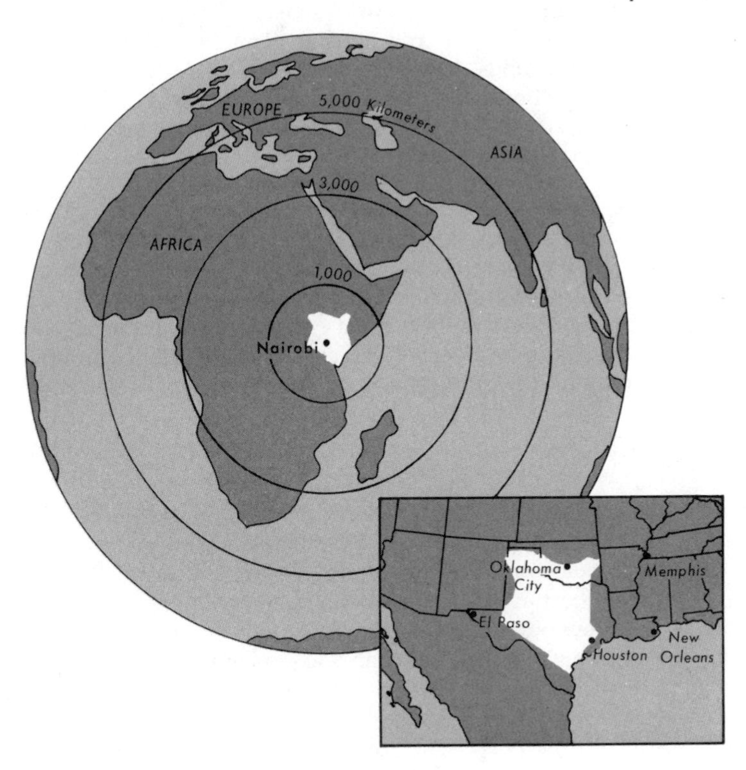

Country

Formal Name: Republic of Kenya.

Short Form: Kenya.

Term for Citizens: Kenyans.

Capital: Nairobi.

Independence Achieved: December 12, 1963.

Flag: Black, red, and green horizontal bands from top to bottom, separated by narrow white stripes; warrior's shield and crossed spears centered on flag.

Geography

Size: Total area of 580,367 square kilometers includes 11,230 square kilometers of water, mainly in Lake Rudolf (known in Kenya as Lake Turkana) and Kenya's portion of Lake Victoria.

Topography: Seven geographic divisions encompassed in two macrodivisions consisting of elevated southwestern one-third of country and outer two-thirds that form arc of low plateaus and plains. Land rises gradually westward from narrow coastal plain in series of plateaus culminating in highlands area, bisected north to south by great Rift Valley. Eastern section of highlands contains country's highest point, Mount Kenya (5,200 meters). Most of north and northeast consists of semiarid and arid plains.

Climate: Less than 15 percent of country, mainly in coastal and southwestern highland regions, receives fairly reliable rainfall of 760 millimeters or more. Most of country experiences two wet and two dry seasons. Total rainfall highly erratic, particularly in areas of low precipitation. Intermittent droughts affect entire country, especially north and northeast. Bracing temperate climate in highlands; high temperature and humidity in coastal area; arid areas generally hot and humidity low.

Society

Population: Census of 1979 enumerated population of 15.3 million, of which 98.6 percent African; by mid-1982 population estimated at nearly 18 million. Average annual growth rate of 4 percent in late 1970s and early 1980s, highest in world. Roughly 15 percent of population urban, much of it concentrated in Nairobi and Mombasa areas. Rural population densities ranged from less than one person per square kilometer in northern and northeastern districts traversed by pastoral nomads to more than 300 persons per square kilometer in parts of central Kenya near Nairobi and parts of western Kenya near Lake Victoria.

Ethnic Groups and Languages: Between 30 and 40 indigenous ethnic groups recognized by 1979 census. Number of African languages (grouped into three different language families) corresponds roughly to number of ethnic groups; sections of several groups speak different languages; some languages used as mother tongues by more than one ethnic group. Official languages, English and Swahili. Five ethnic groups make up more than 70 percent of African population: Kikuyu (more than 21 percent), Luhya (14 percent), Luo (nearly 13 percent), Kamba (more than 11 percent), and Kalenjin (nearly 11 percent). In 1979 census, Asians, Europeans, Arabs, and non-Kenyan Africans made up slightly more than 1 percent of population.

Religion: In 1980 about 73 percent of all Kenyans professed some form of Christianity but only about 62 percent affiliated with a church; smaller proportion engaged to some degree in religious activity. Of all affiliated Christians, more than 31 percent Roman Catholics; nearly 28 percent members of independent African churches; more than 27 percent members of wide range of Protestant churches having institutional connections with North American and European denominations. About

6 percent of population Muslims; about 18.9 percent thought to be adherents of indigenous religions.

Education: Seven-year primary-school system (Standards 1 through 7); no fees, but attendance not compulsory; in early 1980s roughly 95 percent of children between ages of six and 12 in school. Passing of Certificate of Primary Education examination at reasonably high level required for enrollment in secondary school; substantially smaller proportion of students in 13- to 18-year age-group reflects high admission standards and need to pay fees; another sharp drop after first four years (Forms I through IV) of secondary school. Only students passing East African Certificate of Education examinations (ordinary or 0 level) go on to upper secondary school (Forms V and VI) and, after passing advanced (A level) examinations, to University of Nairobi or other institutions of higher education. School system controlled, and to considerable degree supported by, central government; private schools exist at primary and secondary levels; many schools constructed and maintained by local communities under *harambee* (see Glossary) program. In early 1980s literacy rate for males over age of 15 estimated at roughly 65 percent; for females about 35 percent.

Health: Health service infrastructure fairly effective but suffers from urban-rural and regional imbalance, as well as shortage of medical personnel at all levels. Malaria and other tropical ailments, childhood diseases, and parasitic and venereal infections remain serious health problems, complicated by inadequate sanitary conditions and, in some areas, malnutrition.

Economy

Salient Features: Private enterprise-oriented economy. Extensive government participation through variety of parastatal agencies, but heavy reliance on private sector for economic development. Foreign investment welcomed; multinational corporations deeply involved in agriculture, manufacturing, and financial operations; larger multinational undertakings often have government equity participation. Country's principal natural resource: agricultural land. About 85 percent of rural population engaged in agricultural and pastoral activities.

Agriculture: Large number of subsistence farmers, but substantial number of farms produce cash crops; pastoralism overwhelmingly a subsistence occupation. Agricultural sector largest contributor to gross domestic product (GDP—see Glossary); also accounts for largest share of exports. Production of basic foodstuffs usually meets domestic needs. Major crops: maize, wheat, other cereals, pulses, potatoes, coffee, tea, pineapples, sugarcane, cotton, pyrethrum, sisal, and tobacco.

Manufacturing: Diversified range of consumer goods, some intermediate goods; mainly for domestic market. Modern manufacturing developed principally as import substitution industry based largely on processing imported materials. In 1983 almost two-thirds of enterprises still in latter category. Sector accounted for about 13 percent of GDP but employed only about 2 percent of national labor force.

Mining: Wide variety of minerals; as of mid-1983 none had international importance in significant quantities. Principal mineral foreign exchange earners: soda ash, fluorite, and limestone (processed into cement).

Energy: Principal indigenous energy sources: wood and hydrothermally and geothermally generated power. Wood provides most of energy used by rural population. Domestic electric power source important and gradually increasing, but imported oil and petroleum products provide overwhelming amount of energy required by modern sector of economy.

Foreign Trade: Principal exports by value: agricultural commodities (coffee, tea) and petroleum products. Main imports: crude petroleum, industrial materials, machinery, and transport equipment. Principal destinations for exports: Britain, Federal Republic of Germany (West Germany), and Uganda; principal sources of imports: Britain, West Germany, Japan, and Saudi Arabia.

Currency: Kenya shilling (KSh) equal in mid-1983 to about US$0.08 (US$1 equaled about KSh13). Values and financial data often given in Kenya pounds (K£), a denomination not issued as currency; K£ equal to KSh20.

Fiscal Year: July 1 through following June 30. Fiscal year July 1, 1983, through June 30, 1984, expressed as FY 1983/84.

Transportation

Railroads: Government-owned Kenya Railways in 1983 comprised 2,060 kilometers of one-meter-gauge single track; mainly served highly populated zone from east of Nairobi northwestward through Nakuru and Eldoret to Ugandan border. System consisted of main line (1,085 kilometers) from Mombasa to border, where connected with Uganda Railways, and seven branch lines (975 kilometers) mostly serving areas of Kenya's populated zone. Branch line in southeast connected with Tanzanian railroad system, but inoperative since 1977 because of border closing by Tanzania.

Roads: Extensive officially designated road system of about 52,675 kilometers; 6,540 kilometers paved (1981); additional 100,000 kilometers of tracks and elemental roads in rural areas. International trunk roads (3,600 kilometers, two-thirds paved) connected with road systems in neighboring countries. National trunk-road net of about 2,785 kilometers (two-thirds paved) between main urban centers. Primary road system (about 7,750 kilometers, one-fourth paved) linked important provincial centers. Remaining some 32,000 kilometers of roads served local needs.

Ports and Shipping: Major port of Kilindini at Mombasa best equipped port on East African coast. In 1983 facilities included 14 deep-water berths for general, bulk, and container cargo; tanker berths for crude and refined petroleum; large dry dock for vessels up to 18,000 gross registered tons. Port equipment and storage space modern, extensive. Harbor permitted entry of large aircraft carriers. In early 1980s annual cargo averaged about 8 million tons; exports mostly dry cargo; about two-thirds to three-quarters of imports were bulk petroleum and oil products.

Civil Aviation: Government-owned Kenya Airways provided domestic and international services; latter also furnished by about 30 international airlines. Two international airports, at Nairobi and Mombasa; developed domestic airports at Kisumu, Malindi, and Nairobi (latter used mainly by charter operations). More than 200 airstrips throughout country (some paved); access by airplane to many towns, tourist attractions, and isolated farming areas.

Government and Politics

Government: Constitution of 1964 created republic with centralized form of government. Constitution revised and updated in 1969. Popularly elected president names vice president and members of cabinet, who must be members of unicameral National Assembly (158 elected and 12 appointed members). All political candidates must be members of Kenya African National Union (KANU), only legal party since 1982.

Administrative Divisions: Provincial commissioners, answerable to president, administer seven provinces and Nairobi Area. Lower level administrative units are 40 districts, further subdivided into divisions, locations, and sublocations. Elective municipal, town, and county councils have limited powers delegated by national government.

Judicial System: Laws based on Kenyan Constitution and statutes, unrepealed acts of British Parliament applicable to Kenya, and English common law. Court hierarchy consists of Court of Appeal, High Court, resident and district magistrates' courts, and kadhis' courts concerned with Muslim personal law.

Politics: Daniel arap Moi elected Kenya's second president after death of Jomo Kenyatta (August 1978), overcoming opposition from Kenyatta's followers among powerful Kikuyu ethnic group. Moi initially highly popular as result of conciliatory policies toward all groups. Emerging economic and social strains, underscored by air force coup attempt of August 1982, spurred Moi to shore up his position by insisting on personal political loyalty. Early elections called by Moi for September 1983; his control of KANU made reelection certain. New cabinet more responsive to his direction was anticipated.

Foreign Relations: Active in Organization of African Unity and Commonwealth of Nations. Moderate, pragmatic foreign policy; nonaligned but closely associated with Western nations for development aid and investments. Ties with United States expanded after conclusion of Facilities Access Agreement (June 1980).

National Security

Armed Forces: In 1983 Kenyan military establishment of nearly 16,000 personnel composed of army, about 13,000; navy, about 650; and air force, being rebuilt to strength of about 2,000. Air force temporarily placed under army command after airmen involved in 1982 coup attempt; reorganized air force known as 82 Air Force. Military service voluntary; no organized reserves.

Major Tactical Units: Army included five infantry battalions, two armored battalions, one armored reconnaissance battalion, one air cavalry battalion, two artillery battalions, and support units. Air force had one fighter-bomber squadron, one light strike squadron, two transport squadrons, and one training squadron; 29 combat aircraft in 1982 inventory; serviceability poor after coup attempt caused technicians to be dismissed from air force. Navy included seven patrol vessels.

Foreign Military Assistance: Exclusive reliance on Western sources of weapons and training. Britain has maintained close military ties since independence and has supplied training, as well as most army and air force equipment. United States became important partner in late 1970s; Kenya purchased jet aircraft and helicopters; concluded Facilities Access Agreement in June 1980 allowing conditional American military access to certain Kenyan airfield and port facilities. Israel, France, and Commonwealth countries also have sold equipment and provided training.

Defense Expenditures: In FY 1979/80 defense spending KSh817 million, or 16.4 percent of total central government expenditure.

Police and Paramilitary Forces: Kenya Police, a national force, included approximately 14,000 regular personnel and semiautonomous 1,800-man paramilitary General Service Unit; administrative police under local control maintained law and order in outlying areas.

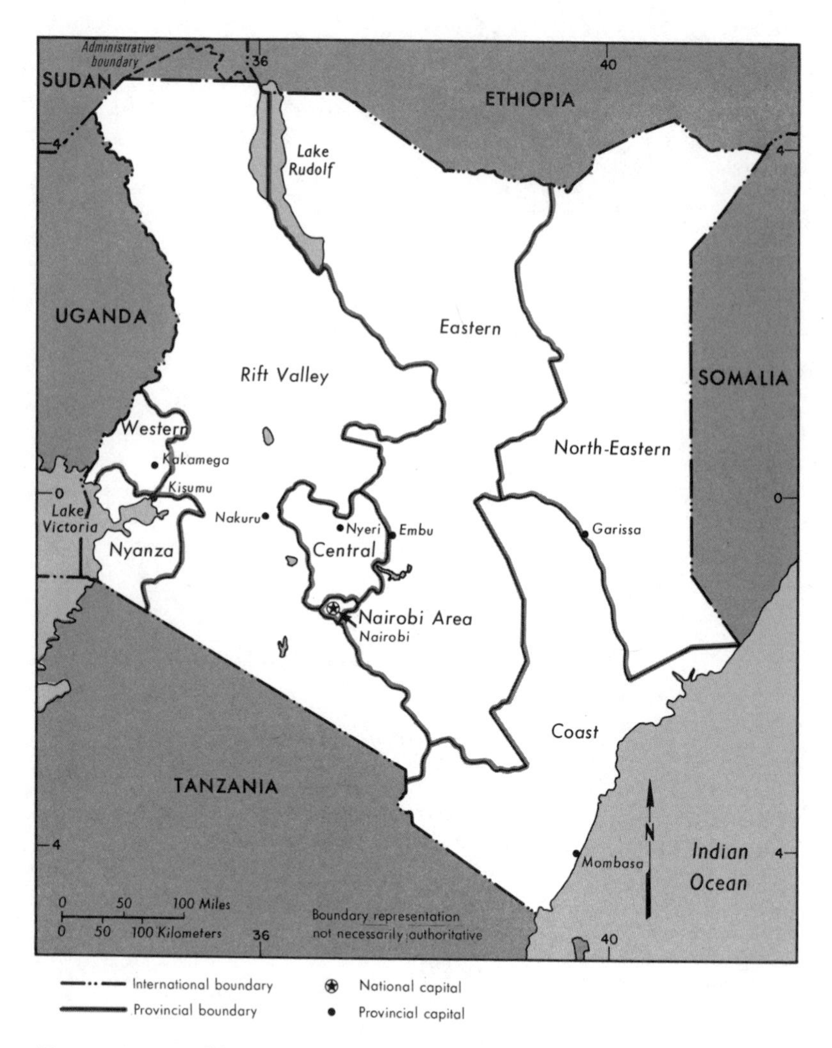

Figure 1. Republic of Kenya, 1983

Introduction

UNIQUE IN MANY ASPECTS among the developing countries of the African continent, Kenya has long been a subject of international interest. Scientific evidence in the form of some of the oldest hominid fossils ever found suggests to paleontologists, such as the famous Leakey family, that the eastern shores of Lake Rudolf in northern Kenya were probably the cradle of mankind millions of years ago. Expressed more simply in biblical terms by a popular modern writer, the area "surely was once part of the Garden of Eden."

Modern Kenya, the heartland of East Africa, encompasses some 580,000 square kilometers, an area slightly smaller than the state of Texas. Bisected by the equator, its southeastern frontier is washed by the Indian Ocean and its southwestern reaches by vast Lake Victoria (see fig. 1). Towering mountains, forests, lakes, mangrove swamps, arid plains that include a desert, and many national parks and game preserves teeming with majestic wildlife mark the country as a showcase of scenic wonders. For nearly a century these attributes have attracted a growing influx of foreign visitors eager to experience the thrill of safari, a term that has virtually become synonymous with the country's name. In the early years adventurers armed with rifles came to bag impressive animal specimens for their trophy rooms. The quest continues, but the guns have been replaced by cameras. Kenyans have capitalized on the striking variety of their topography, climate, and bountiful wildlife, making tourism an important earner of foreign capital.

International attraction to Kenya, however, did not begin with the advent of safaris. This interest dates instead from at least the first century A.D. when the indigenous Cushitic-speaking Africans, who had occupied the area from about 1000 B.C., were visited by Arab traders. Proximity to Arabia eventually prompted coastal colonization, and Arab and Persian settlements were founded there in the eighth century A.D. By then, Bantu and Nilotic peoples had also moved into the area. The Swahili language, a mixture of Bantu and Arabic, developed as a lingua franca for trade between the various peoples of the coastal region. The Arabs were followed by Portuguese explorers in 1498, by Islamic control under the imam of Oman in the 1600s, and by British colonization in the nineteenth century.

Major developments in the precolonial years impressed a fundamental character on the area's economic and cultural patterns as well as on interethnic relations. To some degree, events and processes in the country's early recorded history have had a continuing influence on the entire national culture. But for the great bulk of the people, especially the African leaders who have guided Kenya through its development period, the country's colonial heritage has had the greatest impact.

As a progressing political entity, Kenya is still in its infancy. First organized in 1895 as the East Africa Protectorate within the internationally recognized British sphere of influence, the territory provided the British a secure route from the Indian Ocean to higher priority inland acquisitions. To aid in this process, white settlement in the cool, fertile Kenya Highlands was encouraged, and large numbers of Asians from the Indian subcontinent were imported as indentured laborers to build a railroad through the territory to landlocked Uganda. Although London's intent was to ensure coexistence between the white settlers and the indigenous Africans, this aim was unacceptable to the British immigrants who shared a dream of turning the territory into a "white man's country." As a consequence, increasing demands by the settlers gradually alienated the territory's most fertile land to the Europeans. By the early twentieth century the settlers had gained limited yet significant representation in the administration of their interests. The Asian community was barely represented and the Africans not at all. In 1920 the East Africa Protectorate was officially annexed as a British colony and given its present name.

In the course of the colonial experience, a number of economic, governmental, and judicial institutions were developed in common with the whole of British East Africa, which included the neighboring colonies of Uganda and Tanganyika (present-day Tanzania). Among these were a common market, currency, appeals court, and railroad and harbor administrations. Kenya, however, differed from the other colonies inasmuch as it had a European community large enough to dominate local political affairs and because it soon became the most industrialized of the three. The moves toward institutional commonality fell into disarray and after independence were abandoned.

Colonial society in Kenya was marked by clear physical, linguistic, and cultural distinctions among the indigenous Africans, the Asians, and the Europeans (as all white people were—and still are—designated). The political, economic, and social status of each of these groups stood in inverse relation to its numbers. The Europeans (largely persons of British origin) always constituted less than 1 percent of the total population, but they were politically dominant and insisted on their social superiority. The European settlers in this African environment were farmers and ranchers or businessmen and the purveyors of services who catered to the needs of the agriculturists. The Asians, roughly 2 to 3 percent of the population, were generally involved in urban occupations, mainly commercial activities. After an early and unsuccessful effort to compete for political power with the Europeans, the Asians settled for their place in the middle of the economic pyramid and concerned themselves with their own communal affairs, maintaining only the most public and necessary social relationships with the other communities.

The Africans—96 to 97 percent of the colony's population—remained largely subsistence farmers and pastoral herders or agricultural and domestic laborers, although there were increasing exceptions in the later colonial period. They exercised little or no power on the national scene, were generally at the lower end of the income scale, and were considered by Europeans and Asians alike as social and cultural inferiors.

Although strongly egalitarian in their own social order, Africans for many years acceded to their place in the stratified colonial society because of their pronounced ethnic fragmentation, their initial uncertainty about European intentions, and the potential available to them. Culturally and linguistically diverse, the African population was composed of 30 to 40 distinct ethnic groups ("tribes" in the language of the colonial authorities and a term that has persisted even in independent Kenya). There was little or no relationship between many of the African ethnic groups during the precolonial period; they were either too far apart to have contact with one another, or their mode of life was so different that there was no significant competition for territory. During the colonial era ethnic boundaries were established and, except for some mixing in border areas and urban centers, each African group stayed primarily in a specific region to which its cultural way of life was well adapted. Most Africans thus were barely touched by the colonial economy and society. But the Kikuyu, the most numerous of Kenya's African peoples, became an important exception to this general pattern because of their proximity to the main areas of European settlement in the highlands and Nairobi, the capital city.

In the aftermath of World War I, African interest in the local political process emerged tentatively, especially among the Kikuyu in Nairobi but also among the second largest ethnic group, the Luo. Awareness of their perceived inferior status and a growing determination to alter it were sparked by the harsh wartime experience, continuing losses of land to white settlers, intensified tax and labor demands by the European society, and the spread of education by missionaries.

Direct political participation was not achieved until 1944, when the Kenya African Union (KAU)—the colony's first source of real African nationalism—was formed. Founded as a vehicle to attain the common goal of a united African majority, the KAU never achieved much popular support except among the Kikuyu, whose strong cultural unity had already marked them as the first of the indigenous African ethnic groups to regard themselves as one people. Although the KAU's political approach was generally moderate, its eventual demand for African access to their lost lands—the fertile "White Highlands"—became a revolutionary issue. Because the government was dependent on the production of the white settlers to attain economic development of Kenya, the KAU's demand received little consideration.

After World War II, African political awareness grew, and dissatisfaction with the social, political, and economic order intensified. In the postwar years, when demands for independence swept the continent, the Kikuyu provided most of the leadership, the participants, and the victims as African discontent erupted in the Mau Mau movement, an event of international concern that left an enduring mark on

Kenyan society. Generally interpreted as a rebellion against British colonial rule, violence against the colony's Europeans was insignificant compared with that leveled against fellow Kikuyu in response to the growing disarray of the traditional system of land tenure generated by rapidly increasing population pressures. The state of emergency declared in 1952 by the British government persisted for eight years before the bloody civil war of the Mau Mau period was brought under control.

In the aftermath, the British instituted a program of land reform but banned African political organizations at the national level until 1960. Jomo Kenyatta, the Kikuyu president of the KAU and for many years the leader and symbol of the struggle for independence, was detained by the British and charged with managing the Mau Mau movement. Found guilty in 1953 by the court, a verdict regarded by most Kenyans as a miscarriage of justice, he was incarcerated until August 1961. In his absence the British government began orderly preparations for the advent of Kenyan independence, but ultimate transfer of political authority required the structuring of organized political activity. The African peoples' sole claim to unity lay in their common demand for majority rule, although many anticipated the opportunity to reclaim land in the economically advantageous "White Highlands." In response to London's call for representative political parties, the small groups of pastoral peoples near this economic prize joined coastal Africans who resented the Kikuyu and the Luo and formed the Kenya African Democratic Union (KADU). A second party, the Kenya African National Union (KANU), was organized by the Kikuyu and the Luo with help from most of the other African agriculturists and their urban brethren. Upon his release from detention, Kenyatta became KANU's leader.

After a brief interval of coalition government between the two parties and development of safeguards for the European and Asian minorities, the British conceded that December 1963 was an appropriate time to relinquish their control over the East African colony. KANU's proven electoral strength and its leader's moderate approach assured Kenyatta his role as the sovereign country's first prime minister. A year later when Kenya opted for status as a republic within the Commonwealth of Nations, he became the new nation's first president.

Under the guidance of the charismatic Kenyatta, who served as head of state and chief executive for the next 15 years, Kenya drew international attention as a model of pro-Western, capitalist success and political stability. Surrounded by neighboring countries that were actual or potential sources of instability and conflict, Kenya stood out as an island of moderation and peaceful progress in a sea of unrest. The promised drive to place Africans in positions of authority in both government and private enterprise hitherto filled by Europeans and Asians was handled pragmatically to reward the Kenyan majority without encouraging opportunities for minority critics. Although pursuing a policy of economic and labor "Africanization," significant participation by Europeans and Asians was accepted or at least tolerated in the interest of the public welfare. Nationalization of the economic means of production, an approach frequently used in other newly independent countries, was avoided. The government entered the economic field through the formation of certain parastatal enterprises, and the holdings of non-Africans who chose not to continue under a changing pattern of Kenyan society were gradually purchased by well-off Africans, including vast segments of the prized highlands.

With national development a primary goal, the government promoted rapid economic growth through public investment, encouragement of smallholder agricultural production, and incentives for private (often foreign) investment. In the first decade of independence, gross domestic product (GDP—see Glossary) grew at an annual average of more than 6 percent. Agricultural production increased by more than 4 percent per year, stimulated by the redistribution of former European estates to smallholders, the rapid diffusion of new crop strains, and the opening up of new areas to cultivation. In the social area, improvements in the availability of health services and education were undertaken.

Traditional Kenyan society contained strong elements of economic and political egalitarianism, and all Kenyans were expected to cooperate in a mutual sharing of benefits and to cooperate in a variety of contexts. This communal, cooperative spirit was constantly evoked by Kenyatta and his government officials in exhortations to the people to work together in the spirit of *harambee*, the national motto meaning "let us all pull together." Derived from an African phrase used by gangs of laborers when heavy jobs were to be tackled, it was placed in bold letters on the country's coat of arms and served as a standard against which the performance of government employees, private workers, and peasants was to be measured. Building on this foundation, the government sought to incorporate from any source ideas or principles that were deemed practical and relevant to Kenyan needs. It maintained a practical, independent attitude and did not accept uncritically the tenets of either Marxian socialism or laissez-faire capitalism.

Although the country stood out as one of Africa's steady achievers, the Kenyatta era was not devoid of some elements of discontent. Some of the criticism stemmed from the marked change in socioeconomic status achieved by the new African elite. High positions in the political and administrative systems had provided good incomes to their incumbents. They had also given some enterprising politicians and bureaucrats the knowledge and opportunity to invest in agriculture and in industrial and commercial acitivities. But the regime's detractors were usually less critical of such entrepreneurship, concentrating instead on allegations that some politicians and their kin had benefited from privileged access to good land as well as illegal enterprise and corruption.

The chances of achieving the higher political positions at the national level depended on developing a local power base, winning elections, and gaining acceptance by Kenyatta and his closest advisers. Although not necessarily related to the president by blood or marriage, this loyal entourage was commonly referred to as the Kenyatta "family."

A number of Kenyan critics of the system of government under Kenyatta expressed their arguments in terms of opposition to self-aggrandizement by an elite at the expense of the masses. The president and his "family" tried to accommodate the strong tendency to organize political interests in ethnic terms but sought to prevent the expression of ethnicity in ways that might lead to disintegration of the polity, threaten the position of the "family," or pose barriers to national economic development. These factors explained the evolution of the system of strong central government, a system that operated in a firm, no-nonsense manner.

An important factor affecting the degree of political freedom during the Kenyatta era was the president's conception, derived from the style of decisionmaking characteristic of Kikuyu elders, that policy decisions ought to be based on consensus and that once achieved, such consensus should not be breached. Violations of any explicitly reached or implicitly understood consensus put the violator outside the pale and were therefore subject to sanctions. As he grew older, Kenyatta became affectionately known to his people as "Mzee," a Swahili word for elder and a term loosely translated as the "Old Man."

Although he recognized the need to deal with what his critics regarded as maldistribution of wealth and the problems that stemmed from such inequality, he remained committed to a development policy that stressed growth for his nation. This policy was based on the assumption that in the long run, growth would provide the wherewithal to cope with the problems of economic justice and equity. Allegations of self-interest leveled against his regime from time to time had little noticeable effect on him, for Kenyatta knew that self-interest had never been alien to traditional African values. It was not unusual for Africans in a traditional setting to attempt to maximize their power and wealth and to try to keep what they had been able to gain. Usually, however, it was not the individual alone who benefited but rather his kin group or community. Indeed, if they did not share, the individual could not rely on their support for personal political and economic enterprises. The difference in modern times was that the range of power and wealth had become much greater, and their accumulation markedly distinguished a successful person from an unsuccessful one.

When the octogenarian Kenyatta died in August 1978, Daniel arap Moi, the country's vice president for 12 years, assumed office as interim president in accordance with the provisions of the Constitution. He became head of state and chief executive in his own right the following October when he was elected president of KANU and designated as its sole nominee for president of the republic. A member of the minority Kalenjin ethnic group, the new leader capitalized on his long-term experience in the upper echelons of government and sidestepped Kikuyu and Luo opposition mounted behind the scenes against his role as Kenyatta's chosen successor.

Assuming control of the government, Moi was confronted with a number of social, political, and economic problems. Some of them were functions of factors over which his government could exercise little or no control. Others had been dealt with tangentially by his predecessor or not at all. His first moves included the launching of a campaign to eliminate corruption in the bureaucracy and the large government corporations. This was followed by a consolidation of his power base, facilitated by the 1979 elections for the National Assembly, in which many anti-Moi members were unseated. With his extensive training under the late "Father of the Nation" and his own open style of government, Moi entered the 1980s seemingly secure in his political position. But he warned his people in a statement after the parliamentary elections that "the 1980s will be difficult years, mainly because of external forces," and forecast that period as "a time of austerity."

The basis for the president's somber view was the distinct slump in the rate of economic growth that had started during the last years of the Kenyatta era. In 1973 a worldwide economic slump had begun to limit capital available for national development, and the substantial rise in the cost of importing petroleum essential to Kenya's industry and agriculture had not been offset by the country's export earnings. Moreover, at about the same time, Kenya's economic and political relations with its East African neighbors had deteriorated, and Tanzania and Uganda had contributed less and less to its foreign trade. The rate of growth had slowed, unemployment had risen, and real per capita income had begun to decline.

Moi's prediction of difficulties ahead was certainly appropriate, but external forces have been only partly to blame. Kenya's basic problem—one of long standing—is its high rate of population growth, estimated in 1983 to be the world's highest at about 4 percent annually. This portends that the country's population—estimated at nearly 18 million in mid-1982—will double every 18 years. This prospect is a disquieting threat in a country where the economy is keyed essentially to agricultural output, where 85 percent of its people depend in some manner on agriculture for their livelihood, and where only about 20 percent of the land is classified as potentially arable. Because the arable land is the most densely populated, mounting population pressures have resulted in further subdivision and landlessness in areas of high potential and settlement in semiarid regions not well suited to farming. The production of food crops thus faces serious constraints, and that reality has imparted its toll on real GDP, which has been growing at a rate of only about one-half that of the population increase.

The rapid growth of population has also compounded the worrisome problem of unemployment, unofficially approaching 30 percent of the country's work force. Unemployment is higher in the major towns and cities where the wage-earning sector has been hard pressed to absorb the burdens associated with increasing urban migration. In the course of several years of economic decline, Kenya has suffered from chronic balance of payments deficits, erratic international prices for its export commodities, a reduction in the growth of profitable tourism, an escalating energy bill, and persistently inefficient parastatal activity. The demand for social services, such as those of education and health, has risen correspondingly with the growth of population, placing added pressures on the budget and reducing funds available for national development.

As Kenya's economic difficulties mounted during the early 1980s, a concomitant climate of social unrest was joined by vague political rumblings. Cabinet reshuffles occurred to defuse dissent in government circles, and positive—if limited—moves to assuage public concern were undertaken or at least promised. The attempted coup d'etat mounted by air force personnel in August 1982 was rapidly contained, but international attention was again focused on Kenya—this time raising questions about its political stability. Since the abortive coup, international aid agencies and Western donors have come forward with needed capital and foreign exchange in recognition of the country's economic plight and political vulnerability. A more direct United States interest in Kenya's future has arisen since the Facilities Access Agreement of 1980 was concluded between Nairobi and Washington in conjunction with other measures to protect the strategic oil supply line from the Middle East's Persian Gulf through the Indian Ocean.

Amid the domestic frustrations that have slowed Kenya's efforts at national development, Moi has moved adroitly to deter or counter perceived threats to his style of leadership. Calling for national parliamentary elections to be held in late September 1983, more than a year earlier than decreed by the Constitution, he appeared in midyear to be moving to strengthen his political backing for a new approach in resolving the challenges facing his country. In anticipation of the outcome, the African president has already exhorted his fellow Kenyans to accept and promote a new national philosophy of "peace, love, and unity." When he assumed the presidency after the death of Kenyatta, Moi had stressed continuity of his predecessor's policies through the slogan of *nyayo* (Swahili for footprints or footsteps). Five years later it appeared that the footsteps he expected Kenyans to follow in future years were those of Daniel arap Moi.

* * *

On August 29, 1983, two months after research and writing of this study were completed, Moi was automatically returned to office for a second five-year term as president of the republic. According to the Constitution, the president must be a member of the National Assembly and consequently must stand for reelection in his home district. Because a 1982 amendment to the Constitution had made the country a de jure one-party state, KANU had become Kenya's only legal political organization. Having received the party's nomination as its presidential candidate a week earlier and being unopposed for reelection to the parliamentary body, Moi was declared the winner by the national supervisor of elections without the need for a popular vote. The first new footstep had been taken.

October 1983 Harold D. Nelson

Chapter 1. Historical Setting

Ruins of thirteenth-century Gede Palace near Malindi

ALTHOUGH KENYA MAY have provided the setting for the earliest development of the human species, the ancestors of the modern nation's African population began making their appearance in the region less than 1,000 years ago, and the in-migration of some ethnic aggregations continued into the twentieth century. Culturally and linguistically heterogeneous groups of agriculturists and nomadic pastoralists settled in the physically varied environment of the country's interior, where as many as 40 distinct ethnic categories have been recognized. Among these the Bantu-speaking Kikuyu emerged as the dominant group in Kenya's fertile heartland. The coastal region experienced a different history, coming under Islamic influence as early as the tenth century. Arab and Persian merchants founded towns there whose ports became part of a commercial network linked to the Middle East. Intimate contacts between the Arab and indigenous Bantu cultures on the coast produced over a long period of time the Swahili culture, in which the characteristics of both were assimilated.

The history of Kenya as a political entity began with the region's inclusion in the British sphere of influence in the late nineteenth century and the subsequent establishment of a British protectorate and colony there. The British brought together the country's diverse elements under a unified administration and bestowed on it the name *Kenya* after the 5,200-meter peak in the central highlands that the Kikuyu called *kere nyaga,* the "mountain of whiteness."

The aim of British colonialism in Kenya was to integrate the country into an imperial system and to develop its economic potential, while providing for the security of the indigenous population and improving their general well-being, as defined according to the prevailing mentality of colonial authorities. The political, economic, and social changes brought about by the British were not effected smoothly, however, nor from an African perspective were they uniformly advantageous. An early realization that the climate and fertility of the Kenya Highlands made the region ideal for European settlement encouraged the reservation there of large tracts of the country's best land for the white minority and corresponding restrictions on African and Asian land use. Social pressures engendered by these restrictions and the inability of limited African reserves to meet the land needs of an expanding population—together with growing African resentment of the inferior status accorded them—provoked unrest that contributed to the formation of political action groups, organized on the basis of ethnic affiliation, in the 1920s.

Improvement in the lot of the average African was limited until after World War II when political movements, like that among the Kikuyu led by Jomo Kenyatta, demanded a role for the black majority in

Kenya's government. The determination of the European community to retain exlusive control in a "White Man's Country" and the continued denial of African rights set off a violent reaction during the Mau Mau emergency in the 1950s. The Kikuyu-led insurrection was suppressed, and the lengthy imprisonment of Kenyatta and other African leaders suspected of complicity in it caused a hiatus in organized African political activity until 1960, when the campaign for majority rule within the framework of the colonial regime succeeded in submerging ethnic differences among Africans and in winning the recognition of British authorities.

In 1961 the British government set Kenya on a course that led to majority rule and, at the end of 1963, to full independence within the Commonwealth of Nations. The next year Kenya became a republic under a unitary form of government headed by Kenyatta as its first president, and the principal political parties voluntarily merged under his leadership in the Kenya African National Union (KANU). Radical dissidents and ethnic interest groups fearful of Kikuyu domination followed Oginga Odinga out of KANU during an interlude in the late 1960s, but the rival political movement that they formed was banned in 1969, and Kenya reverted in practice to being a one-party state.

Ethnic antagonisms remained the principal stumbling block to national unity, but Kenyatta's firm, paternalistic rule nonetheless provided the country with a substantial degree of stability during the first decade and a half of Kenya's independent existence. Although the Mzee—the "Old Man," as Kenyatta was familiarly known—held tightly to the reins of power, Kenya maintained basically democratic institutions. Parliamentary debate was sharp and frequently questioned government policies, elections were vigorously contested by rival candidates, and the press was relatively free in its reporting and commentary. A program of "Kenyanization" of government and the economy was instituted, however, gradually forcing the departure of most of the country's European and Asian populations. Operated by an African entrepreneurial elite with close ties to the political elite, the Kenyan economy developed along capitalist lines, emphasizing rapid growth and modern production methods. The favorable orientation of the economy and stable political conditions inspired a confidence in the country's future that encouraged investment. Political opposition, however, focused on substantial inequities in distribution, particularly of farmland, as well as on official corruption.

As an aging Kenyatta became more withdrawn from the everyday conduct of government, decisionmaking was deferred more and more to members of the inner circle of advisers and officials who surrounded him. Rival personalities and factions within KANU maneuvered for position in anticipation of the end of the Kenyatta era. When the Mzee died in office in August 1978, he was succeeded by his vice president and heir apparent, Daniel arap Moi, in an orderly transition of power.

Kenya's Prehistory

Modern Kenya is the site of fossil finds that are considered significant clues in understanding man's early development and history. Deposits in the Rift Valley, dated over 20 million years in age, have yielded anthropoid remains possibly in the ancestral human line, and other primate fossils dated to 12 to 14 million years ago are believed to be of a creature having direct affinity to the hominid family. Fossils from the area of Lake Rudolf (known in Kenya as Lake Turkana) provide evidence that the extinct australopithecine branch of man inhabited Kenya approximately 3 million years ago. Other contemporary specimens discovered in the same general area have been tentatively classified as belonging to the genus *Homo*, of which modern man is the latest representative.

The region took part in the advance in stone toolmaking that occurred during the Acheulean cultural period, which began in East Africa about 400,000 years ago. Characteristic Acheulean hand axes are found in profusion at Olorgesailie National Monument south of Nairobi, an apparent center for the manufacture of stone artifacts over a lengthy period of time some 250,000 years ago. Similar but smaller sites are at Kariandusi and near Lake Baringo, where remains of an advanced form of man, *Homo erectus*, have also been found. Scanty remains of modern man have been discovered associated with a stone industry dated to about 16,000 B.C., but more extensive evidence of his presence in Kenya occurs only considerably later.

Major climatic changes brought generally humid conditions to eastern Africa from about 8000 B.C. Lakes increased materially in size, and their water level rose to about 185 meters above the present-day levels. Archaeological evidence indicates that peoples forming part of a geographically widespread culture based on fishing and using aquatic animals and plants as the principal food sources occupied the lakeshores throughout the succeeding several millennia. From skeletal remains it appears that these people were negroid. Based on known cultural features and the present-day distribution of speakers of the Nilo-Saharan family of languages in Africa, it has been postulated that these early inhabitants of Kenya also spoke a language or languages belonging to the same family; however, no relationship has been established between these earlier inhabitants and present-day Nilo-Saharan speakers in Kenya.

During the third millennium B.C., a drier climatic regime commenced; as lakes and other bodies of water shrank, food sources diminished and the aquatic economy declined. About this time new peoples arrived in the Rift Valley and Kenya Highlands; their skeletal remains have features similar to those of the Cushitic-speaking peoples living at present in the Horn of Africa. The newcomers appear to have coexisted, at least initially, with the negroid inhabitants of the aquatic communities which, however, had been forced to rely more and more on hunting and gathering. Skeletal finds indicate that a third human type, the bushmanoids, also inhabited the area of modern Kenya at roughly the same time.

Cushitic-speaking peoples apparently were the principal inhabitants of the valley and the adjacent highlands from about 1000 B.C. through most of the first millennium A.D. There is evidence that they had domesticated animals, and it is believed that they were primarily pastoralists. They possessed a neolithic culture characterized by distinctive stone bowls and platters, and the presence of stone pestles and grinding stones suggests that they may also have practiced some form of rudimentary agriculture. Hunters and gatherers of negroid and bushmanoid stocks were the principal inhabitants in the forested parts of the Kenya Highlands and the wooded grasslands at lower levels. The first millennium A.D. saw the arrival in these areas of new negroid groups who possessed some knowledge of agriculture and of ironworking. Little is known of these people, but they are believed to have been Bantu speakers, perhaps coming from the south and southwest. Sites that they occupied have been found from Kwale in southeastern Kenya, not far from the coast, westward to the Lake Victoria area.

The Peopling of the Interior

People of three distinct language groups—Bantu, Cushitic, and Nilotic—are found in present-day Kenya (see Ethnic Groups and Languages, ch. 2). The interior of the country, extending from the *nyika* (Swahili for wilderness—applied to the climatically hostile area forming a barrier behind the coast) to Lake Victoria, is populated by intermingled groups of Bantu-speaking and Nilotic peoples, whose ancestors migrated to Kenya after the beginning of the second millennium A.D. The early Cushitic people who inhabited western Kenya and parts of the highlands area were absorbed or driven out during these movements. Elements of the present Cushitic-speaking population, which occupies the northern and northeastern parts of the country, began arriving sometime before the sixteenth century. Somali clans eventually ranged over most of northeastern Kenya. A particularly large influx of Oromo (Galla) people, moving out of Ethiopia, started toward the end of the nineteenth century and continued through the early decades of the twentieth (see fig. 2).

In their oral histories, the Kikuyu, the nation's largest ethnic group, claim that their ancestors came originally from northeast of Mount Kenya in a migration that was probably under way in the fifteenth century. Archaeological discoveries in central Kenya, related to the presumed Bantu-speaking people who entered southern Kenya during the first millennium, indicate that these people preceded the Kikuyu in the region. Linguistic studies further suggest that they may have been the ancestors of several later Bantu groups in the area, including the Kikuyu.

During the three to four centuries after their migration began, the proto-Kikuyu moved slowly southwestward, splitting into new groups that by the late nineteenth century occupied a broad area in the central

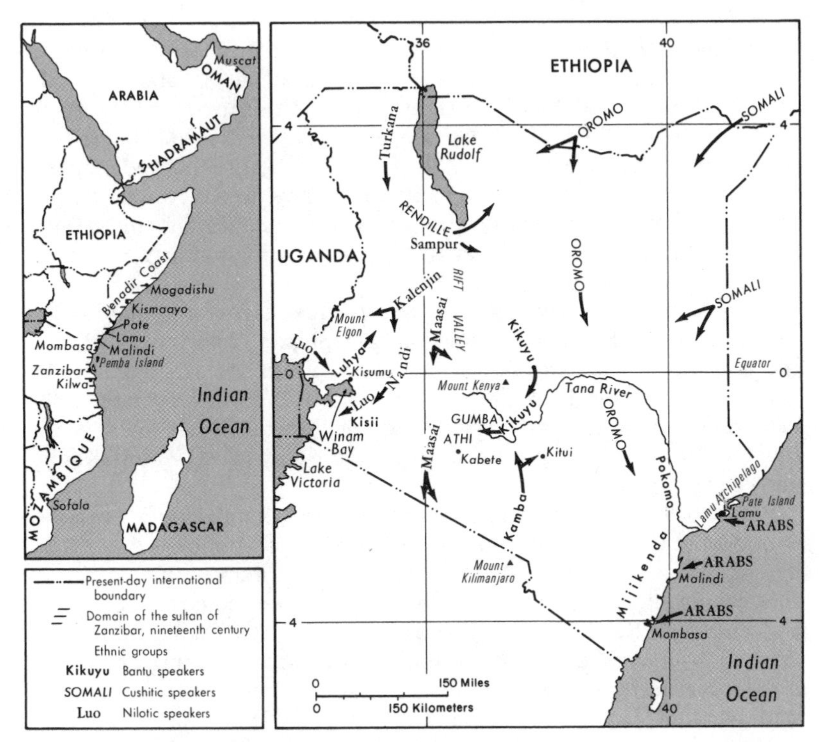

Figure 2. East Africa Coast and the Peopling of Kenya's Interior, Thirteenth to Nineteenth Centuries

part of the highlands. In the course of their movement they absorbed other groups already in place. Such ethnic elements included the short-statured Gumba and the Athi (also Okiek or Nderobo), both hunting and gathering peoples.

The Gumba, believed to have been Cushitic speakers, were primarily hunters in the open grasslands. Oral traditions state that they were skilled at iron working and pottery making, a knowledge of which they imparted to the Kikuyu. The two ethnic groups seem to have lived in a symbiotic relationship, exchanging meat and skins for agricultural products, and considerable assimilation of the Gumba by Kikuyu groups occurred. The expansion of the Kikuyu, however, resulted in friction and eventually war, as land used for hunting was cleared for cultivation. Little is known about the fate of the Gumba after hostilities with the Kikuyu in the mid-nineteenth century.

The Athi were forest dwellers who seem to have had a relationship with the Kikuyu similar to that of the Gumba. They were only partly assimilated by the Kikuyu, however, and groups of them still survive, mainly in Rift Valley Province. The Athi are important in Kikuyu history; it was they who, according to tradition, sold the heartland region of Kabete to the Kikuyu in exchange for cattle.

The Bantu communities that eventually merged to form the Kamba appear to have been in the area of Mount Kilimanjaro about the fifteenth century, and they probably reached the Mbooni Hills, their ethnic heartland in present-day Machakos District, in the latter half of the seventeenth century. Initially hunters and gatherers, they turned to agriculture because of the fertility of the new territory. Population growth led to their expansion to areas less suitable for cultivation, including Kitui to the east, where they returned to hunting and readopted their earlier pastoralism.

Kamba hunting groups discovered the value of ivory as a trade item, beginning the systematic exploitation of elephants and eventually forming two-way trade caravans to the coast. From the late eighteenth century their trade increased greatly, and activities were eventually extended over a wide area stretching north to the Tana River, south into present-day Tanzania, and west to the forests of Mount Kenya and Kikuyu country.

At its peak in the mid-nineteenth century, Kamba trade was the mainstay of the prosperity of the coastal port of Mombasa, but other groups were by then beginning to contest their monopoly. Feuds among the Kamba clans also began to affect trading operations, as did efforts by peoples in the Kenya Highlands to exclude the Kamba from their territory—in part because the Kamba had turned to raiding for slaves. Depletion of elephants by the late nineteenth century had created a new problem, forcing Kamba hunters to go hundreds of miles for ivory. Moreover, a general state of unrest, which endangered caravan traffic, existed in the *nyika*, and caravans traveling safer routes farther south secured much of the interior trade. Kamba trade continued at a much reduced rate until competition from the Uganda railroad, which ran through their territory carrying goods between Mombasa and Kisumu, finally brought an end to well over a century of aggressive Kamba commercial activities.

Bantu-speaking peoples had begun arriving in the Lake Victoria region of western Kenya by about the eleventh century. Sometime during the next few centuries, separate agricultural groups that later came to constitute the Luhya occupied the lakeshore. During the sixteenth century the pastoral Nilotic Luo pushed into the area north of Winam Bay from present-day Uganda, displacing the Luhya eastward. Settled agricultural practices appear to have been adopted by at least some Luo, but by the middle of the next century others were on the move southward along the shore of the lake, conquering new territory as they went. There they came against the Bantu Kisii (Gusii), who were also expanding into this part of Kenya. Territorial adjustments between these three peoples, as well as with Nilotic groups on their eastern fringes, often involved warfare and continued until the imposition of British control early in the twentieth century effectively brought an end to the forcible occupation of land by rival ethnic groups.

The time of entry and dispersion of the ancestors of various other Nilotic peoples in modern Kenya is uncertain. The first groups must have begun their in-migration—from the general area of southwestern Ethiopia—in the early centuries of the second millennium, for the ancestors of the Kalenjin peoples, among them the Nandi, appear to have reached the Mount Elgon region before 1500. By the early seventeenth century Maasai pastoralists were pushing southward through the Rift Valley and are known from oral records to have been at the southern end of the Kenya section of the rift in the eighteenth century, becoming the dominant force in southwestern Kenya. Although weakened by internal warfare, the Maasai were so feared by neighboring groups that few dared challenge their control of the southern valley, plains areas, and surrounding plateaus. Among the latest major Nilotic arrivals were the Turkana pastoralists, who entered northwestern Kenya in the eighteenth century.

The Kenya Coast

The coast of East Africa was mentioned in Greek accounts written in the first and second centuries A.D., listing items of trade from the region that included ivory, tortoiseshell, and spices. Although archaeological evidence of sites dating from before the thirteenth century is lacking, references in medieval Arab documents indicate that Muslim traders had set up an outpost on Pate Island in the Lamu Archipelago some 500 years earlier and that other settlements founded along the coast by Arab and Persian (Shirazi) merchants probably date from the tenth and eleventh centuries. These towns, stretching from the Benadir Coast in Somalia to Sofala in Mozambique, became links in an extensive commercial network connecting East Africa with Southwest Asia and the Indies. Gold brought to the coast from the fields around Great Zimbabwe was shipped from Kilwa in present-day Tanzania, the most important of the Arab colonies. Those farther up the coast at Mombasa, Malindi, Lamu, and Pate in present-day Kenya exported slaves and ivory that had been exchanged by Africans from the interior for salt, cloth, beads, and metal goods. A trading expedition from China is recorded as having reached Malindi about 1417. Although the sultan of Kilwa exercised a loose hegemony over them, the larger Arab towns gradually developed as autonomous sultanates, competing fiercely for a larger share of the region's commerce. The fortunes of the sultanates rose and fell but, by the end of the fifteenth century, Malindi had established itself as the most prosperous trading center on the Kenyan coast, surpassing its rival, Mombasa.

Migration of Arab families to East Africa continued, particularly from the Hadramaut in southern Arabia. Over time a distinctive Islamic culture resulted in the coastal region from intermarriage between indigenous Bantu-speaking Africans and Arab settlers. Physical and cultural integration were accompanied by the development of the Swahili (from the Arabic for "coastal") language, which came to serve as the lingua franca of the East African littoral as well as the mother tongue of the mixed population (see Language and Linguistic Classification, ch. 2).

The Portuguese Presence

The navigator Vasco da Gama called at Mombasa and Malindi on his voyage to India in 1498, initiating 200 years of Portuguese influence along the East African coast. The sultanate of Malindi quickly established friendly relations with the newcomers and opened its port to their trade. Its rival, Mombasa, reacted with hostility to the Portuguese intrusion, however, and in 1505 the town was sacked by Francisco de Almeida, who commanded an expeditionary force that had occupied Kilwa and Sofala earlier that same year. When Mombasa became the center of Arab resistance in East Africa, the Portuguese carried out a second destructive attack on the town in 1529 with the assistance of Malindi, compelling its sultan to recognize the overlordship of the Portuguese crown and pay an annual tribute.

Portuguese control in the region, exercised at a distance by the governor of Goa through allies such as the sultan of Malindi, remained tenuous during most of the sixteenth century. Resentment against foreign influence continued to fester, until in 1589 Mombasa renounced Portuguese suzerainty and accepted the protection of the Turkish corsair Mirale Bey and his fleet. A strong Portuguese flotilla, dispatched from Goa, captured the Turkish vessels and left Mombasa to be looted by the Zimba, a marauding band of African warriors who two years before had destroyed Kilwa. When the Zimba next turned against Malindi, however, they were defeated by the intervention of warriors from the neighboring Segeju tribe. The sultan of Malindi then employed the Segeju in taking Mombasa, moving his court there in 1592 and inviting his Portuguese friends to install a garrison.

In order to strengthen their hold on that stretch of the East African coast, the Portuguese began construction of a massive defense works, Fort Jesus, at the entrance to Mombasa harbor in 1593. For close to four decades thereafter Portuguese dominance was unchallenged until, in 1631, they temporarily lost both the town and the fort to a disaffected Arab sultan. Although these were recaptured eight years later, the Portuguese were soon challenged by the growing power of the imam of Oman (southeastern Arabia) for control of the northern coast. (The imam derived his political authority from his office as religious leader.) In 1660 Mombasa was seized by Omani forces, although the Portuguese held Fort Jesus until 1699 when it fell after an epic three-year siege. An attempt by the Portuguese to regain the fort in 1728 failed. Not until the start of British antislaving activities in East Africa early in the next century was European influence reasserted in the region.

Throughout their 200 years on the Kenyan coast, the Portuguese showed no interest in colonization. The chief concern of the handful of Portuguese in the coastal towns was trade, and the two centuries of their presence left no permanent marks other than a few words bequeathed to the Swahili language and such monuments as Fort Jesus. Indirectly, however, as elsewhere in East Africa, Portuguese influence had a far-reaching impact through the introduction of major food crops from the New World, in particular, maize, cassava, and potatoes. These became staples in much of the region and contributed to the growth of its population.

The Omani Hegemony

After the capture of Fort Jesus and the subsequent expulsion of the Portuguese from Zanzibar, the imam of Oman was able to claim suzerainty over the entire coast of East Africa. His authority there was largely nominal, however, and actual control lay in the hands of the Arab families who ruled the coastal towns. The strongest of these families was the Mazrui, who in 1727 had come to power in Mombasa.

In 1741 the incumbent imam was overthrown in Oman and replaced by Said al Busaidi, who also took the secular title of sayyid (lord) and established a dynasty. The Mazrui took advantage of the change of rulers in Oman and renounced their allegiance to the imam, establishing at Mombasa an independent shaykhdom that eventually dominated much of the coast from Pate in the north to Pemba Island.

In 1806 a strong figure of the Busaidi line, Said bin Sultan, became sayyid in Oman and set about to reassert Omani authority in East Africa. His rise to power coincided, however, with British efforts to curb the slave trade and combat piracy in the Persian Gulf, which caused Britain to exercise a dominating influence over the actions of Said and his successors throughout the rest of the nineteenth century. In 1823, for example, British representatives persuaded Said to consent to an agreement restricting his involvement in the slave trade to his own possessions. The treaty had little impact on the existing slave trade inasmuch as the main movement of slaves in the region ran through territory claimed by Oman or in its coastal waters, but it was intended rather to prevent the expansion of the trade to new markets. Of larger significance at the time was the treaty's recognition of Omani sovereignty from the Benadir Coast southward to Portuguese Mozambique.

By 1824 Said's forces had ousted the Mazrui from the Lamu Archipelago and were poised to attack their stronghold at Mombasa. When the townspeople petitioned the captain of a British naval vessel to guarantee their security, the officer proclaimed a protectorate over Mombasa, considering it an opportunity to stop slaving through the port, although he lacked authorization for such an action. The British government repudiated the arrangement made in its name, as did the Mazrui, who claimed the town. Mombasa fell to the Omani in 1828, although Mazrui held out against them in Fort Jesus for another nine years.

In 1840 Said moved his court from Oman to Zanzibar, where he assumed the title of sultan, but British influence followed him there. Zanzibar was the main entrepôt for the slave trade along the East African coast, prompting the British to impose another treaty on Said in 1845 that limited the trading to the coastal area from Kilwa to Lamu. The trade in the unrestricted area continued to flourish, however. Reports of the horrors of the slave trade made by British naval officers and by European travelers shocked the British public and brought support for the permanent stationing of an antislaving patrol in the western Indian Ocean. British pressure was also increased on the sultan to agree to a further restriction of the trade. Gradually, concessions were made, and in 1873 the reigning sultan, Barghash, agreed to stop the sale of slaves and all slave shipments between ports in his domain. Movement of slaves continued overland behind the coast, but in 1877 the sultan ordered this halted as well. The entry of slave caravans from the interior to the coastal area was also prohibited. To enforce these decrees an armed force led by a British officar was recruited. The measures were far from popular, and in Kenya in 1880 Swahili slave traders at Mombasa attacked a British missionary-operated center for freed slaves, which the traders associated with the sultan's ban on slaving. Discontent over slaving restrictions continued on the Kenyan coast until the end of the century.

Zanzibar became a center of legitimate trade as Said developed the clove industry on the island and actively encouraged trade from the interior. Kenya was largely bypassed—the main interior trade routes ran south of it—but Mombasa was reported to have been prosperous at mid-century, largely because of the ivory and other items collected in quantity by Kamba traders in the interior and directed to the port town. In the following decades elephants in the Kamba and other areas were hunted out, and caravan operations were also disrupted by tribal warfare. The decline in trade that resulted (and the rise of Zanzibar as a commercial center) brought an exodus of merchants and artisans from Mombasa that, together with British antislaving operations, reduced the town to comparatively minor importance. Mombasa did not recover from the decline until the early 1900s, after it had become the starting point for the construction of the railroad to Uganda.

European activities on the mainland were confined largely to missionary work and exploration from the 1840s to near the end of the century, although a few trading concessions conducted limited operations at a number of coastal points. In Kenya the first Christian mission was established in 1846 near Mombasa by Johann Krapf and Johann Rebmann, Swiss serving with the Anglican Church Missionary Society (CMS). In 1862 Krapf, then associated with the Methodist Missionary Society, founded another mission also in the vicinity of Mombasa. Both missions conducted schools that were the first such Western institutions in Kenya.

Efforts to extend mission activities to the interior were frustrated by the local hostilities that kept large areas unsettled. On the coast, after the banning of the slave trade in 1873, the CMS established a settlement for freed slaves at Frere Town outside Mombasa. But little else could be done because the indigenous Muslim population was strongly opposed to the teaching of Christianity and otherwise resentful of the missionaries, whom they considered leaders of the antislavery movement. In the years that followed, however, mission stations for freed slaves were also established by Roman Catholic and Scottish

Presbyterian missionaries. Most of the Europeans—estimated to number 300 in the region by 1885—were involved in missionary work.

The Colonial Period

Until the 1880s little official interest was shown by the European powers in acquiring territory in East Africa. British government policy was to work through regional leaders to create an atmosphere in which trade could grow without the costs that direct administrative control would entail. The only other European power having substantial interests in East Africa was Germany, but the government of German chancellor Otto von Bismarck displayed an equal lack of eagerness for colonial ventures that might require direct government intervention and expenditures. Bismarck himself had ignored demands by German explorers and businessmen for colonial expansion overseas. His main concern was that German trading operations receive adequate protection by local regimes.

By 1885, however, international considerations and domestic policies had brought a change in Bismarck's outlook. His hand was also forced by the activities of Karl Peters, who had founded the Society for German Colonization to promote overseas expansion. In 1884 Peters and two associates went to Zanzibar, proceeding from there to the mainland where they persuaded Arab shaykhs and local African chiefs to sign treaties offering their territories for German colonization. The treaties were presented to, and accepted by, Bismarck the next year, and a subsequent order by the kaiser declared the areas to be under German protection. A charter was issued to the society to administer the new protectorate—whose extent was not defined—which was to be known as German East Africa. The society then ceded its rights to the new German East Africa Company, also headed by Peters. At about the same time, the Germans had obtained a treaty with the sultanate of Witu on the northern Kenyan coast, which they also proclaimed a German protectorate in 1885.

In Britain the government of Liberal prime minister William Gladstone had sought to avoid a direct commitment to Zanzibar and had refused to support the sultan when he protested the German action. The new Conservative government that took office under Lord Salisbury in July 1885 determined to head off further German expansion in East Africa by reconciling conflicting claims in the region. The next year a joint British-German commission, which was convened to decide the extent of the sultan's domain, awarded the islands along the coast, including Lamu Island in Kenya, to the sultan, as well as a strip of land extending inland 16 kilometers that went as far north in Kenya as the mouth of the Tana River. The interior beyond the coastal strip was divided into British and German spheres of influence separated by a line roughly the same as the present-day Kenya-Tanzania border.

Imperial British East Africa Company

In 1888 the privately financed Imperial British East Africa Company

(IBEAC) headed by Sir William Mackinnon was given a royal charter to administer the British sphere. At about this time, the British government concluded that the occupation of Egypt would be long-term and that control of the Uganda region, where the headwaters of the Nile rose, was desirable. A new Anglo-German agreement in 1890, under which Germany secured the island of Helgoland in the North Sea, placed Uganda completely within the British sphere. The German claims to the Witu enclave were dropped, and recognition was given by Germany to a British protectorate over the islands of Zanzibar and Pemba.

Events in Uganda were soon to become an important factor in determining British policy in Kenya. At government urging, IBEAC extended its operations to Uganda in 1890. Failure to find highly profitable trade items there and heavy expenses in administering the area added to the company's already serious financial problems—caused by an initial undercapitalization and the relatively small amount of business on the coast. Because of strong parliamentary opposition, however, the government was unable to offer financial help, and in 1891 it appeared likely that the company would have to abandon Uganda. This brought an outcry from missionary groups, whose efforts had been fairly successful in Uganda, that a British withdrawal would lead to massacres of Christians by the Muslims. Loud opposition to withdrawal was also voiced by the press, and some official fears existed that the French might move to fill the vacuum.

As a result, the British government established the Uganda Protectorate in 1894. Creation of a protectorate so far inland raised questions concerning communications lines to the Kenya coast and the ability of IBEAC to control the interior. The company was experiencing difficulties in the coastal strip, which it managed under a 50-year lease from the sultan of Zanzibar, as the result of free trade provisions imposed by the British government in 1892. Negotiations were initiated, therefore, for the government to take over all IBEAC responsibilities. An agreement was reached in June 1895, and on July 1 the East Africa Protectorate was officially established (see fig. 3). The new protectorate, which was placed under the jurisdiction of the Foreign Office, comprised in general the territory of present-day Kenya lying between the coast and the eastern edge of the Rift Valley and included the leased coastal zone, over which the sultan had expected—and sought in vain—to regain sovereignty.

The East Africa Protectorate and the Uganda Railroad

The East Africa Protectorate was placed under the charge of Sir Arthur Hardinge (who from 1896 had the title of commissioner), then British consul general in Zanzibar. IBEAC had several permanent posts on the route to Lake Victoria and Uganda that devolved to the control of the protectorate. In reality, however, the protectorate at its inception had a reasonably firm grip only on the narrow coastal zone. Its control even there was brought into question almost immediately by a disputed

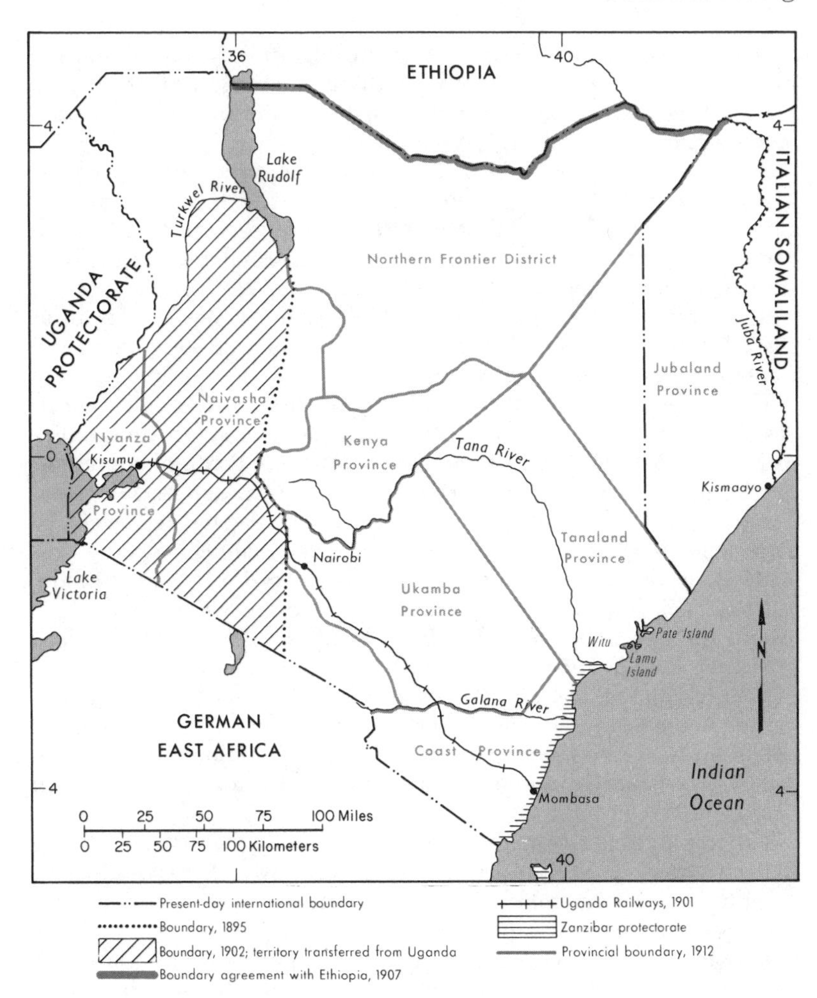

Figure 3. East Africa Protectorate, 1895-1920

succession in the powerful Mazrui family, which erupted into a revolt in 1895 against the claimant formerly backed by the IBEAC. Hardinge was forced finally to call for reinforcements from India before the rebellion was ended the following year. British control of the area was never seriously contested thereafter.

Within the next few years the East Africa Protectorate was divided into provinces (each under a resident commissioner), which were subdivided into districts administered by district officers. The district officer's task was a lonely one, and his functions varied, combining responsibility for political, legal, financial, and military affairs; law enforcement; economic development; and public works. On the coast, Islamic religious courts continued to have jurisdiction over matters involving the personal status of Muslims, but efforts to employ indigenous leaders in administrative capacities under a system of indirect rule proved generally unsuccessful in the long run. In 1902 the King's African Rifles (KAR) was formed to provide military security in the protectorate.

Since the early 1890s the British government had shown interest in the construction of a railroad from the coast to Uganda. After establishment of the Uganda Protectorate, the proposed railroad became of great strategic significance, and in 1895 responsibility for its building was assigned to the new East Africa Protectorate. Work began at Mombasa in December 1895, and the line reached the site of Nairobi in 1899. By the end of 1901 it extended to Kisumu on Lake Victoria and was opened to public traffic in 1902.

The principal obstacle to the advance of the railroad and the imposition of British control was expected to be the widely reputed ferocity of the Maasai. The British officer in charge of Fort Smith (present-day Kikuyu), an outpost bordering on Maasai territory, established a friendship with the chief Maasai leader in the region, however, by giving him support in a local conflict, and thereafter his people presented few problems to authorities there or to the progress of the railroad. This left the British generally free to deal with other ethnic groups through whose territory the railroad ran. The sectional nature of Kikuyu and Kamba society favored the British effort to gain control in their territories. The stiffest resistance actually came from the Nandi, located in the Kenya Highlands to the west of Nakuru. A major military operation was conducted against them in 1895 and another in 1900. Nandi recalcitrance continued, however, and they were finally subdued only in 1905.

The imposition of British control was handled pragmatically during this early period. Some African leaders were extended special treatment to secure their friendship and support, and warring groups were played off against one another. Moreover, the indigenous peoples along the route of the railroad found the British stations useful places for trade and apparently equated the few white men running them with earlier traders from the coast whose operations had always been of a temporary nature.

The expansion of British control after completion of the railroad in Kenyan territory did not follow a grand design but was carried out essentially by the protectorate officials on the basis of their own analyses of local situations. Actions to protect friendly groups from attack, occasional expeditions against slaving (slavery was finally abolished in the protectorate in 1907), efforts to assist traders and caravans that went into unprotected territory, and various other measures gradually extended British control. Such activities in central Kenya involving the Kikuyu brought the establishment of a new post at Nyeri in 1902. Within a few years, other Kikuyu groups and the Embu (in 1906) and Meru (in 1908) around Mount Kenya were subdued without London's prior approval. Farther west, control of the Kisii and other ethnic groups was attained generally by about the middle of the first decade,

A section of the railroad that runs through Kenya, connecting the coast at Mombasa and landlocked Uganda Courtesy CNI News/Bill Chewning

but submission of the last group, the Marakwet (a Kalenjin subgroup) did not occur until 1912. The Somali, Oromo, and various Nilotic peoples of the northern part of the protectorate proved less tractable. A major expedition against the Ogaden Somali in 1900-19001 attained few tangible results, and little was accomplished in succeeding years beyond the establishment of a few outposts.

Construction of the railroad and establishment of the East Africa Protectorate had in large part been effected on strategic grounds. Neither operation was self-supporting, and the British government, although willing for a time to provide grants-in-aid, was pressing for action that would generate revenues in the protectorate adequate to cover local expenditures. Some senior British officials had envisioned colonization of the area by immigrants from the Indian subcontinent (locally called Asians) as a way to bring development, and at the start of the twentieth century the Foreign Office and the protectorate's commissioner, Sir Charles Eliot, supported Asian settlement. Asian traders and entrepreneurs, long established in Zanzibar, already operated in Mombasa and other mainland towns. Moreover, during construction of the railroad, more than 30,000 laborers had been brought from India, some 7,000 of whom elected to remain in the territory under the terms of their contracts. As events developed, however, the possibility of an Asian settler's acquiring good agricultural land disappeared, and the existing Asian community and new immigrants turned mainly to the commercial field as shopkeepers and traders.

European Settlement

The forbidding terrain lying beyond the coast and lack of knowledge of the interior had initially given Kenya the reputation among Europeans of being a barren land. During the 1890's, however, British officials, soldiers, and missionaries began reporting the temperate climatic conditons, fertility, and apparent emptiness of the highland region of western Kenya. This part of the country seemed ideal for white settlement and agricultural development using European methods.

In 1902 Eastern Province of Uganda Protectorate was transferred to the East Africa Protectorate. Primarily, the move was intended to place control of the railroad under one jurisdiction, but consideration appears also to have been given to bringing the uplands of Eastern Province, physiographically part of the Kenya Highlands complex, under a single administration for the purpose of encouraging European settlement there. The transfer included all land from the eastern escarpments of the southern and central Rift Valley westward to Lake Victoria and the northern Rift Valley and some territory to its west.

The decision to favor European settlement was made in 1902 after the policy received the backing of the Foreign Office, and the handful of European settlers in the protectorate persuaded Eliot to end his support for Asian colonization. At the time the entire European population numbered little more than 500, and fewer than 20 were actually engaged in farming. Some additional settlers arrived in 1903, among them Lord Delamere, a British nobleman who was to play a leading role in settler affairs during the next three decades, and the following year Eliot enunciated his so-called White Man's Country policy for the protectorate. A number of Afrikaners recruited in South Africa, together with additional British arrivals, raised the European population to over 1,800 by 1906. By 1914 Europeans numbered over 5,400, about 3,000 of whom were considered permanent settlers. The total increased to more than 16,600 in early 1930, at which time the African population was estimated at over 2.9 million.

The Compartmentalization of Land

An early problem in attracting settlers was the question of land titles. IBEAC had made almost 100 treaties with tribal leaders, but these did not assign land rights. After establishment of the protectorate, responsible authorities in London had recommended against the alienation of land, their opinion being that in a protectorate the land did not actually belong to the crown. Unoccupied land, however, could be assigned for occupation on a land certificate basis not involving a transfer of title. The following year authorization was given for such certificates to be issued for a fixed time period.

European settlers wanted freehold grants, however, and by 1899 the British government had concluded that wasteland and unoccupied land found in such jurisdictions as the East Africa Protectorate and "occupied by savage tribes" actually came directly under the control of the crown; such land, therefore, could be granted to settlers without restrictions. The Crown Lands Ordinance of 1902 made provision for the sale and leasing (for a maximum of 99 years) of such land. The commissioner was given considerable leeway in making rules to implement the ordinance, and Eliot subsequently established provisions permitting an initial allocation of 160 acres, which could be increased to a maximum of 640 acres. The settlers from the beginning objected strongly to the lease's length, which they felt introduced a considerable degree of insecurity, and in 1915 the lease term was increased to 999 years, i.e., to be held in perpetuity.

Of particular significance was the 1902 ordinance's provision that only temporary occupation licenses, limited to one year and a maximum of five acres, might be issued to Africans and other non-Europeans who were considered qualified to use the land. This provision was immediately applied to all Asians seeking to obtain land in the highlands area. Moreover, in the next year specific instructions were issued by Eliot that land for Asian settlement was not to be issued outside town boundaries in a broad area from the eastern highlands to the western edge of the Rift Valley.

Despite Asian complaints the Foreign Office backed Eliot. In 1905 jurisdiction over the protectorate was transferred to the Colonial Office, which initially tried to exercise greater discretion in allowing European settlement when it came at the expense of the indigenous population. But the rules that Eliot had established held until 1915, by which time almost all of the most desirable agricultural land had been alienated to Europeans. The new Crown Lands Ordinance of 1915 perpetuated the restriction by authorizing legal limitations to nonwhites (including Asians) on ownership, acquisition, management, and other matters involving land in the highlands.

Early interpretations of land rights implied that Africans did not have title to any land but that their rights were only those of occupancy, cultivation, and grazing. If African-occupied land was no longer used, it became wasteland and reverted to crown land status and thus could be assigned to Europeans. Advantage was taken of the provision when land containing an African settlement was leased. The settlement was excluded from the lease as long as it was occupied, but as soon as it was deserted, no matter how this might occur, it became crown land and part of the leased parcel.

Supposedly inalienable reserves were established for the Maasai by treaty in 1904, one south of the railroad, the other to the north in the Laikipia Plateau area. They were to be held in perpetuity, and settlers were to be excluded from acquiring any of this land. Gradual divergence in the development of the two Maasai groups caused the government to believe that it would be better for them to occupy one area. There was also considerable settler pressure to move the northern group from the Laikipia Plateau because of its fertile, well-watered land. The move to an enlarged southern reserve was finally effected in 1913 despite opposition from the northern Maasai. The northern area was then thrown open to European occupancy.

The Crown Lands Ordinance of 1915 also authorized the establishment of African reserves, but there was no guarantee of their inviolability even after official proclamation, for the protectorate government had the prerogative of declaring areas of any reserve surplus to African needs and disposing of them. For example, in the Nandi reserve in western Kenya some 44 square kilometers of the best land were taken in 1919 for use in the settlement of British war veterans.

The question of both African and European land security led during the 1920s and 1930s to the impaneling of several commissions of inquiry. Legislation in the late 1930s finally set boundaries for the so-called White Highlands, which enclosed a total area of about 43,250 square kilometers. Existing African land rights in these areas were voided, either with or without compensation. In contrast, certain European holdings in the midst of reserve areas were allowed to continue, although the established rents for such land and the residual land rights were transferred from the government to the appropriate reserve.

At the same time, the original existing African reserves were reclassified as native land instead of crown land. They were delimited and divided into nine units that were allocated to the principal ethnic groups. Certain other specified areas were made available for temporary reserves, and some additional land was designated for African leasehold. The remaining crown land outside the White Highlands was opened without regard to racial background, but this land generally was far less desirable. Population increases and the requirements of subsistence agricultural practices brought growing pressures on the reserves and helped fuel already long-existing African discontent over land.

Economic Development

The lack of important mineral resources was confirmed by early comprehensive surveys, and the British government concluded that agriculture for export was the only way to make the protectorate pay for itself. The most suitable land in the Kenya Highlands was usable both for temperate climate crops and at somewhat lower levels for tropical ones. To the few early settlers with capital, such as Lord Delamere, the answer was obvious: temperate-zone wheat and wool, both items then booming on the world markets. Ecological conditions, however, proved far from similar to those in Britain, Canada, and Australia, and substantial losses were suffered before several years of experimentation brought some success. Meanwhile, smallholders grew a mixture of crops while attempting to determine their suitability. This kind of agriculture contributed little to the overall support of the protectorate, and after about 1905 the administration decided to promote the production of staples. Cotton cultivation was attempted but soon failed. The emphasis placed on coffee, however, brought eventual success. By 1910 high coffee prices on the world market attracted substantial new investment, and by 1920 coffee had become the protectorate's largest earner of foreign exchange.

Coffee growing required only moderate funding in contrast to the large-scale financing required by the sizable plantations. Coffee's continuing profitability encouraged some middle-class British families and even a few aristocrats to venture a new life in the pleasant surroundings of the Kenya Highlands. A new character was also given to smallholder settler operations, which had often been precarious, when maize was found to grow well in the highlands. Although seen essentially as an export crop, the domestic demand also proved great. Nonetheless, maize exports increased, and in 1930 they were second only to coffee as a foreign exchange earner. Another promoted crop was sisal, which became a major export item. By 1914 the economic situation was much improved from the standponts of both settler and administration. The previous year domestic revenues for the first time had met government expenditures. A network of shops and trading posts, spread across the country by a growing number of Asians, helped stimulate the economy.

The African population was reluctant to become involved in the wage economy. The hut and poll taxes imposed on them were intended to secure revenue, but an underlying purpose was also to get the Africans to furnish the labor needed by the settlers. Against this the Africans, generally provided for by their subsistence agriculture, saw little reason to work for cash wages much beyond the one or two months needed to secure money for their taxes. Consequently, the labor turnover was tremendous, adding greatly to the settlers' costs. Moreover, free choice of the working period affected seasonal supply, and settlers demanded government action to force longer labor stints.

When the administration began the practice of informally conscripting labor for public works for which it was unable to hire willing workers, the settlers insisted that it recruit labor for them as well, and local officers cooperated to use varying degrees of pressure to effect this. In 1908 the British government came out strongly against the use of forced labor, but the situation remained relatively unchanged in the protectorate, and officers followed their own judgment as to what constituted involuntary impressment. For the Africans this situation was not improved by the Native Authority Ordinance of 1912, which officially recognized the position of local headmen, perforce friendly to the British, who were frequently accused of abetting forced recruitment.

World War I brought an economic setback for the European population, largely through neglect of farms and a decline in exports, as settlers left for military service. Hostilities on Kenyan soil occurred only in the southern border area and had a minimal effect on the African population, but thousands of Kenyan African soldiers served with other British Empire forces in the difficult campaign in German East Africa.

The greatest African participation in the war was, however, as porters of the Carrier Corps. The road system was unsuitable for motor transport, and tsetse fly infestations practically prevented the use of draft animals. As a result, about 150,000 Africans were recruited or conscripted to provide the needed porterage. Work conditions were poor, and at the same time, East Africa was hit by the worldwide influenza epidemic. More than 40,000 Africans died during their service, including soldiers killed in combat. Adding to the woes of the African population was the serious famine in the protectorate in 1918.

Economic recovery was relatively rapid right after the war, but by 1921 world commodity prices had tumbled (coffee prices, for example, declined by 60 percent and more), bringing hardship to many of the 1,100 settler farms. By 1923, however, export prices were again rising, and farming profitability returned until 1928 and 1929 when locust plagues devastated the country. The world depression of the 1930s, aggravated by a major drought between 1931 and 1934, put not only the farmer but also the government in dire straits. Throughout the depression, however, coffee and sisal production continued to rise, and two new crops, tea and pyrethrum (used in insecticides), brightened the economic picture. The large tea plantations started in the mid-1920s were reaping profits by 1935, and before the end of the 1930s tea was in second place among exports. Pyrethrum, only introduced in the mid-1930s, was producing large earnings within two to three years.

In 1923 the government announced that it would promote cash crops in the reserves. Little came of this, however, because African farmers, more intent on providing for local food needs, showed little interest in producing for the export market. Strong opposition from the settlers to the suggested introduction of coffee cultivation on African farms ended the initiative. The depression, which proportionately had affected customary African market products (such as animal skins) even more than settler crops, brought new support for African export production. African maize output increased greatly during the 1930s, more than offsetting a substantal decline on settler farms, and cotton cultivation was successfully promoted in western Kenya. Finally, in 1937 the introduction of coffee growing in the reserves began, although African cultivation of the cash crop did not attain importance until the mid-1950s.

Political Participation and Evolution

The protectorate's headquarters, established in Zanzibar in 1895, remained there in the early 1900s despite efforts by Eliot, the second commissioner, to have it removed to Mombasa. The protectorate's major problems were nonetheless on the mainland, and by 1902 Eliot was essentially operating out of Mombasa. By that time he was calling for a move to Nairobi, increasingly the center of economic activity after the completion of the Uganda railroad in 1901 and because of the presence of settlers in the Kenya Highlands. The Foreign Office refused the request, and not until 1907, two years after the protectorate had been transferred to the jurisdiction of the Colonial Office, was the move to Nairobi formally made.

Settler political interest brought formation of the Colonists' Association in 1902. In 1903 Lord Delamere, recently arrived in East Africa, formed the Planters' and Farmers' Association (in 1905 renamed the Colonists' Association and after 1910 known as the Convention of Associations). This replaced the earlier body and became the dominant political voice of the settler community. In 1905 the association called for the creation of a representative legislative council, which was authorized by the British government in 1906; at that time the title of the chief administrative officer of the protectorate was changed to governor. The first council formed in 1907 included eight members—six official representatives and two appointed to represent the settlers.

The Asian community, which then outnumbered the Europeans about three to one, was not represented on the council. To promote their interests, Asians had formed the Indian Association at Mombasa in 1900 and a similar body in Nairobi in 1906; the coordinating British East Africa Indian Association was established in Mombasa in 1907. From 1914 the East Africa Indian National Congress (later Kenya Indian Congress) acted as the community's most important political organization.

In 1907 the Colonial Office pressed the question of Asian representation, and two years later A.M. Jeevanjee, a successful merchant residing in Mombasa, was nominated to the council. The protectorate's new governor, Sir Percy Girouard (1909-12), and his successor, Sir Henry Belfield (1912-17), were generally unsympathetic toward Asian demands; and when Jeevanjee's term ended in 1911, no new appointment of an Asian was made. Asians were also denied representation on local government bodies and were ignored in appointments to government commissions, such as those concerned with labor and land. Relations between the European and Asian communities became even more bitter after World War I, as the Europeans insisted on continued exclusion of Asian settlers from the White Highlands, restriction of Asian immigration, and residential and commercial segregation.

Settler demands for more direct representation and a greater voice in managing the financial affairs of the protectorate led in 1919 to approval of the elected Legislative Council, which included 11 Europeans in white constituencies and two appointed Asian representatives. The following year, in which the first election was held, the Colonial Office proposed the direct election of Asians, but the demand of Asian leaders for a common voter roll instead of the proposed communal voter rolls was not accepted. The two Asian members of the council resigned, and members of the Asian community generally boycotted the voting.

In 1920 the East Africa Protectorate was reorganized as the Kenya Colony and Protectorate. The protectorate consisted only of the narrow coastal area formally remaining under the sovereignty of the sultan of Zanzibar. The action setting apart this area served to consolidate the European settlers' hold on the crown colony established in the interior (see fig. 4).

In 1923 the Colonial Office issued the Devonshire White Paper (after the colonial secretary, the Duke of Devonshire) that had far-reaching implications for both Europeans and Asians, declaring that the interests of the African population were paramount and that in any conflict African interests had precedence. Formally titled *Indians in Kenya: Memorandum*, the white paper was published to resolve differences between Europeans and Asians after both parties had claimed that their intention was to protect the best interests of the Africans. This gave the Colonial Office an opportunity to use a reference to the paramountcy of African interests as a way of avoiding a formal commitment to either the Europeans or the Asians. Although the Devonshire White Paper made it clear that the country was actually held in trust for the Africans and, moreover, that the introduction of responsible government, i.e., self-government in the hands of the settlers, was unlikely, the White Highlands remained the preserve of the Europeans.

The Legislative Council, elected by communal voter rolls, consisted, in accordance with the recommendations of the white paper, of 11 Europeans, five Asians, one Arab (another Arab was to be appointed), and one missionary representative for Africans to be appointed at a later date. A representative for African interests (preferably a missionary) was also added to the appointed Executive Council that advised the governor.

The Asian community reacted vehemently to the white paper and refused to vote for, or participate in, the Legislative Council. In 1924 Asians withheld poll-tax payments. This failed as a protest measure, it was claimed, largely because of Asian disunity, and late in the year Asian representatives agreed to join the Legislative Council and the Executive Council.

By 1940 Asians numbered nearly 50,000, more than double the European and three times the Arab population. Discriminatory practices in town property holdings had largely disappeared but not those that prohibited Asians from holding agricultural land in the White Highlands. Moreover, despite their greater numerical strength, Asian representation at the central administration level remained unchanged, and European members of town councils everywhere outnumbered those who were Asian. Frictions within the Asian community continued to weaken its political effectiveness. In 1932 disagreements led to formation of the Federation of Asian Chambers of Commerce and Industry of Eastern Africa, which differed over policy with the East Africa Indian National Congress, but their efforts nonetheless tended to be complementary. Differences between Hindus and Muslims in

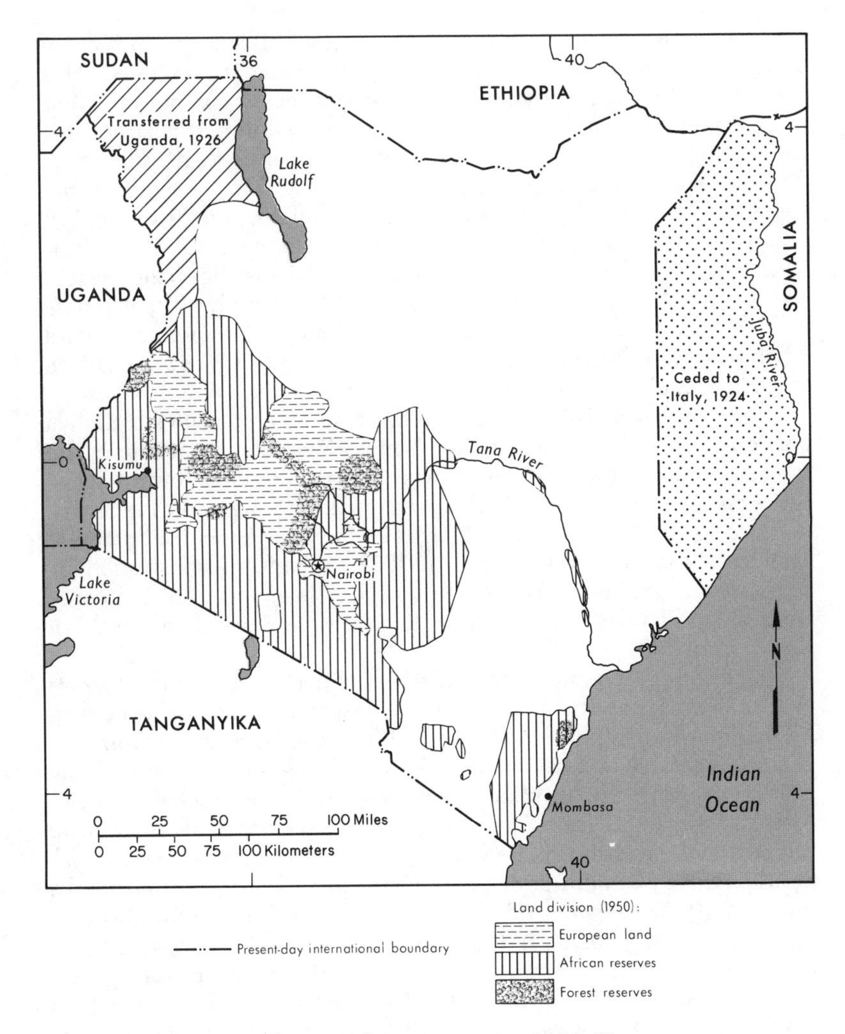

Figure 4. Kenya Colony and Protectorate, 1920-63

the Asian community also led to the formation of a separate Muslim Association by the latter.

The first organized African political activities began in 1919 with the formation of the Kikuyu Association, whose members included the appointed headmen and chiefs in the Kiambu area who banded together to oppose government alienation of land there. The following year the more militant East African Association was founded in Nairobi under the leadership of Harry Thuku, a government employee. This predominantly Kikuyu organization spoke out against compulsory labor recruitment, against increases in the hut tax, and in particular against the requirement that all adult males carry a *kipande* (registration certificate). The Native Registration Ordinance of 1915, enacted by the Legislative Council, had directed universal adult male registration, but because of the war, implementation did not occur until 1920. Buttressed by supplementary work requirement legislation, the system was intended to guarantee an adequate labor supply. The *kipande* included a record of work periods, wages, employer comments, and other matters related to employment. Loss of the *kipande* or failure to carry it could result in heavy penalties.

Stimulated by a visit by Thuku to the Kisumu area, Luo and Luhya mission-educated elites formed the Young Kavirondo Association. The association's activities, however, were soon redirected toward social concerns, and the organization was renamed the Kavirondo Taxpayers' Welfare Association in 1923. Meanwhile the government, alarmed at Thuku's activities, arrested him in 1922. A large demonstration by supporters in Nairobi was fired on by the police, and over 20 people were killed. Thuku was kept in exile at remote outposts in northern Kenya until 1931.

The most prominent of the African political organizations before World War II was the Kikuyu Central Association (KCA) formed in 1925. Jomo Kenyatta (then known as Johnstone Kenyatta) became its general secretary in 1928. In 1929 Kenyatta was sent to Britain to lay a petition before the British government calling for elected African seats on the Legislative Council. He was sent again in 1931 in an unsuccessful effort to bring KCA views and African grievances before a parliamentary committee considering the union of Kenya, Tanganyika (present-day Tanzania), and Uganda. Kenyatta remained away from Kenya until 1946, spending the intervening years studying, lecturing, and holding various jobs in Britain. From his academic work in anthropology at the London School of Economics came a well-received book, *Facing Mount Kenya*, a study of the Kikuyu, published in 1938. In general, however, he usually discussed Kenyan affairs from a trans-ethnic standpoint. Kenyatta also traveled in Europe and in 1932 visited the Soviet Union where, according to his biographer, Jeremy Murray-Brown, he received instruction in revolutionary techniques. During his long stay in Britain, Kenyatta continued to lobby for change in Kenya and also involved himself in the pan-African movement.

During the 1930s the KCA became the voice of an emerging Kikuyu consciousness. Its preeminence stemmed largely from its espousal of traditional Kikuyu customs in a controversy that emerged in the late 1920s over efforts by missionaries to eliminate such practices as female circumcision and polygamy. The emphasis on Kikuyu culture encouraged the development of Kikuyu ethnic identity. Many Kikuyu Christian church groups broke with their missionary leaders, established independent organizations and, of particular significance, set up an independent Kikuyu school system with which the KCA leadership became closely associated.

When Italy entered World War II in July 1940, an Italian brigade crossed into Kenya and advanced toward Lake Rudolf. By the end of the year, however, the Italians had withdrawn to a defense line at the Juba River in the face of a British buildup in East Africa that included Kenyan battalions of the KAR. These units took part in the British offensive launched in February 1941 that within two months had defeated enemy forces in Italian Somaliland and liberated Ethiopia. The KAR also saw action later in the war in Burma. Europeans from Kenya served with British forces on many fronts and, along with Kenyan Asians, in colonial units.

Until the KCA was officially banned in 1940 as a wartime emergency measure, its political activities remained Kikuyu oriented. In the late 1930s other associations were organized by the Kamba and Taita. They likewise were designed to serve tribal aims and, although they shortly associated themselves with the KCA, they retained their ethnic character and outlook. This emphasis on the ethnic aspect of political activity would continue to be a feature of African politics in Kenya.

The detention of more than 20 leaders of the KCA and of the Kamba and Taita organizations in 1940 as possible subversives, together with the banning of the KCA, muted African political activity during World War II. A small number of European liberals began expressing the view that Africans should be directly represented in a new legislature. The Legislative Council, seated in 1944, included the first African appointee, Eliud W. Mathu, one of the founders that year of the Kenya Africa Union (KAU). In late 1946 Kenyatta returned to Kenya as the undisputed leader of the nationalist movement, and in mid-1947 he was elected to the presidency of the KAU at a meeting attended by representatives of most of the major ethnic groups. Kenyatta continually attempted to bring the disparate African political and social organizations into the KAU and to broaden the national character of KAU leadership. Oginga Odinga, a leader of the Luo, joined in 1950. By 1951 the KAU reportedly had about 150,000 members throughout Kenya, but most were Kikuyu, and they still constituted almost the entire executive committee.

Insistent African demands, coupled with official concern over growing African disaffection, led to an increase in the number of appointed African council members to two in 1946, four in 1948, and eight in 1951. Africans still were denied direct election, but from 1948 the colonial governor appointed individuals from names submitted by the partly elected African councils that had functioned in many districts as local administrative bodies.

In 1944 the Electors' Union had been formed to represent the increasingly diversified interests of the European population, replacing the old Convention of Associations as the political voice of the settlers. A principal goal of the new organization was to maintain the unity of the white community by bringing together both farmers and businessmen in the same organization. In a policy statement it emphasized the need for political leadership to continue in European hands. The right of Africans to be represented in the Legislative Council was acknowledged but, significantly, the possibility of direct election was not foreseen for many years—until the African electorate had become qualified in terms of education and economic status. In 1949 the Electors' Union issued its Kenya Plan, which indicated that the European community intended to keep control indefinitely under a hoped-for dominion status similar to that of Canada and Australia.

The political unity of the European community contrasted sharply with the disarray that characterized the African political scene, especially among the politically conscious Kikuyu. By chance, however, an incident in 1949 brought to the attention of the KAU leadership a device for mobilizing mass resistance to colonial authorities. The incident involved the eviction of about 160,000 Kikuyu squatters. In contrast to the usually submissive attitude expressed in similar situations in the past, they presented a solid front against the move and had to be expelled forcibly from the land by the authorities. Their determined resistance was attributed to an oath-taking among the Kikuyu that had welded together the entire community.

Oath-taking in traditional African society was treated with the same general solemnity associated with formal oaths in Western cultures and was held to be just as binding. Indications of a revival of oath-taking created a belief among Europeans that the African population was retrogressing to primitive practices. European fears were heightened by the use of traditional symbols and rituals that were culturally and emotionally abhorrent to Europeans. The result was misinterpretation of the phenomenon and failure to come to grips with the underlying causes of rapidly mushrooming African discontent.

The potential for achieving political unity through oath-taking was immediately realized by KAU leaders and was promoted in Kikuyu rural areas. The response, although great, was not unanimous. Opposition existed among various Christian groups, individuals connected with the administration and their local community supporters, and some better-off African landholders and businessmen. Direction of the rural oath-taking campaign was carried on secretly by an underground group, formerly part of the banned KCA. They were generally political moderates who had preferred change by constitutional means.

Discontent in Nairobi, however, caused by mounting unemployment, brought control of political activities there into the hands of militants, including radical trade union activists ready to use violence to gain self-government, who had taken over the Nairobi KAU branch in 1951. These militants gradually extended their control to some rural areas.

The Mau Mau Emergency

During the late 1940s the term *Mau Mau,* the origin and meaning of which remains unclear, became associated in the minds of the European population with oath-taking and militancy aimed specifically at them. By 1950 security forces were certain that a secret organization bearing the name *Mau Mau* existed. Members, it was believed, were bound together by an oath, and their goal was the expulsion of Europeans from the country. Convincing evidence for the allegation was never produced, however, and Carl G. Rosberg and John Nottingham in their comprehensive analysis, *The Myth of "Mau Mau,"* have suggested that the organization in question was probably the outlawed KCA. In August 1950 the so-called Mau Mau association was officially banned.

During 1951 civil disobedience occurred, and cases of arson and cattle maiming were reported late that year and in early 1952. Worried settlers pressed for a state of emergency to be called, but the administration refused, looking on Mau Mau as a fanatical religious cult rather than a subversive political movement. In October 1952, however, the assassination of Senior Chief Waruhiu brought European demands that resulted in the official declaration of an emergency.

Kenyatta and other KAU leaders were immediately arrested, and he and five others were brought to trial in November. The prosecution attempted to prove a connection between the Mau Mau and the KAU, and the six defendants were charged with belonging to and directing the operations of a Mau Mau society that was dangerous to good government. The trial ended in April 1953 with a verdict of guilty, and maximum sentences of seven years' imprisonment at hard labor were meted out, although one defendant was subsequently acquitted on appeal.

Political considerations weighed heavily in the court's verdict. The presiding judge's finding, which linked Mau Mau and the KAU, may have been influenced by the Lari Massacre, which occurred in March 1953 during the course of the trial. The massacre in fact underlined the point that Africans were the principal victims of the terror. It was carried out by insurgents against villagers described as loyal to their chiefs and the government. Almost 100 people were hacked to death, many animals were killed, and huts were burned in the attack.

An estimated 15,000 insurgents, identified as Mau Mau adherents, withdrew to the heavily forested areas of the central Kenya Highlands. They were organized along military lines, but communications were difficult, and operations were not well coordinated. Although the emergency continued until January 1960, Mau Mau activity had been virtually stamped out by 1956. More than 11,500 Africans, almost all of them Kikuyu, were reported killed in clashes with security forces. Some 1,800 other African civilians died in terrorist actions, and over 500 Africans serving with the government forces also were killed. Sixty-three Europeans in security units were killed, as were 32 settlers, the latter relatively small total seeming to belie the settlers' belief that they were the main target of the Mau Mau. Forty-nine Indians, including civilians and members of the security forces, died as a result of the conflict.

Action not directly of a combat nature also had great impact on the Kikuyu. The dispersed settlement pattern characteristic of the Kikuyu area was completely altered through the concentration of almost 1 million rural people into specially built fortified villages, as part of an operation that was generally completed by 1955. Dwellings formerly occupied by these people were destroyed. The independent Kikuyu school system was closed, and some school buildings were also pulled down. In Nairobi continued unrest and acts of terrorism led the government to institute Operation Anvil in 1954, in which almost one-half of the Kikuyu, Embu, and Meru in the city's population were moved to rural villages. A total of about 90,000 Africans were sent to detention camps during the emergency.

An important outcome of the emergency was a change in official attitudes toward African land tenure and production of commercial crops. Although the colonial administration's Department of Agriculture had advocated changes in African land tenure and consolidation of highly fragmented landholdings since the early 1930s, the influence of settlers who feared African competition in cash crops and the loss of needed cheap labor had prevented any action from being taken. Nonetheless, with government concurrence, limited consolidation through exchange of holdings by some chiefs occurred after 1952, when the recently elected Conservative government in Britain undertook a reassessment of the Kenyan situation and determined to back the colonial administration in its plans for land and agrarian reform.

The proposed reforms were contained in the Swynnerton Plan, which was completed in 1954 at the height of the Mau Mau emergency by R.J.M. Swynnerton, director of the Department of Agriculture, and provided the guidelines for African agricultural development during the remainder of the decade. Official endorsement of land consolidation was given in 1955, at which time financial assistance was also sought from the British government to speed up the process. Aided by the concentration of the Kikuyu rural population in controlled villages, most of the Kikuyu areas had been consolidated, and a large number of freehold titles had been granted by 1959, when reservation of land for the exclusive use of Europeans was legally ended.

Complaints arose over inequities resulting from efforts to meet tight schedules. There was evidence also that not all Kikuyu approved of the scheme, but little opposition was voiced openly because many people apparently believed that in the emergency situation their disagreement would be wrongly construed. An effort was made to protect the interests of detainees, but some lost their land nonetheless.

The Swynnerton Plan also called for a major emphasis on expanding cash crops, a move that would be feasible because of the farmers' new ability to secure financing based on their land titles. A secondary benefit was expected to be the employment of landless people by African landholders. More important from the European viewpoint, however, was the anticipated growth of a landed, relatively well-off African middle class that would have interests similar to those of European landholders and a stake in maintaining the political status quo. New political leadership was expected to emerge from this group to replace that of the presumably discredited KAU.

Substantial development of commercial farming followed land reform. Although spread among a number of crops, the principal advance was in coffee, cultivation of which in the reserves had received full authorization in 1951. The acreage planted to coffee by Africans increased markedly, and the value of production rose from the equivalent of less than US$100,000 in 1954 to over US$6 million in 1960. Pyrethrum production also achieved major gains during this period.

The Resumption of African Political Activity

The arrest of KAU leaders was not followed by the immediate proscription of KAU activities because the government apparently believed that moderates would assume control and operate the party along less militant lines. The new leadership, however, which significantly included individuals from ethnic groups other than the Kikuyu, restated KAU demands. By mid-1953 the administration had concluded that a change in party outlook would not occur, and the KAU was banned. All other African political associations throughout the colony were also proscribed. This proscription was lifted in 1955, but African political organizations were limited to districtwide activities. Moreover, political activity and the formation of political associations continued to be banned in the areas occupied by the Kikuyu, the Embu, and the Meru, except for an advisory council composed of loyalists who had supported the government. Although the effect of the 1953 proscription had been to halt the growth of political institutions on the national level, that of the 1955 order was to strengthen the ethnic aspects of political associations, at the same time acting to stimulate wider local political development.

The political vacuum that existed during these two years was filled in part by the activities of the Kenya Federation of Registered Trade Unions (later renamed the Kenya Federation of Labour—KFL) headed by Tom Mboya, a Luo who became the federation's general secretary in late 1953. KFL political activism, however, was curtailed in 1956 by a threat from the government to cancel the federation's registration.

In 1954 the British government in effect imposed a new constitution on Kenya. Known as the Lyttleton Constitution (after Oliver Lyttleton, the secretary of state for the colonies), it contained the concept of parity in the Legislative Council between European representatives and representatives for the African and Asian communities. Important new provisions were the election of the eight African representatives and the establishment of a multiracial ministerial system in which Africans were assigned one minister and the Asians two.

Elections for the Legislative Council were held in March 1957, and eight candidates were picked from as many African constituencies. In the constituency that included the Kikuyu, Meru, and Embu ethnic groups, however, only loyalists were permitted to vote. The eight men chosen represented a wide range of African groups, but their action in the new legislature was marked by its trans-ethnic character. Six of the new members, including Mboya and Odinga, protested the composition of the legislature on the grounds that the vast majority of Africans were grossly underrepresented, and they demanded an increase in African seats to 15, refusing to accept ministerial appointments until this was agreed to. Their action and the political deadlock that ensued prompted the British government to issue the revised 1958 Lennox-Boyd Constitution (named for the incumbent colonial secretary, Alan Lennox-Boyd), which maintained the principle of multiracialism but increased African members to 14 and Asians to eight. European representation was set at 14, for the first time placing them in the minority. The new charter also provided for an additional four members of each racial group to be picked by the council, acting as an electoral college. The purpose was a hoped-for selection of moderate Africans who would accept ministerial posts, thus attesting to the multiracial character of the government.

The right to organize politically on a national basis was restored in July 1959, with the proviso that organizations had to be multiracial. Earlier in the year the British government had agreed to sponsor a new constitutional conference, and recognition by African leaders of the need for unity at that conference led many to refrain from divisive party activity. The conference, held in early 1960 at Lancaster House in London and presided over by Iain Macleod, the colonial secretary, resulted in the Macleod Constitution, which provided for an African majority in a 65-member Legislative Council. Fifty-three seats, including 20 reserved for the racial minorities, were to be elected by voters on a common roll. The remaining 12 members were to be selected by the council. A majority of the Council of Ministers were to be African, but Europeans were assured three portfolios and Asians, one. The intention of the British government to grant independence within a comparatively short period of time, announced at the opening of the conference, took all participants by surprise, including the African delegates who had expected neither this nor the granting of African majority government.

The reaction of the European participants in the conference to the decisions was mixed. The conference report was rejected outright by the conservative United Party, whose leader stated that the proposals would deal a death blow to Kenya's European community. The moderate New Kenya Party accepted the decisions, but only at the price of British guarantees of funding for African resettlement on land that European farmers wished to sell and security of tenure for Europeans who chose to retain ownership in a multiracial environment.

The unity that characterized the African delegation throughout the Lancaster House conference soon dissipated as disagreement arose over the extent of participation in the new government. In early 1960 the formation of purely African political organizations on a national scale was authorized. Two major parties emerged in which ethnic factors played a part. The Kenya African National Union (KANU) was led by James S. Gichuru, Mboya, and Odinga, who supported continuing opposition to the colonial administration; the party was mainly representative of Kikuyu, Luo, and Kamba. The Kenya African Democratic Union (KADU), headed by Ronald Ngala, Masinde Muliro, and Daniel arap Moi, was basically a defensive coalition of smaller ethnic groups that feared domination by the majority Kikuyu and Luo. KADU's support was based among the Mijikenda and other coastal peoples, the Kalenjin and Maasai, some Luhya groups, and the Somali. Its leaders favored cooperation with the colonial administration, and the party therefore had the support of many in the European and Asian communities.

KANU was in essence the successor of the banned KAU. As early as 1958 Odinga had shocked the Legislative Council by open reference to Kenyatta and a declaration that he and the others convicted with him were the country's genuine political leaders; Odinga and Mboya continued thereafter to press for Kenyatta's release. In April 1959 Kenyatta completed his seven-year term but was immediately placed under detention and kept at Lodwar in the far northwestern part of the country. Nonetheless, in May 1960 KANU leaders nominated Kenyatta to the party presidency, although the action was subsequently disallowed by the government.

Elections under the Macleod Constitution were held in February 1961. The KANU campaign was conducted on a platform stating that if the party were successful, it would not accept ministerial positions until Kenyatta was released and assumed his rightful place as the nation's political leader. KADU's position was less strongly worded but still called for Kenyatta's release. KANU won 16 seats to KADU's nine in the election. Neither party agreed to form a government, creating an impasse that continued for several weeks until KADU joined with the New Kenya Party, the Kenya Indian Congress, and independents to form a coalition administration. KADU's leadership explained that they had decided to participate in order to obtain Kenyatta's freedom. In July 1961 the governor, Sir Patrick Renison, reversed his long-held opposition to the African leader's release and active participation in the independence process, and Kenyatta was freed the following month. In October he became president of KANU without administration objection. The following January he was elected to fill an intentionally vacated seat in the Legislative Council, where he assumed the position of leader of the opposition.

Development of the Independence Constitution

The principal task faced by Kenya's political leaders of all races after the 1961 election was drafting a constitution in order that a transfer of power from the colonial government could be effected. With this partly in mind, KANU and KADU made efforts to reach agreement on their differences in talks during the summer of 1961. The former's arbitrary attitudes, however, raised concern among KADU leaders over dominance of national affairs by the larger ethnic groups after independence. Coupled with an apparent rise in ethnic identity among the groups associated with KADU and a belief that KADU might be able to maintain local control of areas in which such groups lived, the party enunciated its doctrine of regionalism *(majimbo;* Swahili for regions). This concept, which called for a considerable degree of regional autonomy in a federal system, also received the support of New Kenya Party leaders.

Although the regionalism proposed by KADU, as against the centralism favored by KANU, was the major issue at the so-called framework constitution conference finally held in London from February to April 1962, almost equally important were issues concerned with land policy. Regionalism won out in part apparently because of support by the British colonial secretary, in part because of the persistence and intransigency of KADU delegates, and in part because of concern by Kenyatta and KANU leaders that independence would be delayed if they refused to sign. KANU also accepted an expanded land resettlement program proposed by the British government for the preindependence period, although party leaders would have preferred land reform after self-government had been achieved, when the fulfillment of African priorities would become paramount. An interim all-party coalition government, formed after the conclusion of the conference, was left to complete the details of the framework constitution.

Under the provisions of the framework constitution, a general election was held in May 1963 for the new National Assembly, composed of the House of Representatives (117 elected seats plus 12 to be filled later by the assembly) and the Senate (41 elected seats). Regional assemblies were also elected. Voting was conducted in single-member constituencies by voters registered on a common roll. The delimitation of constituency boundaries favored KADU by giving greater representation to less populated rural and pastoral areas whose people supported regionalism, compared with the more heavily populated Kikuyu and Luo areas.

In preelection campaigns KADU emphasized ethnic identification, regionalism, and economic liberalism, while KANU's approach stressed nationalism, centralism, and so-called African socialism. In foreign affairs KANU advocated a completely nonaligned approach, whereas KADU appeared to favor keeping British bases on Kenyan soil. It became clear as the campaign progressed that, although the principle of regionalism had been agreed to in the framework constitution, a

KANU victory would nonetheless force some modification of regionalist proposals and could lead eventually to a centralized form of government.

Although the main contestants in the election were KANU and KADU, a third party, the African People's Party (APP), headed by Kamba leader Paul Ngei, put up a strong fight. Ngei had been a member of KANU but had withdrawn after disagreement over the Kamba district party leadership. The election results gave KANU 70 seats, KADU 32, and APP eight. Independents won two seats, and five seats were not filled because of the boycott of the election by the Somali, whose leaders were demanding the right for their region to secede and join Somalia. In the Senate election, important because of the large number of votes required in that body to amend the constitution, KANU took 18 seats, KADU 16, APP two, and others two; three Somali seats went unfilled because of the boycott. Of the 12 members selected by the National Assembly, 11 were from KANU.

The national character of KANU had been demonstrated by the election returns. The party swept the Kikuyu-Embu-Meru seats and nearly all the seats in western Kenya inhabited by the Luo. It won the large towns, except Mombasa, and took other seats in areas peopled by the Kamba, Luhya, and Kalenjin; the pastoralist Turkana voted solidly for KANU. Two members of the European community were also picked by KANU in the election to fill the special seats in the assembly. In elections for regional assemblies KANU won control of Nyanza, Central, and Eastern regions, and KADU took Western, Rift Valley, and Coast regions; no assembly was elected in North-Eastern Region, inhabited largely by Somali (the regions were renamed provinces in 1964). No major KANU politician ran in the regional elections, however, because of the party's opposition to regionalism.

The Kenyatta Era

Kenya was granted internal self-government on June 1, 1963. Kenyatta, as leader of KANU, became prime minister and selected a cabinet that was well balanced ethnically. Five ministers were Kikuyu, four Luo, one Kamba, one Luhya, one Meru, and one came from Coast Region. A European was appointed agriculture minister, and a European and an Asian were made parliamentary secretaries; the speaker of the House of Representatives was a European, and the deputy speaker an Asian. Kenyatta emphasized the necessity of unity of all ethnic and racial groups for the economic betterment of the entire nation, but in October a KANU-inspired effort to merge KANU and KADU was unsuccessful. In early 1964, however, the KADU leadership announced support for a policy of unity, which had priority over ethnic considerations.

In September 1963 a final conference had been held in London to reach agreement on the constitutional issues dividing the various participants. Although KANU's position in the National Assembly had been strengthened by defections from the other parties (bringing the total of KANU-held seats to 23 in the Senate and to 99 in the lower house), its representatives were unable to prevent the inclusion of significant regional features in the new Independence Constitution (also known in Kenya as the Majimbo Constitution). Thus, when the country attained independence within the Commonwealth on December 12, its governmental system was far more decentralized than that in the colonial period.

Party Politics in the 1960s

The Somali problem in North-Eastern Region was an immediate concern of the new government. Both major parties agreed that the Somali area should not be permitted to secede from Kenya and that the Somali insurgents, called *shifta* (bandits), should be suppressed. In December 1963, however, the government was defeated in a move to secure the extraordinary majority required in the Senate for the continuance of the state of emergency in North-Eastern Region. KADU refused to go along, claiming that its leaders had not been consulted. The Senate recessed, and the government threatened to continue the emergency without authorization. Instead Kenyatta called a hurried meeting with opposition leaders, the Senate was reconvened, and KADU acceded to the government's request.

In late January 1964 the government faced a new problem in the mutiny of some officers and men of an army battalion. The mutiny, put down with the aid of British troops in Kenya, did not seriously threaten the government but forced it, nonetheless, to make a broad reassessment of the military's role in the new nation.

Despite its early 1964 statement of the need for unity, KADU was highly vocal in its opposition to the government. Its fortunes were on the decline, however. Elections were held in North-Eastern Region to fill the vacant Somali seats, and pro-KANU candidates were returned. In a March speech Kenyatta—noting that the membership of the House of Representatives now stood at 105 KANU and 22 KADU—said that the country would soon have only one party. The idea of a one-party system was increasingly mentioned by KANU leaders, with the proviso that the system not be imposed by law but be voluntarily accepted by the opposition members. Moreover, such a one-party system would be distinct, it was argued, from a one-party state imposed by law.

KADU continued to call upon the government to enforce the regionalist features of the Independence Constitution and threatened to take it to court for failing to do so. In August 1964 the government announced its intention to amend the constitution in order to make the country a republic, creating an office of president and abolishing regional autonomy. Kenyatta warned that if the National Assembly would not agree to the amendments, he would go to the people in a referendum.

A heated debate took place on the first amendment dealing with the presidency but, by the time the vote was taken in early November,

Jomo Kenyatta, independent Kenya's first president Courtesy CNI News/Bill Chewning

KADU's strength in the House of Representatives had been whittled away still further by defections, and the proposal carried in that chamber. In the Senate, however, the party still retained more than one-third of the seats. It appeared that the first amendment, which required a 75 percent majority vote there, and the second amendment to abolish regionalism, which required a 90 percent majority vote, would be rejected. Two days before the scheduled vote on the bill to establish a republic, three KADU senators defected to KANU, ensuring the necessary majority. On November 10, before any vote was taken in the Senate, Ngala made a dramatic announcement on the floor of the assembly that KADU had dissolved itself and that its members wished to join KANU. They were welcomed to the government's side, the constitutional amendments were adopted, and the country entered a period of one-party rule.

On the first anniversary of independence, Kenya was proclaimed a republic, remaining within the Commonwealth. Kenyatta became its first president elected, according to the constitutional amendment, by the National Assembly, and Odinga was named his vice president. The cabinet was enlarged and made more representative of various ethnic groups and political opinion in the country. Moi, who had been a leading figure in KADU, received the important position of minister of home affairs.

In early 1965 long-standing disagreements between the generally older, more conservative members of KANU and the party's younger, more radical members on economic and political policies began to surface in struggles for control of local party branches. Formerly, such differences had been smoothed out by Kenyatta behind the scenes or had been kept in hand by the realization that a KANU split could be detrimental to early attainment of independence. At the same time, however, factions also polarized behind Mboya or Odinga, whose rivalry for party influence went back to Legislative Council days. Mboya was favored by moderate elements, and Odinga by those inclined to the left. Charges of foreign influence and of the receipt of foreign funds to promote factional aims were exchanged, although little concrete evidence was ever produced.

Early in 1965 Odinga made a speech in which he said, "Communism is like food to me," a statement taken as significant by many Kenyans and foreign observers alike. He complained that he had been intentionally stripped of all governmental power when he was appointed vice president, and he was increasingly critical of other ministers. The matter came to a head in April 1965 when he accused Mboya and Ngala of being tools of Britain and the United States. Minister of Labour Julius Gikonyo Kiano and others quickly responded and asked Odinga either to stop criticizing them or to resign. Because of Odinga's actions, Kenyatta removed him from a delegation scheduled to attend the 1965 Commonwealth Conference. Relations between Kenyatta and Odinga worsened as the president grew more suspicious of communist influence in Kenyan politics.

In December 1964 Kenyatta had opened a Soviet-financed party training center, the Lumumba Institute, which Odinga had sponsored. The school had Soviet staff members, and leftist elements within KANU were heavily represented in its student body and administration. Radical demands by students and the use of the school by left-oriented legislators to push their views led to criticism in parliament and charges of communism from some. On June 1, 1965, the second anniversary of internal self-government (Madaraka Day), Kenyatta made a major speech denouncing communism and warning of the dangers of communist imperialism. These pressures led the party to close the school in June 1965. In July a group of 27 students who had been trained at the Lumumba Institute entered KANU headquarters in Nairobi and declared all party officers deposed except Kenyatta. They were quickly arrested, and 26 were convicted in September.

The incident increased rumors of an impending coup, rumors that were given credence by statements of various ministers. The rest of the year was characterized by open competition between Odinga and

Kenyatta, who followed one another around the country making speeches. Nonetheless, when Kenyatta reshuffled the cabinet in December 1965, Odinga was retained as vice president. His authority to supervise elections, however, was transferred to another minister.

That same winter a number of military coups took place throughout Africa, and there was serious unrest in neighboring Uganda. Recognizing that some of the army takeovers had been directed against dishonest and extravagant politicians, Kenyatta took action against members of the Maize Marketing Board who were involved in irregularities and suspended Ngei, the Kamba leader, from his ministerial duties while corruption charges against him were being investigated. The government also announced that during 1965 over 100 other officials were tried and convicted of abusing their positions.

In order to strengthen his position against the leftists, Kenyatta had Mboya introduce in the National Assembly a motion of confidence in the government. Despite Odinga's protests, the motion, proposed in February 1966, was carried. The same month the organizing secretary of KANU, John Keen, published an open letter to the president in which he criticized the "appalling" state of the party. He noted that the last delegates' conference had been held in October 1962 and the last secretariat meeting in February 1964. He asserted that the party was heavily in debt and that the staff had not been paid for seven months. He asked that Mboya be relieved of either his ministerial or his party post as secretary general and suggested that a commission of inquiry look into KANU's role in the one-party state. These statements, coming in the wake of other criticisms of the party and Odinga's growing disaffection, persuaded Kenyatta to call a conference of delegates and district officials for March 1966.

On the eve of the conference the government expelled a number of diplomats accredited to Nairobi from communist countries. The press reported that they had been attempting to buy delegates' votes and had been in close touch with Odinga supporters. The party's conservative group was in full control, and Kenyatta, who dominated the conference, was reelected party president. Odinga was removed from his post as party vice president; other party officeholders believed to be radicals were replaced, and new party vice presidents were elected in each province and Nairobi Area. They included two ex-KADU leaders, Ngala and Moi, who were elected vice presidents from their respective provinces. Mboya was reelected secretary general in a contest with Masinde Muliro, the former KADU leader who had lined up with the left wing. After winning in a preliminary vote for vice president of Central Province, Bildad Kaggia, the prominent Kikuyu leftist and former head of the Lumumba Institute, was defeated by Gichuru. The outcome of the conference was to expel the left from positions of influence and to increase ethnic and geographical representation in the party's major offices.

In April Odinga resigned as vice president, making a long statement in which he criticized the government on a large number of points.

He asserted that it ignored the "common man" and represented foreign interests. His resignation was followed by that of a minister and two assistant ministers. Several labor union officials also resigned from KANU and lined up with Odinga. A total of 30 representatives and senators, including one appointive member, resigned from KANU, and on April 26 the formation of a new party, the Kenya People's Union (KPU), was announced. Odinga was named president, and Kaggia deputy president.

KANU responded to these events vigorously and issued a series of statements denouncing the dissidents. A plan was devised to expel the Odinga group from the National Assembly. Because this could not be done by a simple vote, it was decided to amend the constitution so that a person who had been elected to the assembly under one label would be required to vacate his seat if he switched to another party. The amendment was directed solely against KPU members; former members of KADU were not affected since members of absorbed or disbanded parties were excluded from the provisions of the amendment. Upon hearing this proposal, 13 KPU members reconsidered and asked for reentry into KANU.

Although KPU had not yet received government registration as a political party, the speaker of the House of Representatives recognized it as an opposition party for purposes of debating the proposal. The amendment was easily passed with the aid of the repentant KPU members—who were subsequently told they would not be reaccepted into KANU—and the KPU seats were declared vacant; by-elections to fill these seats were scheduled for June.

KPU members generally fell into three categories. They included Luo supporters of Odinga; politicans representing local interests usually in more remote areas who felt that KANU and the government had neglected to consider local problems; and the radical element, mostly younger men, who disagreed with KANU policies concerning landownership, education, and what they labeled "capitalist control of the means of production." Most if not all of the radicals had supported Kenyatta, their main complaint being against party leaders at the middle level and their influence on Kenyatta. The break with KANU, however, raised the question of alternative national leadership.

The formation of KPU ended the one-party state but was to have little effect on the course of Kenyan politics. By-elections were set for three two-day periods in June 1966. KPU was handicapped in its campaign by a delay in the official registration of the party. The party was also at a disadvantage because of government control of the radio, and broadcast information on KPU was given the general public only indirectly in connection with the reporting of KANU activities. Press coverage was somewhat better and was generally extensive for larger rallies in city areas.

Although some campaigning by higher KANU party and government officials occurred, KANU candidates by and large were left on their own with little assistance from the central organization. Only one-third of the eligible voters participated. The results, however, were overwhelmingly in support of KANU, which won eight of the 10 Senate seats and 12 of the 19 House seats. One of the seven seats won by KPU went to Odinga by a large majority. Total KPU membership in parliament thus amounted to only nine, of whom six were Luo, two were Kamba, and one was from a minor ethnic group in western Kenya. (In December 1966 the constitution was amended making the National Assembly a unicameral body.) During the next three years the government took actions that were detrimental to KPU activities in local areas, including the refusal to register party branches and nominations for elections on various technicalities and the detention of more active members under public security regulations.

On July 9, 1969, Mboya was assassinated for motives never fully determined. His killer was a Kikuyu and, although Mboya, a Luo, had been a strong supporter of Kenyatta and KANU, many of the Luo viewed his death as an ethnic affront. Luo-Kikuyu enmity increased rapidly in the next few months. It was capped in October 1969 when KPU was banned, and its principal leaders, including Odinga and the party's other members of parliament, were detained. These actions occurred after a visit by President Kenyatta to Kisumu, during which a large crowd of Luo reportedly menaced his safety and was fired on by security guards. In an explanatory statement the government accused KPU of becoming subversive, intentionally stirring up interethnic strife, and accepting funds from foreign agencies to promote KPU activities. The proscription in effect brought a return to the single-party state.

Kenyanization and Economic Policy

When independence was achieved in 1963, Europeans and Asians were firmly entrenched in control of Kenya's economy, the result not only of their competitive advantage over the African majority but also of restrictions imposed on African participation during the colonial period. Although the transfer of land to African ownership had begun with British assistance before independence, Europeans still occupied the best agricultural areas in the White Highlands. Asians were dominant at every level of the business community, from that of the large-scale merchant to the small shopkeeper. Meanwhile, fewer than one in three of those in the Asian community and a much smaller percentage of permanently resident Europeans had accepted the option to become Kenyan citizens.

Noncitizen Europeans and Asians operated the country's financial institutions, its industries, and most of its services and included most of those engaged in the liberal professions, such as medicine and law. After independence African leaders condemned the overwhelmingly disproportionate presence of noncitizens in the economic life of the country as an unwanted legacy of the colonial period that compromised Kenya's sovereignty and barred the African majority from making material progress. In Kenyatta's words, "A country is never fully independent until its economy is controlled by its citizens."

Accordingly, a policy of Kenyanization was proposed that required the replacement of noncitizens by citizens in all sectors of the economy. It not only aimed at giving positive assistance to citizens in obtaining property or gaining employment but also discriminated actively against noncitizens. In principle, the program was not racially motivated, formally distinguishing between citizens and noncitizens engaged in economic activity rather than between Africans and non-Africans, but in practice Kenyanization was clearly intended to further African interests by eliminating competition from better trained, better financed Europeans and Asians. African owners, it was anticipated, would in turn hire African employees, unlike entrepreneurs in the typically family-operated Asian businesses. Meanwhile, priority would be given to training Africans to take over skilled positions from noncitizens.

Kenyanization efforts first focused on ensuring for Kenyan nationals preference in hiring in the civil service and, as they became qualified, for executive and technical positions in large foreign-owned firms. Implementation of the program on a broader scale, involving the displacement of noncitizens, was advanced in two specific pieces of legislation, the Kenya Immigration Act of 1967 and the Trading Licensing Act of 1968. The 1967 act repealed the ordinance that had allowed noncitizens temporary residence on renewable four-year work permits. Under the new law noncitizens could apply to remain in Kenya only if their skills were not available in the African work force. Under the provisions of the second act, licenses to conduct commercial enterprises were progressively withdrawn from Asians and reissued to Africans. The act also limited those areas where "noncitizens"—specifically Asians—could legally engage in business. Wholesale, retail, and export-import trade was reserved exclusively for citizens, and a deadline of January 1, 1969, was set for noncitizens to liquidate their holdings. Businesses owned by noncitizens in Nairobi and Mombasa were excluded initially because of the size of foreign involvement in those cities, but restrictions were gradually imposed there as well. Noncitizens were expected to leave Kenya as soon as possible after their affairs had been settled.

Some 15,000 Asians who had retained British passports after independence left Kenya in the months immediately after enactment of the Kenyanization legislation, most of them heading for Britain. To stem the sudden influx, the British government limited entry to the holders of 1,500 immigration vouchers that were to be issued annually to Asians in Kenya holding British passports. India, meanwhile, barred entry to Asians holding British passports. By 1970 the number of Asians in Kenya, which had been 200,000 at independence, was reduced to 140,000, less than one-half of whom had obtained Kenyan citizenship. Five years later, only 100,000 Asians remained, of whom 20,000 were on the waiting list for vouchers to emigrate to Britain. Many of the potential emigrants were deprived of the means to earn a livelihood, while others made illegal arrangements with African proxies to operate their businesses. Even Asians who held Kenyan citizenship reportedly suffered from official harassment, and some had their Kenyan passports canceled.

By the mid-1970s Kenyanization of retail trade and road transport was virtually complete, although as elsewhere in the private sector non-African citizens played the dominant role. The influence of large multinational corporations, which furnished a large share of the investment and technology needed for economic development, was strengthened in the intervening years, during which the corporations were supportive of Kenyanization through their hiring practices. Foreigners, mostly British, still occupied more than one-third of management and about two-thirds of all professional-level posts in foreign-owned corporations. But by the mid-1970s, as more Africans acquired the requisite education and experience and as British nationals who had remained in top managerial positions were repatriated, about 75 percent of middle- and high-level positions in government and modern private enterprise were held by Africans, and close to 90 percent of public employees were Africans. Although the last of the British officers on secondment to the Kenyan armed forces and police were relieved in 1975, government administration still relied significantly on a small cadre of expatriate personnel in professional grades.

The Kenyanization of European-held farmland was both more complete than had been possible with managerial and professional positions and less traumatic than had been the exodus of Asian aliens. A large part of British economic assistance to Kenya after independence was used to buy out European settlers through the Land Transfer Program and to facilitate the resettlement of African farmers. According to the letter of the law, sales were voluntary, but the Kenyan government warned that "severe action" might be taken against noncitizens who delayed in disposing of their landed property. In 1974 the number of African-owned farms in what once had been known as the White Highlands had reached 1,400 as compared with only 58 in 1963, and the process of transfer of land from noncitizens was completed by the end of the decade. Many of the large estates were acquired intact by African buyers, who continued to operate them in the same manner as their previous European owners had. Despite the turnover in proprietorship, about 120,000 hectares of prime farmland remained in the possession of Europeans who had become Kenyan citizens.

Kenyanization also furthered the development of an educated and prosperous African elite that owed its rise to the regime. It included not only government and party officials and members of the legislature and the civil service, many of whom had benefited from their public positions to become successful in business, but also successful businessmen and landowners who had used their newly acquired wealth to gain entry into public life. The connection of government and business through interlocking political, professional, and entrepreneurial elites seemed to ensure public support for various enterprises and to attract investment to them.

Opponents of the regime criticized the government for its gradualist approach to Kenyanization. Odinga in particular spoke in favor of forced expulsion of noncitizens and outright expropriation of their property. He and others considered to represent the left wing of Kenyan politics also urged public control of businesses given up by the Asians and redistribution of land vacated by Europeans to smallholders, alleging corruption and favoritism in the reissuing of commercial licenses and the sale of property to politically well-connected Africans.

The prevailing economic philosophy in postindependence Kenya differed markedly from that in many other emerging African nations in placing primary reliance on private enterprise to generate rapid growth. KANU's preindependence manifesto and the government's subsequent paper on African socialism in Kenya had stated that nationalization would be resorted to only in cases of extreme urgency, when foreign-owned firms were clearly operating to the detriment of national interests. The concept of African socialism itself was defined in Kenya as one that promised equality of opportunity but did not guarantee equality of results.

By the late 1960s this liberal policy was modified somewhat to meet the demands of the Kenyanization program, which required the government to increase the degree of public participation in key sectors of the economy. Private enterprise, however, remained the dominant element. At the same time, by granting liberal provisions for the repatriation of profits, Kenya succeeded in attracting substantial foreign investment and in generating an exceptionally high overall rate of growth, averaging 6.5 percent annually during the period 1964-72. The advantage was partially offset by a parallel population growth rate of more than 3 percent and, although per capita growth persisted despite the population rise, it neither provided a cure for unemployment nor alleviated the poverty of the lowest income groups in rural areas.

In 1974 the World Bank (see Glossary) cited Kenya as one of the 30 countries whose economies were worst hit by the increase in world oil prices. The rate of growth dropped markedly, and in 1975 real income declined for the first time. The dominant features of the Kenyan economy in the second half of the decade were a deteriorating foreign trade balance and a high rate of inflation, both related to energy costs. A fortuitous boom in export commodity prices in 1976 and 1977 reversed this trend temporarily, but underlying structural problems—slowing agricultural growth, dependence by the modern sector on costly fuel imports, and limits to export substitution development—posed an obstacle to sustained growth (see Economic Development, ch. 3).

Foreign Relations and Conflicts

The direction of Kenya's foreign policy was determined in the first decade after independence by imperatives that had their origin in the colonial period. Notably, these included close political and economic ties to Britain, institutional and economic links with Tanganyika and Uganda, confrontation with Somalia over the largely Somali-populated territory in northeastern Kenya, and the need to maintain and extend export markets. As in other matters, Kenyatta's was the controlling voice in the formulation of foreign policy, which reflected his moderation, caution, and pragmatism and emphasized African solidarity and Kenya's reliance on the West for technical assistance and investment.

Kenya chose to exert its influence abroad through membership in international and regional bodies. It maintained its attachment to the Commonwealth, was admitted to the United Nations (UN) shortly after independence, and participated in the Organization of African Unity (OAU). The East African Community was viewed at its inception as a vehicle for eventual regional federation. Kenya benefited from Commonwealth trade preferences and was included in the Lomé Convention, ensuring preferential treatment for its imports by member states, after Britain joined the European Economic Community (EEC) in 1972.

Despite its Western orientation and the special nature of its relations with Britain, Kenya stressed its adherence to a policy of nonalignment in the East-West confrontation. Additionally, it sought to win guarantees of a nuclear-free zone in Africa and in 1974 joined India in appealing to Britain and the United States to withdraw plans for establishing a naval base at Diego Garcia and to acknowledge the Indian Ocean as a zone of peace. Kenya also supported programs intended to redress the existing international economic order, which it regarded as disadvantageous to countries like itself whose economies were dependent on the production of raw materials for export to the industrialized countries.

The OAU was regarded by Kenya as the primary channel for cooperation among African states. In chorus with other African leaders, Kenyatta had demanded immediate British action in 1965 to restore a legal government in Southern Rhodesia. He had refrained, however, from voicing his views on white minority rule in southern Africa as strongly as had some other OAU heads of state. Kenya's stand on southern Africa hardened after the appointment of Njoroge Mungai, the president's confidant, as foreign minister in 1969. Within the OAU, as well as in the UN and the Commonwealth, Kenya assumed an activist role in efforts to enforce the UN-decreed boycott of Southern Rhodesia and to prevent arms sales to South Africa and in 1972 threw its political support behind national liberation movements in Southern Rhodesia and Namibia (South West Africa).

Relations with Major Powers

Because of its moderation and the independence of its positions from outside influence, Kenya became a recognized force within the Commonwealth. Kenya in turn made use of its Commonwealth connections to gain additional technical assistance and to bring collective diplomatic pressure to bear on Britain to require a settlement based on black majority rule in Southern Rhodesia. The implementation of the Kenyanization program put Kenya at loggerheads with Commonwealth members Britain and India. British legislation restricting the flow of Asians into Britain and India's refusal to admit Asians holding British passports brought loud charges from Nairobi that those countries were attempting to sabotage the program. The breach in Anglo-Kenyan relations was closed when a bilateral agreement was reached, limiting the rate at which Asians would be forced to leave Kenya. A subsequent Anglo-Indian agreement on the passport issue that allowed temporary admission into India of expelled Asians claiming British nationality served also to relieve the acute tensions that had developed between Kenya and India. The well-being of Asians in Kenya remained, however, a sensitive issue in Kenya's relations with India.

Despite the continuing friction with Britain over what Kenya contended was London's responsibility for events in Southern Rhodesia, the two countries retained their special relationship and, although Kenyan spokesmen were regularly critical of the British position on southern Africa, their attitude appeared to be governed by the same practical approach followed in other matters. Britain was Kenya's most important trading partner and its largest source of private investment. Britain was the primary donor of technical assistance and economic aid and also supplied most of Kenya's military equipment and training. In exchange, British military units were permitted to conduct exercises on Kenyan territory, often in conjunction with Kenyan forces.

Kenya's first contacts with the United States came through the American Federation of Labor-Congress of Industrial Organizations (AFL-CIO), which had contributed financial support to Mboya's union in the days before independence. Mboya's American ties were valuable for relations between the two countries when he later became a cabinet minister and secretary general of KANU. After independence Kenya's government was particularly sensitive to American activity in Africa, and in 1965 it condemned United States involvement in the Congo (later Zaïre). Odinga and others associated with him sought to portray the United States as an imperialist power in order to encourage a tilt in Kenya's foreign policy in favor of the Soviet Union. After Odinga's fall from power in 1966, most prominent Kenyan political figures maintained an openly friendly attitude toward the United States. Relations between the two countries continued to develop along cordial lines in the 1970s, a major impetus to this course stemming from Kenya's basic economic policy encouraging free enterprise and foreign investment (see United States, ch. 4).

Kenyatta demonstrated repeatedly his distaste for communism and his sensitivity to attempts by foreign powers to influence Kenyan international affairs. Relations with the Soviet Union were complicated from the start by Odinga's enthusiasm for closer ties with communist countries. In part to counter the effect of aid received from the United States by Mboya, Odinga before independence had sought financial aid and scholarships from the Soviet Union. As vice president in 1964 he led a mission to Beijing (Peking) and Moscow, where he signed aid and technical assistance agreements without the approval or prior knowledge of the cabinet. China offered an interest-free development loan and a smaller direct grant. Initial Soviet aid consisted of a shipment of obsolete weapons that the government ordered returned because of their unsuitability. This incident, combined with evidence that arms were reaching dissidents in North-Eastern Province from Soviet-equipped Somalia, started Soviet-Kenyan relations off badly.

The Soviet aid procured by Odinga had also included assistance for health care and education. A modern hospital, for instance, was constructed and equipped with Soviet aid at Kisumu, Odinga's hometown. The Soviets also agreed to Odinga's request to build and provide instructors for the Lumumba Institute, where ideological training could be given to KANU activists. Although plans for the hospital and school were allowed to proceed, the government announced that it would not accept into the armed forces the several groups of Kenyans that had been sent under Odinga's patronage to East European countries for military training, particularly as pilots. While some Kenyan students who had gone to the Soviet Union for academic training returned voicing pro-Marxist sentiments, others came back loudly denouncing Soviet racism. Both reactions were disturbing to the Kenyan government and further prejudiced relations with the Soviet Union.

The government had also grown concerned about the involvement of the embassies of communist countries in Kenya's internal politics, which generally took the form of bankrolling Odinga's activities, and 10 communist diplomats were expelled in March 1966. The Soviet Union lost its only significant level of influence in Kenya when Odinga's fall from power was confirmed by his resignation as vice president and by the defeat of his faction at the polls in 1966. Despite the animosity toward the Soviet Union generated by these events and by Soviet military assistance to Somalia, Nairobi retained proper diplomatic relations with Moscow, but the Soviets thereafter adopted a much lower profile in Kenya.

The East African Community

Kenya's economy had benefited greatly during the colonial period from its access to the less developed markets in Uganda and Tanganyika. After 1920, when the latter came under British administration, the three territories constituted in effect a common market in which goods, services, capital, and labor moved freely across their common borders. In 1923 Kenya and Uganda formed a customs union that was joined by Tanganyika in 1927. Their external customs departments were integrated in 1949, when a common income tax system was also introduced. Railroads and harbors were administered by single authorities as were the postal service and telecommunications. The East Africa Currency Board, established in 1919, formulated a regional monetary policy and issued a common currency. An inter-territorial appellate court exercised jurisdiction over the region. Policy questions of mutual interest were resolved at an annual meeting of the three colonial governors until 1948 when a permanent regional administration, the East African High Commission, was created. It was renamed the East African Common Services Organization (EACSO) after Tanganyika became independent in 1961 but continued to function essentially in the same manner.

As Kenya and Uganda approached independence, however, the unity achieved under EACSO began to disintegrate under pressure of the members' competing economic interests. The modern sector, particularly its industrial component, had developed more rapidly in Kenya, and as a result Kenya enjoyed a substantially favorable balance of trade with its partners. In 1964 Uganda and Tanzania (the name adopted after merger of Tanganyika and Zanzibar that same year) sought agreement on a quota system to regulate Kenyan imports in order to foster development of their own infant industries. When the Kenyan government failed to ratify the proposal, Uganda and Tanzania unilaterally imposed restrictions on Kenyan goods and on travel, and in 1965 the decision was made to create separate currencies. Disappointed by a turn in events that was so clearly in conflict with their declarations in favor of African unity, the leaders of the three nations agreed in September 1965 to a solution that would retain the advantages of common services and preferential access to combined internal markets while seeking means to redress the imbalance in the pattern of trade. A commission was appointed under the chairmanship of Danish economist Kjeld Philip to examine the current and long-term problems of East African cooperation. The report of the Philip Commission formed the basis for a treaty, which came into force in December 1967, formally establishing the East African Community (EAC).

With minor modifications, the institutional structure of the EAC was patterned on that of the EACSO. Executive authority over community matters was vested in the three heads of state, acting jointly as the East African Authority. A minister for East African affairs with cabinet rank was appointed by each of the three governments to collaborate with his counterparts in coordinating the work of five councils on which they were joined by other ministers responsible for relevant portfolios in their respective governments.

The treaty provided for a uniform system of taxation and fiscal incentives for investment. The partners pledged to maintain a common external tariff. Although the treaty created an instrumentality for progressing toward a common market in the long run, its short-term aim was one of narrowing the trade gap between Kenya and the other two members. The East Africa Development Bank was established to promote balanced industrial growth in conjunction with the World Bank. Common services included the East African Railways Corporation, East African Airways (EAA), the East Africa National Shipping Line, and other similar community agencies for river and road traffic, harbors, and posts and telecommunications that were carried over from the EACSO.

Fissures appeared almost immediately in the EAC edifice, however. The EAC was not popular in official circles in Kenya which, it was felt, bore too much of the burden of operating expenses and had been called on to make more than its share of sacrifices to accommodate the less developed economies of Tanzania and Uganda. Given that disparity, Kenyans had difficulty in viewing the EAC as an association of coequals. Nor did the different personalities and political assumptions of Kenyatta, Tanzania's Julius Nyerere, and Uganda's president, Milton Obote, contribute to close cooperation. Controversies arose over the financing of community agencies and the methods of operating them, over the division of gains and responsibilities, and ultimately over the purpose of association. Kenya, for example, sought expanded markets for its superior manufacturing capacity, while the Tanzanians urged economic interdependence. Kenya's economy was capitalist, Tanzania's socialist. Kenya prided itself on its democratic institutions, while Tanzania unfavorably contrasted Kenya's "neocolonialist" approach to development with its own policy of "self-reliance." Tanzania charged that Kenya was unduly influenced by the United States, while Kenyan leaders were troubled by Tanzania's interaction in many areas with communist countries. Kenya anticipated the creation of a common market, free of restrictions, that would allow it to increase its regional industrial advantage in cooperation with foreign-owned corporations. Tanzania looked for acceptance of central planning for allocation of goods and coordination of production. When Nyerere charged that Kenya's capitalist orientation prevented the restructuring of the EAC along these lines, Kenyans responded that Tanzania was sabotaging progress toward a common market and reprimanded its president for his socialist dogmatism.

Although Tanzania insisted that continued joint management of community services was essential to any future consideration of dropping trade quotas or of movement toward a common market, it was delinquent in its remittances to support their administering agencies, and Uganda's bill went unpaid. The East African Railways Corporation ceased to operate as a single unit in 1974 after disagreement on financing and standards of equipment maintenance. When Tanzania rejected Kenya's application for community action to enlarge port facilities at Mombasa, Kenya refused to make further payments to the EAC harbor authority which, like other services, soon splintered into separate national systems.

The violent events that took place in Uganda after the military coup there in 1971 put a further strain on regional cooperation in East Africa. In January of that year Obote's government was toppled by army units led by Major General (later Field Marshal) Idi Amin Dada. The ousted Ugandan president was granted asylum in Tanzania by Nyerere, who made no secret of his sympathy for Obote and his personal animosity for Amin. Armed clashes between Ugandan and Tanzanian soldiers occurred on several occasions along the border, and in September 1972 Obote supporters used Tanzania as a base for an ill-fated invasion of Uganda. Fighting continued until October, when a peace was arranged between Tanzania and Uganda through Kenyatta's mediation.

The conflict between its EAC partners affected Kenya in two ways. First, at the executive level the EAC was virtually paralyzed because of Nyerere's refusal to attend any meeting in which Amin participated. Second, Kenya's bilateral relations were also troubled.

The Kenyan government was disturbed by continuing signs of instability in Uganda, the threat to Kenya's security posed by the Ugandan military, the Soviet arms that were reaching them, and the unpredictability of Amin's actions. The situation in Uganda also had an economic impact on Kenya, which had profited not only from its own trade with the landlocked country but also from the transit of goods between Mombasa and their destinations in Uganda.

Relations with Uganda were further strained by the disappearance of Kenyans working and studying there, who were apparently caught up in the waves of indiscriminate killings perpetrated by Ugandan soldiers. Although Kenya continued formally to adhere to a policy of offering neither criticism nor praise of the Amin regime, relations turned decidedly for the worse in February 1976, when Amin laid claim to the large section of western Kenya that had been ceded to the East Africa Protectorate during the colonial period and closed Uganda's border with Kenya. In July ties deteriorated to the verge of war when Uganda charged Kenya with complicity in the Israeli commando operation that liberated hostages held at the Entebbe airport. Talks in November 1977 between Moi and Amin brought an agreement reopening the border to trade. Two months later Peter Mungai Kenyatta, the president's son and an assistant minister of foreign affairs, was dispatched to Kampala to reassure Amin of Kenya's "brotherly" and "friendly" attitude toward Uganda (see Tanzania and Uganda, ch. 4).

In the early 1970s Tanzania had taken additional steps to limit Kenyan imports in order to conserve foreign exchange and protect domestic producers. Measures included putting a stiff licensing fee on imports and insisting that shipments from Kenya be delivered either by air or by sea. In addition to protesting these restrictions, Kenya complained that Tanzania was importing goods from outside the EAC, particularly cement from China, that were available in Kenya. The Tanzanians responded that China had offered better terms of trade, but it was not difficult for the Kenyans to see in this trend a departure from EAC movement toward a common market.

The weakening of the EAC infrastructure and the growing barriers to its trade with Tanzania led Kenya to strengthen its economic ties with other countries in eastern Africa and to improve transportation and communications links with them. Commercial contacts with Zambia in particular had been improving since the late 1960s as that country sought outlets to the sea free from dependence on Southern Rhodesia.

Initially, most Zambian traffic was routed through Tanzania to Dar es Salaam, but serious overcrowding there caused much Zambian cargo to be shifted to Mombasa. Tanzania, in retaliation for the loss of business at its major port, cut off truck traffic from Zambia to Kenya briefly in 1974. Early in 1977, Tanzania closed its border with Kenya to all commercial and tourist traffic.

Within the EAC framework, public utilities in Kenya had registered net losses. Road transport to Tanzania had been severely restricted. All international and intercontinental flights on EAA, the flagship line of the EAC, were routed to Dar es Salaam, while the international-class airports at Nairobi and Mombasa were limited to interregional flights. Every attempt to expand their capacity in order to bring tourists from overseas directly to Kenya was frustrated. In January 1977 Kenya acted unilaterally to dissolve the EAA, forming Kenya Airways as its national carrier with EAA equipment in Kenya and opening its major airports to international traffic. Tanzania at first refused to recognize Kenya's right to split the system and denied landing rights to Kenya Airways aircraft, but Kenya's action had effectively sealed the fate of the EAC.

In the months that followed, some effort was made to reorganize trade relations and restore transportation links but, despite World Bank mediation, no mutually acceptable formula could be found for salvaging the EAC. The regional association was dismantled, and a commission was assigned to distribute assets and sort out liabilities among the onetime partners.

Somalia and the Shifta Conflict

Kenya's only outstanding dispute with a foreign country at independence was Somalia, independent since 1960, which had irredentist claims on the Northern Frontier District (NFD), including postindependence North-Eastern Province. Although poor and arid, the area constituted nearly one-fifth of Kenya's territory and was the home of about 200,000 ethnic Somali and Oromo. Somalia's concern for these mostly nomadic people reflected its policy of pan-Somalism, in line with which Somalia sought the unification of all Somali-inhabited areas, including the NFD and the Ogaden region in Ethiopia.

Even after British control had been established in Kenya, Somali clans were still migrating into the trans-Juba region, extending their range southwestward to the banks of the Tana River. In their movements the Somali paid no regard to political boundaries, and those who crossed the Juba River, where the British sphere of influence began, maintained their contact with fellow clansmen in Ethiopia and Italian Somaliland. Kenya's border with Somalia was a result of the secret arrangements that brought Italy into World War I on the side of the Allies. In 1916 Britain promised to cede part of its own colonial holdings in compensation for Italy's exclusion from the postwar division of German colonial territory already agreed to by Britain and France. A treaty drawn up in 1920 and ratified in 1924 provided that Italy take over the area west of the Juba River up to 41° east longitude, including the port of Kismaayo. Known as Jubaland, it was incorporated into Italian Somaliland the following year. The new colonial boundary left a Somali-populated area within Kenya that was equal in size to the ceded territory. Although a number of Somali had settled in towns or as farm workers elsewhere in the colony, British authorities prohibited the nomads from moving over the internal frontier of the NFD as a precaution against ethnic conflict and the spread of interclan warfare. Other barriers (including taxation at a higher rate) were erected as well, setting the Somali apart from the rest of the African population.

These distinctions, all of which indirectly recognized the Somali as an alien element in Kenya and therefore emphasized their ties with Somalia, remained in effect until Kenya's independence and continually reinforced the Somali sense of exclusiveness. The Somali in the NFD were convinced that their interests were neglected by colonial authorities, and they expected them to be similarly neglected by an independent Kenya. They looked to fellow Somali across the border for political leadership, particularly after Somalia's independence.

Somalia's constitution stated prominently in its preamble that it promoted "by legal and peaceful means, the union of the Somali territories," and its fundamental laws provided that all ethnic Somali, no matter where they resided, were citizens of the republic. Somalia did not directly assert sovereignty over adjacent territories in Kenya and Ethiopia but rather demanded that Somali living there be granted the right to self-determination. At the London talks on Kenya's independence in 1961, Somali representatives from the NFD called on Britain to arrange for the region's separation from the colony before Kenya was granted self-government. The British government appointed a commission to ascertain popular opinion on the question in the NFD. The results of its investigation indicated that separation from Kenya was almost unanimously supported by the Somali and their fellow nomadic pastoralists, the Oromo. These two peoples, it was noted, represented an overwhelming majority of the NFD's population.

Despite considerable diplomatic activity by Somalia, the British government decided not to act on the commission's findings. Anxious that independence negotiations proceed smoothly, the British were reluctant to alienate Kenyan nationalist leaders, who were all opposed to giving away a large part of their country. It was also felt in London that the federal format then proposed in the Kenyan constitution would provide a solution through the wide degree of autonomy it allowed the predominantly Somali region within a federal system. This solution did not ease Somali demands for unification with Somalia, however, and even regional autonomy disappeared when Kenya amended the constitution and introduced a centralized form of government in 1964.

The denial of Somali claims led to steadily increasing unrest in the NFD. Adapting easily to life as *shifta* (bandits), Somali dissidents conducted a guerrilla campaign against the police and army for more than four years. Kenya's charges that the guerrillas were trained and equipped with Soviet arms in Somalia and that their activities were directed from Mogadishu were denied by the Somali government. But it could not hide the fact that Somali radio exerted an influence on the level of guerrilla activity by the militant tone of its broadcasts beamed into Kenya.

Meanwhile, clashes between Ethiopian police and Somali in the Ogaden had grown steadily in scope, eventually involving small-scale actions between army units along the border. In February 1964 armed conflict erupted along the entire length of the Somali-Ethiopian frontier. A cease-fire was arranged in April under OAU auspices, but the potential for future hostilities remained high. Consequently, Ethiopia and Kenya concluded a mutual defense pact shortly after the latter became independent in December, in response to what both countries perceived to be the continuing threat from Somalia.

Under OAU auspices a number of efforts were made to settle the differences between Somalia and its neighbors. The resulting agreements between Kenya and Somalia were usually honored for a time, until some reported incident in North-Eastern Province once more inflamed public opinion on both sides. The propaganda level would then rise and with it the level of hostilities. This situation eased only after a change in government in Somalia brought Mohamed Ibrahim Egal to office as prime minister in 1967. Without relinquishing Somalia's commitment to uniting the Somali people, Egal sought rapprochement with Ethiopia and Kenya through the good offices of the OAU, hoping to create an atmosphere in which the questions of self-determination for Somali outside Somalia could be peacefully negotiated. After a meeting between Kenyatta and Egal, diplomatic relations were restored in January 1968, and the state of emergency in effect in North-Eastern Province since before independence was at last relaxed. Tensions were so reduced that Kenyatta by mid-1968 could refer to them in the past tense as "a little quarrel."

The military junta that took power in Somalia under Major General Mohamed Siad Barre after a coup in 1969 pledged to continue that country's peaceful relations with Kenya. Nevertheless, Kenya remained mindful of Somalia's long-range goal for the unification of "Greater Somalia," and its caution was heightened by the knowledge that the Soviet-trained and Soviet-equipped Somali army was nearly three times the size of its own. Misgivings about Somalia's intentions seemed to be confirmed in 1974 by a revival of guerrilla activity in North-Eastern Province by the clandestine United Liberation Front of Western Somalia. The Kenyan attorney general, Charles Njonjo, heatedly invited Somali dissidents to "pack up their camels and go to Somalia" if they were not satisfied with their lot in Kenya. Protests were also directed at Somalia for allowing the installation of Soviet bases on its soil in violation of the zone of peace that Kenya (among other nations) sought to establish in the Indian Ocean region.

Kenya reaffirmed its alliance with Ethiopia after Haile Selassie was deposed by a military government in 1974. Kenya's fear of Somali subversion proved more compelling than even that of Soviet influence in the region, sustaining the alliance after Somalia expelled the Soviets in 1977 and after Ethiopia was drawn within Moscow's orbit. During the Ogaden war in 1977-78 Kenya openly sympathized with Ethiopia against Somalia. Although Somalia tried to assure Kenya that it wanted peace along their common border, the Kenyans took the renewal of fighting by *shifta* insurgents early in 1978 as a more reliable indication of Somali intentions. Citing unrest in the region, Kenya had already undertaken to upgrade its armed forces with purchases of military equipment from the United States and Britain.

Middle East Relations

Arab pressure on OAU members after the Arab-Israeli 1973 war persuaded countries in Sub-Saharan Africa that, like Kenya, had previously enjoyed cordial relations with Israel to reevaluate their foreign policy in the Middle East. Relations with Israel had been based on trade and on the investment, technical assistance, and military training that the Israelis provided under a 1965 cooperation agreement. Kenya's view of the Arab world, by contrast, was conditioned by Arab support for Somalia's irredentist claims on its territory.

Kenya severed diplomatic relations with Israel in November 1973. After the break Kenya took a leading role in African efforts to obtain Arab financial assistance for development projects. Officially, Kenya stated that it would give its diplomatic support in the UN and OAU to Arab objectives as a matter of principle and not because it expected dividends. But privately, Minister of Foreign Affairs Mungai made it plain to the governments of Arab oil-producing states that his country deserved special consideration in return for backing the Arab position against Israel. Its economy hard-hit by the rise in world oil prices, Kenya later criticized those same Arab governments for a lack of sensitivity to developing countries in Africa, but no attempt was made to restore formal diplomatic relations with Israel.

Relations with the Arab states were complicated by the apparent increase in Palestinian influence in Uganda during the tense period in relations between that country and Kenya after the Entebbe affair in 1976 and, more significantly, by Arab aid to Somalia in 1977-78. There seemed to be little linkage, however, between the Somali question and Kenya's attitude toward a Middle East settlement. Nairobi applauded Egyptian president Anwar al Sadat's peace initiative with Israel in November 1977, but the following February Kenyan military aircraft intercepted two Egyptian transports that had overflown Kenyan airspace carrying supplies to Somalia.

The Political Personality of Jomo Kenyatta

The imposing figure and paternalistic rule of Jomo Kenyatta gave the Kenyan political system its stability, direction, and essential unity. His importance stemmed from a long history as the spokesman of Kenyan nationalism, his imprisonment by colonial authorities, his organization of Kikuyu and national political movements and, not the least, his commanding personality, which literally dominated Kenyan politics and government. He was the symbol of Kenyan nationhood and in every respect deserved to be considered the "Father of the Nation."

Kenyatta was a man of many contradictions. Although detained during the emergency in the 1950s for allegedly managing the Mau Mau insurrection, his actual connection with the Mau Mau had always been ambiguous, and convincing evidence was never presented to substantiate contact between him and the insurgents. Still it was he, rather than they, who was recognized in the years leading to independence as the leader of Kenya's struggle for national liberation. As prime minister of the self-governing colony, he had worked with British authorities to ensure a smooth transition of power and had sought the cooperation of European moderates and African loyalists. Characterized as a nationalist rather than as leader of the Kikuyu, he had attempted to create a unified African political movement. As president of an independent Kenya, he had advanced non-Kikuyu as his number-two men—Mboya and Odinga (both Luo) and later, Moi (a Kalenjin). Kenyatta insisted on maintaining a semblance of national representation at the ministerial level of government, but he put his trust in the Kikuyu "old guard," a tight coterie of favored ministers and advisers drawn from members of an official family related to him by blood, marriage, or long association, most of them from Kiambu. He resisted ideologically motivated solutions. Although he promoted a concept of African socialism, he encouraged Kenya's free enterprise economy. In a de facto one-party system, Kenya's political institutions continued to develop along democratic lines.

Kenyatta was basically a cautious conservative, a pragmatist who sought to ensure a balance in his policies and the appearance of balance in the composition of his government. Especially in the early years of his regime, he rarely announced a decision without first verifying that it had popular backing; when necessary he appealed to the Kenyan people in mass rallies against opposition politicians. Although successful throughout his career in molding public opinion, Kenyatta was confident enough of his position in later years to insist on pushing through a particular policy "whether people like it or not." Because of his personal prestige, wide public support, control of the party apparatus, and command of the powers of government, his regime was able to withstand ethnic and ideological pressures building up in the country and mounting criticism of corruption in official circles.

Government functioned at two levels: the first, the formal government structure; the second, the inner circle of mainly Kiambu old guard who surrounded the president. It was among this latter group that decisions were made and presented to the formal government for implementation. In 1974 it included holders of five of the nine most important ministries and several potential rivals for the future leadership of the country. Some were connected with the Gikuyu [Kikuyu]-Embu-Meru Association (GEMA), which administered the *harambee* (literally, let us all pull together) program for social welfare and development among the Kikuyu. As an organization it was also dedicated to keeping political power in Kikuyu hands. Among the most influential were Njoroge Mungai, Kenyatta's personal physician and foreign minister from 1969 until his defeat in parliamentary elections in 1974; Oxford-educated Eliud W. Mathu; and Mbiyu Koinange, a Kiambu traditionalist who was minister of state in the Office of the President and Kenyatta's brother-in-law. Kenyatta's youngest wife, Mama Ngina, a keen businesswoman and his closest adviser outside the government, reputedly controlled political patronage.

Kenyatta's exact age was unknown, although he was generally believed to have been born about 1890. In poor health, he withdrew more and more from the everyday routine of government in Nairobi after 1969, dividing his time between his family farm at Gatundu and the provincial state houses at Nakuru and Mombasa, which became Kenya's executive capitals and centers of political intrigue when the president was in residence. From these locations Kenyatta maintained absolute control of the country's political machinery. Increasingly shielded by his inner circle of advisers, however, the president became remote from public opinion, particularly regarding the growing resentment of corruption in high places, but he could still be a powerful force in forming it.

There was no prime minister, and the president acted as his own head of government. During his extended absences from Nairobi, the cabinet seldom met as a collective body. The National Assembly remained an arena for conflict solution, where policies handed down by the government were vigorously debated and then invariably approved, but Kenyatta referred to its deliberations as "a kind of theater." Moi, the only non-Kikuyu close to the center of power, assumed responsibility for much of the day-to-day conduct of government and represented Kenya in negotiations with foreign leaders.

In 1975 Kenyatta was elected to his third term as president. As his health further weakened, the question of succession became uppermost in the concerns of the old guard, who were determined to preserve their influence in the post-Kenyatta era. The Kiambu core, which included top civil servants and senior military officers, as well as prominent politicians, tried to agree on a Kikuyu candidate, but they remained disunited themselves. Moi's high stock with Kenyatta only served to widen the split in their ranks.

Government and Opposition in the 1970s

The banning of KPU and Odinga's detention after the Kisumu incident in October 1969 seemed to have a quieting effect on the country. Kenyatta reopened the political process by decreeing that candidates for the approaching parliamentary election would be selected by KANU members voting in primary elections to be held in December. More than 700 candidates were approved by the party to contest 158 seats in the National Assembly. They held the field alone: no other party was functioning that might offer candidates, and independents were barred from presenting themselves.

Coming so soon after a period of intense political unrest, the general election in February 1970 demonstrated the vitality of democratic institutions in Kenya, albeit within the context of a de facto one-party system. Nearly half of the incumbent members, including five ministers and 14 assistant ministers, went down to defeat at the polls. The results were taken, however, as a vote of confidence in the government. Several former KPU leaders had been released from detention before the election and readmitted to KANU, and two of them were selected to stand for the assembly. Only one opposition member from the outgoing parliament retained his seat. The openness of the election and the subsequent inclusion of a number of Luo in the ministerial ranks of the new government helped to ease tension among that group, on which the recent unrest had focused.

In March 1971 the government moved rapidly against an attempted armed coup. There was no immediate suspicion that it was ethnically based, and the plotters appeared to have no following in the population. Thirteen suspects were brought to trial, during which the prosecutor, without naming names, implied that a few men in high places were implicated with them. When the country's two highest ranking officials of Kamba background—one, the army chief of staff and the other, the chief justice—were later cited in testimony, they resigned.

During the next four years, the government was free from outward challenge. The period of relative calm was broken in the summer of 1974, however, when the country experienced its first serious industrial unrest. In August the government with the cooperation of the trade union banned strikes and demonstrations, and the University of Nairobi and Kenyatta University College, where students had taken advantage of the disturbances to press demands for better accommodations and less stringent academic requirements, were closed.

Parliamentary elections were called for October. As in 1970 the more than 700 candidates nominated by KANU were the only contenders for seats, but they represented a wide variety of factions within the party. The common theme for all KANU candidates was support for Kenyanization and for the expansion of education as proposed in the government's Development Plan 1970-74, but personalities rather than issues dominated the contest. Typically, candidates stressed their connections in Nairobi as proof that they could deliver more to constituents than could their opponents. Government-supported candidates spent money freely during the lively campaign. Endorsement by GEMA virtually guaranteed election in predominantly Kikuyu constituencies. The approximately 4.4 million voters who cast ballots represented about 80 percent of those eligible and included newly enfranchised 18-year-olds. A secret ballot was used for the first time. Under election regulations, each party contesting elections was to have a separate ballot box at the polling place but, because KANU was the only party in the field, voters had the choice of only one box in which to cast their ballots. Following the pattern set in previous general and local elections, a high proportion of incumbents lost their places. Also, as in earlier elections, charges of intimidation, corruption, and vote fraud were rife after the votes had been tallied.

Even though limited to approved KANU candidates, voters could exercise a clear political choice at the polls among factions and personalities wearing the party label. In addition to GEMA, representing Kikuyu interests, a rival progovernment faction led by Attorney General Njonjo gathered around Moi, the front-runner, to succeed Kenyatta. The so-called TJ Group (which included onetime protégés of Tom J. Mboya) was dedicated to carrying on Mboya's tradition under the leadership of his brother, Alphonse Okuku Ndiege. Jean Marie Seroney, the recognized leader of the Nandi (an element of the Kalenjin group), was a popular parliamentarian who not only opposed Kikuyu dominance but was also a particular adversary of Moi, also a Kalenjin but of the Tugen group. Among the most vocal critics of the government during the election campaign was Josiah Mwangi Kariuki, who in 1974 was probably the most popular figure in Kenya after Kenyatta himself. Kariuki, an assistant minister in the outgoing government and formerly the president's private secretary and leader of KANU's youth movement, drew strong support from Kikuyu dissidents who resented the influence and exclusivity of the Kiambu circle around Kenyatta. He had come to disagree with the government on a number of basic issues that bore on Kenya's orientation to a free enterprise economy. Odinga, a fixture of the discredited pro-Soviet left, was barred from reentering KANU and was therefore prevented from being presented as a candidate for office, but several of his followers were in the running, and one of them defeated the government's candidate in Odinga's home constituency.

The assembly seated in 1974 was younger and contained a larger percentage of academically and technically trained members, teachers, and trade unionists than the one that it replaced. In all, a small but vocal group of about 20 members, some of whom were associated with Seroney, Kariuki, and the Odinga faction, could be depended upon to offer consistent opposition to the government bench. Both the Kikuyu old guard and the pro-Moi faction were amply represented in the new government, in which places were distributed among the ethnic groups but from which the TJ Group and the Kikuyu dissidents were excluded. Confrontation between the president and parliament had been anticipated in July when, without consultation, Kenyatta decreed that Swahili would have official status and its use allowed in parliamentary debate. Some members who were outside the government pointed out that, according to the constitution, English was the official parliamentary language, reflecting the country's multiethnic character. An amendment to the constitution was duly passed to back up the presidential decree, but criticism was made at the time of the president's methods in attempting to circumvent the constitutional process.

The lines of confrontation became more sharply drawn in November when Kenyatta postponed the opening of the new parliament in order to prevent Seroney, a frequent critic of the president's inner circle of advisers, from being elected deputy Speaker of the House of Representatives. Support for Seroney, who had no connection with the government, had gained impetus after rallies at which Kariuki had brought into the open charges of corruption by members of the official family. Kariuki accused government ministers of accepting bribes from foreign businesses in the form of a percentage of their profits, and he had implicated Moi and Mama Ngina in similar dealings. Delaying the opening of the legislative session had also served the purpose of preventing Kariuki from questioning the government on the issue in the National Assembly. Moi responded to Kariuki's attack on him by warning against rumormongering based on accounts in the foreign press. At the same time, foreign newspapers and periodicals reporting the incident were ordered seized.

Kariuki, a onetime Mau Mau detainee who had gone on to become a student at Oxford, broadened his attack to challenge the capitalist structure of the country's economy. Foreign investment, he charged, was a corrupting influence which, together with a landholding system that allowed a few Africans to own large estates while the rural masses went landless, was setting the stage for class conflict in Kenya. His opposition to the government and his denunciation of those in the "ruling circle" carried all the more weight and made him more dangerous to the old guard because he was a Kikuyu.

The period was marked by a number of acts of violence. In the worst of them a bomb was exploded at a Nairobi bus station, killing 27 bystanders. At Gatundu, Kenyatta's cattle were maimed in Mau Mau fashion. Both incidents were blamed on the clandestine Maskini (literally, poor people) Liberation Organization (MLO). Kariuki had no known links with the MLO, but the old guard was quick to accuse him of contributing to the tense atmosphere in which these acts had taken place. The National Assembly convened on February 4, 1975, and Kenyatta was elected unanimously to a third term as president. Seroney, who during the interim had assured Moi that his criticism was not directed at Kenyatta personally, was chosen as deputy Speaker. Kariuki was not present at the opening session.

Kariuki was last seen alive escorted by senior security officers on the day before parliament opened. His mutilated body was found two weeks later. His funeral was turned into a violent demonstration of opposition to the government by students and the unemployed. Many Kenyans were convinced that the government was implicated in Kariuki's murder, and not even the president was exempted from suspicion in the affair.

In March a 15-member parliamentary commission was impaneled to investigate Kariuki's death, but its work was hampered by the refusal of police cooperation. In a report issued two months later, the commission recommended the dismissal from office of the commander of the General Service Unit, Benjamin Gethi, who was with Kariuki on the day that he disappeared. Three others were cited in connection with the murder, and an additional investigation was requested into the roles of five others. The names of two of those in the latter group, including that of Koinange, were expunged from the report on the president's order. Njonjo criticized the report in the National Assembly, and his proposal that it be "adopted" instead of "accepted" was defeated only by a narrow margin. Several ministers who voted with the majority against the attorney general's amendment were shortly dismissed from the government. Criminal charges were never brought in the case.

The Kariuki affair marked a watershed in Kenya's political history. The obvious government cover-up only heightened suspicions of government responsibility. The investigation of his murder and the disregard for its findings revealed deep divisions in Kikuyu ranks, even among those from Kiambu, as the old guard found itself pitted against the younger men. As enraged younger members of parliament became bolder in questioning the government's actions, the government became less tolerant of its opposition. Seroney's allies and friends of Kariuki hammered away at inequitable land distribution and mismanagement of public lands. Martin Shikuku, who was named to chair a committee to investigate land use, broadened its scope to probe related instances of corruption and ethnic favoritism.

The government, which chose to disregard charges of corruption directed against its members, counterattacked in the National Assembly, attributing unrest to agitation by "students" and "communists." Drawn into the fray, Kenyatta dismissed his critics as "animals." Shikuku's investigation was halted, and his committee was abolished. As if to spite the critics, a government-sponsored constitutional amendment was proposed and passed after a bitter debate allowing the president to pardon a former minister, Paul Ngei, who had been convicted of corruption in office.

In October 1975 the government turned forcibly on its parliamentary opposition. Seroney and Shikuku were arrested outside parliament and deprived of their seats. Two months later another vocal opposition member, 26-year-old Chelegat Mutai, was sentenced to 30 months in prison for allegedly inciting sisal workers in her constituency to violence, and her seat was also declared vacant. Several others involved in the investigations of Kariuki's death and government corruption, including Mutai's colleague, George Anyona, were detained on suspicious charges, one of them sentenced to a two-year prison term on an old charge of wife beating. Some concluded that there was no legal way left open to challenge the government. When parliament was reconvened after a recess, its energies were devoted to dealing with the breakup of the EAC.

Daniel arap Moi, Kenyatta's successor as president of the republic
Courtesy Ministry of Information and Broadcasting, Kenya

The Question of Succession

The crucial problem facing the government establishment once the opposition had been stilled was to ensure that the political system would survive Kenyatta. Under the constitution, the vice president took over if the president died or was permanently incapacitated, but his powers were circumscribed to arranging for a presidential election within three months. Candidates were to be nominated by the recognized political parties—of which only one, KANU, existed in 1976.

The question of succession was brought into the open, complete with strong ethnic overtones, during a party rally held at Nakuru in the autumn of 1976 where a constitutional amendment was discussed that would have entrusted interim presidential authority to the Speaker of the National Assembly, rather than to the vice president (Moi), during the 90-day period between the death or resignation of the president and the election of a successor. Introduced by Kihika Kimani, the member of parliament from Nakuru who had been a government stalwart during the debate on the Kariuki affair, the measure was backed by GEMA. But many believed that it was prompted by Kenyatta himself to test the waters and that it reflected his will. The proposed amendment was actively opposed at the rally, however, by a group of 98 members of parliament who would have possessed sufficient voting strength to defeat the measure had it been introduced in the National

Assembly. This group was led by Njonjo, Moi's chief partisan within the inner circle, and by Stanley Oloitipitip, the minister of natural resources who had characterized the proposal as being "unethical [and] immoral." It was Njonjo who brought the debate to a sudden halt, when speaking in his capacity as attorney general, he reminded delegates at the rally that speculating about Kenyatta's death was a treasonable offense.

The old guard still had political capital to invest in blocking the succession of a non-Kikuyu to the presidency. The question of who would succeed Kenyatta as president of Kenya had become one of who would succeed him as leader of KANU. In the absence of another party, KANU would nominate a candidate who would be unopposed, and it was reasonable to assume that the deputy leader of the party, who followed Kenyatta as party president, would receive the nomination. Since 1966, however, when the multiple vice presidency was introduced, KANU had not had a clearly defined second-in-command. In the meantime KANU had become moribund, something to be mobilized for rallies and elections but lacking direction or responsibilities. It had gone for 10 years without elections for party offices, and the last party convention had been held in 1971.

Under the plan devised by Kenyatta after the defeat of the constitutional amendment on the presidency, grass-roots elections were to be conducted in late 1976 to select delegates who would in turn elect a single national party vice president. Rival slates of candidates were committed to Mungai, representing the old guard, and Moi, and places on them were sought by politicians eager to identify with one or another camp and to assure themselves of a political base for the future. The ethnic element was important in the voting, which extended over several weeks, but was not considered decisive. As a result of the grass-roots vote, Mungai could count on the support of delegations from eight predominantly Kikuyu constituencies, and Moi from eight in the Kalenjin belt. The remaining 25 were split or undeclared. Moi had strong support from Maasai districts and in Coast Province and also from Kikuyu farmers in Rift Valley Province. He had also won the backing of some of Mungai's rivals in the Kikuyu hierarchy. His chief opponents outside Mungai's Kikuyu constituencies were found among young party activists who, although not necessarily favoring Mungai as an alternative, resented Moi's business interests and landholdings; he had additional opponents among the Luo and former KPU members who were die-hard supporters of Odinga.

The campaign leading up to the party convention to win over uncommitted delegates accentuated the deep divisions within KANU. On April 2, 1977, the day before the scheduled election for which delegates had already assembled in Nairobi, Kenyatta from his residence at Gatundu suddenly canceled the vote, leaving the question of succession unresolved. Some sources, in fact, believed that this was the intention of the aging president, who feared that Moi, his personal choice to succeed, might be defeated. He announced that a general election would be conducted in 1979.

On August 22,1978, Jomo Kenyatta died of natural causes brought on by the advance of old age. Having assumed transitional executive powers as prescribed in the constitution, Moi, in the absence of another candidate, was declared president on October 10. Mwai Kibaki, a prominent member of Kenyatta's inner circle but not one of the Kiambu group, was named vice president. Koinange, the leader of the Kiambu old guard who had earlier sought to prevent Moi from becoming president, was retained in the cabinet but in a position of much less importance than that which he had held previously. Moi set out as his administration's priorities to heal ethnic cleavages and remove the "tribal" factor from Kenyan politics, to stamp out corruption, and to deal with unemployment. Political detainees, including Seroney, Shikuku, and Anyona, were released by presidential order (see Post-Kenyatta Developments, 1978-79, ch. 4).

* * *

A scholarly comprehensive survey of the country's history through the 1970s is not available, but Clarendon Press' three-volume *History of East Africa* and selected chapters in the multivolume *The Cambridge History of Africa* put Kenya's past in the context of a broader regional history. *Zamani: A Survey of East African History*, edited by Bethwell Ogot and J.A. Kieran, offers topical essays on the subject. Godfrey Muriuki's *A History of the Kikuyu, 1500-1900* provides background material on Kenya's largest ethnic group. A detailed study of the establishment of the British presence is contained in G.H. Mungeam's monograph, *British Rule in Kenya 1895-1912*, while Charles Miller relates the story of the building of the Uganda railroad in *The Lunatic Express*. Elspeth Huxley's *A New Earth: An Experiment in Colonialism* and her two-volume biography of Lord Delamere, *White Man's Country*, give a sympathetic portrayal of the colonial experience from the standpoint of the European settler community. In *Colonialism and Underdevelopment in East Africa*, E.A. Brett views the same phenomenon from a critic's perspective. Jeremy Murray-Brown's *Kenyatta*, the standard biography of the father of Kenyan nationalism and the country's first leader, is essential reading for an understanding of modern Kenya. *The Myth of "Mau Mau"* by Carl G. Rosberg and John Nottingham is a definitive work on that subject. Cherry Gertzel's *The Politics of Independent Kenya, 1963-8* offers a guide to the formative years in Kenya's political development, and Ogot's *Historical Dictionary of Kenya* is a helpful reference work for further reading. (For further information and complete citations, see Bibliography.)

Chapter 2. The Society and Its Environment

Bao, a game of great skill and formalized ritual popular throughout Kenya

SOCIAL RELATIONS IN KENYA in the early 1980s were ordered by ethnicity and regionalism on the one hand and significant differences of wealth and power on the other. Playing a variable part in the internal structures of ethnic communities were groups based on descent from a common ancestor (lineages or clans) and ties of kinship between particular individuals. Ethnic differences were often called into play in politics, and they affected the relations between individuals in many daily encounters, but ethnic solidarity could be ephemeral, responding to particular economic and social situations. Increasingly in Kenya the relations of individuals or sets of persons to others have depended on the relative wealth and power of the persons or groups involved. Ethnicity has taken second place in the relations between Kenyans of different ethnic groups, and connections of common descent and of kinship have become less important than differences of status and income in the relations of members of the same ethnic group. Wealth, status, and power were still competed for, and many Kenyans continued to look to their own ethnic groups and kin for allies in that competition.

Kenya's 1979 census recognized between 30 and 40 ethnic groups. Of these, only five were fairly large, ranging in size from 10 percent to more than 20 percent of the population. These groups, in addition to being internally differentiated in terms of wealth, power, and other indicators introduced in the colonial era and persisting after independence, were often divided into subethnic groups based on differences of dialect, location, economic adaptation, and other indicators of cultural significance, some old, some new. Except in the major cities (Nairobi and Mombasa) and in a very few of the larger towns, ethnic membership and regional residence usually went together. Nevertheless, relations between members of different ethnic groups within the marketplace and workplace did occur in urban centers and even in some rural areas. Except in a few cases they were friendly, but such relationships were often limited to the business at hand. Sociability, intermarriage, and the like were usually carried out with members of one's own group. Even if contacts between members of different groups were rarely marked by hostility, some relations were usually easier than others. People speaking closely related languages, coming from the same region, and having a tradition of ancient connection have often been able to interact more easily than peoples who did not have such bonds. Nevertheless, the common experience of different groups in the same region in modern Kenya has sometimes permitted them to bridge gaps in language and to overcome a history of animosity.

Beginning in the colonial period, despite the limits—legal and other—on the kinds of economic activities Africans could undertake, the levels of education they could aspire to, and the sorts of lives they could lead, a process of social and economic differentiation took place. That process and the development of social stratification were speeded up toward the end of the colonial era and have become even more marked since independence. This has been particularly true of the Kikuyu, who have experienced large and visible differences of power, income, education, and life-style among members of the political and economic elite, the varied middle stratum, the small shopkeeper, the urban worker, and the ordinary peasant. But differences and stratification, if more recent and less complex, have occurred among all African ethnic groups except a few very small ones on the margins of Kenyan society.

Differences in power and wealth have not always gone together, but since independence at least, power held by virtue of participation at the highest levels of government has frequently entailed wealth, usually acquired by investment in economic enterprises. At the same time, those who have directed their attention first to economic activity have often carried weight in political councils. In any case, those who have political power and wealth usually have the respect of the less fortunate ones. Some analysts have suggested that people in the middle stratum may be frustrated by their sense that access to better opportunities seems to have become increasingly limited. These Kenyans, however, have not challenged the basic premises of a differentiated and stratified social order calling for a large measure of private enterprise.

The developing economy that has been linked in various ways to the growth of marked social, political, and economic differences was no longer advancing as rapidly in the late 1970s and early 1980s, and the opportunity for social mobility, which has softened the sharp edges of difference, has declined. The problem has been complicated by Kenya's very rapid population growth—an estimated 4 percent, the highest in the world. The growth has put a heavy burden on the already inadequate infrastructure of education and health, and the result may be increasing dissatisfaction with the social and economic order. Efforts to deal with population growth were under way, but they would not prevent a doubling of the population by the turn of the twenty-first century, a rate that would not be matched by economic growth.

Physical Setting

Kenya lies astride the equator on the east coast of Africa (see fig. 1). Its total area of 580,367 square kilometers includes 11,230 square kilometers of water, contained mainly in Lake Rudolf, known in Kenya as Lake Turkana (6,405 square kilometers), and the country's portion of Lake Victoria, known in Kenya as Victoria Nyanza (3,955 square kilometers).

The most striking physiographic distinction in Kenya is between the area of higher land, encompassing roughly the southwestern one-third of the country, and the remaining two-thirds, consisting of low plateaus and plains (see fig. 5). The highlands include the only large area—other than the coastal belt—that can count on generally reliable rainfall;

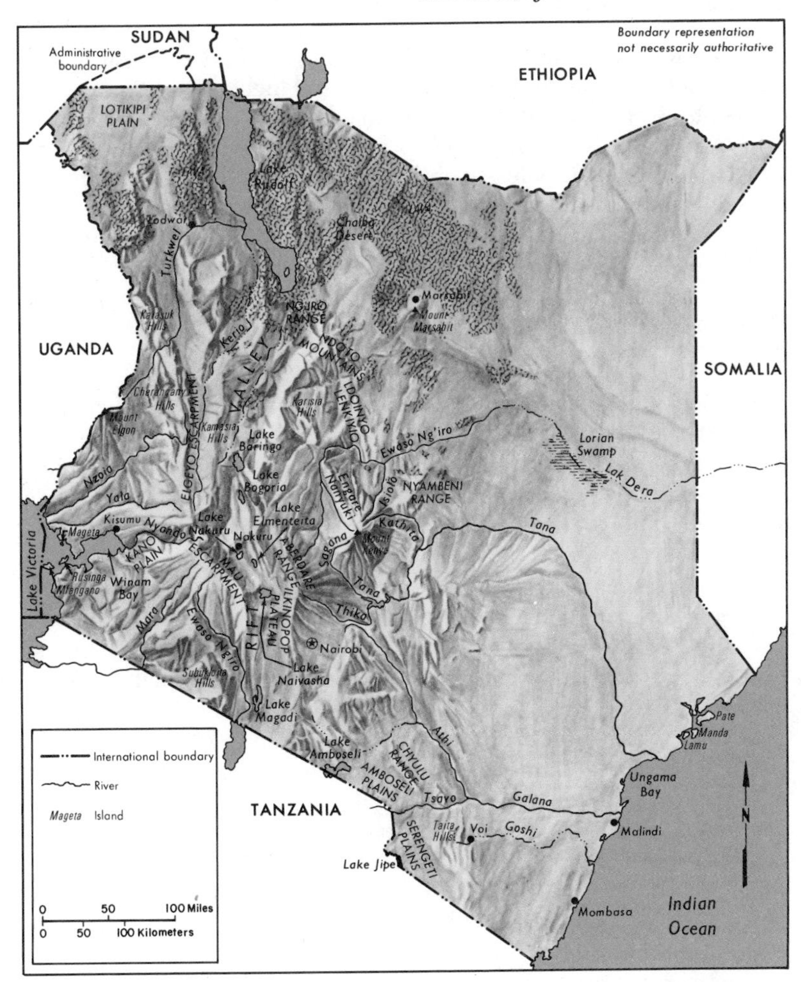

Figure 5. Terrain and Drainage

they also contain most of the good soils, and the great majority of the settled population lives there. In contrast, the outer arc of lower land is peopled almost entirely by nomadic pastoralists living in a terrain covered mostly by semiarid vegetation and receives highly variable rainfall that in many places rarely exceeds 250 millimeters a year.

The country's number and variety of large animals are an important tourist attraction. Efforts (of varying degrees of success) to conserve and protect this significant natural resource have led to the establishment of parks and game reserves in different parts of the country.

Geographic Regions

Kenya is characterized by highly varied terrain and climatic conditions that range from moist to arid. The three principal climatic subdivisions include a narrow coastal belt along the Indian Ocean, which has rainfall adequate for agriculture; a central highlands region and the adjacent lower plateaus to the west that border Lake Victoria, which also have adequate precipitation for crops; and the rest of the country, which usually receives less than 500 millimeters of rain annually and is usable chiefly as rangeland (see Climate, this ch.).

The country may be divided into seven major geographic regions that intersect the principal climatic subdivisions (see fig. 6). Topography, rainfall, and soil conditions combine to produce substantial differences in natural vegetation (see fig. 7).

Coastal Region

The Coastal Region exhibits different features in its southern and northern parts. The shoreline, south of the Tana River delta, formed largely of coral rock and sand, is broken by bays, inlets, and branched creeks. Mangrove swamps line these indentations, but along the ocean are stretches of coral sand that form attractive beaches. A rise in the ocean level relative to the land in this area led to the formation of islands in certain places. The most notable of these is Mombasa. The sheltered configuration and deep water of the creeks around Mombasa led centuries ago to its use as a harbor and to its later development as East Africa's most important port (see The Kenya Coast, ch. 1; Transportation, ch. 3).

Not far off the shoreline a barrier reef, broken only at a few points, parallels the coast. Immediately inland from the coast a narrow plain is succeeded by a low plateau area that reaches an elevation of about 150 meters and after a few kilometers terminates in a line of discontinuous ridges. Rainfall in the subregion is adequate for agriculture which, in addition to fertile soils of dried-up lagoons in certain parts of the low plateau, has fostered a rather dense farming population (see Agriculture, ch. 3).

The principal physiographic feature of the smaller northern section of the region is the Lamu Archipelago, also formed by the inundation of the coastline as a result of a rise in the ocean level. This area was historically a major center of Arab trade. The northern part is less heavily populated than the south, in part because of the smaller amount of rainfall.

Coastal Hinterland and Tana Plains Region

The coastal hinterland forming the southern part of this region is a relatively featureless plain broken only in a few places by small hills. The plain rises very gradually westward from an elevation of about 150 meters to about 300 meters, where it meets the Eastern Plateau Region. Rainfall is low, and the area is sparsely populated, mostly by nomadic pastoralists. Part of this hinterland falls within the *nyika* (wilderness), an area of bushland and thicket inhabited largely by wild animals.

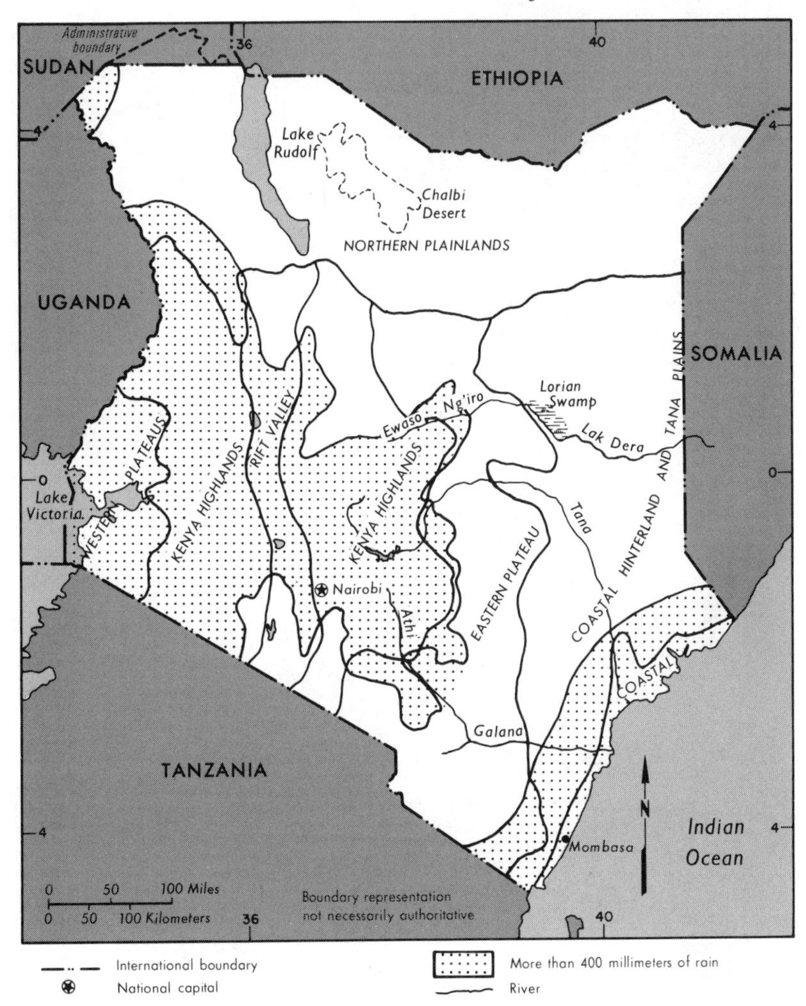

Source: Based on information from Irving Kaplan et al., *Area Handbook for Kenya*, Washington, 1976, 53.

Figure 6. Geographic and Climatic Regions

The Tana Plains section of the region—equally featureless and deficient in rainfall—extends northward from the upper part of the Coastal Region to the Northern Plainlands Region. The Tana Plains' eastern edge and their western limits are marked by the higher elevation of the Eastern Plateau Region. The vegetation is mainly bush and scattered trees. The population consists of nomadic pastoralists. Considerable sections of the area along the perennial Tana River have been irrigated. A major feature of the Tana Plains is the great Lorian Swamp.

Eastern Plateau Region

The Eastern Plateau Region consists of a belt of plains extending-

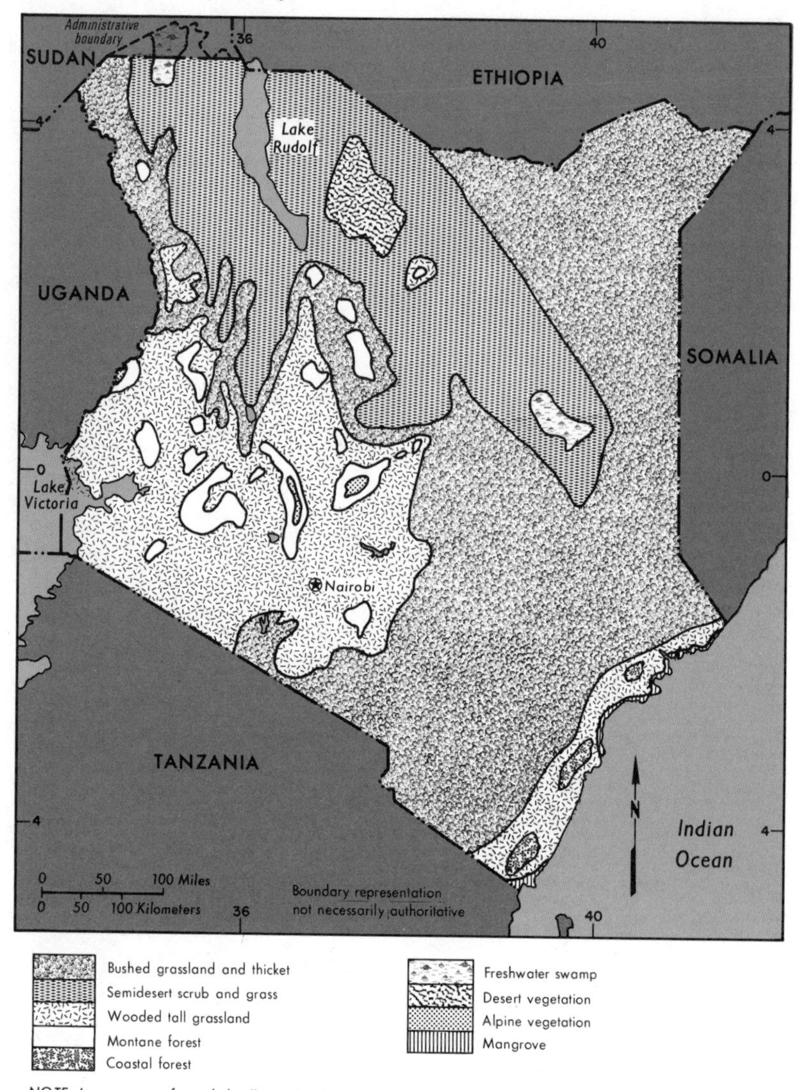

Source: Based on information from Irving Kaplan et al., *Area Handbook for Kenya*, Washington, 1976, 63.

Figure 7. Present-day Distribution of Natural Vegetation

north and south to the east of the Kenya Highlands. Elevations are mainly between 300 and 900 meters (notable exceptions are the Chyulu Range and the Taita Hills, which rise to over 2,100 meters). The monotony of the region is broken by numerous scattered hills and pinnacles, some craggy, others domed and smooth. The southern part

Rural settlement at Kalacha Dida near Mount Marsabit in Eastern Province
Courtesy Barbara Hately-Smith

of the region includes the Amboseli and Serengeti plains and is the site of the Amboseli and Tsavo national parks.

Rainfall is relatively low, particularly in the more northerly sections. The Chyulu Range and the Taita Hills have greater precipitation, but rainfall in the former is highly unreliable. At times the seasonal Namanga River pours a large amount of water onto the flat Amboseli Plain to form Lake Amboseli, which at its fullest has an area of about 114 square kilometers. During the dry season the lake disappears, and the area becomes a dusty plain. Much of the vegetation in the region is bushed grassland and thicket that gradates in the north into semidesert bush and grass. The higher elevations of the Taita Hills, however, have woodland growth.

Northern Plainlands Region

The vast Northern Plainlands Region consists of a series of arid plains and includes within its limits Lake Rudolf and the Chalbi Desert. Rainfall in the area west of the lake is under 250 millimeters; in some years it is almost negligible. Streams flowing through the area in the rainy season to empty into Lake Rudolf dry up at certain times of the year. Water holes remain, however, and at other points water lies only a short distance below riverbeds. The area is inhabited by the nomadic Turkana, who graze their camels, goats, and sheep on scattered bush and grass. Lake Rudolf is the site of fishing activity.

Significant features east of Lake Rudolf include the Chalbi Desert, Kenya's only true desert. The plains around Mount Marsabit consist of a vast lava plateau. Erosion on those plains farther east has dotted the landscape with hills of varying shapes and sizes.

The area east of the Chalbi Desert is generally arid and ordinarily supports vegetation only of the semidesert kind. Certain spots are more favored, including Mount Marsabit, which at higher elevations may receive up to 760 millimeters of rain annually and has an upper forest cover. Foothills of the southern Ethiopian highlands extending into Kenya also have more rainfall, and several perennial rivers flow south-southeastward from these hills onto the plains. The area supports a sparse nomadic population except for a few cultivators in the Marsabit area and the Ethiopian foothills.

Kenya Highlands Region

The Kenya Highlands Region comprises the complex of high land in west-central Kenya. It consists of two major divisions lying east and west of the great north-south Rift Valley. Each major section has a number of subdivisions, but the whole area is tied together by the common denominators of markedly higher altitude, cooler temperatures, and generally greater precipitation than found in other regions. A striking feature on the eastern edge of the highlands is Mount Kenya, the country's highest point, which rises to 5,200 meters.

Among the more important subdivisions of the eastern highlands is the area east of the Aberdare Range, which is populated by the Kikuyu, the country's largest ethnic group. Much of the original forest in this area has been cut down, and the land is cropped intensively.

To the west of the Rift Valley many upper elevations in the southern part of the highlands remain covered by forest. Small farms dot the area at somewhat lower levels. Forest also still covers large areas of the northern part of the western highlands. The local population grows wheat and maize, and cattle are grazed on the area's rich grassland. On the northwestern edge of the highlands lies Mount Elgon, an extinct volcano rising to over 4,320 meters above sea level.

Rift Valley Region

The great Rift Valley of eastern Africa, formed by a long series of faulting and differential rock movements, extends in Kenya from the Lake Rudolf area in the north generally southward through the Kenya Highlands and into Tanzania. In the vicinity of Lake Rudolf the valley floor is about 455 meters above sea level, but southward it rises steadily until in its central section in the area of Lake Naivasha the elevation is close to 1,890 meters. From that point southward it drops off to about 610 meters at the Kenya-Tanzania border.

The central section of the valley, about 65 kilometers in width, is rimmed by high escarpments. To the east is the Ilkinopop Plateau, some 610 meters above the valley floor, and east of that plateau lies the Aberdare Range, which has elevations above 3,960 meters. On the valley's western side are the Mau Escarpment, rising to nearly 3,050 meters, and farther north the Elgeyo Escarpment and the Cherangany

Hills, the latter having elevations of over 3,350 meters. The valley floor has been subjected to extensive volcanic activity, and several cones rise high above it; the area remains one of latent volcanism, hot springs and steam emerging at numerous spots. Volcanoes and lava heaps divide the central section into compartments in which lie a series of lakes that have no outlets. Their content ranges from the alkaline but relatively fresh water of lakes Baringo and Naivasha, both of which support fish populations, to the higher soda content of lakes Elmenteita, Bogoria, and Nakuru and the almost solid and commercially exploited soda ash of Lake Magadi.

The northern and southern parts of the valley receive a yearly rainfall averaging between 250 and 560 millimeters. They have semidesert vegetation consisting of grass, bush, and scattered trees and are inhabited by nomadic pastoralists. The more elevated central section around Nakuru has higher precipitation, and the vegetation includes wooded grassland. The heavier rainfall in this part, especially close to the escarpments, allows the cultivation of grain crops.

Western Plateaus Region

The Western Plateaus Region forms part of the extensive basin in which Lake Victoria lies. It consists mainly of faulted plateaus marked by escarpments that descend in a gentle slope from the Kenya Highlands Region to the shore of the lake. The region is divided by the secondary Kano Rift Valley into northern and southern components having somewhat different features. This faulted valley lies at a right angle to the main rift running through the highlands and is separated from that valley by a great lava mass. The lake intrudes into the Kano rift for about 80 kilometers to form Winam Bay, at the eastern end of which is Kisumu, the country's fourth largest town and a major lake port. East of this arm of the lake is the low-lying Kano Plain, which suffers periodically from drought and floods. Good soils and generally adequate rainfall for crops have led to a very high concentration of rural population in this region.

Climate

A little less than 15 percent of Kenya's total area receives an annual rainfall of 760 millimeters or more. Still less of the country—between 12 and 14 percent—can expect an average rainfall between 560 and 760 millimeters a year. More than 70 percent of the area usually records less than 560 millimeters annually, and a considerable part receives less than 250 millimeters annually (see fig. 8). Mean monthly rainfall is often erratic, and annual variations are striking and can be serious, especially in drier areas. Thus at Lodwar in northwestern Kenya, where the mean annual rainfall is about 150 millimeters, as much as 500 millimeters and as little as 25 millimeters have been recorded in a year. Droughts affecting all of Kenya, but especially its drier areas, have occurred on the average every eight to 10 years for a period of two to four years. The most recent one occurred from 1972 to 1976.

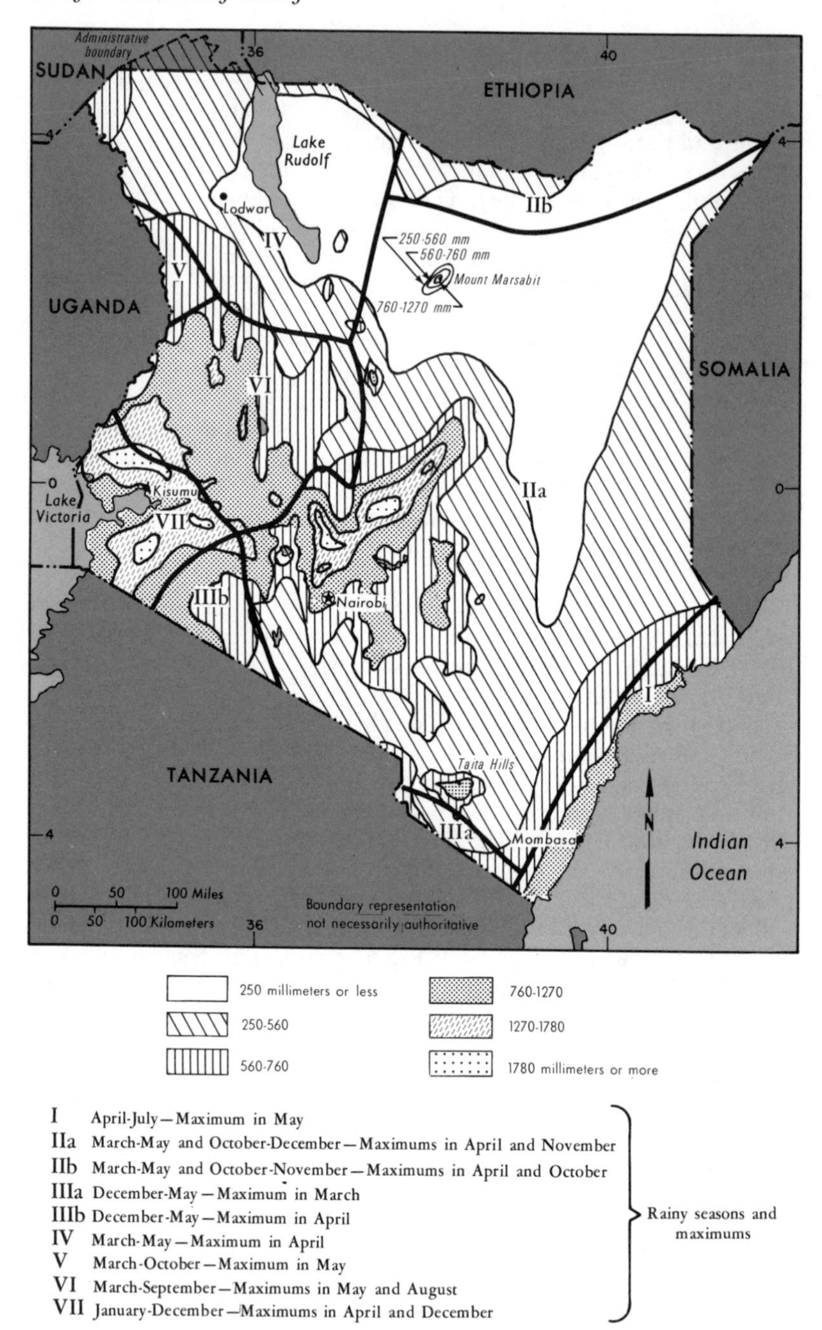

Source: Based on information from Irving Kaplan et al., *Area Handbook for Kenya*, Washington, 1976, 61.

Figure 8. Mean Annual Rainfall

Among the factors responsible for the geographic variation in rainfall are the variations in topography and the sources and flow of the major air masses overhead. Very important locally are the diurnal temperature changes associated with Lake Victoria. The principal air masses are the northeast and southeast trade winds, which vary in intensity and direction. Usually by late December the northeast trade winds flowing from the Arabian Peninsula (and on the west from the Sahara) being a dry season that lasts until about March. During March southeast trade winds sweeping across the Indian Ocean begin to deposit rain over Kenya, and in April rainfall occurs throughout the country. By July a second period of dry weather ensues—except in the western parts of the country. Dry conditions then prevail until September or October, when a reinstatement of the low-pressure belt over Africa and convergent trade winds bring what are known in Kenya as the small rains. These continue into December, when the seasonal cycle starts again.

The relative difference in temperature gain and loss and in altitude between Lake Victoria and the surrounding land results in the area between the lake and the Kenya Highlands' receiving at least two inches of rain in every, or almost every, month of the year and in the absence of a pronounced dry season. The effects of the larger air masses are still felt, nonetheless, and periods of higher rainfall are regularly recorded in April and December. To the north of this area, regional conditions also result in a wet season that lasts usually from March to September or October and a drier or dry period during the intervening months.

There are great variations in average temperatures, and altitude again is a major factor. The Kenya Highlands offer a cool, bracing climate, much of the highlands having a mean annual maximum temperature between 22°C and 26°C and a minimum between 10°C and 14°C. Nairobi, at 1,658 meters, has a mean annual temperature of about 18°C. The humidity in the highlands is about 90 percent in early morning. By midafternoon it drops substantially to about 40 percent in the dry season and to between 50 and 60 percent in the rainy season. The combination of moderate temperatures, adequate rainfall, and good soils brought tens of thousands of white settlers to the highlands during the colonial era.

Away from the highlands, as the elevation decreases, average temperatures increase. A zone immediately around the highlands has mean annual maximum temperatures between 26°C and 29°C and minimums between 14°C and 18°C. Beyond this zone the low plateaus of eastern Kenya and the northern plains register mean annual maximums between 30°C and 34°C and minimums from 18°C to over 22°C. One area to the west of Lake Rudolf and another along the Somalia border have mean maximum temperatures above 34°C; the latter area has recorded an absolute maximum of 46°C. The Rift Valley experiences temperatures similar to those in eastern Kenya. The humidity in the semiarid to arid areas usually is between 60 and 70 percent in early morning. It decreases by midafternoon to roughly 40 to 45 percent and in some places to as low as 30 percent.

A zone along the coast experiences both high temperatures and high humidity. The hottest months are January through March; at Mombasa the mean monthly temperature is about 28°C during this time. Beginning in June and extending through August, a cooler period sets in when afternoon temperatures may average about 28°C and night temperatures may drop to below 21°C. Little variation occurs, however, in the humidity, which throughout the year is above 90 percent early in the morning and usually between 60 and 70 percent in midafternoon. Sea breezes blow relatively steadily during the year, providing some relief.

Drainage

The principal drainage pattern centers in the Kenya Highlands Region, from which streams and rivers radiate eastward toward the Indian Ocean, westward to Lake Victoria, and northward either to Lake Rudolf or to the arid terrain of northern Kenya, where they disappear. A secondary drainage system is formed by rivers in the southern highlands of Ethiopia, which extend into Kenya along the eastern section of their boundary. These rivers are all seasonal, and those that receive sufficient water at flood times to reach the sea do so through Somalia. Minor internal systems are associated with the lakes in the Rift Valley.

The two largest perennial rivers, and the only navigable ones, are the Tana and the Galana (the latter known locally in its course from west to east as the Athi and the Galana), both of which empty into the Indian Ocean. The Tana River, approximately 725 kilometers long, rises in the southeastern part of the Kenya Highlands and enters the sea at Kipini. About 320 kilometers of the Tana's lower length are navigable by shallow-draft launches.

The Tana basin includes much of the flow from the Aberdare Range and Mount Kenya. In the Tana River's lower reaches the gradient is extremely gentle, banks are low, and flooding occurs during high water. As the river nears the coast, it develops many backwaters and at times may change course. The upper course of the river has a number of falls that have the potential, partially exploited by the early 1980s, for hydroelectric power development (see Electric Power, ch. 3).

The Galana River rises in the southeastern part of the Kenya Highlands and with its tributaries flows into the Indian Ocean north of Malindi. It is navigable by canoe for approximately 160 kilometers inland, where further travel is impeded by the rapids of Lugards Falls.

Several smaller rivers originate in the foothills of the eastern Kenya Highlands area within the Tana River basin. They usually disappear in the semiarid region east of the highlands but at times of heavy flooding manage to cross the area and empty into the Tana River. South of the Galana River, the Goshi River (called the Voi in its upper course) has a length of about 210 kilometers, but only about 80 kilometers of the lower course is perennial.

The western slopes of the Kenya Highlands are drained by a number of generally parallel rivers that empty into Lake Victoria. The largest rivers include the Nzoia, which drains the Cherangany Hills and the eastern slope of Mount Elgon, and the Yala, which eventually reaches the lake through Lake Kanyaboli and the Yala Swamp. Yala Falls—and Selby Falls on a tributary of the Nzoia—have considerable hydroelectric power potential. The Mara River, having its source in the Mau Escarpment in the southwest part of the highlands, flows southward, enters Tanzania, and turns westward to Lake Victoria.

The northern part of the Kenya Highlands east of the Rift Valley is drained by small rivers that disappear in the arid land to the north and by the larger, eastward-flowing system of the Ewaso Ng'iro. The Ewaso Ng'iro usually terminates in the great Lorian Swamp in the Tana Plains, but at times a heavy runoff floods the swamp, and the waters flow eastward as the Lak Dera into Somalia.

Demography

The 1979 census yielded a population of 15.3 million, 98.9 percent of which was African. The total constituted an increase of more than 40 percent over that enumerated just 10 years earlier. By mid-1982 the population was estimated at nearly 18 million, and the annual rate of natural increase was calculated at 4 percent, the highest in the world. If that rate persists, Kenya's population will have nearly doubled by the year 2000 and more than tripled by 2020. The rate of population growth poses problems for a country whose sustained rate of economic growth is not likely to be that high; it also raises the demand for educational and health facilities, which may not be met. The bulk of Kenya's people, in the early 1980s still roughly 85 percent rural, was concentrated in the country's southwestern quadrant and along the coast, the only areas capable of supporting a relatively dense agricultural population. But these regions either were already saturated or were likely to be by the year 2000, and the remainder of the country could not accommodate the prospective growth except under radically changed technological conditions in agriculture.

The High Growth Rate and the Age Structure

High rates of natural increase usually reflect the continuation of a customarily high birth rate and the decline of the death rate, particularly that part of it accounted for by infant mortality. In Kenya the estimated crude birth rate of 50 per 1,000 people in 1948 (when the first census was taken) persisted through subsequent censuses until that of 1979 when it was estimated to have risen to 53 per 1,000. The estimated crude death rate decreased from 25 in 1948 to 14 in 1979. The infant mortality rate dropped from 184 per 1,000 live births in 1948 to 87 in 1979, well under the estimated African average (in 1982) of 121 infant deaths per 1,000 live births.

The persistence of a high birth rate reflected the continuing value placed by most of Kenya's people on having children. Kenya's small urban population and well-educated (secondary school or beyond) women have fewer children, a tendency supported by the easier availability of family-planning facilities in urban areas (see Population Policy and Practice, this ch.). The lower birth rate in this comparatively small category has been offset by the improved standard of nutrition and hygiene of most of the still largely rural population, making for a larger number of live births. At the same time, these improved standards—and the availability of antibiotics—have diminished the death rate generally and the infant mortality rate specifically.

The rates of growth have not been uniform for all of Kenya's ethnic groups. Broadly, those groups whose home districts lie in the more densely settled, climatically favorable southwestern quadrant have had higher rates. There have been variations, however, accountable for in part by differences in values, levels of education and vulnerability to disease vectors (see Education; Health, this ch.). In the larger, much less densely settled, semiarid to arid parts of Kenya, growth rates have not been nearly so high and in some cases have been so low as to require special explanation. In an earlier period, between the censuses of 1962 (just before independence) and 1969, the growth rate of the major coastal ethnic group seemed to be lower than average, but it approximated the mean in the 1969-79 intercensal period (see Ethnic Groups and Languages, this ch.).

Kenya's annual rates of growth in the 1970s and early 1980s have generated a young population. In the 1979 census 48.5 percent of the population was less than 15 years old (see fig. 9). By mid-1982 the proportion under 15 years was estimated at 50 percent; the proportion of those over 65 years was estimated at 4 percent. Kenya is thus one of the dozen or so countries in the world where the segment of the population usually thought of as constituting the work force is exceeded by the segment comprising those thought of as dependents. Children under age 15 do contribute to some extent to the household economy in farming and nomadic communities, but the contribution is not great. The closer the country comes to achieving universal primary education and the longer life expectancy at birth becomes (it was 55 years in the early 1980s), the greater will be the burden on the working-age population. Given the situation in the early 1980s, even a very successful effort to limit population growth during the decade would not have significant effects on growth and the age structure until well after the year 2000.

Density Distribution, Urbanization, and Migration

Kenya's average population density in 1979 of 27 persons per square kilometer masks a great deal of variation (see fig. 10). The special Nairobi Area and the district encompassing Mombasa aside, densities ranged from 395 persons per square kilometer in Kisii District to one per square kilometer in Marsabit District. The two urban areas had densities of 1,210 per square kilometer (Nairobi) and 1,622 per square kilometer (Mombasa). The more densely populated districts (having

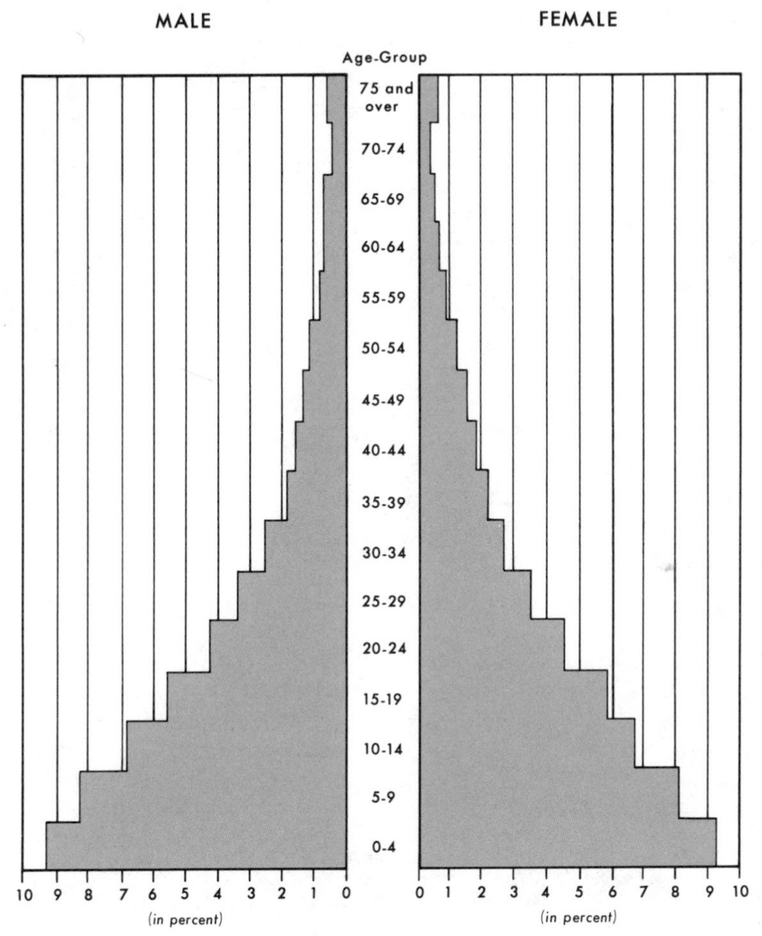

Source: Based on information from Kenya, Ministry of Economic Planning and Development, Central Bureau of Statistics, *Statistical Abstract, 1981*, Nairobi, 1981, 15.

Figure 9. Age and Sex Structure of the Population, 1979

more than 100 persons per square kilometer in 1979) constituted about 8 percent of the land area. In these districts lived about 58 percent of the population. If several other comparatively small areas in which the density approaches 100 per square kilometer are added, then more than 70 percent of the population lived in less than 11 percent of the land area. Most of this densely settled territory lies in the southwestern quadrant, i.e., the Kenya Highlands and Western Plateaus geographical regions and, to a lesser extent, in the south-central portions of the Rift Valley. A secondary area of concentration lies along the coast.

Except for a few coastal towns established by Arab traders and rulers, there were no urban centers in Kenya until the arrival of the British

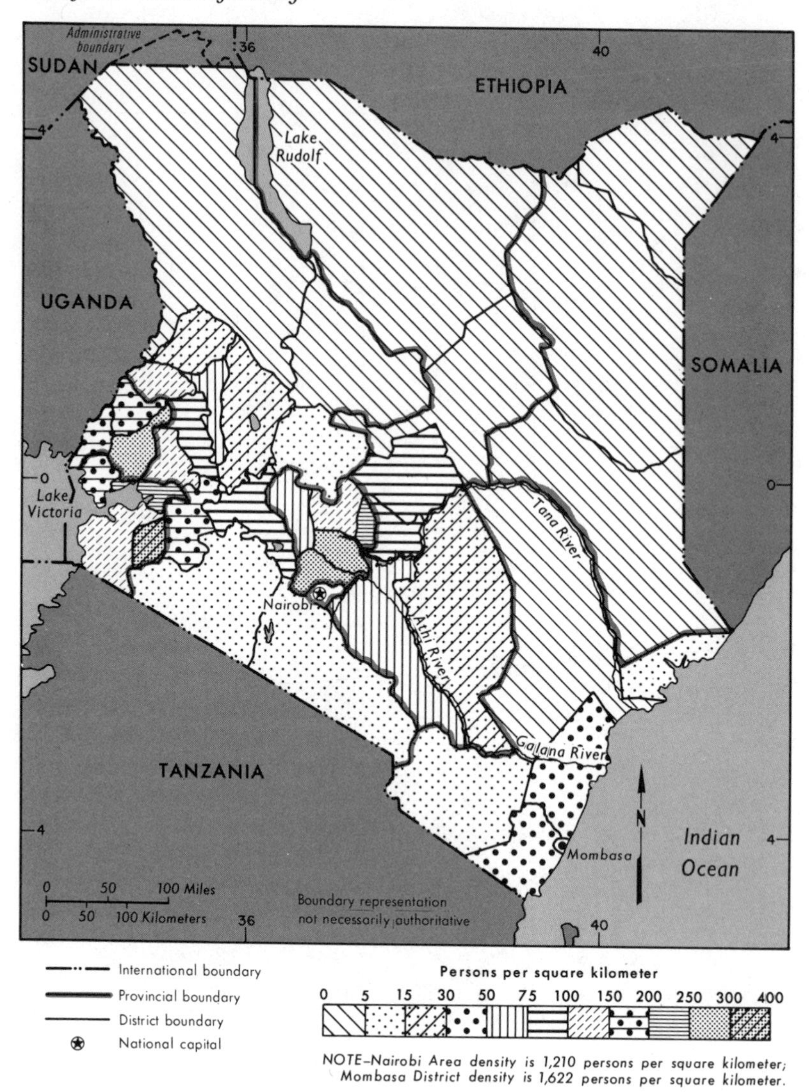

Source: Based on information from Kenya, Ministry of Economic Planning and Development, Central Bureau of Statistics, *Statistical Abstract, 1981*, Nairobi, 1981, 13.

Figure 10. Population Density by District, 1979

toward the end of the nineteenth century. Despite the growth of the urban population during the colonial era and since independence, Kenya has remained predominantly rural. In 1969 roughly 10 percent of its people were considered urban, i.e., living in towns of 2,000 persons or more. By 1979 that proportion had risen to nearly 13 percent and may have approached 15 percent in the early 1980s.

Aerial view of Nairobi, Kenya's national capital and East Africa's largest urban center
Courtesy Kenya Tourist Office, New York

Motorized traffic in downtown Nairobi reflects the pace of the bustling city.
Courtesy The Lamp, Exxon Corporation

Results of the 1979 census describing the distribution of the urban population were not available in mid-1983, but it was clear that more than one-half of the roughly 2 million persons in urban areas lived in Nairobi and Mombasa. In 1979 the Nairobi Area (which includes a zone outside the city proper) had a population of nearly 828,000, about 62 percent higher than that enumerated in 1969. The Mombasa District (including a zone outside the city), about one-third the size of the Nairobi Area, had a population of a little more than 341,000, an increase of 38 percent over that of 1969. According to the 1969 census, only nine other towns had populations exceeding 10,000; only one of these, Nakuru, approached 50,000. It is likely that several towns exceeded that figure in 1979, and one or two, Nakuru and Kisumu, may have approached or exceeded 100,000. In 1969 roughly 10 percent to perhaps 25 percent of the people in towns between 10,000 and 50,000 were Asians, Europeans, and (especially in the coastal town of Malindi) Arabs. Although a number of these inhabitants have undoubtedly departed, they have been replaced by a larger population of Africans.

Before independence and until the early 1970s, Nairobi and Mombasa had been the chief magnets for African rural-urban migration, and their African populations, unlike those of smaller towns, were ethnically mixed, although local groups, e.g., the Kikuyu in Nairobi, were represented more heavily than others. Because industry had been entirely in the hands of non-Africans (chiefly Europeans) during the colonial era, most of it had been located in Nairobi and its neighboring towns, which had conditions congenial to Europeans, and to a lesser extent in Mombasa (despite its uncomfortable climate) because of its significance as a port. This pattern persisted, especially in Nairobi, in the first decade of independence, in part because many of the Africans in the higher reaches of government were Kikuyu from the area. Opportunities, real or imagined, in industry, government, and commerce continued to draw Africans of all ethnic groups and of varying qualifications to Nairobi. By the early 1970s, however, the government responded in conjunction with private business to the complaints of Kenyans elsewhere that new industries ought to be more widely distributed; beginning in the mid-1970s steps were taken to place such industries outside of Nairobi. Some other towns, e.g., Kisumu and Webuye in western Kenya, are likely to grow a little more rapidly, but they will probably not approach Mombasa, let alone Nairobi, in size in the foreseeable future. Moreover, they and other towns serving agricultural areas or acting chiefly as administrative centers are not likely to become as ethnically heterogeneous as Nairobi or Mombasa.

The opening up of parts of the Kenya Highlands (restricted to European occupation in the colonial period) to African settlement led to limited permanent migration from some areas, particularly Kikuyuland, to the Highlands and the Rift Valley, but there has been no massive shift of population. Most migrants leave the rural areas for urban centers in search of work. If they find a way of surviving in the towns, either through regular wage labor or participation in the infor-

Swahili poster in a family planning center in Kisumu says, "This mother needs to space her births."
Courtesy World Bank Photo/Kay Chernush

mal sector, they may become permanent urban dwellers (see Employment, Wages, and Prices, ch.3). Some Kenyans are second-generation urbanites, and a few are third-generation townspeople. In the colonial era the migrants were typically males between 15 and 50 years of age, who might stay for considerable periods but who saw themselves as temporary. That distorted age and sex structure has begun to change. Households are established, and children are born in the towns. Nevertheless, even if many migrants remain in the towns for protracted periods (10 to 15 years or more), they maintain links with their rural homelands and send money there. Not uncommonly, a man may have a wife and children in a town and another family in the rural area from which he stems.

Population Policy and Practice

The Kenyan government early demonstrated an awareness of the problems posed for economic development by the high rates of population growth. In 1967, four years after independence, the National Family Planning Program was announced. Even before independence, local family-planning groups had merged in 1961 to form the Family Planning Association of Kenya. Despite this relatively early start and the announcement by the government in 1968 of its intention "to pursue vigorously policies designed to reduce the rate of population growth through voluntary means," population limitation programs had achieved very little success through the 1970s. This failure reflected an inadequate supply of facilities, personnel, and contraceptive materials, as well as a low level of demand for the services offered.

From its inception the family-planning program has been under the control of the Ministry of Health and has been carried out in conjunction with the mother-and-child-care program in the same facilities. At the end of the 1960s and through the first half of the 1970s, shortages in trained personnel and facilities were apparent in the rural areas, where most of the people lived. Under the third Development Plan 1974-78 and the fourth Development Plan 1979-83, these shortages were to be alleviated, and some progress was made to that end. Nevertheless, as of mid-1980 only 30 percent of the Ministry of Health's rural health facilities offered daily family-planning services. Another 16 to 17 percent offered part-time services, and more than one-half of the total did not provide any services. At the same time, goals were set for numbers of new visitors to the family-planning clinics and for acceptors of contraceptive devices or medication. These goals had been set in terms of non-Kenyan models, and they were eventually revised downward. Even so, they were not met.

Despite the training of substantial numbers of paramedical personnel and the establishment or upgrading of facilities to provide family-planning services, many rural families were not being reached in the late 1970s, and there were indications that this continued to be the case in the early 1980s. Research showed that roughly 70 percent of the acceptors of family-planning devices came from within 6.5 kilometers of a service point (as the dispensing facilities were called), whereas only about one-half of the rural population lived that close to a facility offering family-planning services. A substantial proportion of such facilities did not offer services on a daily basis. If a woman lived outside the six- to seven-kilometer radius, visiting a service point usually entailed walking two or more hours each way, a considerable burden on the busy rural woman. In 1982 many Kenyans complained that they did not know where the service points were, that they were too far away, or that contraceptives were not available at some facilities. The unavailability of contraceptives appeared to reflect poor management of their distribution and transportation problems affecting either the materials or the travel of the personnel who had the authority to distribute them.

The association of family planning with mother and child care, although sensible from one point of view, had its drawbacks: nurses and other medical personnel concerned with family planning also dealt with curative medicine to which they tended to give priority. Moreover, only nurses were permitted to dispense contraceptives at most service points—when available. In short, despite increased numbers of nurses and paramedical aides, there were still in the late 1970s few who were primarily involved in family planning. The norms for staffing were raised in 1980, but it was not clear that newly added personnel would be devoted chiefly to population control (see Health, this ch.).

Even if shortages of facilities, personnel, and contraceptive devices were to be rectified in the near future, the population explosion would not be curbed soon. The major obstacle lay in the lack of demand, i.e., in the value that most Kenyans placed on numbers of children, a value manifest in high fertility rates even among the minority who were aware of and used modern contraceptive methods. In the late 1970s that value had begun to change only among the small number of Kenyan women who had been educated through or beyond the secondary level (see Education, this ch.).

In a sample of Nairobi women interviewed in the Kenya Fertility Survey of 1977-78, nearly 60 percent were aware of various modern methods, but the values of these urban women did not appear to have changed. They used contraceptives to space their children better, not to limit their numbers.

In the rural areas the increase in awareness and use of modern contraceptives between the survey of 1966-67 and that of 1977-78 has been minimal. As in the urban areas, those who do use them are concerned with spacing rather than limitation. There were even indications that rural women had slightly increased the number of children they hoped to have.

Efforts to provide information to rural women on the nature and availability of family-planning techniques had not been effective up to the early 1980s. In the latter half of the 1970s much emphasis was given to the work of family-health field educators who were expected to educate the population face-to-face and to recruit patrons of both the mother-and-child clinics and the associated family-planning service points. They had far more lasting success in bringing women to the former than to the latter. Radio programs and other media used to propagate the family-planning gospel failed to make a significant impact. Some Kenyans seemed to find the radio programs "Panga Uzazi" (planned parenthood) more confusing than informative.

Most specialists in the field think that in the long run, economic development and its attendant processes—urbanization, education of women, and diminishing significance of children in the labor force and as supporters of their aged parents—will lead to a declining birth rate. In the Kenyan case, however, the rapidity of population growth is an obstacle to development. In these circumstances, the effort to curb growth must rely on the increase (and more efficient use) of facilities, personnel, and contraceptive materials and on a much more effective campaign to familiarize Kenyans, particularly in the rural areas, with the need for and practice of family planning.

Ethnic Groups and Languages

Africans, who constitute more than 99 percent of Kenyan nationals, are divided into more than 30 recognized ethnic groups ranging in size from a few hundred to more than 3 million persons. Small numbers of Asians (local term for those of Indian or Pakistani origin), Arabs, and Europeans (whites of whatever origin) are also nationals of Kenya. Somewhat larger numbers in these three categories who were not nationals and Africans from neighboring states together constituted a little more than 1 percent of the total population in 1979 (see table A).

The ancestors of the country's indigenous peoples came to the area in small groups from different directions at various times over a period of more than two millennia (see The Peopling of the Interior, ch. 1). Languages representing three of Africa's four language stocks are therefore spoken in Kenya. They are Niger-Kordofanian, Nilo-Saharan, and Afro-Asiatic. The number of languages equals or exceeds that of ethnic groups, posing a major problem for a state seeking to integrate its diverse populations. Efforts to deal with it have been made by declaring Swahili a national language, but the expansion of the use of standard Swahili has been slow.

With some exceptions, groups speaking languages of a given stock have made generally similar ecological adaptations to their environments. Such adaptations reflect both the culturally embedded orientations they brought with them on their arrival in the area and their responses to the opportunities offered (or the exigencies imposed) by local environments.

Thus all groups speaking Bantu languages (of the Niger-Kordofanian stock) have long been primarily cultivators. A few groups near major bodies of water have turned to fishing for much or all of their livelihoods. They therefore live in that comparatively limited part of Kenya that will sustain cultivation or fishing. Although Bantu-speaking groups constitute at least two-thirds of the indigenous population, they occupy less than one-fourth of the land area (see fig. 11).

Nearly as uniform in their quite different adaptation are the Cushitic-speaking peoples (well under 5 percent of the population), most of whom are pastoral nomads continuing a mode of livelihood characteristic of the areas in Somalia and Ethiopia from which they stem. The speakers of Cushitic languages (of the Afro-Asiatic stock) are thinly distributed over nearly one-half the country.

The peoples speaking Nilotic languages (of the Nilo-Saharan stock) are more varied. As a whole they constitute somewhat more than one-quarter of the population and inhabit roughly the same proportion of the country's land area. But the Western Nilotic-speaking Luo, cultivators and cattle keepers, are much more densely concentrated than the Southern Nilotic-speaking Kalenjin. The latter, despite a tradition of keeping cattle, have long been involved in mixed farming and, except for a few groups, have given up a pastoral nomadic way of life, as have the Eastern Nilotic-speaking Teso. Much more sparsely settled are the Eastern Nilotic-speaking Maasai, largely pastoral nomadic people, and related peoples occupying the more arid sections of the Rift Valley and the near desert in the northwest.

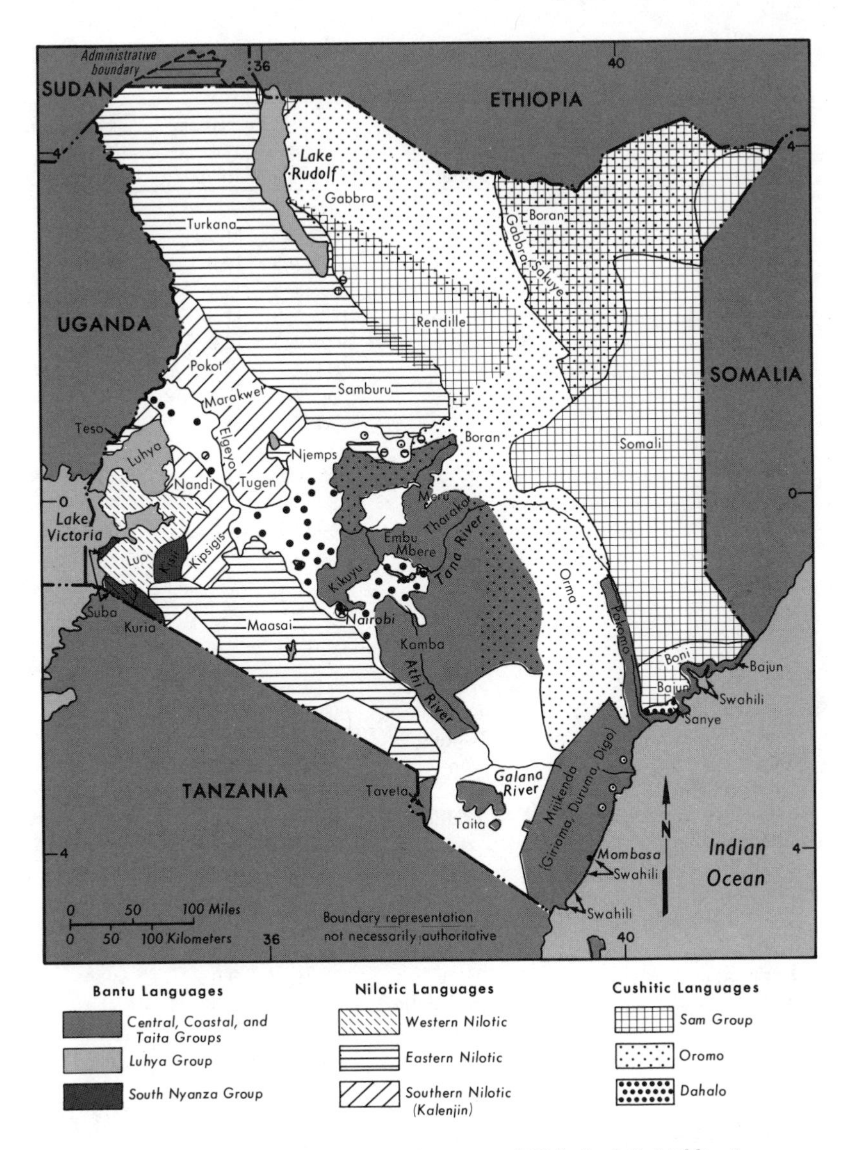

Source: Based on information from Bernd Heine and Wilhelm J.G. Möhlig, *Language and Dialect Atlas of Kenya*, I, Berlin, 1980.

Figure 11. Distribution of Principal Ethnic Groups

Language and Linguistic Classification

Of the several branches and families of the Niger-Kordofanian language stock, only the Bantu family—widespread throughout Africa south of 5° north latitude—is found in the country. Except for a few speakers on the southern Somali coast, Kenya is the northeasternmost limit of the Bantu linguistic distribution. Subgroups of Bantu languages

Table A. Ethnic Composition of Kenya, 1979

Ethnic Group	Language Family	Number	Percentage of Nationals	Percentage Difference since 1969
Kenyans				
Kikuyu	Bantu	3,202,821	21.2	45.1
Luhya[1]	-do-	2,119,708	14.0	45.9
Luo	Western Nilotic	1,955,845	12.9	28.5
Kamba	Bantu	1,725,569	11.4	44.1
Kalenjin[2]	Southern Nilotic	1,652,243	10.9	38.8
Kisii (Gusii)	Bantu	944,087	6.2	34.5
Meru	-do-	840,504	5.6	57.6
Mijikenda[3]	-do-	732,830	4.8	40.1
Somali				
Somali[4]	Cushitic	155,695	1.0	513.6
Degodia	-do-	93,035	0.6	49.0
Gurreh[5]	-do-	83,083	0.5	68.7
Ogaden	-do-	25,642	0.2	-72.1
Ajuran[5]	-do-	22,006	0.1	41.6
Hawiya	-do-	1,604	—	-60.1
Gosha	-do-	1,852	—	-36.7
Total Somali	-do-	382,917	2.5	51.3
Maasai	Eastern Nilotic	241,395	1.6	55.8
Turkana	-do-	207,249	1.4	2.0
Embu	Bantu	180,400	1.2	53.4
Taita	-do-	153,119	1.0	41.1
Oromo (Galla)				
Boran	Cushitic	68,894	0.5	102.0
Orma	-do-	32,197	0.2	97.0
Gabbra	-do-	30,553	0.2	89.7
Sakuye	-do-	1,824	—	-58.3
Total Oromo (Galla)	-do-	133,468	0.9	88.3
Teso	Eastern Nilotic	132,487	0.9	54.4
Kuria	Bantu	89,169	0.6	48.9
Samburu	Eastern Nilotic	73,625	0.5	34.4
Mbere	Bantu	61,725	0.4	25.3
Suba[6]	-do-	59,668	0.4	n.a.
Pokomo	-do-	39,741	0.3	13.0
Bajun	-do-	36,971	0.2	51.6
Rendille	Cushitic	21,794	0.1	16.4
Tharaka	Bantu	9,682	—	-81.2
Taveta	-do-	7,676	—	21.4
Njemps	Eastern Nilotic	7,546	—	15.6
Nderobo[7]	-do-	7,200	—	-65.8
Swahili/Shirazi	Bantu	5,646	—	-43.3
Boni/Sanye[8]	Cushitic	4,170	—	5.0
El Molo	-do-	538	—	n.a.
Asians	n.a.	32,554	0.2	-46.6
Arabs	n.a.	18,861	0.1	-22.1
Europeans	n.a.	4,445	—	14.3
Others[9]	n.a.	57,318	0.4	2.3
Total Kenyans	n.a.	15,142,971	99.7[10]	40.8[11]

Table A—Continued

Ethnic Group	Language Family	Number	Percentage of Nationals	Percentage Difference since 1969
Non-Kenyans				
Africans[12]	n.a.	71,818	n.a.	20.8
Asians	n.a.	46,046	n.a.	−40.1
Europeans	n.a.	35,456	n.a.	−3.4
Arabs	n.a.	20,285	n.a.	450.0
Others[9]	n.a.	10,213	n.a.	520.0
Not stated	n.a.	343	n.a.	n.a.
Total Non-Kenyans	n.a.	184,161	n.a.	2.4
TOTAL	n.a.	15,327,132	n.a.	n.a.

—means less than 0.1 percent.

n.a.—not applicable.

[1]Luhya consists of 16 groups: Bukusu, Dakho, Kabras, Khayo, Kisa, Marachi, Maragoli, Marama, Nyala (lake), Nyala (east), Nyole, Samia, Tachoni, Tiriki, Tsotso, and Wanga. Population figures for these groups were not available.

[2]Kalenjin consists of a number of groups of which seven were recognized in the 1969 census: Kipsigis, Nandi (including Terik), Tugen, Elgeyo, Pokot, Marakwet, and Sabaot (including Koney and Pok). Of these, the Kipsigis, at nearly 40 percent, and the Nandi, at more than 20 percent, were by far the largest. Of the others, only the Tugen exceeded 10 percent.

[3]Mijikenda consists of nine groups: Giriama, Duruma, Digo, Chonyi, Rabai, Ribe, Kambe, Jibana, and Kauma.

[4]Persons who identified themselves only as Somali were so listed in the census, although like the others subsumed under Somali, e.g., Degodia, they were also members of specific sections.

[5]Many Gurreh and Ajuran, although Somali in origin, apparently spoke Oromo rather than Somali as a mother tongue.

[6]The Suba were not distinguished in the 1969 census and were probably then included with the adjacent Luo.

[7]The nomadic, hunting, and gathering Nderobo spoke one of two Nilotic tongues, either Eastern Nilotic Maasai or Southern Nilotic Nandi.

[8]Boni/Sanye appears to involve the lumping of at least two categories speaking different Cushitic languages.

[9]Others includes persons who have not stated ethnic group or race. In the case of Kenyans, the majority is probably of African origin. In the case of non-Kenyans, the composition is not certain.

[10]The remaining 0.3 percent is made up of groups each of which constituted less than 0.1 percent of the Kenyan population. Note that Kenyan nationals constitute 98.8 percent of total population.

[11]This national average does not include non-Africans and "others."

[12]Includes Africans from neighboring countries, particularly Tanzania and Uganda. Some Africans, particularly nomadic peoples who are closely related ethnically to Kenyan groups, may not have indicated their non-Kenyan provenance.

Source: Based on information from Kenya, Ministry of Economic Planning and Development, Central Bureau of Statistics, *Statistical Abstract, 1981*, Nairobi, 1981, 14; and Irving Kaplan et al., *Area Handbook for Kenya*, Washington, 1976, 86–87, 91.

in Kenya have not been firmly established, but adjacent languages appear to be closely related in linguistic terms. Hence Kikuyu, Kamba, Meru, and several other languages clustered north, northeast, and east of Nairobi are often referred to as the central Bantu tongues. But the precise relationship of these languages to each other and to Bantu tongues elsewhere in Kenya continues to be debated, as does the extent to which a category of people recognized as an ethnic group by the census speaks dialects of the same language or different languages. The same sorts of problems arise in connection with other commonly recognized clusters—coastal Bantu, the Luhya tongues, the Taita group, and the South Nyanza group. For example, at least one section, the Maragoli, of the heterogeneous people called the Luhya speaks a language thought by some linguists to be more closely akin to that spoken by the Kisii (Gusii) of the South Nyanza group than it is to languages spoken by other Luhya groups.

Aside from Arabic, used by some indigenous Muslims for religious purposes, the only branch of the Afro-Asiatic stock embracing Kenyan languages is Cushitic, otherwise represented in Ethiopia and Somalia. Somali, present in at least two dialects, has the largest number of Cushitic speakers in Kenya. Of the two Somali dialects spoken in Kenya, Common Somali is spoken as a first language by the great pastoral nomadic majority, and Central Somali by the much smaller group of cultivators (who also understand Common Somali). Oromo (commonly called Galla until the mid-1970s) is spoken in several dialects apparently corresponding to the several sections recognized in the census. Several other Cushitic languages are spoken by relatively small numbers of people. Rendille and Boni are usually considered closer to Somali than to Oromo; by contrast the language of the people called Sanye in the census and commonly lumped with the Boni is considered closer to Oromo.

The Nilo-Saharan stock has been less fully accepted by specialists than the other two, and its constituent branches and families are less firmly fixed. Specifically, the position of the subgroups here classified as Eastern Nilotic and Southern Nilotic was considered uncertain by some linguists who preferred to call them Para-Nilotic. The Nilotic languages in Kenya have been divided into three clusters: Western Nilotic, represented by the Luo, the only non-Bantu-speaking group of substantial size; Eastern Nilotic, represented by the Maasai (and two related dialects, Samburu and Njemps, distinguished on sociological rather than purely linguistic grounds), Turkana, and Teso; and Southern Nilotic, comprising the Kalenjin tongues. All of the Kalenjin people speak closely related languages, but some languages of recognized sections of the Kalenjin, e.g., Kipsigis and Nandi, are mutually intelligible dialects of a single language, whereas Kipsigis and Pokot are not.

Two kinds of multilingualism are to be found in Kenya. In the first kind, the mother tongue of a participant in an ethnically mixed exchange will be used; in the second, a language not native to the speakers will be employed. For example, in multilingualism of the first sort, Luhya may use Luo in a conversation with Luo, and Embu and Kamba may use Kikuyu in exchanges with native speakers of Kikuyu. In the first instance, the mother tongues of the participants belong to different language families. In the second instance, Embu is so closely related to Kikuyu that some scholars consider it a dialect of the latter, and some dialects of Kikuyu and Kamba also appear to be quite close.

Multilingualism of this first kind is not uncommon in border areas between two or more ethnic or subethnic groups. It occurs chiefly in the context of economic or other brief transactions. Much more rarely, friends of different ethnic groups may use the language of one group. In the still-infrequent instances of inter-ethnic marriages in rural areas, one spouse (usually the one marrying into an alien community) will learn the language of the other, which is the domestic language. This kind of multilingualism also occurs in urban areas in the marketplace and the workplace where one ethnic group is dominant and clearly sets the tone.

The second kind of multilingualism usually involves the use of English or Swahili, sometimes both. Both have official status, but the contexts in which they are employed and the positions of typical users have differed. According to the Constitution, "the official languages of the National Assembly shall be Swahili and English, and the business of the National Assembly may be conducted in either or both languages." Nevertheless, all bills and related memorandums, acts of parliament and related legislation, financial resolutions and related documents, and proposed or actual amendments are to be written in English and must be quoted in English in the proceedings of the National Assembly. This restriction on the use of Swahili reflects an uncertainty that English legal language can be translated into Swahili in such a way that both versions will carry exactly the same meaning. But it also reflects a continuing ambivalence about the value of Swahili as opposed to that of English, the use of which has long been a mark of high status.

Swahili, a Bantu language much modified lexically (and to some extent in other ways) by contact with Arabs, developed as a common mother tongue along the coast and in Zanzibar by the thirteenth century. It has easily incorporated foreign words—Arabic, Hindi, Persian, and English among them—adapting them to fit the Swahili sound system and its grammar. Several dialects are spoken as first languages in Kenya, each tied to a specific local community, e.g., the dialect called Mvita, used in Mombasa. There are others in Tanzania, including the Zanzibari dialect, Kiunguja, which provided the basis for spoken standard Swahili. Standard Swahili was developed in the 1930s by the Inter-territorial Language (Swahili) Committee for the East African Dependencies on the basis of earlier work when missionaries and educationists felt the need for a standard version of the language and for an accepted Latin orthography. The use of Swahili as a second language in missions and schools, by the colonial authorities, and by Europeans and Asians to communicate with Africans led to the emergence of several much simplified dialects (or pidgins) that were not satisfactory for educational, administrative, and religious purposes. There were also written forms, some in Latin script and one (used chiefly by Muslim religious figures) in Arabic script. The latter was still in use, but the Latin form, standardized in the 1930s, was much more widely employed.

The development of standard Swahili and its Latin orthography did not obviate the continuation of nonstandard dialects among those for whom Swahili was a second language, particularly if they acquired it informally, as many of them did. Among these are Kisetla (literally, [European] settler Swahili; used in exchanges with Africans—also called kitchen Swahili) and Kihindi (literally, Indian Swahili). The dialect called Kishamba (literally, the language of the fields or rural Swahili—sometimes called upcountry Swahili) is in fact several dialects, the variants depending upon the mother tongues of the speakers and the extent to which any substantial number of them have been formally educated in standard Swahili. The Swahili of relatively uneducated Kenyans aside, there were (at least up to the early 1970s) variations in the form used in various publications of the press and on the radio, although these tended to be closer to standard Swahili.

The use of Swahili as a national language was not given high priority in the first decade and a half after independence. Although the question was raised soon after independence and again in the late 1960s and early 1970s, a concerted drive to make Swahili a national language (reflected in the educational system) did not begin until the mid-1970s. The extent to which this has been carried through has not been reported (see Education, this ch.). This reflects the wishes of some important ethnic groups to retain their native languages in a country in which ethnicity has been important in organizing social and political relations.

One category of Kenyan Africans, Muslims, whatever their ethnic origin, seems to be willing to use Swahili in many contexts, although Muslims may retain some knowledge of their mother tongues. Apparently they consider Swahili closely linked to Arabic, even if few know how to write it in the Arabic script. But the failure to encourage the use of Swahili also reflects the peculiar place of English as a mark of education and status. It often happens that precisely those Kenyans who have received formal training in Swahili also know English and hold positions in the public or private sector with which the use of English is associated. These people use Swahili only when they must.

In a sample survey of Kenyans undertaken in the late 1960s, it was found that 42 percent claimed to use Swahili alone as a second language; 10.3 percent claimed to use both Swahili and English as second languages; and 7.7 percent claimed to know both Swahili and a vernacular other than their mother tongue. This survey did not indicate the kind of Swahili used nor did it indicate claimed competence or relate variety and competence to age and sex. A separate survey undertaken about the same time suggested that comparatively small percentages in most ethnic groups claimed to "speak very well, fluently, or could talk on any topic." Exceptions were samples of Kikuyu and Pokomo. Other groups in the coastal area or its hinterland, e.g., some of the Mijikenda and the Taita, are said to be well acquainted with Swahili. Some groups seem to resist acquiring Swahili, e.g., the Luo, who have a relatively high proportion claiming competence in English.

Of the slightly more than 10 percent of Africans who claim to know both English and Swahili, most probably use English in speaking to their superiors or equals and Swahili only to those (usually subordinates or others in economic transactions) who they think cannot speak English. With some exceptions, e.g., the late Jomo Kenyatta, those who have considerable competence in both English and Swahili are likely to be young and to have had a substantial amount of formal education. Their Swahili may therefore approach the standard version. That has not always been the case, however, because some primary schools did not use Swahili at all (at the time of the surveys), and the secondary schools certainly did not (see Education, this ch.).

Because many women and older men had little or no education at the time of these surveys, they either did not learn Swahili (or had acquired it informally), spoke a dialect quite different from the standard form, or could claim only a limited degree of competence. As increasing numbers of women receive more schooling, and as generations of males acquire more education than their fathers, greater competence in a Swahili more closely approximating the standard form may become more widespread. A more recent survey than those of the late 1960s was not available.

Ethnic Groups

The correspondence between language and ethnic group varies. In general, language serves as a marker for both objective and subjective definitions of an ethnic group. People speaking a single language in a country like Kenya tend to be perceived by others as members of a single group, and those sharing a language make that fact a significant part of their self-definition as a group. Some culturally similar groups speaking dialects of the same language define themselves as different, however, and may be so defined by others for social, historical, or ecological reasons. Conversely, speakers of distinct but closely related languages may be considered and deem themselves part of a single group, at least in some contexts.

No ethnic group ("tribe" in the language of the colonial authorities and in the postindependence lexicon of Kenyans as well) is culturally and linguistically homogeneous except perhaps for a few of the very smallest ones. Moreover, no Kenyan group was characterized in the precolonial era by a centralized political order that encompassed all or even most of those speaking the same language and sharing a common culture. Even if all of the members of an ethnic category considered themselves descended from a common ancestor, which members of many such categories did not, they were divided into a number of local small-scale political systems (sometimes under a chief with limited powers). If their numbers were great or if they were spread over a large area, they may not even have been aware of the existence of other like peoples. Moreover, linguistic and cultural similarity did not necessarily preclude armed conflict. In effect, the ethnic categories used by the colonial authorities, often for administrative convenience, did much to define ethnic groups as they stood, at least officially, in the latter half of the twentieth century. In some important cases, current ethnic categories were first established in the 1930s and 1940s, largely as a consequence of the awareness and aspirations of the local elites in the independent groups that constituted the new categories.

Of the five largest ethnic groups, each having more than 1 million persons and together constituting more than 70 percent of Kenyan nationals, two—the Bantu-speaking Luhya and the Southern Nilotic-speaking Kalenjin—are of recent vintage, having emerged in the colonial era to bring together local entities of similar language and culture. The degree of relatedness between any two of the several components of either the Kalenjin or the Luhya varies. Moreover, members of these components, which still persist, do not have an equally intense sense of affinity to the larger, more comprehensive group. In both rural and urban areas, for example, the Maragoli, one of the largest entities usually assigned to the Luhya, may disclaim membership in the latter, in part because their language differs from that of most Luhya. At the same time, however, their numbers are large enough that they do not perceive themselves to be an overwhelmed minority as the smaller Luhya groups might without the Luhya identification.

The other three of the five largest groups—Kikuyu, Luo, and Kamba—have a longer historical identity, but even they were not aware of the outer limits of their groups until the colonial era. There is still some question of the boundaries between the Kikuyu and groups such as the Meru, Embu, and Mbere. In Nairobi, non-Bantu speakers and others not of the central Bantu-speaking peoples may tend to lump members of the smaller groups with the dominant Kikuyu. All three of these large groups were divided by dialect differences and cultural variation and were organized into small-scale, not always friendly, political units. Further, given their size even in the colonial period, different sections of these large groups were variably affected by the changes of the era. Thus, although the Kikuyu in general can be said to have felt the impact of the European presence earlier and more intensely than any other of the major groups, those of Kiambu District, immediately adjacent to Nairobi, were probably more strongly affected than Kikuyu of other districts.

The 10 next largest ethnic groups, ranging in number between more than 100,000 and nearly 1 million, together constitute more than 25 percent of Kenyan nationals. One, the Mijikenda (literally, nine towns), is an officially recognized entity comprising nine groups, distinguished in many contexts by themselves and by others. The two largest of the

Mijikenda groups are the Giriama and the Digo. The term *Mijikenda* is clearly Swahili, as is the other term, *wanyika* (literally, those of the bush; considered pejorative), applied to them. Although their Bantu languages are very closely related and the groups have been treated as a unit for some time, the degree of their solidarity is not known.

Two other groups, the Somali and the Oromo, consist of peoples independently counted in the 1969 and 1979 censuses but grouped together here. All the groups who are considered Somali are certainly seen, and perceive themselves, as such in some situations. The other names offered in the census refer to various levels of descent groups in terms of which the Somali, in Kenya as in Somalia, are organized. Thus, the Hawiya constitute one of six clan-families (groups of clans) in which almost all Somali are grouped. Three other Somali names used in the census—Degodia, Gurreh, and Ajuran—are in fact sections of, or associated with, the Hawiya, as are other groups not noted in the census but recognized by ethnologists or linguists in Kenya. The other group, the Ogaden, noted in the census (and others not noted), are sections of the very large Darod clan-family. The Ogaden in particular are to be found not only in Kenya but also in Somalia and Ethiopia. The Somali-speaking Gosha cultivators may be freed slaves in origin and do not appear to be attached to a Somali clan-family.

The sections below the level of the clan-family were the focuses of economic and political organization in the preindependence era in both Somalia and Kenya, and conflict between sections was not uncommon. Awareness of Somali nationality dates from the late colonial period and has been connected with Somali irredentism, but that awareness has not eliminated sectional loyalties. A comparison of the 1969 and 1979 censuses nevertheless suggests that significant numbers of some sections chose to identify themselves as Somali in the latter census. The sharp drop in the number of Ogaden—by far the largest group of Somali in the 1969 census—and the huge increase in the category of Somali (comparatively small in the 1969 census) may be attributed to a change in identification.

The groups collectively called Oromo have been separately enumerated in all censuses through 1979, but their relationship has long been noted, and the term *Galla*, not their own, has often been applied to them. In Ethiopia, Oromo speakers constitute the largest single ethnolinguistic category but are segmented into a number of culturally quite different groups. Many of them have insisted on using their own name, Oromo, for themselves, particularly since the onset of profound change in Ethiopia beginning in 1974. There is no indication that the use of the name has spread to the related groups in Kenya. The Orma have been in Kenya for some hundreds of years and have no significant links with Oromo of Ethiopia. The Boran, by contrast, have maintained a regular connection with Boran in Ethiopia, and sections of them have, like many nomads, ignored the international boundary in the course of their regular movements.

Smaller groups (under 100,000 members) and segments of larger ones are assimilated to some degree by more populous groups adjacent to or surrounding them. In some cases assimilation extends only to the convenience of identification in the census (such identification may, however, be imposed by the census taker); in others it involves taking on a good part of the way of life and the language of a neighboring group. Sometimes, however, a group uses the language of neighbors and aspects of their culture but retains its own identity.

Portions of the Gurreh and the Ajuran (Somali in origin and still socially and culturally Somali) had nevertheless adopted the Oromo tongue of their neighbors as a home language. The Ajuran, perhaps in response to the surging Somali nationalism of the time, were showing signs of readopting Somali identification in the 1960s. Some of the Rendille, all of whom had been camel nomads, had taken to herding cattle in the less arid southerly reaches of their territory, adjacent to the Samburu. They had adopted many of the herding techniques and the language of the latter and perhaps some aspects of their social organization. It is possible, moreover, given the apparent low Rendille growth between 1969 and 1979, that some have begun to identify themselves as Samburu.

A clue to the possibility of assimilation of one group by another is provided by comparison of the censuses of 1969 and 1979. Some groups show either negative rates of growth or positive rates well below the average growth of 40.8 percent over a period of 10 years. A degree of assimilation of some of these groups by others may account for their decline, but other factors are responsible for the decline of several groups. In only a few cases, however, is direct evidence available. It is likely that the already small group of Oromo-speaking Sakuye, living among Bantu and larger Oromo groups, has been absorbed by one or the other. The actual decline in numbers of the Bantu-speaking Tharaka may also be ascribable to assimilation by adjacent groups, Meru or Kamba, each of which shows growth above the average. The term *Swahili* applied to a group (as opposed to its application to the language) has not been popular because it has carried the implication of servitude. People who formerly acknowledged the term *Swahili* may no longer be willing to do so, and many may have been enumerated as "other," i.e., African, their tribe not specified. The decline of the Nderobo is more easily explained. Hunting and gathering peoples scattered in various parts of the Rift Valley and immediately adjacent areas, each Nderobo group typically spoke the languages of a nearby pastoral group, either Maasai or Kalenjin, although at least one group spoke an Eastern Cushitic tongue. They were nevertheless identified as Nderobo as long as they maintained their way of life. When, as they have increasingly done, Nderobo take to keeping cattle (or, more rarely, to cultivation), their identity changes.

The very low rate of growth of the Turkana must be ascribed to a low birth rate and a high death rate. Very much affected by drought in the 1970s, they lost not only a great many cattle but also a great many children and other family members. Their situation was made

The nomadic Somali transport their portable shelters and household possessions by camels when their herds move on.

worse by the incursion of raiders from Uganda in the difficult period generated by the Idi Amin Dada regime and its fall. Many Turkana were killed in the course of these raids.

The relatively low rates of growth of some other pastoral groups may also be attributed to drought and to the relative lack of health maintenance and curative facilities (see Health, this ch.). All Kenyans are affected to some extent by drought, but pastoral peoples, especially those in the north, suffer most grievously. There are instances of what seems like extraordinary growth among pastoral groups., particularly the Somali and the Oromo. That growth may be traced in part to movements across Kenya's borders with Ethiopia and Somalia that are ascribable to the ordinary exigencies of nomadic pastoralism. The 1979 census indicated many Boran on the Kenyan side of the border, whereas the 1969 census did not. But both Ethiopia and Somalia experienced internal turmoil in the late 1970s, and there was warfare between Ethiopia and Somalia in Ethiopia's Ogaden in 1977 and 1978. Some of the Oromo and many Somali enumerated in Kenya in 1979 may have fled their usual pastures in Ethiopia and Somalia. The Bajun, a Swahili-speaking group of coastal and island dwellers (fishermen and boatmen) in southern Somalia and northern Kenya, also showed a considerable increase in Kenya, which may reflect movement from Somalia. Finally, nomads have always been hard to count, particularly in the thinly administered northern areas, and what may appear to be extraordinary growth may simply be a consequence of an undercount in 1969.

In addition to the groups listed in the census, there are others that ethnographers and linguists have been aware of but that have probably been lumped with a neighboring or surrounding group. For example, enclaved among the Kisii are the Nubi (numbers uncertain but described as small), who are descendants of people brought from southern Sudan and northern Uganda as soldiers early in the colonial era. The Nubi speak a locally modified Arabic at home and use Swahili as a mode of communication with their neighbors. Few speak Kisii as a second language. Nubi are Muslims in an area where vitually all others are adherents of the indigenous religious system or some form of Christianity. The Suba, originally Bantu speaking, who live adjacent to the Luo in southwesternmost Kenya and, for the most part, speak their language, were not separately recognized in the 1969 or earlier census. They were presumably enumerated as Luo. In the 1979 census they were listed separately.

The fact that some groups are not independently listed in official documents such as the census may reflect a decision on the part of the groups concerned to identify themselves for official purposes as part of their larger neighbors. It may, however, reflect official decisions to continue to use categories received from the colonial power and to ignore smaller groups even when the latter, e.g., the Nubi, are clearly separate from their neighbors and think of themselves as such. Why the Suba were recognized is not clear, although they are larger than most unrecognized groups.

Each of the three non-African categories in Kenya is heterogeneous with respect to citizenship, origin, involvement in Kenyan society, economy, politics, and degree of intragroup communal organization and segmentation. The majority of non-Africans are not Kenyan nationals, but the proportions vary, as does the extent to which each of the ethnic categories has changed in size.

The Asians, both those who hold Kenyan citizenship and those who do not, have lost the greatest numbers. From roughly 150,000 at independence, they have declined to about one-half that number. The decrease of resident Asians, i.e., those who had a long-term stake in the country, is even greater inasmuch as about 9,000 of the Asians who are not Kenyan nationals are Indian nationals, generally professionals, who live in Kenya under contract for a limited period. Those who are neither Kenyan nor Indian nationals have British citizenship.

All but a few of those categorized as Asians in the census originated in the Indian subcontinent, either in what is now India or, more rarely, in Pakistan or are descendants of such persons. For the most part, Asians who are Kenyan nationals were born in Kenya as were most who have remained there but did not choose Kenyan citizenship. Although all are officially called Asians, Africans frequently use the term *Indian* for the Swahili *Wahindi*, a name the people themselves do not care for.

Caste is much attenuated among Asians in Kenya, but differences in wealth and education are significant. The most important divisions among Asians, however, are those established by religious differences. Religious statistics postdating the exodus of roughly one-half the Asian population of 1969 were not available in the early 1980s, but it was likely that Hindus, originating largely in Gujerat, remained the largest single group. Muslims, originating in either Gujerat or the Punjab, constituted about one-fourth of the Asian population in 1969, but they were (and remain) divided into five distinct groups: Sunni Muslims, three Shiite groups—the Khoja Ismaili (followers of the Aga Khan and thought to be the most numerous), the Bohra, and the Ithna Ashariyya—and the Ahmadiyya. The last group is perhaps the smallest and considered outside the acceptable range of variation by most other Muslims. In addition, there are in Kenya Roman Catholics (chiefly Goans in origin), Sikhs (originally from the Punjab), Jains (a small ascetic group stemming from Hinduism millennia ago), and Parsis. All religious groups and Muslim subgroups are essentially endogamous. Given these religious divisions and the differences based on wealth and education, there has not been a great deal of Asian solidarity, although the pressures to which Asians have been subject have led sporadically to a sense of common fate and to intermittent cooperation (see The Social Order, this ch.).

In 1969 there were more than 40,000 Europeans in the country, of which not quite 10 percent were Kenyan nationals. In 1979 there were nearly as many Europeans, and slightly more than 11 percent were citizens of Kenya. That growth in proportion reflected both absolute growth in the number of citizens and a small decline in the number of nonnationals. There has been a considerable turnover in the European population, particularly among those who do not hold citizenship. Most nonnationals were from Europe and North America working for local affiliates of foreign-based industrial, financial, and commercial enterprises. Others were specialists employed by the Kenyan government, or they represented foreign governments, international agencies, and special interest groups, such as missions. Some of these persons have spent long periods in Kenya.

In the colonial and early postcolonial eras, the tone of the European community was set by the British, although there had always been non-British Europeans in Kenya. The exact composition of the European population—nationals and nonnationals—was not available in 1979, but there were probably far more non-British Europeans and Americans among the nonnationals than there had been 10 years earlier. Those Europeans who have taken Kenyan citizenship are largely British in origin.

Arabs who were Kenyan citizens claimed descent from either Arabs who came to the coast before the arrival of the Portuguese in the fifteenth century (so-called old Arabs) or those who came with the rise of the Omani dynasty in Zanzibar and on the coast in the nineteenth century (so-called true Arabs). Others have claimed Arab descent but were often not recognized as such by the old or true Arabs. Those identifying themselves as Arabs, whatever their origins, were usually the products of a long history of Arab unions with African women.

The precise reason for the decline in the numbers of Arabs who are Kenyan nationals is difficult to determine. Some may have decided that the "Kenyanization" policy begun in 1967-68, although not in principle applicable to citizens, had affected them adversely (see Kenyanization and Economic Policy, ch. 1). It is more likely that they identified themselves in the 1979 census as Africans (tribe not specified), as some Arabs had begun to do even before 1969. The substantial increase in the numbers of Arabs who were not Kenyan nationals is attributable to the arrival of Arabs from the Arabian Peninsula, most of them probably Yemenis.

In general, non-Africans have been much more urban than Africans. A breakdown for 1979 was not available, but in 1969 nearly 95 percent of all Asians, who tended to be engaged in commerce at various levels and who had been prevented from owning land in the colonial era, were urban. After independence their continuation in retail trade was discouraged, and it is likely that the small proportion that lived in rural areas as traders has declined, leaving Asians generally even more urban than they were earlier. In 1969 roughly 79 percent of all Arabs were urban, living mainly in towns along the coast. That proportion has probably not changed significantly. Of the Europeans, 63 percent were urban, according to the 1969 census. In 1979 the Europeans who were not Kenyan nationals were probably much more urbanized because of their jobs. Europeans who were Kenyan citizens were probably less urbanized.

The Social Order

Most of Kenya's ethnic groups have shared modes of social organization and relations based on descent, kinship (by blood or marriage), seniority (whether generational or chronological), and neighborhood. The expression and relative emphasis given each of these modes varied a great deal in the precolonial era and underwent change even then as trade, warfare, migration, and other factors affected all or part of an ethnic group. For example, some Bantu-speaking groups took on the system of age-sets (see Glossary) of the Kalenjin and Maasai peoples with whom they made war and peace, but others did not. Social structures changed still further under the impact of the colonial order as Africans in different communities became involved in varying degrees in the colonial economy, largely as wage laborers but also, despite restrictions, as cultivators of cash crops. Moreover, chieftainship of a different kind, i.e., at the lowest rung of the colonial system of authority, became a source of income and power. As time went on, some Africans entered government service at a low level, but at wages that were good by the local African standards then prevailing. Political and economic changes were accompanied by others induced by missionary activity and by the availability of Western education, no matter how

Maasai herders watching over their grazing animals near Kajiado ward off the early morning chill with blankets of traditional design.
Courtesy The Lamp, Exxon Corporation

limited. All of these factors gathered weight as the colonial system continued, and they were accelerated after World War II. Even before the war and certainly after it, sections of the Kenyan population most affected by these alterations—and most involved in the modern economy—sought political change that would give them greater latitude and opportunity. Although politically active Africans often used traditional symbols and complained of the violation of indigenous institutions, many were already acting in terms of relations and groups different from the precolonial ones, or they were using old institutions in new ways.

Some elements of indigenous social systems had either disappeared or were much attenuated by the end of the colonial period. This was true of age-sets, which were significant in the political and military organizations of the Kalenjin and Eastern Nilotic-speaking (Maa-speaking) Maasai and Samburu peoples and in certain other pastoral nomadic groups and some Bantu-speaking peoples, such as the Kikuyu. In a modified form, age-sets lasted into the postcolonial era among some of the nomadic pastoralists, but these were peoples on the fringes of the national society and economy. Among the sedentary groups involved in the modern economy and affected by missionary activity and the gradually increasing availability of education, age-sets had diminished in importance before World War II and in some cases even earlier. Personal experience of them could be elicited only from a few elders in the early 1980s.

Descent groups (lineages and sometimes clans) occurred universally. They were holders of land rights, political units, regulators of marriage, and congregations for significant collective rituals. In a much modified form, descent groups have retained a degree of importance in most ethnic groups. Among pastoral nomadic peoples, such as the Somali, in which descent groups were significant in intra-ethnic raiding and warfare and as political entities, they apparently have remained of great importance. Among the Kikuyu, by contrast, individual ownership of land was introduced relatively early, and social differentiation in terms of wealth has become pervasive. Consequently, descent groups have had little significance in the modern era. But this has not been the case for all sedentary peoples. The Luo had a very strong and complex descent group system; although modified, it persisted at least into the early 1970s and functioned not only in the rural areas but also in the urban environment.

The elements in a Kenyan descent group system are patrilineages and, sometimes, patriclans and subclans. A patrilineage consists of males and females who are descended in the male line from a common male ancestor and who can, in principle, trace the connection to that ancestor and thereby to each other. Lineages vary in genealogical depth. That is, the living members of a shallow lineage may trace their ancestry only to a common grandfather or great-grandfather. Lineages of greater depth may trace to a common ancestor as far as 12 generations from its living adult members. In some systems lineages of lesser depth nest within those of greater depth so that the deeper lineage contains two or more of those at the level below it. The systems in Kenya vary with respect to the number of levels of nesting lineages within the overarching maximal one, but few are very elaborate. The Luo, however, are an exception. Some 12-generation maximal lineages among the Luo have as many as 100,000 members, and there are several levels below it down to two- or three-generation lineages. The maximal lineage in the Luo case functions in the rural areas chiefly as a regulator of marriage: male and female members of the same maximal lineage may not marry. Lineages of a shallower kind are landholding groups, and others at intermediate levels have other functions. In Nairobi lineages of varying depths are the basis for different levels of Luo associations culminating in the overall Luo ethnic association.

In some groups lineages are typically shallow but are parts of patriclans (sometimes divided into subclans). Common clan membership implies a common ancestor, but the genealogical links cannot be traced, nor is an effort made to do so. Typically, clans are dispersed throughout the territory of an ethnic group. They are sometimes exogamous, and common membership of a clan provides points of contact for anyone traveling outside his or her home territory. Occasionally, the clans have some religious significance, but by and large the functioning political, economic, and religious units are the constituent lineages.

Members of the same lineage are kin, but the operation of kinship in Kenyan society takes into account not only one's patrilineal kin but also those traced through one's mother and the kin acquired by marriage. Both are of a lineage other than one's own. Moreover, relationships of daily economic and social significance with kin acquired through one's father are usually restricted to members of the minimal lineage and to members of their households who are of other lineages. From this point of view every individual has a different set of kin. Aspects of kin relations between any two persons are governed in part by standard expectations of proper behavior, but these also have been changing. Moreover, each individual has a certain degree of freedom in choosing which of these relationships will be fostered, based on personal preference and possible advantage. In general, relations between kin have remained important; in particular, kinship may provide a basis for interdependence between two persons in their effort to cope with modern economic and political circumstances. Sometimes a better off kinsman will become the patron of his (usually) younger kinsman in the latter's efforts to make his way economically or politically.

In precolonial times a neighborhood or local community, often consisting of members of several different lineages, was the unit of sociability and cooperation for working the fields or herding; it might also have engaged in certain kinds of religious activity. The neighborhood has retained its importance in present-day Kenya, but its membership has become more differentiated than it once was. Its religious composition may vary; many of its males are working in other places or are engaged in activities that preclude their participation in a cooperative group. Moreover, some have achieved an income and status that make it unseemly to take part in the comparatively egalitarian work group. It is not uncommon for an urban wageworker to send money to a wife in the rural area so she can hire men to do the work that he alone or he and other men of the neighborhood would formerly have done. Although there have always been differences of wealth and status in any local community, these features have different bases in the modern era, and the life led by a member of a local elite may be quite different from that of the ordinary peasant. There is a chief, a teacher or two, one or more workers at the rural health facility, and perhaps others whose jobs and educations give them status and interests that distinguish them from ordinary peasants even when they are from the same or a nearby community.

In the precolonial era men and women were members not only of descent groups and neighborhoods but also participated by virtue of that membership in groups of larger scale covering a larger territory. They owed allegiance to a chief or to a set of elders, although in Kenya such persons rarely had the kind of authority associated with some African rulers. Within that larger group men and women would marry, go about their business peaceably, participate in those rituals relevant to the chiefdom, and engage in economic and other exchanges characteristic of the group. These entities, although autonomous societies, were not isolated. Their members interacted, not always peacefully, with other sections of the same ethnic group. Politically independent sections of the same people were not necessarily or typically required to renounce armed conflict with one another.

Ethnic groups were not isolated, nor were their boundaries or composition fixed. They encountered others in their migrations and expansions, processes that continued into the early twentieth century. When they settled, they often found another ethnic group exploiting a different, but neighboring, ecological niche. In these circumstances ethnic groups exchanged what they produced for what they needed, and sometimes women of one group married men of the other. At times, however, relations were hostile. If two groups were competing for the same territory, or if one group thought it could get what it wanted, e.g., cattle, without giving anything in return, warfare or raiding would take place. But hostility was not perpetual. Relations between the Kikuyu and the Maasai, for example, varied between warfare and peaceful exchange in the many decades that they were in contact before the arrival of the Europeans. Whether the relations between any two ethnic groups were hostile or peaceable, one group would often augment its numbers by absorbing sections of another. Sometimes the absorbed people were taken in as equals; often—initially at least—they were taken in as dependent groups that over several generations would become integral parts of the assimilating groups.

The existence of the colonial state established relations between ethnic groups that had never been in contact before, and the changes wrought in the colonial era and thereafter brought people into competition for opportunities and rewards that had not been available earlier. The Luo, in the course of their arrival in western Kenya and the movements that led to their settlement in their present location, had contacts—some hostile—with sections of the Kalenjin, Luhya, Kisii, and others but none at all with the Kikuyu in central Kenya. By the time of national independence, many observers and many Kikuyu and Luo perceived these two groups as the major competitors for power and economic rewards in Kenya. This was partly a function of their size—the Kikuyu were the largest group and the Luo the second largest (until the 1979 census). But it was also a consequence of the movement of substantial numbers of Luo into Nairobi, particularly during the Mau Mau period when many Kikuyu were forced to leave a city they had come to consider peculiarly their own. But the Kikuyu and the Luo have not been the only groups to see the competition for power and economic advantage in ethnic terms.

From the point of view of local elites, the most obvious power base in their own struggle to achieve national status has been the ethnic group. From the point of view of ordinary people, those who exercise extraordinary power and have acquired great wealth are most easily identified in ethnic terms, even if the more sophisticated outsider sees that only a small portion of an ethnic group has acquired power and wealth. Moreover, in the competition for jobs, it is easier for a Luo, for example, to think that a job given by one Kikuyu to another is a matter of ethnic preference when in fact the two Kikuyu in question are relatives and the preference is a matter of kinship rather than ethnicity.

It is only in certain circumstances that an ethnic group is cohesive. Given the degree of differentiation in power, wealth, and status among the Kikuyu, intra-Kikuyu conflict—couched in sectional terms, e.g., between the Kiambu and other Kikuyu, or in class terms—has been as salient or more so than conflict between the Kikuyu and others. Other groups are perhaps not so pervasively stratified as the Kikuyu, but there are differences that occasionally make for conflict. Sections of specific ethnic groups often find themselves in competition for one advantage or another—where shall the new hospital or secondary school be built?—and may demonstrate solidarity with one another only intermittently.

Nevertheless, although ethnic solidarity and inter-ethnic hostility come and go and although ethnic alliances in the political sphere have shifted over the years, one irrefutable fact remains. Most Kenyans feel comfortable with those whose mother tongue they share, who have the same general understanding of how the social world is supposed to work, and who (even with the religious and educational differentiation that has taken place) react in similar ways to certain situations and symbols. There are inter-ethnic marriages and inter-ethnic friendships, but they are not frequent. Some well-educated people may be adamantly opposed to having ethnicity define their associations, but even among the educated in the cities, friendships are very likely to be with educated persons of the same ethnic group.

Inter-ethnic relations that occur in the cities are often limited to the workplace or marketplace. In some cities, however, residential propinquity requires neighborly interaction. Whether in the market or the neighborhood, some inter-ethnic relations are more amiable than others. Kikuyu and Kamba, for example, speaking closely related languages and living in closely adjacent territories, seem to get along more easily than do Kikuyu and Luo or Luhya and Kikuyu, despite the fact the latter are both Bantu speakers. The Luo and Luhya, speaking very different languages but neighbors in western Kenya, accommodate each other more easily and often take the trouble to learn at least a few words of each other's language if only as a gesture of amiability. When a Luo and a Luhya converse, it is not unusual to hear words of both languages in the midst of some combination of English and Swahili.

Differences of wealth, status, and power were present in varying degrees in all Kenyan ethnic groups in precolonial times, but their bases differed from those that developed in the colonial period and afterward, and their magnitude was much less. Age (or genealogical seniority) and sex played a part in determining who exercised authority and received deference. In principle, all males had a chance to become an elder. Except in unusual circumstances, women did not exercise public power, but senior women who had borne children and were past the childbearing age were entitled to some deference. Chiefs, who often inherited their posts—but only after demonstrating certain capacities—were also accorded deference; they were typically better off than most of their people with respect to cattle (important even among cultivating peoples) and other forms of wealth. Warriors and traders (in those societies where long-distance trading was important) could acquire wealth and, with it, influence and prestige. They could convert their wealth and influence into power over particular persons by becoming patrons of poorer persons, who might be kinsmen. But a man with cattle, wives, and dependents did not live much differently from his less fortunate neighbors. Given the agricultural technology and modes of landholding in earlier times, there was a practical limit to the land a man and his dependents could work, and there was a limited market for its products. Moreover, a man's rights in land or cattle would eventually be partitioned among his heirs. If he was wealthy, his sons had a head start. Above all, cattle—the chief form of wealth or investment—were perishable. Disease, drought, and raids could destroy a man's wealth. In short, the economy and technology of earlier times precluded the accumulation of great wealth over generations.

Beginning even before World War I but continuing more quickly after the war, new kinds of differentiation and stratification began to develop among African groups. The differentiation took place on two levels—between regions (and therefore ethnic groups) and within regions or ethnic communities. Throughout the colonial period there were substantial restrictions on the jobs and other economic opportunities open to Africans, either because they had been preempted by Europeans and Asians or because the colonial authorities saw fit, for various reasons, to limit the kinds of crops Africans could grow and the kinds of activities they could engage in. Toward the end of the colonial era, many of these limits were eased or removed, and some Africans moved rapidly into the niches that became available. Nevertheless, until national independence there were ceilings on the range of differentiation and stratification. The highest levels of power and the economy were closed to Africans. After independence Africans achieved the highest reaches of governmental authority, and a com-

Kikuyu village in a rural area of the Kenya Highlands

bination of government policy and practice explicitly directed at permitting Africans to acquire wealth opened still other opportunities, sometimes at considerable cost to non-Africans.

The differences between regions, which have persisted into the last quarter of the twentieth century, were based in the first instance on the area's suitability for cash crops. The lowland sections of Eastern Province (where portions of the Kamba live), the lowland areas of Coast Province (home of some of the Mijikenda), and the lowland areas of Nyanza Province (home of a portion of the Luo) were, for one reason or another, unsuitable for the cash crops available in the second quarter of the twentieth century, or they required a technology or kind of labor that made their cultivation uneconomic. Regions were also distinguished by the extent to which the inhabitants had access to wage labor, particularly of a more remunerative kind (within the limits set by the colonial order). A third distinguishing element was the availability of Western education, at the time offered only by missionaries. Given the limited range of jobs open to Africans between the two world wars, a little education went a long way if literacy and an acquaintance with arithmetic were firmly acquired and if Africans became acquainted with the English language. As time went on, access to education became more widespread; for those willing to migrate, jobs became available. But early access to all the elements that made a region potentially richer than others—and that gave individuals a chance to differentiate themselves economically from their fellows—was characteristic of the area containing Nairobi, the White Highlands, and the Kikuyu.

Although one region provided greater opportunities for the development of wealth than another, and in some cases continues to do so, not all of the region's inhabitants benefited. There is a higher proportion of Kikuyu at the upper and middle levels of income and power; but most Kikuyu either remain smallholders with very little land, are landless agricultural laborers, or are engaged in the urban labor market and the informal economy, earning comparatively low incomes. At the same time, there are in all of the agricultural areas and wherever there are towns of any size a small minority of well-off landholders, who are usually involved in mercantile enterprises and frequently hold political office or work in the civil service.

With some exceptions the precursors of the upper and middle social strata in postindependence Kenya owed their situation to a combination of land acquisition and what colonial authorities, and Kenyan officials after them, called progressive farming. Others had sources of income outside farming, usually in the form of wages but sometimes through mercantile activity. Often the income gained from wage labor was converted into land acquisition and agricultural inputs. Sometimes the income gained from wages went into the formation of a trading enterprise, but such an enterprise could also be initiated or sustained on the basis of cash crops that commanded a good price for several years. For Africans who had their roots in land and who were limited in the range of their investments and job opportunities, landholding remained at the core of their enterprise. Few were prepared in the colonial era to abandon agriculture entirely.

Economic historian Gavin Kitching, on the basis of case studies of Africans who did reasonably well in combining these kinds of activities, has summarized the factors contributing to their success. "We see a universal access to formal education, usually through mission schools. . . . Individuals then had opportunities to obtain the better paid jobs . . . an opportunity strengthened by the fact that . . . gaining an education brought . . . Africans into contact with Europeans . . . who . . . could act as their patrons." But access to education and patronage had to be taken advantage of. For many, an element of good luck was apparent. But all of the case studies tell of Africans who showed considerable initiative, and many of them indicated a degree of ruthlessness. In many instances an enterprising African ran into indigenous social and cultural barriers. For example, the acquisition of land often required getting around then-current patterns of landholding or refusing to participate in the kind of redistribution of wealth that was considered desirable in some communities.

National independence opened the highest levels of power, status, and the economy to Africans. They not only became the rulers of their country, but also many of those who occupied the highest posts had in their own backgrounds (or those of their fathers) the entrepreneurial experience of the colonial era; they saw independence not as a chance to change the emerging socioeconomic order but as an opportunity to allow Africans to be dominant in it. To this end, accommodating laws were enacted, and institutions were developed. Europeans and Asians formerly were at the highest rungs of the economic ladder. The citizenship laws and other actions limiting the range of European and Asian economic activity put within the reach of Africans possibilities in commerce and industry hitherto unavailable to them (see Kenyanization and Economic Policy, ch. 1). The sale of many European landholdings opened large sections of what had been the White Highlands to Africans, some of whom were in a position to acquire substantial holdings. Moreover, credit was made available to prospective African investors to establish their own businesses. Others had acquired enough capital to invest in European-held enterprises, and in some instances these came entirely into the hands of Africans. Some Africans moved into the highest levels of European-controlled enterprises. Many of these people in commerce, industry, and government held a good deal of land, either because they had acquired it at some stage of their entrepreneurial careers or because they invested in it for avocational and retirement purposes. It was not uncommon for large farms held by big businessmen and high government officials to be comparatively less productive than the smaller holdings of the less wealthy.

Unlike the situation in some African countries where rulers and civil servants had used their positions to acquire interests in land and in commercial and industrial enterprises but were involved in them only to the extent of collecting the income, Kenyan government officials and civil servants took a substantial interest in the businesses in which they invested. Their official positions had given them a base from which to engage in economic enterprise, and some of the opportunities that came their way were owed to those positions and to contacts who could help them, i.e., act as their patrons in the same way that district officers and missionaries had acted as patrons of their fathers or uncles. But they had to be prepared to take advantage of opportunities and patronage.

Prospective patrons in turn were willing to give a hand to those who showed promise and the probability of loyalty. There had always been a degree of competition at the political level, and loyal clients could be helpful. To many Kenyans the probability of loyalty seemed greater from kin because the bonds were not wholly those of convenience. Nevertheless, patron-client relationships across kin and ethnic boundaries did exist.

The upper and middle strata of Kenyan society were also marked by the presence of some who had not started as politicians or civil servants but had begun as entrepreneurs or sometimes as professionals. Some of these entrepreneurs had very little formal education but a great deal of acumen and drive. It was only later in their careers that they were appointed or elected to political positions, although they may have exercised considerable influence in less public ways.

Inevitably, businessmen entering the competition for economic opportunity—and lacking helpful connections—saw existing practices as barriers to the realization of their ambitions. From their perspective, credit should be more easily available to those who were not in government. Some saw ethnic favoritism as an obstacle to their success.

Even among those who were already at the highest levels, there were differences of interest. Some Kenyans still worked for European-controlled companies and saw a continuing role for such companies in the economy. Others preferred that these firms come under African control. Further, some observers have argued that there has been an element of ethnicity in the outlook of some Kikuyu who had arrived at (or were very near) the apex of the system. In the view of these observers, these Kikuyu feel that they are entitled to rule, an outlook that those of a different ethnic (or within Kikuyu, subethnic) origin have rejected. Those who are not at such exalted levels but have done reasonably well and aspire to do better may criticize the workings of the system, but they do not reject it. Only a few intellectuals, some of them professed Marxists, claim to be fundamentally opposed to it.

Beyond the small minority at the top, there has been a larger minority that has constituted a middle class or, in the language of some observers, a petty bourgeoisie. In the rural areas and the smaller towns where many of the middle class live, they may make up the highest stratum. Some are well-off farmers and traders; others are local administrators, teachers, nurses, or successful artisans. All of them have some education, and they all live differently from the ordinary peasant. They are given a degree of respect and deference by the peasantry, and they are quite aware of their difference from the mass of Kenyans who either engage in subsistence agriculture or scrape together an uncertain income from a combination of low-paid wage labor and subsistence cultivation. This middle stratum has by no means been homogeneous with respect to income, education, or outlook. But they have shared a status above that of the peasants, and they have tended to see Kenyan society as offering still further opportunity—if not for themselves, then for their children.

It is in this middle class that some analysts see the potential leaders and core followers of a significant opposition to the elite (see Political Setting, ch. 4). The burden of that opposition is that the policies and actions of the elite limit the realization of the aspirations of members of the middle stratum and, for that matter, of peasants and workers. At the same time, these middle-class people—local politicians and entrepreneurs, particularly—are often dependent on the patronage of the elite to gain particular advantages.

Religion

Kenyans have been subject to decades of missionary activity and responses to it in the form of African independent churches and to centuries of Islamic influence centered on, but radiating from, the coast. For most Kenyans, religious belief and practice is an amalgam of elements, variously integrated, of Christianity or Islam on the one hand and practices and outlooks characteristic of indigenous religious systems on the other. Some groups on the periphery of Kenyan society, usually nomadic groups, have been little touched by missionary influence or have resisted it. Some, particularly the Somali, are Muslims, but theirs is an Islam closely connected with their Somali ethnicity rather than a religion that ties them to other Kenyan Muslims. Data on religious adherence provide useful if limited guidance to the religious outlooks and behavior of those who call themselves Christians or Muslims. The *World Christian Encyclopedia* is the most authoritative source of statistics covering all manifestations of Christianity, and it also provides data on non-Christian religious bodies and adherents. Its statistics for 1970 seem to be firmly based, but it also has estimated numbers for 1975 and 1980.

The encyclopedia estimates that in 1980 about 73 percent of all Kenyans were professed Christians. Only 62 percent, however, were affiliated with a church of some kind, the remainder being defined as nominal. But of those who were affiliated, 20 percent were thought to be inactive, i.e., they did not meet the minimum requirements of their churches for attendance or participation. In short, roughly one-half of all Kenyans had some kind of active connection with institutional Christianity. These data included the entire Kenyan population, but the proportion of Christians (professed or affiliated) among Africans was probably not substantially different, given the very small number of non-Africans in the country. Of these, only Europeans and the very few Goans were likely to be Christians.

Adherents of indigenous religions were estimated to account for 18.9 percent of the total population in 1980. Obviously, they constituted a slightly greater proportion of the African population. Muslims made up 6 percent of the population, of which the great bulk were Africans; the rest were Asians and Arabs. The remaining 2.1 percent of the population consisted of Ba'hais, Hindus, Jains, Sikhs, nonreligious persons, Jews, and Parsis, listed in order of estimated size. Inasmuch as Hindus, Jains, Sikhs, and Parsis were Asians, with few exceptions (African converts to Arya Samej, a Hindu reform sect), it is likely that their numbers were smaller than those estimated. The nonreligious people were chiefly Europeans. The Ba'hais, the largest of the miscellaneous religious groups, were mainly Africans, the religion having had a number of converts among the Luhya.

Of Kenya's 10 largest ethnic groups, five had a substantial Christian majority in 1972, by profession if not by affiliation; 94 percent of the Luhya, 89 percent of the Luo, 82 percent of the Kisii, 77 percent of the Kikuyu, and 61 percent of the Kamba were Christians. These proportions may have increased by the early 1980s. Of the remaining five large ethnic groups, one, the Somali, is entirely Muslim. The Kalenjin and the Mijikenda are mixed, religious adherence varying from group to group. One of the Kalenjin sections, the Pokot, remote and to a substantial extent pastoral, was still strongly oriented to its indigenous religious system in 1972. More than one-half the members of two other sections, the Tugen and the Elgeyo, were said to adhere to the indigenous system. Perhaps most affected by Christianity were the two largest groups, the Kipsigis and the Nandi, but neither had as many Christian affiliates as did the Kamba. Of the Mijikenda, the Digo were more than 90 percent Muslim and the Duruma about 25 percent. The Giriama, a very large section of the Mijikenda, had held out against the influence of both Christians and Muslims; more than 80 percent of its members were estimated to adhere to the indigenous system in 1972. More than 75 percent of the pastoral nomadic Maasai were thought to adhere to their indigenous religion, and more than 50 percent of the Meru did likewise. As for smaller groups, the great mass of the pastoral nomadic Turkana and Samburu still practiced their local religions, as did the Mbere, a central Bantu-speaking people related to the Kikuyu and the Meru.

Indigenous Religion

Although faith in and the practice of the full complex of any indigenous religion have become less common, they still occur. Moreover, views held by Christians and Muslims of the way the world works and how to get it to work to one's advantage are often strongly affected by notions rooted in indigenous religion. Broadly, such religions, despite significant variations, are concerned with the effects of spirits and other sources of extraordinary power on the welfare of the living. Rituals have been oriented toward gaining the help of spirits in individual, family, or community efforts to acquire valued goods, or toward placating the spirits if they are deemed responsible for misfortune. But spirits, whatever their character or attributes, are not alone in exercising power to help or to harm. Some men and women—witches or sorcerers—are also thought to have such powers, either by natural proclivity or by acquiring certain skills in the manipulation of words and material items.

An indigenous religious system is inherently local: the congregation is the family, the lineage, the clan, the community or, sometimes, the chiefdom, depending upon the occasion of the ritual. Although people of the same ethnolinguistic category may share the same names for, and conceptions of, certain deities and spirits and the same general outlines of belief and practice, many of the spirits worshiped or placated are local—the ancestors of specific lineages or spirits associated with certain places or natural features. Among almost all peoples there is belief in a high god, often associated with creation, sometimes with nature (the sky, the sun, or the rain). Only rarely is the high god appealed to directly, although ultimate power may be attributed to him. The spirits regularly communicated with in most indigenous religions are the ancestral spirits, a pattern consistent with social systems that, formerly at least, placed considerable emphasis on the significance of descent from a common ancestor for social, legal, political, and economic relations, as well as religious ones. For many peoples, including Christians and Muslims, links with, and rituals directed toward, ancestral spirits are still of some importance but decreasingly so except among groups in which lineage structures retain their significance. Partly as a consequence of Christian (and Muslim) influence, even those who still think of themselves as adherents of indigenous systems pay more explicit attention to the high god.

Belief in the activity of witches seems to persist even when other elements have faded. Witches are believed to exercise psychic power that enables them to harm others. They may be either men or women, but more often it is women who are accused of witchcraft, frequently against other women and their children, a consequence in part of the tensions between co-wives of the same man. In general, witches, whatever their sex, are thought to have inherited their powers, but the behavior and characteristics attributed to them vary from one ethnic group to another. For example, some groups think of them as exercising their power unconsciously, others as doing so deliberately.

Some persons are believed to be able to harm others (and sometimes to protect them) by using drugs or herbs or manipulating material things derived from or connected with the victims. Such persons have usually been referred to as witch doctors or medicine men. In Swahili the term is *mganga* (pl., *waganga*). *Waganga* may act in preventive or curative fashion, preparing amulets and other items to ward off the actions of witches or malevolent natural spirits or dispensing herbs to deal with certain illnesses.

Given world views that leave little or nothing to chance or to disinterested nature and that conceive of several sources of affliction, it is necessary to turn to a diviner to determine who or what is responsible for a particular affliction and, in some cases, to suggest what is to be done to deal with its source, whether witch, angry ancestor, or something else. The material apparatus of divination varies, but a significant attribute of many diviners is their understanding of the usual points of conflict in social relations in the community and of the particular tensions of their clients.

Varieties of Christianity

In 1970 there were more than 200 separate Christian denominations represented in Kenya; over 150 of them were African independent churches. By 1979 there were more than 220 of the latter. Christian churches in Kenya may be placed in seven categories. The largest includes only the Roman Catholic Church, to which 19.6 percent of all Kenyans (31.6 percent of all affiliated Christians) belonged in 1980. Of these a small number were Pentecostals. The next largest was the much more heterogeneous set of African independent churches of which 17.1 percent of all Kenyans (27.7 percent of all affiliated Christians) were members. Of nearly equal size was the cluster constituted by the Protestant churches, to which 17 percent of the population (27.4 percent of all Christians) belonged. Classified here is the full range of churches, e.g., Presbyterian, Methodist, Lutheran, Baptist, and Assemblies of God, that maintain institutional connections with and varying degrees of dependency on personnel and other support from sources in Europe and North America.

Separately listed is the Anglican Church to which 5.8 percent of all Kenyans (9.4 percent of affiliated Christians) belonged. Roughly 2.4 percent of the population (3.9 percent of all Christians) were affiliated with orthodox churches. The largest of these, the African Orthodox Church, has institutional connections to the patriarchate of the Orthodox Church in Alexandria. There were also two small groups labeled, respectively, marginal Protestants and Catholics (non-Roman). Marginal Protestantism included churches such as Christian Science and Jehovah's Witnesses, originating in the Western world, which accept sources of revelation in addition to the Old Testament and New Testament. Jehovah's Witnesses, however, were banned in 1968. Catholics (non-Roman) included those churches that had detached themselves from the Vatican after 1700 or were like Roman Catholics in their sacraments and hierarchy but have seceded from Protestant or Anglican churches.

Colonial authorities and the Protestant churches were reluctant to have the missions engage in direct competition with each other in ways that might have untoward consequences for colonial and missionary authority. As a result, there was rarely more than one Protestant mission in an area, at least initially. The consequent ethnic homogeneity of most Protestant churches changed gradually in the late colonial and postindependence periods as people moved around more freely and experienced other churches in urban areas where Roman Catholic, Anglican, and various Protestant churches were to be found. Roman Catholicism and Anglicanism were more widespread, as were the Pentecostal denominations.

Most of the African independent churches arose initially as responses of local congregations to perceived shortcomings of mission organization, or out of religious needs not met by mission teachings or practice. The first such split, as early as 1914, involved Luo members of a local Anglican mission. In the 1920s and 1930s locally led schismatic groups proliferated, and they continue to do so. Because independent churches established their structures and symbols in the course of conflicts between mission churches and local cultures, they tended to be restricted to persons of a single ethnic group or closely related neighboring groups, although there were exceptions. The need for opportunities to exercise leadership has generated splits within already independent churches, as have other tensions within each church and in the changing societies in which they were embedded. Only a few independent churches have been able to build large memberships. The largest is the African Independent Pentecostal Church, which had nearly one-half million members in 1972. Begun among the Kikuyu in 1925, it had difficulties with the colonial authorities in the conflict-ridden 1952-60 period. Considerable growth has taken place since independence. Among the markedly stratified Kikuyu, it seems to appeal to the less affluent. The largest group—150,000 members, mainly Luo—to have split from the

Roman Catholic Church in Africa is the Maria Legio of Africa, which was established in 1962, apparently in reaction to the changes called for by the Second Vatican Council.

Some independent churches differ from mission-connected churches mainly in having come under early African pastoral and lay control. A number of the churches that emerged in the 1920s and 1930s in Luo, Kikuyu, and Luhya areas did not have substantial doctrinal differences with mission-established churches but wanted the churches to be under African control, at a time when European missionaries were far from ready to relinquish their power. Others, however, are more African in belief and practice whether because they have incorporated features of indigenous systems or have developed forms of faith and worship reflecting the changing African experience and problems of their adherents. Certainly, the Christian missions directly attacked expressions of African values, and some independent churches, although accepting aspects of Christianity, were reasserting African values, such as the Kikuyu independents who reacted to Christian condemnation of female circumcision and polygny in the 1920s and 1930s. Still others found the ritual of Protestant churches colorless and established churches characterized by more expressive activity. Singing, dancing, and street processions are features of some of these groups. An important characteristic of some of the independent churches is the healing role played by their leaders and other members.

Beyond the differences in doctrine, organization, and practice within Christianity, many (perhaps most) adherents of Christian churches retain beliefs and engage in practices deriving from aspects of indigenous religious systems. In certain African churches, indigenous elements are directly incorporated into the faith. In other churches, indigenous practices are separately followed, e.g., divination to determine the sources of certain afflictions that are generally thought to be the result of witchcraft or, more rarely, the actions of ancestral spirits.

Islam

Islam in Kenya is organizationally fragmented along ethnic and sectarian lines. The great majority of African and Arab Muslims are of the Sunni division of Islam, whereas Asian Muslims include Sunnis and Shiites, the latter divided into several separate communities. Among the African adherents of Islam, ethnic differences in organization, belief, and practice separate the Somali and other northeastern pastoral nomads (the Oromo Boran) from the Swahili-speaking Muslims of the coast and those, such as the Pokomo and some of the Mijikenda, influenced by them.

Belief and practice among African Muslims may range from the strict and exclusive Islam, including strict attention to Islamic law, of urban peoples in Mombasa, Malindi, and Nairobi to the bare profession of the Islamic faith by some in the rural areas with few, if any, consequences for their behavior. Between these extremes lie most African

Muslims, who pay heed to many of the demands of the faith, e.g., fairly regular daily prayer and fasting during the lunar month of Ramadan. At the same time, African Muslims may traffic with the spirits of their ancestral religion. Because women are customarily less involved in the more formal observances of Islam, e.g., attendance at noon prayers at the Friday mosque, they may be more often attached to non-Islamic practices. Somali belief and practice, particularly among the nomads, has differed to some extent from that required by Islam, either because ancient Somali ritual has persisted or because pastoral nomadism makes it difficult to submit to the rigors of Islamic practice. Moreover, Somali Islam is marked by the importance of religious orders and the cult of the saints (who are often, in fact, simply ancestors of Somali lineages). Such orders and the cult are common in North Africa and in parts of West Africa but not elsewhere in Kenya. Whatever the discrepancies between the demands of Islam and Somali practice, their Islamic identity is integral to the Somali conception of themselves.

Education

At independence the new government was faced with what it considered a pressing need to train middle- and upper level African staff for government service and for the commercial and industrial sectors of the economy it wished to develop. At the same time, the public expected that primary education for all would be provided; national and local leaders had steadily pressed demands for such education on the colonial authorities. The lack of funds to achieve both goals simultaneously, as well as the shortage of trained teachers to maintain adequate standards if the primary system were expanded too rapidly, led to an early decision to give priority to secondary, technical, and higher education.

Despite the reference to technical and vocational education in early pronouncements, the government emphasized academic training leading to higher education. This fact was not missed by students or parents, who insisted on academic preparation in the expanding primary-school system, a demand that could not be adequately met, given the lack of training of many teachers. Little government action was taken before the mid-1970s to provide either useful training at the primary level for the many who would not go further or extensive vocational education at the secondary level. The problem of primary-school graduates able to work only as unskilled labor persisted into the early 1980s. At the same time, many who had an academic secondary education but could not go on to higher education were considered overqualified for some jobs and lacked the qualifications for others that may have been available.

In the first few years after independence, the educational system inherited from the colonial era was somewhat modified, but it continued to be oriented to the British system on which the colonial one had been modeled. The higher reaches of the system were made more accessible to Africans, but the passing of stringent examinations was

Islamic mosque in Nairobi

required to move from one level to another, thus permitting only a minority to go on to secondary school and a still smaller group to postsecondary education. Moreover, until 1974 attendance at all schools required the payment of fees. In that year fees for the first four years of primary school were discontinued, and those for the last three years were eliminated in 1979.

Although the central government is ultimately responsible for educational policy, which is carried out by the Ministry of Basic Education, and furnishes most of the funds for primary and secondary education, local government has been directly involved in aspects of school construction, administration, and financing. In particular, local councils play a part in hiring personnel, and local communities construct *harambee* secondary schools. The term *harambee* (literally, let us all pull together; signifying self-help) applies to a variety of community projects, among the more common of which is school construction and operation. Government-built and government-operated secondary schools have not met the growing demand, particularly as increasing numbers have attended and completed primary schools, and local communities have been encouraged to construct their own. *Harambee* collections and work projects are also held to build and maintain primary schools. The central government bears the costs of teachers' salaries and equipment. In addition to government and *harambee* primary and secondary schools, there are a number of privately run secondary schools.

Since the mid-1960s Kenya's school system has had at its base a seven-year primary school (Standards 1 through 7) (see fig. 12). Attendance has been neither universal nor compulsory, however. Those who complete seven years of schooling take the examination for the Certificate of Primary Education. Those who pass it at a certain level may go on to lower (sometimes called junior) secondary schools, a four-year (Forms I through IV) program, at the end of which students take the examinations for the East African Certificate of Education (ordinary or 0 level). Passing a junior secondary examination—taken voluntarily—at the end of Form II provides a credential for students who do not complete the full four years. Students' scores on the 0-level examinations in principle determine whether they can go on to higher (often called advanced) secondary education (Forms V and VI). Some of those who cannot go on to the advanced forms may go either to a teachers' training school (for primary-school teachers) or to a technical-vocational secondary course. Most do not go further than Form IV, but they are often the source of the large numbers of untrained teachers employed by the primary schools.

Until 1981 higher education within Kenya was available at two institutions, the University of Nairobi and Kenyatta University College, the latter formally attached to the university. Both were controlled by the Ministry of Higher Education. The primary function of Kenyatta University College was the training of secondary-school teachers, although some training was also accomplished by the Faculty of Education at the University of Nairobi. In 1981 two schools, Kagumo and Siriba, which had been devoted to the training of primary-school teachers, were transferred from the Ministry of Basic Education to the Ministry of Higher Education and converted to the training of secondary-school teachers. Unlike Kenyatta University College, which offered both two-year diploma courses and the baccalaureate in education, and the Faculty of Education at the university, which offered bachelors' degrees, the new teachers' colleges were to offer only the diploma, at least initially.

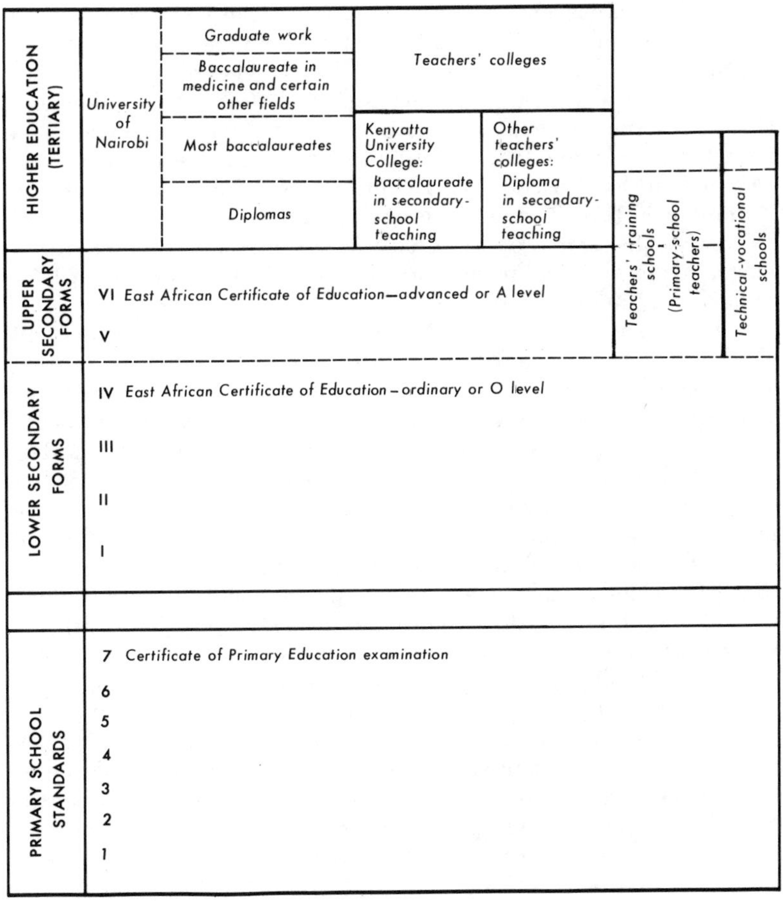

HIGHER EDUCATION (TERTIARY)

University of Nairobi

Graduate work

Baccalaureate in medicine and certain other fields

Most baccalaureates

Diplomas

Teachers' colleges

Kenyatta University College: Baccalaureate in secondary-school teaching

Other teachers' colleges: Diploma in secondary-school teaching

Teachers' training schools (Primary-school teachers)

Technical-vocational schools

UPPER SECONDARY FORMS

VI East African Certificate of Education—advanced or A level

V

LOWER SECONDARY FORMS

IV East African Certificate of Education – ordinary or O level

III

II

I

PRIMARY SCHOOL STANDARDS

7 Certificate of Primary Education examination

6

5

4

3

2

1

Figure 12. Structure of the Educational System, 1982

Two other schools, Kenya Polytechnic in Nairobi and Mombasa Polytechnic, have an anomalous status. They are intended to be post-secondary institutions and to cater particularly to students already in the labor force who are seeking to upgrade their qualifications and status. Apparently they have many part-time students of that kind, but much of the students' course work is at the secondary-school level. The courses offered at Kenya Polytechnic seem to be at a more advanced level than those offered at the Mombasa school, however. At both schools, most of the programs last for two years and include commercial as well as engineering and technical courses.

There was a spurt in the numbers of children attending primary school immediately after independence, but fees were still required, and growth in enrollment was not as great as it might have been. In 1966, when the seven-year primary system came into effect, a little more than 1 million children (the great bulk of them African) were in the primary schools. Through the late 1960s and early 1970s, growth in enrollment was steady but slow as more Africans were willing and able to pay the fees and as the population continued to increase at a rapid rate. When fees for the first four years were abolished, however, a great spurt took place—from an enrollment of 1.8 million in 1973 to 2.7 million in 1974. Thereafter, growth continued at a steady pace until 1979 when fees for the last three years of primary school were no longer required. Enrollment jumped from not quite 3 million in 1978 to nearly 3.7 million in 1979.

It has been estimated that by 1980 more than 95 percent of all children between six and 12 were attending primary school and that a substantial number of children above the age of 12 also attended. This was a consequence of the fact that many children did not begin school at the expected age of six. Moreover, some children repeated Standard 7 in an effort to achieve a higher grade on the examination for the Certificate of Primary Education. There were variations by province in the proportions of all children attending primary school and in the numbers of boys and girls enrolled. In 1980 the densely populated Central (Kikuyu and related peoples) and Western (Luhya) provinces sent most of their children to school, as did the less densely settled but centrally located Eastern Province (Kamba and Taita). These were closely followed by Nyanza Province (chiefly Luo). Rift Valley Province (Kalenjin and some pastoral nomadic peoples) was not too far behind. Curiously, the Nairobi Area did not stand very high, but this may have reflected a tendency of Nairobi families to send children to their home areas for primary education. Lowest by far was North-Eastern Province, largely populated by Somali and Oromo pastoral nomads who were also Muslims. The next lowest was Coast Province, the population of which was largely nomadic, Muslim, or both. Although the pattern has been changing, many Muslims have been reluctant to send their children to secular schools because many schools were linked to missionary activity. Islam and nomadism taken together have been formidable barriers to the secular education of children.

The number of males enrolled has slightly exceeded the number of females in all ethnic groups. Males made up 52.5 percent of total enrollment in 1980, but that did not vastly exceed the proportion of males to females (50.3 percent males) in the five- through 14-year age brackets in the 1979 census. The variation in enrollment by sex from province to province has corresponded roughly to the variation in proportions of all students enrolled. Central, Western, and Eastern provinces had slightly higher proportions of girls enrolled than the country as a whole; Nyanza and Rift Valley provinces were only slightly lower than the national total. Despite Nairobi Area's lower standing in the proportion of all children sent to school, it did send nearly as many girls as it did boys. North-Eastern Province sent far fewer girls

Modern buildings and garden on the University of Nairobi campus

than boys to primary school—nearly three-fourths of its children in school were male. Somewhat better but still well below the proportions for the country as a whole was Coast Province—nearly 40 percent of the children in its schools were female.

The primary-school curriculum established in 1967 was essentially an academic one: children were to be taught how to read and write and given some knowledge of the world. Although reference was made to the development of manual dexterity, vocational or technical training was not part of the curriculum, nor was agriculture. Some attention was given in all standards to arts and crafts and to domestic science (for girls). The focus was on English, mathematics, and science. For the most part English was a subject only in the first three standards but was increasingly used as the language of instruction beginning in Standard 4. Local languages were usually used in the first three standards, and some attention was given them in formal courses at the same time. Schools in some districts used Swahili as the language of instruction, and it was taught as a subject in Standards 4 through 7. The formal teaching of mother tongues and Swahili was often much weaker than the teaching of English, and that appeared still to be the case in the early 1980s.

Enrollment in secondary schools, including those devoted to teacher and vocational training, grew by nearly 130 percent between 1973 and 1980, an overall rate greater than the 116 percent growth of primary enrollment in the same interval. Nevertheless, secondary-school enrollment remained much lower than that of primary schools—in 1980 roughly 11 percent of primary enrollment. The difference was chiefly a matter of policy. The requirements for entrance into secondary schools were set high enough to eliminate all but a small proportion of those who completed the examination for the Certificate of Primary Education.

There were three kinds of academic secondary schools: government-supported—referred to as maintained—schools, of which there were numbers in each province and several national elite schools; assisted schools—the *harambee* secondary schools; and unaided, i.e., private schools. Some of the private schools were considered very good, but most Africans preferred to go to the maintained schools, despite the face that fees were charged and other costs were involved. In general, the maintained schools admitted those who scored highest in the examinations, but a quota system gave special consideration to students from "less advantaged" districts. Quotas were formally announced in 1981 but had been in effect for some time before that. *Harambee* schools, having been constructed by local communities, were normally restricted to candidates from those communities. Usually they were not as good as maintained schools—they frequently had fewer trained teachers—or as some of the private schools. Their students typically had not done as well on the admission examination as those who went to the maintained schools, nor did nearly as large a proportion of *harambee* school students go on to upper secondary school. The proportion of private secondary-school students who entered upper secondary forms was also relatively small.

In 1980 about 46 percent of all secondary-school students went to maintained schools, of which a very small proportion attended the national elite schools; the proportion of secondary students in maintained schools was estimated to have risen to nearly 49 percent in 1981. Students in *harambee* secondary schools in 1980 constituted 23 percent of the total, and students in private schools 31 percent. The 1981 estimates show a slight increase in *harambee* school students, and those in private schools a more substantial decrease to 27 percent. Apparently, the number of students in private schools has been diminishing steadily since 1978, a consequence of cost, but perhaps more important, a result of growth in the number of places available in maintained and *harambee* schools.

There has been a very sharp drop in the numbers of students after Form IV and the 0-level examinations. The number of students in Form V in 1980 was roughly 20 percent of those in Form IV in the maintained schools, and the proportions were much smaller in *harambee* schools (less than 2 percent) and private schools (about 4 percent). The numbers in Form VI diminished further but not so drastically. After the completion of Form VI, students take the advanced (or A level) examinations that permit them, if their scores are high enough, to seek admission to the university.

The number of secondary schools and students oriented toward academic programs has been far greater than the number devoted to teacher training and technical subjects. In 1980 there were well over 400,000 academic secondary students but only a little more than 12,000 in primary teacher training and fewer than 9,000 in technical schools. Secondary schools provided a degree of training in nonacademic subjects, particularly those white-collar skills useful in business. The lack of government-supported vocational schools has led to the establishment of a number of *harambee* institutes of technology, but these institutes enrolled only a little more than 2,000 students in 1981. The courses in greatest demand were in secretarial skills, accountancy, and masonry.

The approximate equality in enrollment of males and females achieved in the primary schools has fallen off sharply in the secondary schools. In the first two forms the difference has not been so great—slightly more than 40 percent of the students in 1980 were female. Thereafter, the proportion of young women declined until they constituted less than 30 percent in Form V and Form VI. The decline after Form II may be attributed to the fact that females beyond the age of 15 begin to be eligible for marriage.

The University of Nairobi, the principal provider of higher education in Kenya, offers a full range of programs for the baccalaureate degree, ranging from the standard liberal arts and the science programs to agriculture, medicine, and law. Of the nearly 5,500 undergraduates enrolled in the 1980-81 school year, more than 25 percent were in the arts program, nearly 17 percent in the science program, and about 14 percent in the medical school. Engineering and commerce programs were each attended by nearly 10 percent of undergraduates. Agriculture (including food science, technology, and forestry), veterinary science, and law also drew fairly large numbers. Other programs (architecture, economics, design and fine arts, dentistry, and pharmacy) attracted smaller numbers. The university also offered graduate programs under many of the same departments (faculties, in local terminology). In 1980 a school of journalism was instituted at this level. The faculty of education offered graduate courses at the University of Nairobi, but undergraduate teacher training for posts in secondary schools was carried on at Kenyatta University College. In the 1980-81 school year, students enrolled in all graduate courses numbered under 900.

The university also offers diplomas requiring one or two years of study (in contrast to the three or more years required for the baccalaureate). Although the range of programs offered had once been fairly wide, only two programs, advanced nursing and adult education, had students in 1980-81. In earlier years other programs, such as urban and regional planning, had also attracted students, but these were either no longer offered or no longer sought.

In the last years of the colonial era and the first years after independence, many young Africans were sent to Europe and North America for university-level education in an effort to obtain quickly a cadre of trained people. By the 1970s this practice has declined sharply. By the early 1980s, although some Kenyans went overseas, few if any were supported by the Kenyan government. Foreign governments often offered stipends, and some Kenyans could pay their own way.

The University of Nairobi grew gradually but steadily in the 1970s from nearly 4,600 students (of whom roughly 4,000 were undergraduates) in the 1973-74 school year to more than 6,300 (of whom nearly 5,500 were undergraduates) in the 1980-81 school year. Kenyatta University College, having taken over the education of secondary-school teachers, grew at a slightly faster rate—from a little more than 1,200 students in the 1975-76 school year to nearly 2,300 in 1980-81. By far the greatest number of these students were working toward baccalaureates in education. Some were studying for diplomas in the same field, but by 1982 all new candidates for diplomas were to enter Siriba and Kagumo, newly raised from primary- to secondary-teacher-training colleges. Also at Kenyatta University College were a few graduate students in education.

The tendency for the number of men to exceed that of women in secondary schools, especially in the upper forms, became even more marked at the university level. In the 1980-81 and 1981-82 academic years, there were more than three times as many men as women enrolled as undergraduates, and the difference was even greater among graduate students. The disparity varied from course to course; it was least in dentistry, the liberal arts, and commerce and greatest in engineering and science.

Health

In 1983 Kenya's health infrastructure compared favorably with that of other countries in East and Central Africa. Nevertheless, overall shortages of health personnel and facilities—and rural-urban and regional disparities in their distribution—persisted. Efforts to deal with these problems and to reorganize the health-care system were under way, but it would take some time to achieve an adequate system, and the continued rapid growth of population made the task even more difficult.

Although the rate of mortality in general, and that of infant mortality in particular, has declined and life expectancy at birth as risen (to 53 years in 1979), the incidence of debilitating disease has remained high. From time to time epidemics break out in some regions. Accurate information on the incidence of disease is lacking because only some of the sick come to the attention of the medical authorities. It is known, however, that some of the more common diseases owe their occurrence to insect or animal carriers or are waterborne or water related. The direct and indirect causes of disease owe their ubiquity to environmental conditions, some of which are controllable by either concerted effort by the health authorities or changes in the way of life in particular communities.

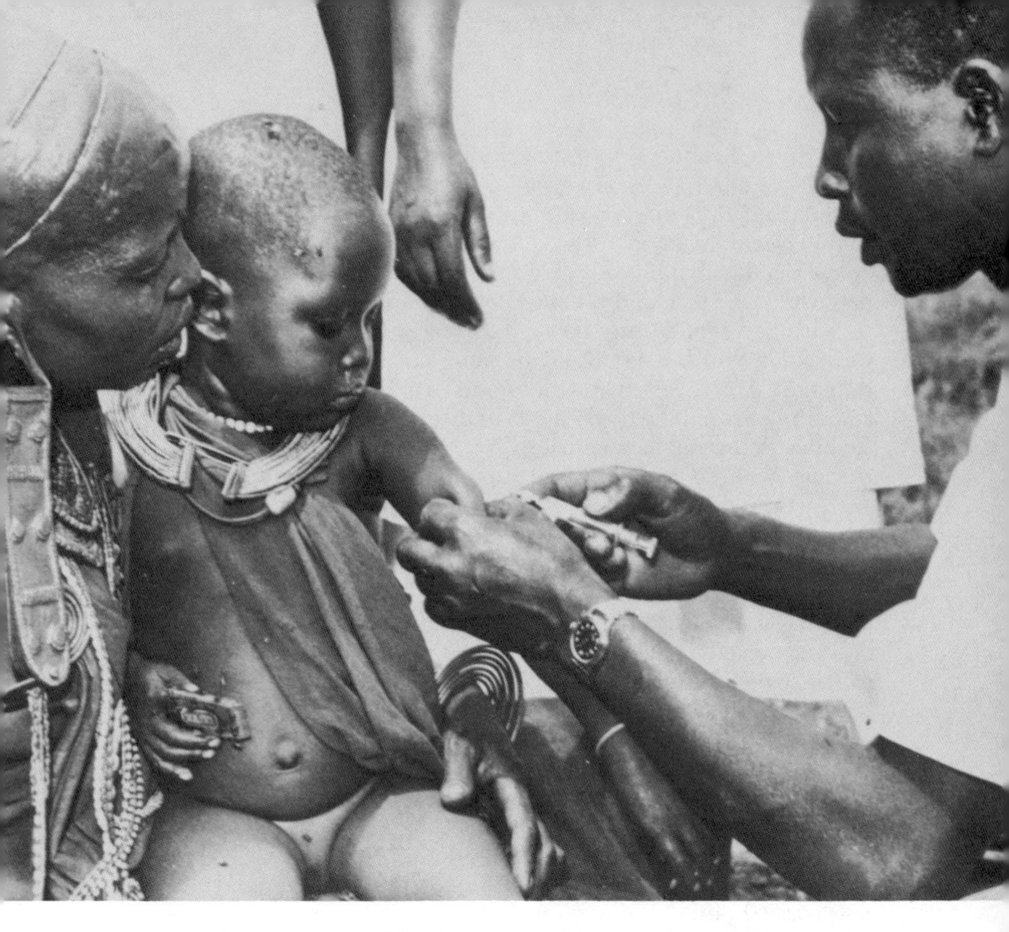

A rural health nurse administering measles vaccine to a Kenyan child
Courtesy United States Agency for International Development

The idea of preventive medicine through the control of the environment on the one hand and by inoculation and similar practices on the other has captured the attention of government and health authorities. This has led to some action, particularly in cases where international entities, such as the World Health Organization, have given aid and encouragement to specific projects. For example, smallpox has been eradicated in Kenya, as it has been in the rest of the world, and measles vaccine has been administered to many Kenyan children. But the distribution of medical facilities and personnel and the availability of vaccines have been such that many Kenyans have not been reached. Environmental sanitation and community hygiene are even more problematic in the rural communities in which most Kenyans live. In general, the authorities and health professionals and subprofessionals at all levels have been more concerned with curative than with preventive medicine, and it would be difficult for them not to be, given the shortages of medical facilities and personnel. In the late 1970s and early 1980s health personnel were also expected to pay attention to family planning, an urgent issue in light of Kenya's rate of population growth, but they often lacked the time to do so.

Outpatient cases in district hospitals and in health care facilities below that level indicated the range of diseases that affected the entire population in 1978, and the incidence of various diseases has probably not changed significantly through the early 1980s. Some diseases that were known to be significant in some areas were not shown in the statistics. Moreover, some observers have suggested that the paramedical personnel who do much of the diagnosing at local health care facilities do not do so adequately.

More than 30 percent of all reported illnesses were diagnosed as acute respiratory infections. Many of the sufferers were infants and young children. Not included were tuberculosis (reported in other sources as fairly frequent in the cities and towns) and pneumonia, which made up less than 2 percent of all cases. More than 24 percent of all patients had malaria which, despite efforts to eradicate the disease-bearing mosquito, has continued to be a major problem, particularly in the lower areas near water (on the coast and near Lake Victoria, but elsewhere as well). Diseases of the skin constituted about 17 percent of the cases. Insect activity, inadequate personal hygiene and, to a lesser extent, nutritional deficiencies were responsible for diseases in this category. Diarrheal diseases, so common among infants that many cases are not reported, probably have had a higher incidence rate than the nearly 9 percent indicated. The same may be said for intestinal worms, reported to be 6 percent of all cases. Well below these (at 2.7 percent) was gonorrhea. Some of the groups that suffered acutely from this venereal disease were, however, subjects of concerted and at least temporarily successful efforts to deal with it. Other diseases together made up less than 5 percent of all cases. Nearly 6 percent of all visits to health care facilities were the result of accidents. Some wounds were a consequence of violence, but cutting instruments have very commonly been used in the rural areas, and it was likely that most damage was accidental. Other reports suggested that tetanus has been a common occurrence.

A number of children's diseases formerly prevalent in developed countries of the West are still problems in Kenya. For example, data for Nairobi Area show that a fairly large number of cases of measles, mumps, and whooping cough were reported throughout the 1970s. Other diseases often found in nontropical areas and reported from Kenya include poliomyelitis, cerebrospinal meningitis, infectious hepatitis, and syphilis. Among the diseases more common in Africa are schistosomiasis (snail fever), filariasis (transmitted by flying insects and prevalent on the coast), and kala-azar (transmitted by infected sand flies and common in the northern Rift Valley and in Eastern province). The occurrence of cholera is intermittent. There were outbreaks in 1974 and 1981, the latter affecting all but North-Eastern and Eastern provinces. It was brought under partial control but broke out again in some areas. The first major outbreak of trypanosomiasis (sleeping sickness) since the 1960s occurred in 1980 in the Lombwe Valley of South Nyanza District, where a game reserve is located. The disease is not widespread in Kenya; Lombwe Valley is apparently the only significant locus.

Many of these diseases, e.g., malaria, schistosomiasis, and the various forms of dysentery, are not usually fatal for adults, although they may be so for infants and children. They do, however, sap the energy of those who suffer from them and disable people for varying lengths of time. Many of these diseases are water related, i.e., the carriers either live or breed in the water (in the case of schistosomiasis and malaria) or the causes of disease are directly waterborne, as in many forms of dysentery. Stringent sanitation techniques, difficult to establish in rural areas, would make a difference.

In the early 1980s most health facilities were under the director of medical services of the Ministry of Health. Below the director were the provincial medical officers of health and the district medical officers of health. The provincial and district medical officers, all physicians, were primarily administrators and were specifically concerned with the operation of the provincial and district hospitals in their jurisdictions. Their direct involvement in, or supervision of, health care activities in their jurisdictions was minor.

In the rural areas, health facilities functioned within rural health units, each of which consisted of a demarcated area within a district. In 1980 such a unit served an average population of nearly 55,000 persons, but there was considerable variation. In principle, each rural health unit had as its chief facility either a district hospital or a rural health center which, in addition to providing the usual outpatient services, supervised the rural health subcenters and the dispensaries within its area and acted as a referral point from them. A rural health center often had several beds for normal obstetrics cases and a few beds for patients requiring observation before being referred to a hospital. It also provided a full range of mother-and-child clinics and family-planning services. In 1980 about 57 percent of the 254 rural health units had rural health centers as their headquarters. Roughly 23 percent had hospitals, and about 20 percent had dispensaries. Some of these were to be upgraded to health centers so that each rural health unit would have either a hospital or a rural health center. District hospitals had outpatient facilities attached to them, but they existed primarily to provide specialized care to patients referred to them by rural health centers. But the dispensaries constituted the core of rural health services. Health service subcenters offered services similar to those of the dispensaries, i.e., primarily diagnosis and treatment of ailments brought to them by outpatients. When diagnosis was difficult or treatment failed, they were expected to refer patients to health centers.

Physicians were usually available only in hospitals. The head of a rural health center (a clinical officer) was trained for three and one-half years (in contrast to the five years required for a baccalaureate in medicine at the University of Nairobi) but was expected to do much of the work done by a physician in the Western world. Working for the health center chief were several enrolled community nurses, the local term for an assistant nurse. Registered nurses were usually found only in hospitals or as public health nurses. Enrolled community nurses were usually in charge of dispensaries, but there were not enough of them in some areas; thus a so-called patient attendant, who had comparatively little training, served instead. A rural health center was supposed to have a public health officer attached to it who would be concerned with preventive health measures in the area served. In 1980 not all rural health centers had such officers, however, nor did they all have a family-health field educator whose primary concern was family planning. Most rural health centers did have midwives or assistant midwives attached to their mother-and-child clinics. Clinical health officers were supposed to exercise a degree of technical supervision over the subcenters and dispensaries in the area served by the rural health center, but they were usually too busy to do so.

In addition to the health personnel attached to specific facilities, there were other health posts in each district. These included a public health nurse, a nutrition officer, and a health education officer. The last two positions were often not filled.

Given the shortages of personnel and the inability of those who were expected to provide technical supervision and continuing education, the Ministry of Health in 1980 planned a reorganization of the rural system in an effort to cope with some of the system's problems. A management team consisting of a public health nurse, a clinical officer, and public health, nutrition, and health education officers were to accomplish the kinds of educational and supervisory tasks that others had been unable to do. Moreover, the district medical officers of health were to be relieved of their hospital administrative duties so that they could provide more attention to the work of the management teams. The extent to which this proposed reorganization had been carried out by mid-1983 could not be determined.

As the situation in the rural area suggested, there was a general shortage of health personnel in the rural areas, and there were few physicians there. Most physicians were located in the major cities of Nairobi and Mombasa. The proportion of those in private practice in the early 1980s was not available, but it was likely that it was less than the 70 percent noted in 1973. A larger proportion of the physicians employed by the government were in the urban areas. Many of them had been engaged in private practice as well until it was forbidden by the Ministry of Health in 1981. The prohibition eventually led to a physicians' strike in May 1981, when they demanded higher pay and allowances to compensate for the income they had earned in private practice. Some of their demands were acceded to, but when they continued to strike, the government ordered them back to work.

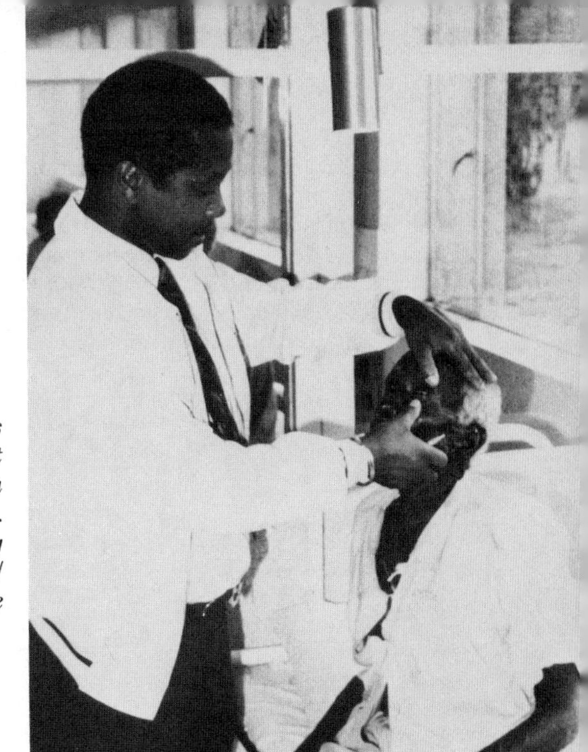

A Kenyan clinical officer checks the progress of a surgical patient in the Eye Wing of Nakuru Hospital. Courtesy United States Agency for International Development/ Emmett George

In addition to the hospitals and other facilities paid for by the government, there were a number of private institutions supported by large-scale commercial and agricultural interests, or sponsored and supported by Christian and other religious groups. Missionaries operated several hundred rural health centers and dispensaries in the early 1980s, and the Aga Khan, head of the Khoja Ismaili Muslims, had sponsored several hospitals.

* * *

There is considerable literature dealing with Kenya's population growth. *Kenya: Population and Development,* a World Bank country study prepared by Rashid Faruquee and others, provides a thorough overview of the problems and prospects. A substantial number of works on many of Kenya's ethnic groups tend to focus on issues peculiar to the group under study, and many of them are based on field research in the colonial or immediate postcolonial period. They are essential for understanding the specific reactions of particular peoples to change, but they only occasionally deal directly with such change. An example is the work of Robert and Barbara LeVine and of Sarah LeVine on the

Kisii (Gusii). An interesting exception is David Parkin's *The Cultural Definition of Political Response,* which deals with the relation of Luo culture and social organization to their behavior in Nairobi. Two works that deal in detail with the development of social stratification are Gavin Kitching's *Class and Economic Change in Kenya* and Nicola Swainson's *The Development of Corporate Capitalism in Kenya, 1918-77*. (For further information and complete citations, see Bibliography.)

Chapter 3. The Economy

Fishermen on Lake Victoria

THE KENYAN ECONOMY, in 1983 a mix of private and public sector enterprise, has been described by an economic mission of the World Bank as a pragmatic blend of laissez-faire capitalism and indigenous African socialism (the traditional economic, political, and social philosophy regulating the activities of African rural society). Since independence there has been a major reliance on private enterprise to develop the economy, but in various ways the government has stepped in to prevent unbridled private entrepreneurship. At the same time, it has modified traditional customary practice as necessary to solve the new situation faced in the development of a modern, monetized economy. Perhaps the most fundamental of the latter changes has been the broad-scale introduction of private ownership of agricultural and pastoral land through registered title. There has also been large-scale government involvement in the economy through a variety of parastatal organizations and activities. This participation has resulted largely from a combination of nationalistic, political, and economic motives: inadequate local private capital, a shortage of indigenous managers, a need for foreign investment, and a desire for Kenyan control of economic activity. Doubts existed in the government in 1983, however, concerning the effectiveness of some parastatals, and there appeared to be a rising sentiment for turning over various operations to the private sector.

Natural resources to sustain and expand economic activity are limited. Mineral wealth is of only minor consequence and, although hydroelectric potential is of considerable significance, it has offered only a partial solution to growing energy requirements. The most valuable natural asset is agricultural land. There has been visible progress in industrialization, but agriculture has continued to be—and was expected to remain in the foreseeable future—the mainstay of the economy, the principal source of employment, and the basis of the livelihood and welfare of a majority of the population.

For well over a decade after independence the economy had generally prospered. Growth during that time was sparked in large part by the opening up of new agricultural land, the accompanying increased production of cash crops, and the expansion of import substitution manufacturing. In 1983 these options no longer existed; most of the new land had been occupied, and most of the economically desirable import substitution plant was in place. Instead, the economic outlook was clouded by major problems, none of which appeared to be of a short-term nature. The most serious of these issues faced by the government in its efforts to revitalize development included the continuing adverse effects of the high cost of oil imports essential to the modern sector, the future supply of food for a rapidly increasing population, and the growing trade and current account deficits.

Economic Development

Programmed economic development began after World War II when the colonial government initiated a 10-year plan covering the period 1946-55. This was followed by consecutive three-year plans that carried up to independence. These plans have been criticized as being little more than proposed lists of government undertakings rather than programs for general economic development. The criticisms, however, ignored the fact that in a free enterprise economy the government was unable to incorporate private sector investment into a central national plan other than indicatively. The colonial administration was in effect limited to programming its own projects but was able additionally to provide direction and encouragement to private development activities through measures such as partial support through loans, tax incentives, and tariff protection. The economic philosophy prevalent in Kenya in the colonial era was that private investment—domestic, foreign, or both—was expected to play the leading role in development. From 1946 to 1963 private capital (largely foreign) added materially to productive facilities, including plants that processed foods and manufactured beverages, tobacco products, leather and shoes, chemicals, cement, paints and varnishes, ink and other stationery items, steel containers, and vehicle tires. Among the most important, with government equity participation, was the refining of petroleum.

The postindependence government has continued the earlier emphasis on the private sector's role in development, in marked contrast to the actions of many other Sub-Saharan African countries after independence. An atmosphere favorable to local and foreign capital has been maintained, although in the latter case investment has been welcomed only if it was considered likely to benefit the domestic economy. Development plans in general have been comprehensive, presenting targets toward which public and private investment should be directed and laying out the investment programs that the government proposed to carry out. An active incentives policy has been pursued with respect to development by the private sector, and a large amount of credit has been made available to the sector for investment.

The first plan after independence, the Development Plan 1964-70, was drawn up rather hastily; a revised, more detailed version covering the period 1966-70 was issued in mid-1966. Three further plans, for 1970-74, 1974-78, and 1979-83, had been implemented through mid-1983. Although government programs have not been carried out fully, they have made substantial additions to economic infrastructure—particularly through development of hydroelectric power facilities and expansion and improvement of the road network—and, in the social field, to health and educational facilities. Many of the new additions to the manufacturing sector have been privately financed, including a significant amount of foreign investment funds, but the government has also participated directly, as in the development of industrial estates, the sugar industry, and other projects. Existing and newly created statutory bodies have actively supported industrial development. Prominent among these was the Industrial and Commercial Development Corporation (ICDC). In agriculture various government development projects have been carried out, including those in the tea industry and irrigation. A main effort of the plans has been the establishment of services and the provision of funding to aid private agricultural development.

The major policy aims of the plans have been attainment of a fast overall growth rate and equitable distribution of the benefits from development. They were to be accompanied by "Kenyanization" of the economy (see Kenyanization and Economic Policy, ch. 1). The achievements during the years immediately after independence were impressive. Agricultural production increased rapidly as uncultivated high-potential farmland was put into use, and output of the major staple, maize, rose markedly after the introduction of hybrid strains. Manufacturing also grew at a high rate, and economic infrastructure expanded significantly. Real growth in the gross domestic product (GDP—see Glossary) from 1964 to 1972 averaged 6.5 percent.

In the early 1970s the economy began confronting a series of external and internal problems that affected growth, which in the period 1972-80 varied substantially in different years and declined overall to an average of 4.1 percent for the period. External factors essentially beyond Kenya's control played an important part. They included the increase in world oil prices, the subsequent worldwide inflation and recession, greatly increased interest rates on external borrowings, and the collapse of the East African Community (EAC), which resulted in the loss of the important Tanzanian market for manufactures. Internally for a variety of reasons (for example, weather and government policies), basic food crop production became erratic. A greater concentration of manufacturing production on supplying the domestic market also occurred, and vital exports of manufactured goods declined. Rising inflation, an overall deterioration in terms of trade, and growing adverse current account balances occurred. Other domestic pressures on government funds, including growing demands for social services, also mounted. In 1980, faced by a shortage of funding, the Development Plan 1979-83 was scaled back.

Government involvement in the economy has increased since independence. In the preindependence period government participation was mainly through what has been called "a plethora of statutory bodies." The latter were particularly prominent in agriculture where they engaged, among other things, in the development and marketing of the main cash crops (coffee, tea, maize, wheat, and sisal) and meat and dairy products. A number of fully owned government enterprises engaged in other activities, such as repair of railroad rolling stock, shipbuilding, and food processing. Government participation has been greatly expanded since independence through the growth of the so-called parastatal sector (including in the economic field a wide range of enterprises having partial to full government equity holdings, operations supported by regular budgetary appropriations, and enterprises in which the government has an interest through long-term loans). Parastatal activities ranged from advisory and regulatory to production, marketing, and financial operations. In late 1982 there were 323 such parastatals, of which 147 were statutory boards, 47 were fully government-owned companies, and 36 had majority government holdings. In the remaining 93 the government held minority interests, either directly or indirectly through another parastatal. Overall, the parastatals gave the government control of a substantial part of the economy.

The parastatals have had mixed results in their operations. Some, such as those in electricity, financial activities, tea production and marketing, and the port operations at Mombasa, have been quite profitable. In the case of the crop marketing board concerned with maize and wheat, profitability has fluctuated, affected by weather variability, government pricing policies, and other factors. Parastatals set up after the collapse of the EAC, including Kenya Railways and Kenya Airways, started under handicaps that continued to affect operations in 1983. Management factors appeared to account for poor results in some cases, such as in the Kenya Meat Commission (KMC), which was reported near bankruptcy at the beginning of 1983. In the early 1980s the number of parastatals requiring government outlays to meet deficits was reportedly increasing. The government had expressed concern over the situation, and in October 1982 President Daniel arap Moi declared that a reexamination of the growth of the public sector and of the use of investment funds was in order. Noting the inefficiency of some of the parastatals, he stated that a number of the public enterprises could be more productive and profitable if they were owned and run by private Kenyan citizens.

Information on progress toward the goal of equitable distribution of the benefits of economic expansion both among families and regionally—the second major aim of the development programs—remained rather limited in 1983. During the period 1964-81 the GDP increased from K£330.1 million (for value of the Kenya pound—see Glossary) to K£2,582.3 million, or approximately eightfold. However, per capita GDP rose less than four and one-half times (from K£36.3 to K£156.4) because of the increase in population (see table 2, Appendix). A comprehensive examination of employment, incomes, and equality in Kenya carried out through the International Labour Office at the beginning of the 1970s noted that after independence certain groups had benefited substantially from the rapid growth of the economy. They included the comparatively small group of Kenyans who had taken over former expatriate-held high-level jobs. A large group of African settlers had benefited through acquisition of formerly white-held farmland, and independence and economic growth had provided new entrepreneurial opportunities for Africans in commerce, transportation, construction, small-scale business, and various services. Additionally, the real incomes of modern sector urban employees had increased markedly. However, at the time a majority of smallholders had received little benefit, and the economic situation of the urban and rural unemployed, as well as that of the urban poor, had changed little.

Covering the agriculture year October 1974-75, the Central Bureau of Statistics carried out the Integrated Rural Survey, which was intended "to provide a broad baseline description of the socioeconomic factors dominating the small-scale households . . . with holdings of less than twenty hectares." Data from this and later surveys (including those of urban households) and from private studies have shown that in 1974 about 29 percent of the population was below an income poverty line (variously adjusted) of Ksh2,000 per annum (for value of the Kenya shilling—see Glossary). The proportion in poverty of the largest population segment, the smallholder, which made up some 72 percent of all Kenyans, was also 29 percent. In absolute terms that meant that almost 3 million people were below the poverty line out of a total of almost 7.4 million smallholders. The people found by the survey to be the worst off were the nomadic pastoralists, 85 percent of whom were below the poverty line. In percentages, however, they constituted only some 5 percent of the total population. In sharp contrast to the rural people (estimated at the time at 90 percent of total population), 32 percent of whom were poor, less than 5 percent of urban residents were in that category.

In an analysis of the main studies on poverty in Kenya, economist Arthur Hazlewood has pointed out impreciseness of available data, the regional complexity of the poverty situation, and the relativity of the latter with respect to different groups in the population. Despite the statistical fact of poverty, he noted that chronic hunger and starvation were not features of Kenyan rural areas. Most cultivators produced their own food, and the food supply of a very large number of smallholders had been improved by the spread of hybrid maize cultivation. The promotion and expansion of cash cropping had also greatly benefited these Kenyans. There was undoubtedly an accumulation of good land into large holdings—an unknown amount was not farmed intensively—landlessness increased, and the overall trend of the terms of rural-urban trade was favorable to the urban population. But the conclusions of various analyses, other than Marxian, were that postindependence economic development brought considerable benefit to smallholders as a group. The analyses also showed, however, that some 60 percent of smallholders who had the largest incomes received most of the benefits and that in real terms the poorest 40 percent made no gain. It also appeared likely that the absolute number of poor people may not have declined because of population growth, although the proportion had.

Agriculture

Agriculture, the country's most valuable productive asset, provides a livelihood for roughly 85 percent of the population that resides in the rural areas. It is the largest single contributor to GDP and during the 1970s accounted annually for about 36 percent of total GDP in constant (1976) prices. Since colonial times agricultural exports have also been the main source of foreign exchange (see Foreign Trade and Balance of Payments, this ch.). Agricultural production was divided into large farm and smallholder sectors, the line between the two being, as officially defined, holdings over or below 20 hectares. The large farms, which numbered more than 3,700 in 1980 and occupied almost 2.7 million hectares, engaged in the commercial production of crops. The smallholder sector consisted of about 1.7 million farms that averaged about two hectares each; they encompassed in all close to 3.5 million hectares. About three-fifths of these small holdings were subsistence operations, another one-fifth were used in general for commercial production, and the remainder were farmed primarily for subsistence but also carried on some commercial farming operations.

From national independence until the mid-1970s the agricultural sector generally produced sufficient basic foodstuffs to meet domestic needs. Between 1964 and 1973 production grew in real terms at an estimated average annual rate of 4.2 percent, or more rapidly than the population growth rate. Between 1974 and 1979, however, the average annual real growth rate declined to 2.7 percent, largely as the result of higher prices for agricultural inputs caused by the effects of increased world oil prices, which reduced their use, erratic local weather conditions, production disincentives, including inadequate producer prices and, in the case of maize, the government's inability to handle bumper crops. In 1980 food shortages forced the importation of large quantities of maize, wheat, and milk. In 1981 the government noted that rapid expansion of the population—at an estimated 4 percent a year—and emergence of a shortage of unexploited, good, arable land threatened to create a serious imbalance between the domestic requirement for food and the available supply. The demand for food was expected to expand rapidly during the decade, impelled primarily by the continuing rapid growth of the population. Proposed solutions to recover and maintain a broad self-sufficiency in foodstuffs were detailed in *Sessional Paper No. 4 of 1981: On National Food Policy*. The paper stressed, among other things, that the responsibility for feeding the country must be shared by the private sector which, along with the government, also owned, controlled, and managed the national resources.

Soils, Land Use, and Tenure

The country's finest soils are found in the Kenya Highlands and on the plateaus that slope westward from the highlands to Lake Victoria. They provide Kenya with some of the best agricultural land in Africa. Other good soils are found along the Indian Ocean coast. Many of the highland soils have formed on volcanic rock. Often well drained and having a high humus content, they cover large areas consisting of rich, dark red to dark brown friable clays and sandy and clayey loams highly suitable for intensive cultivation. The plateaus also have large areas of dark red and reddish-brown soils, generally rich in humus, that include easily workable clays and loams. Soils of the coastal zone are varied. They include loamy and loose sands of calcareous nature that formed on elevated coral plateaus and, on higher ground somewhat farther inland, others of sedimentary origin having differing humus contents; some of these latter soils are relatively fertile. Rich clay loams also occur at points along the coast in the beds of dried-up lagoons.

The better soils generally receive adequate amounts of rainfall for cultivation (see Geographic Regions, ch. 2). However, roughly 80 percent of the country's soils are located in areas having semiarid and arid climates. They are sandy in nature, and those in the vast northern half of the country are shallow, imperfectly weathered, and frequently stony. They support varying amounts of natural vegetation suitable only for extensive grazing. Somewhat better soils are found in the semiarid zone skirting the country's higher elevations, and others lie beyond the coast. Both usually receive enough precipitation to support subsistence agriculture. These areas, however, have long been used by pastoralists mainly for raising livestock. Population pressures have been forcing cultivation of larger areas, but this has been accompanied by growing herds of cattle that have caused serious overgrazing in many places and steady soil erosion.

Of Kenya's total land area of 569,137 square kilometers, roughly 20 percent was broadly estimated to be of high or medium potential for crop cultivation, forestry use, or intensive livestock raising. Marginal land in semiarid areas usable for rain-fed subsistence agriculture and livestock husbandry constituted perhaps 10 percent. The remaining 70 percent was largely semidesert used by pastoralists for extensive livestock grazing. Actual land use in 1980 as estimated by the Food and Agriculture Organization (FAO) included 4 percent (about 22,770 square kilometers) that was devoted to cultivation of annual and permanent crops (coffee, tea, and sisal) or was in fallow. Another 6.6 percent (about 37,560 square kilometers) was in permanent pastures, and 4.4 percent (about 25,040 square kilometers) was forest as broadly defined by FAO and including land expected to be forested. Some 85 percent (about 483,770 square kilometers) was classified simply as other land.

In 1983 land was held under three regular forms of tenure: customary, freehold, and leasehold. Customary land tenure, based on practices of the country's various ethnic groups, governed all landholding and use before the colonial period, with the exception of a narrow coastal strip then controlled by Swahili-speaking people whose Muslim land laws prevailed. In precolonial agricultural regions, areas of land were in general owned by the lineage (see Glossary) or the clan and controlled by a chief or group of elders. Rights of the individual to land were usufructuary, but the right to pass on land to heirs was usually recognized. Large areas of these customary lands were allocated to white settlers by the colonial administration (see The Compartmentalization of Land, ch. 1). The remaining agricultural, or potentially cultivable, land was largely set aside in reserves for the African population. In areas occupied by pastoral peoples, customary use rights related to grazing areas, water holes, stock trails, and the like. Customary practices continued to prevail in most of the reserve lands (redesignated Trust Lands after 1963) after independence. However, the Constitution vested all land rights in the Trust Lands in the local county council, which was given freehold title to the land in its own name (see Local Government, ch. 4). Customary tenure practices continued, but in case of disputes a county-designated land tribunal acted as arbitrator. Another body, the council's land committee, had the power to make allocations of land.

Although freehold titles to agricultural land were given to European settlers, there was little support in early colonial times for titles for African farmers. In 1933 a land commission recommended that individual titles be issued, but little was done until the Mau Mau emergency of the 1950s brought a changed attitude on the part of the government and the conclusion that individual African land titles were a precondition to rapid agricultural development. Such titles would provide the farmer with a reason to invest time and labor in farm improvements and give him additionally the collateral for credits to expand operations (see The Mau Mau Emergency, ch. 1). An important aspect of this new approach was land consolidation, bringing together small parcels to give the titleholder adequate land to produce a better living for his family. For instance, it had been found in 1955 that some 38,000 landholders in Kiambu District, north of Nairobi, had an average of eight separate parcels each. The land registration practices of English law were adopted to carry out the consolidation and entitlements. The Kenyan government has continued actively to promote land registration through the Registered Land Act of 1963, which in general also follows pertinent English law.

Individualization of land through registered titles proceeded slowly during the 1950s. The process, adjudication, consolidation, and registration were carried out in the reserve lands, but there appears to have been little support for the effort from the African population. In 1960 the government officially removed the distinction between reserve land and that held by Europeans—the so-called Scheduled Areas, totaling 3.1 million hectares and containing one-fifth of the best agricultural land—thus permitting individuals of any race to acquire title. As part of an independence package, funds were provided by the British government in 1962 to purchase 1 million acres of this land from European owners for use in the settlement of Africans who would have registered ownership. This became known as the Million-Acre Scheme. Kenyan government purchase of other land and individual purchases also occurred. Registration of Trust Lands has also proceeded, and at the end of 1980 almost 8.3 million hectares, constituting about 64 percent of registrable Trust Lands, had been registered, adjudicated, or was in the process of adjudication.

The pastoral areas of the Trust Lands presented a different situation with respect to registration of titles. The Land (Group Representatives)

Act of 1968 provided the vehicle for implementing registration in these areas. Under the act, group ranches were set up and headed by elected representatives who were registered as corporate owners of the ranch. Observations of the seminomadic Maasai in Narok District have indicated that where cultivation is important, there has been a tendency to subdivide ranches and seek individual ownership. In some cases, individuals and families have secured large holdings for which they hold regular titles.

Crop Production

Kenya's tropical climate, modified by topography and adequacy of rainfall, permits the cultivation of a variety of crops ranging from tropical to temperate (see Climate, ch. 2). In 1983 important temperate crops included maize, wheat, millet, sorghum, rice, other food grains, beans, potatoes, oilseeds, cotton, and tobacco. Subtropical and tropical crops, mainly consumed domestically, were sugarcane, cassava, and bananas, as well as a number of major export commodities that included coffee, tea, pineapples, sisal, pyrethrum, wattle, and cashew nuts. Reasonably reliable data on crop production were limited to certain ones produced for sale (see table 3, Appendix).

Maize, the principal staple, was grown widely by subsistence farmers and also by the large market-oriented farms. Estimates of overall production have been only rough, and published data relate to purchases by the parastatal National Cereals and Produce Marketing Board to which, by law, all maize for sale, except that used locally, had to be offered. Smallholder producers might retain on their farms up to 80 percent of the crop for their own consumption, and in effect the board's purchases served mainly urban centers and some small rural areas where for various reasons production was inadequate. Until the mid-1960s maize output had not met total domestic demand, and there were regular imports. From about the middle of the decade this situation was changed by the introduction of hybrid varieties. There followed a dramatic increase in production (increases in sown area also played a part) and substantial surpluses. The latter have varied greatly, however, influenced by weather, producer prices, availability of fertilizers and credit, as well as other factors.

A major disincentive to production had been introduced when the board was unable in the bumper harvest years of 1976 and 1977 to buy all the grain offered because of a lack of storage space. Farmers were left with large surpluses and cut back sharply on the area planted in 1978. Their negative attitude was further strengthened by discontinuance of the existing seasonal credit system for farmers and by the board's reduction of its maize purchase price. Sales to the board declined from nearly 565,000 tons in 1976 and 424,000 tons in 1977 to 236,000 tons in 1978 and were only slightly higher in 1979. The producer price was raised substantially in 1980, and a new credit system was introduced. There was a positive response from the farmers, but the increased area under cultivation was offset by highly unfavorable weather conditions. The estimated total harvest was under 1.6 million tons, and sales to the board dropped below 218,000 tons. During the favorable conditions of 1981, however, about 2.1 million tons were produced, and board purchases amounted to almost 473,000 tons. Prices were again increased for the 1982 season, and total production reached an estimated 2.7 million tons. The amount purchased was unavailable. However, the board's storage facilities had been considerably expanded.

Since 1966 the government has maintained a strategic stock of maize for use in droughts and other emergencies, that is, mainly to meet urban needs. In early 1980 the reserve, depleted by demands that arose because of the reduced 1979 crop and low amount purchased, totaled only 44,100 tons (the minimum essential reserve was considered to be 180,000 tons). The low harvest of 1980 forced the importation of about 360,000 tons of maize to meet requirements; some additional imports were also made in 1981 to restore emergency stocks. The government's goal in the early 1980s was a reserve of 360,000 tons, which was estimated to be adequate for one year's consumption by 3 million people.

Wheat, introduced early in the settler period, was the most important cereal crop after maize (see Economic Development, ch. 1). Production was largely concentrated in Uasin Gishu, Nakuru, and Narok districts in the Kenya Highlands and mostly on farms larger than 20 hectares. Kenya's goal in the colonial period had been to produce sufficient wheat to meet its own demands and those of Uganda and Tanganyika (later Tanzania); this was finally attained in 1964. Domestic demand began increasing rapidly from the mid-1960s, however, as urban food tastes changed, a trend that continued into 1983 and had been amplified by the growing size of the urban population. Wheat production increased in the late 1960s and early 1970s, and export surpluses occurred. But demands for wheat products rose more rapidly than the domestic wheat output (by well over 7 percent a year as against 5 percent between 1977 and 1980), requiring wheat imports that reached over 139,400 tons in 1981. In 1979 the government, with World Bank (see Glossary) assistance, began a long-range project in Narok District to increase wheat production; in 1983 implementation was still in progress.

The principal industrial crops were sugarcane, cotton, oilseeds, and tobacco. The production of sugar had grown into a major industry that in the early 1980s more than met domestic needs. The first commercial sugar mill began operations in 1922 at Ramisi on the southeast coast. Another was established at Miwani in 1923 on the Kano Plain, east of Kisumu. Both enterprises were privately owned. At independence their combined output of 30,000 to 35,000 tons a year was meeting only slightly more than one-half of the annual demand. As part of an undertaking after independence to attain self-sufficiency in sugar production and also to benefit smallholders associated with cane production, the government constructed sugar factories at Muhoroni (1966) and Chemelil (1968), both on the Kano Plain, and at Mumias (1973) in the Nzoia River valley of Western Province. Production capacity was further expanded by construction of a factory in Bungoma District of Western Province that went into operation in 1979 and another on the Kano Plain that started production in early 1980. All sugar companies had a nucleus estate, or core farm, that provided the principal amount of sugarcane required for processing. The estate production was supplemented by a large number of outlying farms, some of large size but mostly operated by small farmers who usually cultivated less than two hectares of sugarcane each. In 1979 total sugar output of almost 296,000 tons surpassed domestic consumption for the first time. In 1980 output reached 401,000 tons, and almost 95,000 tons were exported. Production declined in 1981 to 366,800 tons but still substantially exceeded total consumption that year of 324,000 tons.

Since colonial times cotton has been primarily a smallholder crop. It can be cultivated in many parts of the country's arable area and is of particular importance because it can be grown on marginal agricultural land where it offers the farm family the possibility of raising a cash crop. In the early 1980s about 45 percent of the crop was grown in Western and Nyanza provinces and another 40 percent in Central and Eastern provinces. The remainder was grown in areas of Coast Province, in the Kerio River valley in Rift Valley Province, and on government irrigation schemes. These government undertakings included a small project at Hola on the Tana River and the large Bura irrigation project under expansion in the same general area in 1983. Smallholders engaged in cotton growing were estimated to number about 100,000. Individual areas planted in cotton were usually between one-half and one hectare.

During the 1960s cotton production was generally below 15,000 tons a year and through the mid-1970s was only slightly higher, averaging 16,000 to almost 17,000 tons annually. In 1975, as part of a program to produce sufficient cotton to meet domestic textile-manufacturing needs. the government initiated the Cotton Development Project. The project has included the provision of free seed, interest-free credit to permit purchase of pesticides and to secure tractor plowing, and a number of increases in producer prices. In 1978 and 1979 output rose to over 27,000 tons and in 1980 reached a record of over 38,000 tons. In 1981, however, production declined to less than 26,000 tons. Reasons given for the drop included delayed payments to farmers for cotton delivered to the Cotton Seed and Lint Marketing Board, but perhaps a more important reason was the effect of a national campaign in 1981 to increase food production, which was believed to have resulted in the diversion to food crops of more than one-quarter of the some 168,000 hectares of land intended for cotton.

Of the crops grown primarily for export, coffee and tea were the most important in the early 1980s. Other included cashew nuts, pineapples, pyrethrum, sisal, and wattle. Coffee was the largest earner of foreign exchange among agricultural commodities, and in most years before 1980 it had also been the largest single-item exchange earner. The industry included both large estates and smallholder operations. Historically, the development of coffee cultivation had favored estate production by white settlers, and not until the 1950s did African smallholder cultivation slowly begin to increase (see Economic Development, ch. 1). The restrictions that had held back African participation no longer applied after national independence, and African holdings grew rapidly in number. In the early 1980s there were an estimated 300,000 smallholders, who collectively owned nearly 60,000 hectares, compared with holdings of 13,000 hectares at independence. In contrast, estates that had grown steadily through 1961 when they had 30,000 hectares in coffee showed little change thereafter. In 1982 the planted area of the 690 estates was only slightly over 29,000 hectares.

Kenyan coffee is predominantly of the arabica variety and has been widely recognized for its high quality. It is grown mainly in Central, Nyanza, and Western provinces at altitudes ranging from about 1,500 to 1,900 meters. Limited commercial development in Western Province of the robusta variety, used in the manufacture of instant coffee, was undertaken in about 1958, but the effort was discontinued in the late 1960s at a time of depressed coffee prices. Renewed interest developed during the 1977-78 period of high general coffee prices, which resulted from damage to the Brazilian coffee crop, and some rehabilitation of existing robusta tress occurred. The use and import of instant coffee has continued to grow in Kenya, and in 1980 the government began encouraging further rehabilitation, new plantings, and expansion of robusta cultivation to other climatically suited areas. It has been estimated that annual production of some 10,000 tons of coffee beans would be required to operate profitably an instant coffee processing plant.

Coffee production is affected by weather and disease, as well as world prices, and annual production has tended to fluctuate. In the early 1970s production was about 60,000 tons a year but increased during the decade as the planted area expanded and new trees came into production. In 1976 output reached 80,000 tons. In 1977 it jumped to 97,000 tons as growers took advantage of the Brazilian crop loss and high prices to increase sales. The normal country export quotas, set to regulate the world coffee market by the International Coffee Organization (ICO). of which Kenya was a member, were temporarily suspended. Meanwhile, Kenya's coffee output, despite a subsequent sharp drop in the world price, continued at a high level, totaling over 90,000 tons in both 1980 and 1981. Smallholders accounted for almost 58,000 tons in 1981. The ICO quotas were reinstituted in 1980, and for 1981 Kenya had a final quota allotment of about 67,200 tons. For 1982 the amount was set at 70,000 tons. About 4,200 tons were consumed domestically, and permissible exports to nonquota countries (among others, the Soviet Union, Eastern Europe, and China) usually totaled another 2,000 to 3,000 tons. A mounting unsold surplus was developing.

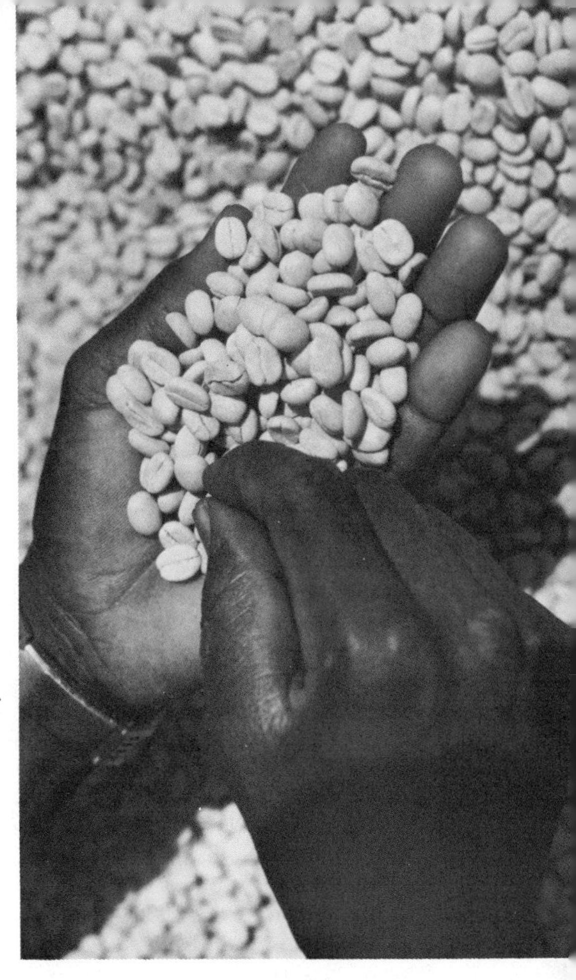

Premium-value Kenyan coffee, a major source of foreign exchange
Courtesy The Lamp, Exxon Corporation

Since the mid-1960s tea has been the second largest agricultural commodity earner of foreign exchange. Tea grows well in the higher altitudes (1,800 to 2,100 meters) of various parts of the Kenya Highlands, including districts in Central, Eastern, Nyanza, Rift Valley, and Western provinces. The first tea was planted in 1903 and developed as an estate crop, which by 1950 produced almost 7 million kilograms of leaf tea. Smallholder participation was negligible until after independence (in 1963 smallholder production had amounted to only about 400,000 kilograms out of a total of 17.8 million kilograms). However, tea appeared to be an excellent vehicle for promoting smallholder participation in cash crop production. An active expansion program was initiated in 1964 under the direction of the Kenya Tea Development Authority (KTDA), which was established that year and charged with bringing new areas into cultivation, constructing and managing tea-processing factories, and handling marketing. Through June 1982 the KTDA had completed five tea-planting programs and had increased processing facilities from one to 33. The total smallholder area planted to tea in 1982 was about 54,689 hectares compared with some 4,400 hectares in 1965; the number of growers had increased during that time from some 20,000 to about 150,000. The area devoted to tea on smallholdings averaged somewhat under 0.4 hectare per family. The programs have been materially assisted by funds received from the World Bank, the Commonwealth Development Corporation, the European Investment Bank, the Organization of Petroleum Exporting Countries (OPEC), and others.

The plantation area under tea also expanded in the postindependence period from 17,969 hectares in 1963 to over 27,000 hectares in 1980. In the early 1980s, although plantations accounted for only about one-third of the area in tea, they produced 40 percent or more of the processed tea. However, this situation was attributable principally to the immaturity of many of the smallholder plantings. Overall tea production increased markedly from 56.7 million kilograms in 1975 to 99.3 million kilograms in 1979. In the latter part of 1980 and in early 1981 output was affected, particularly in smallholdings, by drought. Production totaled only 88.9 million kilograms in 1980 and 88 million kilograms in 1981. The KTDA, on completion of its planting program in 1982, had raised the question of whether further plantings should be made, or whether it would be preferable to emphasize increased unit production and improvement in the quality of the tea. Both proposals would help bring larger incomes to the growers, which was believed necessary to maintain smallholder interest in producing tea rather than other crops. No decision on the issue had been reported through mid-1983.

Irrigation

Kenya has not had an indigenous tradition of irrigated agriculture, although European observers in the late 1800s reported small irrigated areas along the Perakera River near Lake Baringo. At the time, land was readily available for cultivation in the more populated agricultural parts of the country, and the need for irrigation was essentially nonexistent. In the first decade after independence, estimates of irrigable land ranged from about 160,000 to 200,000 hectares, but a major study of water resources by foreign consultants, published in 1979, arrived at a figure of 540,000 hectares. The irrigable land was found mainly in the Tana River and Lake Victoria drainage basins, each having an estimated 200,000-hectare potential. The Rift Valley potential was set at 70,000 hectares, and the Athi-Tsavo basin in southeastern Kenya accounted for 40,000 hectares. The remaining 30,000 hectares was along the Ewaso Ng'iro, which drains an area mainly north and northeast of Mount Kenya (see Drainage, ch. 2).

The first organized irrigation schemes were started during the Mau Mau emergency as projects to utilize the labor of detainees. Economically, the only viable early scheme has been the Mwea settlement and irrigation project, which utilizes the waters of the Thika River in the upper Tana River basin. From a small area first cropped in 1956, land at Mwea under irrigation increased to about 2,000 hectares in crop year 1960-61. A decade later the total had increased to over 4,300 hectares, and continued expansion increased the cropped area to 6,313 hectares in 1980-81. In the latter year individual plots numbered 3,150. The main crop was rice, of which some 30,000 tons (paddy) were produced in 1980-81. The remaining two earlier schemes were located on the Perakera River near Lake Baringo and at Hola on the middle reaches of the Tana River. Both were small undertakings, the first producing onions and chili peppers, the second essentially a pilot cotton-growing project. Their operations have had to be subsidized regularly by the government.

In the late 1960s two other small government irrigation schemes were established as pilot projects. One at Ahero in the central part of Nyanza Province was intended to provide data for the establishment of a major sugarcane scheme on the Kano Plain; the other at Bunyala on the Nzoia River in Western Province was planted in rice to determine the best use for land being reclaimed from the nearby Yala Swamp. These projects continued to be active in 1983 but produced relatively small quantities of paddy rice; both were economically nonviable and were government subsidized. A sixth national irrigation project, the West Kano scheme, commenced production of paddy rice and sugarcane in crop year 1977-78. Figures available through 1980-81 showed an expanding area of coverage and generally increasing production, but information on financial operations was lacking.

These various irrigation schemes operated under the National Irrigation Board (NIB), established in 1966 to control and carry out the development and improvement of national irrigation undertakings. Under the Development Plan 1974-78, the NIB began a large-scale irrigation project (planned irrigated area, 6,480 hectares) on the Tana River at Bura, near the earlier Hola Project. Financial constraints that faced the government in the late 1970s slowed implementation of the scheme, but in early 1983 roughly 1,200 hectares were under cultivation and another 1,000 hectares awaited clearing for cropping. About 75 to 80 percent of the project infrastructure had been completed, and 930 settler families were living at the project. In 1982 about 800 hectares had been planted to cotton, and 400 hectares to maize. The required reliable water flow for this major undertaking had been ensured by the contruction of the Masinga Dam on the upper Tana River. The storage reservoir behind the dam was filled to the planned size—45 kilometers in length and 120 square kilometers in area—in mid-1982 making it the largest man-made lake in East Africa.

The irrigation schemes carried out that are under the administration of the NIB have been costly with respect to return, employment created, production, and benefits to the farmer (who was paid based on the net return from operations). In the Development Plan 1979-83 the government did not make any new commitments to large-scale projects but instead emphasized the promotion of small-scale and private projects. The Small-Scale Irrigation Unit established in the Ministry of

Agriculture in 1977 has initiated a considerable number of such projects, mainly in the upper and lower Tana basin. Since 1979 provincial irrigation units have also been involved. Substantial foreign financial and technical assistance has been received in the program. The total cropped area in all government schemes was about 10,000 hectares in 1980-81, of which more than 60 percent was in the Mwea project. There were at the time 5,289 plotholders in all.

The private sector has pursued irrigation at a faster pace than has the government; in 1980-81 an estimated 16,000 to 18,000 hectares were under private irrigation. Most of the area was on the slopes of Mount Kenya and consisted of coffee plantations and commercial estates producing pineapples, other fruits, and vegetables primarily for export. Small village irrigation schemes were established along the Tana River, assisted financially by foreign church groups; churches in Kenya have helped in organization and management. Other small private and cooperatively operated areas existed in the Lake Baringo area of the Rift Valley, and presumably others of a traditional furrow-irrigation character were developed in suitable areas of western Kenya.

Livestock

As of 1983 a comprehensive enumeration of the country's livestock had not been conducted. But based on rural ground and aerial surveys, the estimated number of large livestock, according to the Central Bureau of Statistics' *Economic Survey, 1982,* was in the range of 24.5 to 29 million. The total consisted of 12 to 13.5 million cattle, 11 to 14 million sheep and goats, about 1 million camels, several hundred thousand donkeys, and roughly 100,000 pigs. There were also about 27 million domesticated fowl. Based on the same techniques used for the overall estimate, it appeared that about one-half the cattle and most of the sheep and goats were kept by pastoralists, as were virtually all donkeys and camels. Their herds varied considerably in composition; those of the north and northeast, where grazing was sparse, had more camels and goats. In other areas where water and browse were more abundant and accessible, cattle and sheep predominated. Rift Valley Province, which had a large pastoral population (including the nomadic and seminomadic Maasai, various Kalenjin groups, and the Turkana), had the greatest number of cattle, estimated at about 6.5 million head.

Smallholders also accounted for a large number of cattle, most of the relatively small pig herd, a considerable number of sheep and goats, and almost all of the poultry. Livestock raising in this case was mainly a supplementary subsistence undertaking and part of mixed farm operations, although some animals were produced for market sales, including milk. Pastoralists relied on livestock for both subsistence and cash income. Marketed production by both groups increased over time but was not usually a primary goal. Pastoralist group ranches in some instances began to raise cattle for marketing, but traditional attitudes, which placed a high value on ownership of cattle as a store of wealth, status symbol, and safeguard in times of famine, remained

Maasai cattlemen beside a new watering trough constructed with foreign aid to Kenya's long-term livestock development program
Courtesy World Bank Photo/James Pickerell

widespread. The commercial production of beef and dairy products was largely centered on the ranches and mixed farms in the former Scheduled Area. Ownership of most of these had been European in the colonial period but subsequently passed largely into African hands. In 1980 almost 430,000 head of beef cattle and over 275,000 dairy animals were owned by commercial operations. There had been a slow downward trend in numbers of beef and dairy animals during the 1970s: beef cattle were decreasing from a high of over 500,000 head in 1969, and dairy animals from a high of some 308,000 in 1972.

Commercial and dairy herds were largely of quality stock, consisting mainly of European breeds or mixed breeds developed using the indigenous boran zebu strain. In contrast, almost all smallholder and pastoralist cattle were of indigenous zebu breeds. Although relatively hardy and disease resistant, they were low in meat and milk yields. In almost all small-farm regions and particularly in the pastoralist areas, the numbers of livestock were reported to be greater than the amount of browse would permit; consequently, overgrazing and undernutrition were widespread.

Wildlife abounds in the 20,000 square kilometers of Tsavo National Park, one of 15 in Kenya that attract many tourists each year

Courtesy CNI News/Bill Chewning

A very large part of the cattle, sheep and goat offtake, as well as of dairy products, was consumed by the producers' households. Until the early 1970s the principal provider of meat to the general market was the parastatal Kenya Meat Commission (KMC). Private slaughterhouses began increasing in number from about that time. They paid better prices than the KMC and also made prompt payment to the seller, in contrast to the frequent delays by the latter in paying for deliveries. As a result, the number of cattle and calves delivered annually to the KMC for slaughter declined from over 200,000 in 1971 to only some 60,000 in the early 1980s. In the case of sheep and lambs, the number dropped from 65,000 in 1970 to fewer than 10,000 head in 1981. The delivery of goats declined during the same time from over 47,000 to 1,000.

Kenya has long been noted for the great numbers and variety of its wildlife. Wild animals have been of considerable value to the economy as a major tourist attraction and have helped generate a significant share of tourism's foreign exchange earnings. In the early 1980s the estimated total of herbivores (elephants, buffalo, antelopes, giraffes, zebras, and others), which formed the overwhelming portion of the wildlife, was about 3 million. Most of these animals were found in the country's many national parks and game reserves. Although impressive in size, the herds no longer were of the great dimensions that characterized them in the early 1900s. Responsible for the decline in numbers were the increase in the human population and the accompanying expansion of settlements and cultivation that encroached on the natural habitat and cut off many of the regular animal migratory routes. An increasing number of domestic livestock also brought competition for water and forage. Most predators in the more heavily settled regions were killed off or driven away. For instance, the lion was only rarely found in much of western Kenya and the heavily populated parts of the Kenya Highlands.

Early legal and subsequent illicit killing also played a major role in wildlife reduction. Heavy inroads were made during World War I, and especially during World War II, when game animals were a major source of food for the labor force, troops, and prisoners of war. Poaching also became a major factor in the decline of certain species, such as the elephant. Although carried on partly for food, most of the economically damaging poaching was for illegal commercial sales—for example, cheetah and leopard skins, elephant tusks, and black rhinoceros horns, which were prized in southern Arabian countries for dagger handles and in the Far East as an aphrodisiac. Government antipoaching activities appeared to have attained considerable success, and some recovery in numbers was reported by the 1980s, except for the rhinoceros, which declined further in numbers in 1981 to fewer than 900 animals. Most regular hunting of wild game had been banned in 1977. By 1983 animal numbers grew to the point that serious damage was being done to crops in some areas, and demands arose to permit hunting again on private land. No action on these requests was reported through mid-1983.

Forestry

Kenya's forest resources are located principally in the Kenya Highlands, but small forested areas are found in the coastal area and in a few scattered places throughout the country where climatic conditions are favorable (see Geographic Regions, ch. 2). About 94 percent of these resources in 1983 were in forest estates and plantations owned by the central government or by local county councils but under the control of the Forest Department. In 1980, department estimates of forests under its administration placed the total area at approximately 18,600 square kilometers, or 3.2 percent of the country's total land area. Of this total, 16,910 square kilometers were indigenous forest (9,530 square kilometers of closed forest, 3,390 of dense woodland, 1,500 of bamboo forest, 2,040 of savanna open woodland, and 450 of mangrove forest). Some 1,680 square kilometers were plantation forests. In addition, approximately 1,240 square kilometers of indigenous forest were privately owned. The total actual area of standing indigenous forest in 1981 appeared, however, to be about 25 percent less than the Forest Department's area computations indicated, according to calculations based on satellite remote-sensing techniques. This placed the amount at some 13,700 square kilometers. Adding the 1,740 square kilometers of plantations (in 1981), actual forest stands occupied about 2.7 percent of Kenya's total land area.

The first major program to protect forests in water catchment areas in the Kenya Highlands was initiated after establishment of the Forest Department in 1902. Widespread destruction of forest for agricultural purposes had long been going on in the lower fringes of the highlands, but the upper forest regions at the time were essentially uninhabited, and large reserved areas were established with little difficulty. Until 1925 the main effort to perpetuate existing forest resources was through natural regeneration of cutover areas or replacement of felled stock with the more valuable indigenous species. The latter required up to a century to reach maturity, however, and in 1926 the emphasis changed to development of commercial plantations of fast-growing exotic pines and cypresses that had been found adaptable to conditions in Kenya. These softwood exotics, which in 1981 covered an area of 1,500 square kilometers, were the source of most sawn timber, construction materials, plywood, and pulp—the latter produced and processed into paper at a pulp and paper mill that opened at Webuye (formerly Broderick Falls) in Western Province in late 1974. Exotic hardwood plantations (135 square kilometers in total area) included eucalyptus species and wattle, both introduced early in the twentieth century from Australia. The former were used for poles and firewood; the latter was a source of tannin, extracted from the bark, and was used otherwise for poles, as firewood, and to produce charcoal. The easily grown eucalypti were also planted widely by farmers and gave a new appearance to the countryside in many places.

Plantation development has been aided substantially by external financing. Between 1968 and 1980 the World Bank supported reforestation of 740 square kilometers. A further project, approved in 1982, in which Italy and Switzerland were also participating, provided for the planting of 64 square kilometers annually for four years. The output of the plantations has largely met the requirements of the modern urban sector. However, the preeminence of wood for fuel in the rural areas, where most of the population resides, has caused a steady drain on the indigenous forests, and serious deforestation has been reported in various parts of the country (see Wood and Vegetable Residues, this ch.). The government has long encouraged farmers to establish woodlots to furnish poles and firewood. In late 1982, as part of a renewed effort, the government announced it was establishing six agroforestry centers. Financed by the United States Agency for International Development (USAID), the goal was 1 million seedlings a year, which would be distributed to farmers for planting on their holdings.

Fisheries

The fishing industry contributed only a small proportion of the monetary GDP (somewhat over 0.2 percent annually in the period 1971-81). Throughout Kenya about 31,000 fishermen were engaged in commercial operations, and an additional unknown but large number of individuals handled marketing and related activities. In the subsistence sector, the imputed value of fishing was about one-tenth of that in the monetary sector. Nonetheless, fresh and preserved fish were important food items, especially for the highly populated areas of western Kenya in the vicinity of Lake Victoria, where the Luo were active fishermen (constituting about 90 percent of the total in the region), and along the Indian Ocean, where marine catches provided fish for Mombasa and other coastal towns, villages, and settlements. Iced fresh fish were supplied from both sources to Nairobi and some other towns inland. However, in most interior rural areas where only preserved fish were available, consumption was negligible, apparently because of the lack of supplies.

The main fishery resources in 1983 were the Kenyan part of Lake Victoria, Lake Rudolf, and the coastal and offshore waters of the Indian Ocean. Since February 1979 Kenya has claimed an exclusive fishing zone extending 200 nautical miles from the coast. Together these sources have regularly accounted for about 93 to 95 percent of the total annual fish catch. Of less significance were the small lakes of the central and southern Rift Valley, a few other small lakes, and the main rivers, including the Tana and Galana in eastern Kenya and the Nzoia and Yala in the western part of the country (see Drainage, ch. 2). There were also numerous small fish ponds, but their estimated production was less than 600 tons a year. A considerable potential for fish farming existed, and during the 1950s the colonial government had promoted the construction of fish ponds, an effort that continued after independence. Estimates of the number of ponds varied greatly; one estimate in the late 1970s set the total at about 9,000. However, most farmers had little knowledge of methods and management, and the needed government extension services were extremely limited. In the early 1980s most ponds appeared to be untended, and yields were believed to be very low.

Lake Victoria has been the largest producer of fish. From the late 1960s to the mid-1970s the annual harvest ranged roughly from 15,000 to 17,000 tons. Expansion of fishing activities by the local population led to a rapid rise in output thereafter to almost 31,000 tons in 1979 and over 39,000 tons in 1981. The main catches included various tilapia species, species of the genus *Haplochromis*, and a small anchovy-like fish. In the late 1970s some 18,000 fishermen were reported operating on the lake, either individually or in small groups. They sold their catches to numerous small private dealers. Because of the lack of ice, only about one-third of the catch was used fresh; the remainder was sun dried, salted, or smoked.

Lake Rudolf at independence was largely unexploited; its great distance from the heavily populated parts of the country and the lack of good roads had discouraged serious foreign interest. The local people were pastoralists, and any fishing was for subsistence. In the early 1960s the government trained some local Turkana in fishing practices. The reported commercial catch grew gradually to more than 3,700 tons in 1969. A fishermen's cooperative was organized in 1971, and production through 1976 usually ran between 4,000 and 5,000 tons a year. In 1977 and 1978 the catch rose to about 15,000 tons, apparently stimulated by the development of export markets for dried and salted fish, mainly in Zaïre. In the late 1970s and early 1980s, however, increasing internal problems in Uganda affected the transportation routes to Zaïre. This, together with a worsening economic situation in that country, appears to have been largely instrumental in a gradual drop in the Lake Rudolf catch to 10,900 tons in 1981. Major hindrances to development of the lake's fisheries for the domestic market were the lack of ice and cold storage facilities and the absence of a good road to the markets for fresh fish. In 1981 an ice plant was reported under construction at the lake, financed mainly by the Norwegian Agency for International Development. The agency was also reported to be financing improvement of the main road south to Kitale from which good roads ran to Kisumu and Nairobi, both large consumers of fresh fish.

Marine fishing was carried on mostly in inshore waters along the country's 400-kilometer-long coast (roughly 600 kilometers in actual shore length, including inlets and coves). The fish catch averaged somewhat over 4,000 tons a year between 1976 and 1981. According to the Fisheries Department, roughly one-fifth consisted of deep-sea (pelagic) species, and the remainder were bottom-dwelling (demersal) species taken within a zone extending only a few miles from the shore. Varying quantities of spiny lobsters, shrimp, crabs, oysters, other mollusks, squid, and sharks were also taken. Game fishing was an important foreign exchange earner. In addition to the reported catch, foreign crew-operated private freeze-trawlers based at Mombasa fished inshore waters for shrimp, and various foreign tuna boats landed catches at Mombasa for freezing and transshipment.

Small-scale fishermen using some 2,000 canoes and dhows accounted for most of the catch. But a number of private commercial enterprises were active in both fishing and marketing, and the government was involved in commercial fishing through Kenya Fishing Industries (KFI). KFI was founded in 1971 as a joint undertaking of the Industrial and Commercial Development Corporation (ICDC), principally with Japanese fishing interests, to set up freezer, storage, and transshipment facilities for tuna fishers. Use by foreign fishermen declined after the rise in world oil prices in the mid-1970s, and ICDC acquired full ownership during 1977 and 1978. In 1979 KFI ordered two vessels of approximately 250 gross registered tons each for deep-sea, long-line tuna fishing. These vessels have cold storage facilities and can operate at sea for three months or more. In late 1981 KGI was reportedly considering building a processed-fish packing and fish meal plant in Mombasa to reduce the substantial imports made each year. The plant appeared to be still in the planning stage in early 1983.

Manufacturing

The manufacturing sector produces a diversity of consumer goods and intermediate products, ranging from biscuits, confectionery, flour, and sugar to cement, fertilizer, paper, plastics, petroleum products, and motor vehicles. Through the early 1980s the sector's rate of growth was higher in real terms than that of the GDP as a whole. In the period 1964-78 growth averaged about 9.5 percent compared with 5.9 percent by the GDP. At the end of the decade and in the early 1980s, however, growing balance of payments problems led to restrictions on the importation of raw and semiprocessed materials (see Foreign Trade and Balance of Payments, this ch.). This had a major impact on production because only about one-third of the country's manufacturing industries used locally procured materials. At the same time, for whatever reason, the rural population demand for manufactured goods stagnated or grew only slightly. A marked drop in output occurred, and the rate of growth in real terms declined to 4.5 percent in 1981. During 1982, associated with efforts to improve the balance of payments position, import licenses for raw materials and supplies for manufacturing were cut back heavily. The action reportedly had a serious impact on production.

Manufacturing has accounted for roughly 13 percent of annual GDP compared with an average of about 35 percent for agriculture. Creation of manufacturing jobs has been a major objective of the government's development efforts. In the 1964-81 period the number of wage employees in the sector rose from 61,000 to 117,000 in private enterprise operations; in 1981 there were additionally about 30,000 others in public sector manufacturing activities. Although manufacturing has been of undoubted importance to the economy, its actual contribution to employment has remained relatively small, the number employed in the sector constituting only about 2 percent of the country's total labor force.

Little development of modern manufacturing occurred until World War II. This has been attributed in part to the smallness of the local market and in part to the limited financing available for new enterprises. A leading factor, however, appeared to have been the general feeling in British government circles that the East African colonies should be primarily sources of raw materials and markets for British manufactures. But also significant were the generally successful efforts of British industrialists, whose goods were marketed in Kenya, in blocking the establishment of competitive operations there. A prime example was the prevention of the opening of textile mills in the colony, proposed at various times by interests in India. The very few modern plants started during this time were concerned almost entirely with the processing of agricultural raw materials. They included sugar and vegetable oil mills, breweries, various other food-processing facilities, and cotton gins. The main exception was the production of soda ash (see Mining, this ch.).

Attitudes in the British home government toward industrialization in the colonies changed after World War II. Substantial savings had been accumulated in Kenya during the war years, and an inflow of foreign investment funds began. The domestic market had expanded with the increase in wage labor, and new demands for consumer goods had appeared and continued to grow in the 1950s. By the time of national independence the country had a well-developed manufacturing sector. Production was largely of import substitution goods aimed not only at the Kenyan market but also at the broader common market that encompassed Tanzania and Uganda (see Foreign Relations and Conflicts, ch. 1). Multinational corporations were extensively involved in the expansion, especially in the establishment of the larger enterprises. Their entry into the Kenyan market was based on a number of reasons, not the least of which was the capitalist character of the economy. More specifically, however, the goal of a substantial number, especially after independence, was to establish subsidiaries that would introduce or expand the sale of the products of the parent company. Profits, reduction in shipping costs and, in some cases, the availability of raw materials were also significant considerations.

The establishment of new enterprises and expansion of existing facilities continued after independence, financed by both Kenyan and multinational sources. Throughout the 1970s import substitution continued to be the main thrust of the new operations, encouraged by government policies that gave them strong protection from foreign competition. Various devices were used to do this, including tariffs, selective quotas, licensing, and export rebates. The success of the policies was apparent in a comparison of manufactured goods imports for 1972 and 1978 that showed a drop during the period from 44 percent of total imports to 31 percent. Concentration on the domestic market was also indicated by a decline in exports of manufactured goods relative to total output from 23 percent to 11 percent. The emphasis on a protected market has a number of negative features, according to observers, tending to result in inefficient operations, higher costs for the consumer, and goods that are not competitive in foreign markets, the latter factor reducing exports and foreign exchange earnings.

Mining

More than 100 useful minerals have been found in Kenya, ranging from barite, copper, diatomite, gold, gypsum, kaolin, and limestone to magnesite, magnetite, salt, soda ash, vermiculite, and wollastonite. A variety of precious and semiprecious stones, including aquamarine, garnet, ruby, sapphire, and tourmaline also occur. But none of the major minerals used by the industrialized countries had been discovered in internationally significant quantities through mid-1983. Only about 15 minerals, other than gemstones, were actually exploited, and the mining industry's contribution to the economy was very moderate (see table 4, Appendix). The main foreign exchange earners were soda ash (anhydrous calcium carbonate) and fluorspar (fluorite). Limestone and coral rock were present in great abundance. Processed into cement, they also brought in large export earnings.

The source of soda ash, which is used in glassmaking, the manufacture of soaps and cleansers, and various industrial processes, is Lake Magadi. Large quantities of salt, mostly used domestically, are also recovered from the lake. The lake, which has no outlet, is situated in the Rift Valley about 120 kilometers southwest of Nairobi. Its bed, dry except during the rainy period when it is covered by 10 to 20 centimeters of water at most, consists of a vast deposit of the mineral trona (from which soda ash is produced), estimated at over 100 million tons. The deposit was built up over a great length of time from materials leached from the surrounding lava, a process that still continues. The deposit has been exploited by the Magadi Soda Company, founded in 1911. In part delayed by World War I, the first commercial production of trona started only in 1915 and soda ash in 1919. In 1926 the original company was acquired by a British firm, Imperial Chemical Industries, and subsequent to independence the Kenya government secured a minority interest. Soda ash exports go almost entirely to other African states and to Middle Eastern and Far Eastern countries.

Limited quantities of fluorspar, a mineral used mainly in the open-hearth production of steel, in processing aluminum, and in the manufacture of various chemicals, were mined in the late 1960s. In 1971 the newly formed Kenya Fluorspar Company, a joint venture of ICDC, the Continental Ore Corporation of the United States, and Associated Portland Cement of Kenya, began development of a large deposit of fluorspar, estimated at over 9 million tons, near the town of Eldama Ravine in the Kerio River valley of Rift Valley Province. Production increased steadily and reached a peak of 124,000 tons in 1977. World prices for fluorspar declined in the late 1970s, and production decreased. But in the early 1980s prices improved, and earnings rose substantially on lower quantities exported.

World prices have been a major factor in Kenyan mining development. Examples include copper, moderate-sized deposits of which have been located. From the early 1950s copper ore was exported, but by the mid-1960s a decline in the world price accompanied by high production costs resulted in virtual discontinuance of mining. Since the early 1970s copper has not been listed in usual mineral production statistics. Another example is mullite, used in spark plugs and refractory porcelains. Kenya was the world's largest producer of this mineral in the late 1940s. During the 1950s, as the result of cost factors, the Kenyan product was no longer competitive, and mining of the deposit, near Taveta in Coast Province, ceased in 1961.

Energy Sources and Use

In the early 1980s Kenya's principal indigenous sources of energy were wood (and charcoal) and hydrothermally and geothermally generated electricity; alcohol, produced in quantity from domestic molasses for blending to make gasohol, became potentially an important new source in late 1982.There were no known domestic deposits of coal or lignite, nor had petroleum been discovered, although small amounts of natural gas had been found during explorations for oil. Estimates of contributions to the country's overall energy consumption were necessarily very rough, but wood and charcoal were believed to account for 48 to 50 percent of the total, and domestically generated electricity for 7 to 8 percent. Most of the remaining energy was furnished by imported petroleum and petroleum products, estimated to acount for about 40 percent of overall consumption. The rest consisted of electricity imported from Uganda and small but increasing amounts of imported coal (and some coke), used mostly by the country's cement plants, which in 1983 were in the process of converting from oil.

There was a sharp demarcation between the sources of energy used by the 85 percent of the population living in rural areas and energy used by the modern sector. In rural consumption the basic energy sources were overwhelmingly wood and charcoal. Some kerosine (commonly called paraffin in Kenya) was also used for illumination and a small amount of cooking. In the modern sector petroleum and petroleum products usually supplied over 80 percent of the energy consumed; electricity provided roughly 15 percent, and coal, coke, wood, and charcoal supplied the remainder. Proportions varied somewhat depending on natural factors that affected the quantity of hydroelectric power produced.

Wood and Vegetable Residues

Wood supplied about 84 percent of the energy used by rural households, and charcoal accounted for almost 6 percent. Most of these materials were used for cooking and the rest for heating at certain times of the year. Charcoal was an essential fuel for many families in urban areas, and some wood was also burned there. The total amount of wood needed to satisfy demands was growing at a rate roughly paralleling the increase in the population. In mid-1982 the minister of energy estimated the annual requirement at some 18.7 million tons. About 13 million tons were being furnished by forest and woodlot sources on a sustained basis. The remaining 5.7 million tons were obtainable only through the diminution of the country's tree stock. By the mid-1980s the estimated demand was expected to exceed the total available domestic supply. Some crop wastes, cow dung, and other organic materials were used locally for fuel. Bagasse (sugarcane waste) was used by the country's sugar factories for fuel.

Electric Power

At the beginning of the 1980s about 6 percent of Kenya's population had access to electricity. This was available through an interconnected generation and distribution system that served mainly the heavily populated corridor stretching from east of Nairobi westward to Kisumu and the Ugandan border and a region along the coast centered on Mombasa. Four towns outside this national net, Lamu and Garissa in eastern Kenya and Homa Bay and Kitale in the west, had their own generating and local distribution facilities. Most of the power came from hydroelectric generation. The country's rivers had an estimated total generating potential of about 6,000 megawatts, but about one-half of this was in small rivers impracticable to develop because of cost factors. Foreign specialists assessing the remaining potential concluded that utilization of only some 800 megawatts was economically feasible as of 1983. The Tana River accounted for about 625 megawatts of the total, and completed installations amounted to 347 megawatts. Among other rivers, the Turkwel in the upper Rift Valley had the largest potential, estimated at about 120 megawatts.

Geothermal energy (natural steam under pressure) was the only other significant domestic source for generation of electricity. Explorations begun in the mid-1950s located several potential sites in the Rift Valley. From 1970 investigations were intensified, assisted by the United Nations Development Program, and resulted in the location of a major geothermal source at Olkaria, south of Lake Naivasha. Tests indicated a generating potential of 100 to 200 megawatts of electricity at the site. The increase in world oil prices after the mid-1970s gave a new competitiveness to geothermally generated power and stimulated drilling that in 1978 produced wells at Olkaria capable of generating over 40 megawatts of power. In 1980, with external financing from the World Bank and the Commonwealth Development Corporation (CDC), construction was started on a power station to house two 15-megawatt generators, together with transmission lines and other requirements. The first of the generators went into operation in August 1981 and the second in December 1982. Funding for a project that included the provision of a third 15-megawatt generator was under negotiation in mid-1983 with the World Bank, the CDC, and the European Investment Bank.

In mid-1983 installed generating capacity totaled about 538 megawatts. Hydroelectric generation accounted for 346.5 megawatts and geothermal power for 30 megawatts. The sole thermal power station, at Kipevu near Mombasa, generated 98 megawatts. Gas turbines at Nairobi and Kipevu accounted for 30.1 megawatts, diesel stations in the interconnected system for 31.5 megawatts, and isolated diesel plants for 2.2 megawatts. Under an arrangement with the Uganda Electricity Board, another 30 megawatts were available to the Kenya system annually, but the amount of power actually supplied varied. Additionally, there were private power-generating facilities having a combined capacity of close to 40 megawatts. The amount of power generated grew substantially in the 1970s as new hydroelectric facilities were completed on the Tana River. Total output rose from 513.4 million kilowatt-hours in 1970—an additional 247.2 million were received from Uganda—to over 1.7 billion kilowatt-hours in 1981 (Uganda supplied 194 million kilowatt-hours that year). The electricity supply potential was further increased in 1981-82 by the completion of the two geothermal generating units and the new Masinga Dam facility on the upper Tana River. The Development Plan 1979-83 included a start on the construction of a power plant on the Tana River near Kiambere. Substantial foreign funding was required for the project, but this had not been ensured as of mid-1983.

About 80 percent of the power distributed went to Nairobi and Mombasa; the capital city and its vicinity used about 56 percent, and Mombasa about 24 to 25 percent. Among the main consumers, households accounted for 27 percent of annual power sales in the period 1979-81. Industrial use had increased during this time from 33 percent to almost 39 percent. Consumption by the commercial sector, the other main user, declined relatively from 30 percent in 1979 to less than 26 percent in 1981. Rural electrification schemes have brought electricity to various areas, but the programs have not ordinarily been economically viable because of installation costs resulting from the wide dispersal of rural households and the small amount of electricity used, which was the result of the inability to pay for more than simple lighting. The government has promoted rural electrification and in effect has sudsidized the schemes as a way to stimulate local commercial and industrial activities and, thereby, potentially to reduce movement to the urban centers.

In mid-1983 three companies were involved in the operation of the electric power system: the East African Power and Lighting Company (EAP&L), the Kenya Power Company (KPC), and the Tana River Development Company (TRDC). The first was privately run, although the government has had a majority stockholding since 1970. The others were fully government owned but were staffed and managed by EAP&L. EAP&L, which operated four small hydroelectric plants and the system's steam, diesel, and gas turbine units, was also the sole distributor of electricity throughout the country. The company was founded in 1922 through the merger of private power companies in Nairobi (established in 1907) and Mombasa (1909). KPC was set up in 1955 by EAP&L primarily as a means to obtain funds for expansion of the power system and to finance the construction of a transmission connection with the power system in Uganda, which at the time was also owned by EAP&L. KPC assumed ownership of two EAP&L hydroelectric plants on the Tana River, selling their output and the power acquired from Uganda to EAP&L. The government initially held a one-third interest in the KPC undertaking; it acquired full ownership in 1971. KPC has been the implementing agency in the development of the Olkaria geothermal power project.

The TRDC was also established by EAP&L in 1964 as a way to secure loan capital for development of the hydroelectric potential of the Tana River. The government, which originally held a one-third interest, secured full ownership in 1971. The TRDC built the country's three largest hydroelectric facilities (at Gitaru, Kamburu, and Kindaruma), which in 1983 together had an installed capacity of 280.5 megawatts. A fourth fully government-owned agency, the Tana and Athi Rivers Development Authority (TARDA), has also been involved since 1982 in supplying electricity to EAP&L from generators at Masinga Dam on the Tana River, which were installed as part of that multipurpose project.

Petroleum

Sedimentary deposits in northeastern Kenya and off the east coast are geologically considered promising sources of oil and natural gas. Various United States and European oil companies have engaged sporadically in exploratory work that started in North-Eastern Province in 1954. Only traces of natural gas had been found, but foreign interest continued and explorations were undertaken at various times during the 1960s and 1970s; the first drilling began in the early 1970s. In 1980 the government awarded a contract to Kenya Cities Service, a consortium of American companies, to explore for oil in the offshore area between Malindi and Lamu. Drilling by this group began at the end of 1981, but through mid-1983 discoveries, if any, had not been reported.

Most of the petroleum products used in East Africa in the colonial period were imported through Mombasa. In 1960 the port was selected as the site of the new East African Refinery, which would use existing distribution channels to provide its products to Uganda, Tanganyika, Rwanda, and Burundi, as well as Kenya. Since it opened in November 1963, the plant has produced a variety of products, including gasoline, kerosine for lighting and cooking, jet engine fuel (more than 80 percent sold to foreign airlines at Kenyan airports), light diesel fuel (used increasingly by motor transport), and heavy diesel and fuel oils. The plant's initial processing capacity of about 2.8 million tons of crude oil a year was increased to 4.2 million tons through completion in 1974 of improvements in processing operations and some extension of facilities. The initial throughput of 1.5 million tons in 1964 rose to almost 3 million tons in 1974 and 1975 but declined to about 2.6 to 2.7 million tons (62 to 64 percent of capacity) annually during the 1977-81 period. An exception occurred in 1980 when output was raised to over 3 million tons as an offset to reduced hydroelectric power generation because of water shortages.

From 1964 to 1973 the refinery exported about 55 percent of its output, and receipts covered approximately the cost of the petroleum products used in Kenya; imports and exports were relatively in balance in monetary terms. In 1973 oil and oil products imports required less than 1 percent of the country's foreign exchange earnings. Since 1973, despite the dramatic rise in world oil prices, a steady increase in the use of petroleum products has occurred. At the same time, declining exports have been affected by factors that included the breakup of the East African Community (EAC), difficulties with Tanzania, and the economic situation in Uganda. Oil products exports declined to less than 44 percent of refinery output in 1981, and after adjustment for receipts, Kenya's oil and oil products import costs were equivalent to 57 percent of total merchandise export earnings (see Foreign Trade and Balance of Payments, this ch.).

For several years after the opening of the Mombasa refinery, its products were transported to Nairobi by railroad. After completion of the paving of the Mombasa-Nairobi road in 1968, an increasing quantity was carried by road transport, and by 1974 the latter acccounted for about one-half of the 1 million tons moved annually. In view of the serious and increasing damage to the road caused by the tanker trucks, as well as the expense of maintaining the road, the government in 1974 set up the wholly state-owned Kenya Pipeline Company to construct and operate a 449-kilometer pipeline from the refinery to Nairobi. Partially financed by the World Bank, the line, consisting of 14-inch steel pipe and having an annual throughput capacity of about 1 million tons, began commercial operations in February 1978 transporting gasoline, kerosine, and diesel fuels. Four pumping stations moved the products from sea level to a tank farm at Nairobi, 1,800 meters in elevation; 10 days were required for a product to traverse the distance.

Transportation

In the early 1980s the transport system was one of the best developed on the continent in terms of meeting the needs of the majority of the country's population, who inhabited the central highlands and the southwest. It included rail, road, and air facilities, limited inland waterway transport (on Lake Victoria), a major seaport at Mombasa, and an oil pipeline running from a refinery at the port to Nairobi (see fig. 13). The vast, sparsely populated areas east and north of the highlands, however, were generally served only by scattered roads and a few dirt runway airstrips. The route of the country's only main rail line, constructed in the early colonial period, traversed the heavily populated corridor that ran from Mombasa to Nairobi west to the Ugandan border. In 1983 the line also formed an important transport route to the Indian Ocean for Uganda and other interior states in the region. Expansion and upgrading of the road network from the mid-1960s had stimulated a rapid growth of that transport mode, which by the early 1970s had become the dominant form of inland transportation. Steamer service on Lake Victoria, especially the rail ferry service, had been economically quite important during the EAC period. Since 1977 Kenya has operated a domestic service in its territorial waters, mainly involving movement of agricultural products from Homa Bay to Kisumu for transshipment by rail.

Railroads

Kenya's public railroad system, Kenya Railways, began operating as a national railroad only in 1977. From 1948 until that time the system had formed part of (with the railroads of Tanganyika and Uganda) first the East African Railways and Harbours Administration and then, from 1967 when the EAC was established, the East African Railways Corporation (EARC). During the 1970s there was a growing divergence of national interests and an inability to agree on a common plan for operating and developing the EARC, accompanied especially from 1974 by maintenance problems that were damaging to operations. In January 1977 the Kenyan government announced that it had withdrawn from the EARC and would operate its rail system independently. This move was formalized in January 1978 when the Kenya Railways Corporation (KRC) was set up as a fully government-owned parastatal body responsible ultimately to the Ministry of Transportation and Communications. The corporation operates both Kenya Railways and the transport system on Lake Victoria.

The KRC system in 1983 comprised 2,060 kilometers of one-meter-gauge single track. Somewhat more than one-half (1,085 kilometers) constituted the main line, which ran from the port of Mombasa through Nairobi, Nakuru, and Eldoret to the Ugandan border. The main line, when originally built in the late nineteenth century, had run from Nakuru to Kisumu on Lake Victoria, from which a connection with Uganda, one of the primary reasons for the railroad's construction, was made by boat. The growth of European settlements in the western part of the former White Highlands in the early 1900s and the advantages of a direct rail line to Uganda led to the building, during 1925 and 1926, of the main line section through Eldoret. Branch lines were also built to serve European farming communities in the highlands, including lines to Kitale and Solai in 1926, Nyahururu in 1929, and Nanyuki in 1930. On the section between Nairobi and Mombasa, branch lines had been opened to Lake Magadi in 1915 for exploitation of the lake's mineral deposits and to Taveta on the Tanzanian border. The latter line was originally constructed principally to aid the British campaign against German East Africa during World War I. Subsequently,

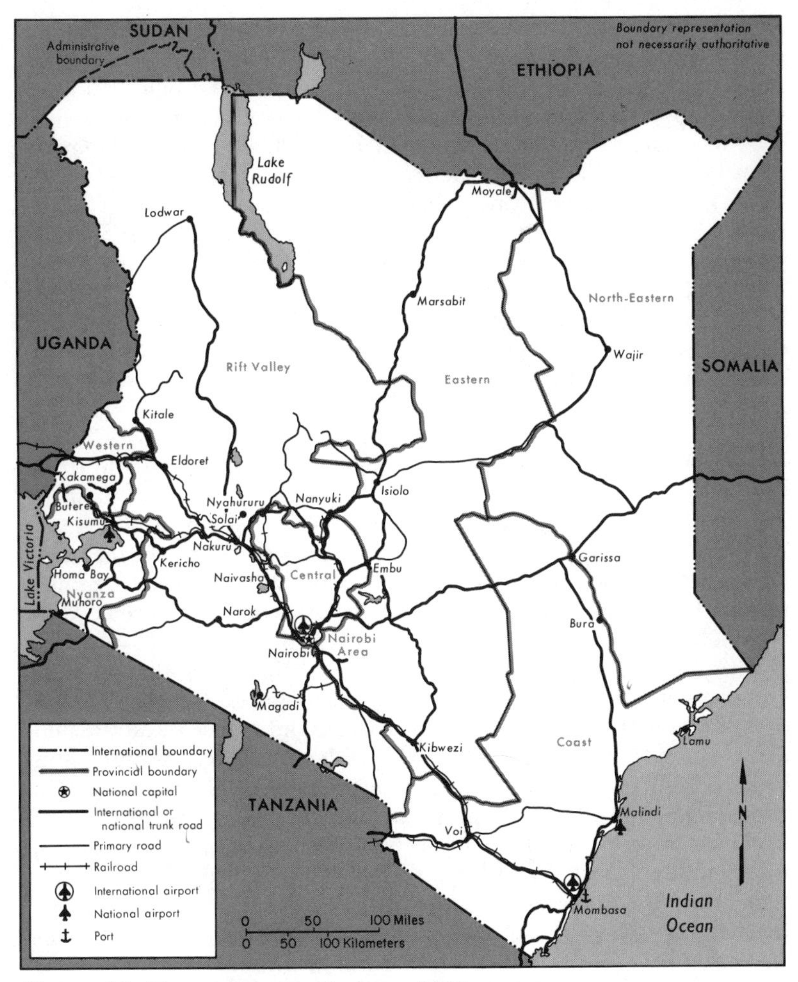

Figure 13. Transportation System, 1983

this line was extended into Tanganyika and became a major route for shipment of agricultural products from the rich Arusha-Moshi area in the northern part of that colony to Mombasa. In 1977, largely as an outcome of the collapse of the EAC, Tanzania closed the line at its border; it remained closed in mid-1983. The branch lines totaled 975 kilometers. From 1930 to mid-1983 new construction had not been carried out on the rail system. However, it was reported in 1982 that Saudi Arabia was to provide financial assistance to build a rail extension in the Kerio River valley.

Until the late 1960s the railroad had enjoyed a virtual monopoly on freight traffic, aided by government measures that greatly limited road transport. Completion of a paved road from Mombasa through Nairobi to the Ugandan border in 1969, paralleled by an increase in issuances of road-transport operating licenses, brought growing road competition. Further road development in the 1970s, as well as railroad equipment shortages and operational problems from 1974 through 1978, led many shippers to turn to road transport which, although more expensive, was faster and more reliable. In 1977, after the establishment of Kenya Railways as an independent operation, the government provided some KSh100 million to revitalize rail services. New equipment included 26 main-line diesel locomotives and 1,200 freight cars, most of which had arrived by 1979. Additional equipment, maintenance facilities, track improvement, and other features were financed through loans from the Federal Republic of Germany (West Germany), Sweden, the African Development Bank, and the World Bank. Dieselization, which had started in 1958, was completed in 1980. That same year Kenya Railways had 335 locomotives of all types, compared with 221 in 1977; freight car units numbered 13,748, as against the 1977 total of 11,179; and there were 552 passenger cars compared with 515 of the earlier period.

Transit traffic through Kenya has been an important part of Kenya Railways' operations. Two-way movement of Ugandan goods, including some traffic to and from Rwanda and Burundi, totaled over 1.3 million tons in 1971, one-third of Kenya's railroad tonnage at the time. More than 300,000 tons of Tanzanian traffic was also handled that year. The EARC's operational problems (beginning in 1974 and continuing in the first years of Kenya Railways), growing economic difficulties in Uganda, deterioration of Uganda Railways' services, and inadequate transshipment facilities at the Kenya-Uganda border resulted in a precipitous drop in the Kenyan system's Ugandan traffic to 149,000 tons in 1979. Tanzanian traffic had also declined and was stopped completely in 1977 by Tanzania's closing of its border with Kenya. A major outcome of these problems was that a large part of the transit traffic was lost to road transport. Analyses of transport cost factors in Kenya have shown that for long hauls, rail transport has been much more cost efficient. As a measure to help the KRC, the government planned to construct two truck-weighing stations between Mombasa and Nairobi to control truck load limits and reduce unfair competitive practices. This action was also designed to reduce wear and tear on the roads. In western Kenya for this latter reason, the government in mid-1983 was prepared to ban all road movement of logs by trucks to the Webuye paper mill. A container terminal had also been built at Nairobi (another was to be constructed at Eldoret) to promote freight movement by rail.

Roads

At independence the new government inherited a relatively extensive, but uncoordinated, road system, which consisted principally of gravel and earth roads; of the some 42,000 kilometers of roads in 1963, less than 1,800 kilometers (about 4 percent) were asphalt surfaced. This situation was mainly the result of colonial policies that had favored rail transport, while discouraging road transport development through

Development of Kenya's road system has provided essential transportation services to rural areas, where the bulk of the country's population resides.
Courtesy Barbara Hately-Smith

a highly restrictive operator-licensing program. From the mid-1960s the government began easing the restrictions, at the same time undertaking a major road improvement program and the development of a national trunk-road system to link Nairobi and the other major towns. In 1968 asphalting of the last section of the road from Mombasa to Nairobi was completed, and in 1969 paving of a stretch from Eldoret to the Ugandan border opened a continuous surfaced highway across Kenya. By 1974 almost all major urban centers also had been connected by asphalt highways.

Part of the early development program was the construction or improvement of feeder roads from certain agricultural areas to the main roads. Notable was the opening up of the country's tea-growing regions, in which World Bank funding played a significant role, and the development of access roads to the various settlement schemes. Other similar roads constructed in the course of the decade opened up the country's sugarcane-growing regions and provided road access to various tourist centers. In 1974 the government initiated, with substantial foreign financial and technical aid, the Rural Access Roads Program (RARP) to provide improved access to markets from high-potential farming areas. The goal was 14,000 kilometers of newly constructed roads and upgraded rural tracks. The project was also specifically developed as a labor-intensive undertaking to create employment in rural areas. Reportedly about 4,500 kilometers had been built by the end of 1981, of which 1,400 kilometers were graveled. Foreign evaluations have attributed marked success to this program and have recommended consideration of the methodology to other developing countries.

By mid-1981 the officially classified road network totaled some 52,675 kilometers, of which 6,540 kilometers (about 12 percent) were paved. Roughly 100,000 kilometers of tracks and unclassified roads were also estimated to exist in rural areas. The classified road system was divided into five main categories. From the standpoint of upgrading, improvement, and new construction, three have received special attention. They were the international trunk roads (3,600 kilometers, two-thirds paved in 1981), which run to neighboring Ethiopia, Somalia, Tanzania, and Uganda (work was also under way in 1983 on a modern road to southern Sudan); national trunk roads, which made up another 2,785 kilometers (two-thirds paved); and the primary road system (total length 7,750 kilometers, of which one-quarter was paved), which links important provincial centers. The remaining roads (secondary and minor) totaled almost 32,000 kilometers; they served local needs, tying rural centers together and providing general access roads for rural areas. Less than 3 percent of these roads were paved. Some 7,500 kilometers were classified as special roads, encompassing those in the various special-access programs.

Ports and Shipping

Located at Mombasa on Mombasa Island and the adjacent mainland in a naturally sheltered inlet, Kenya's major commercial port of Kil-

The modern harbor at Mombasa, Kenya's major port on the Indian Ocean, teems with ships and cargo-handling cranes.
Courtesy The Lamp, Exxon Corporation

indini was in 1983 the best equipped and most modern port on the East African coast. Its facilities were important not only to the country's own economy but also to landlocked Uganda, Rwanda, and Burundi and to eastern Zaïre and southern Sudan, whose foreign trade transited the port. Mombasa had for centuries been a harbor for Indian Ocean dhow traffic (see The Kenya Coast, ch. 1). Its start as a modern port began in 1895 with the construction of a jetty to off-load supplies for the new Mombasa-Lake Victoria railroad. The first deep-water berths were added between 1926 and 1931. After World War II, facilities were gradually expanded, and in 1983 Kilindini possessed 14 deep-water berths, which included facilities for handling general, bulk, and container cargo—the latter at three specialized berths, one of which also handled roll-on-roll-off cargo. In addition, there were two tanker berths for the bulk transfer of crude and refined petroleum. The port was well equipped with cranes, forklift trucks, tractors, trailers, and other equipment. It offered extensive covered and open storage facilities, including a large cold storage facility, and had direct connection with Kenya Railways. In early 1978 a large dry dock capable of carrying out maintenance work on vessels up to 18,000 gross registered tons had been added to the port facilities. In addition to servicing foreign ships, the new dry dock permitted for the first time complete domestic maintenance of Kenyan merchant and naval vessels. The entrance to Mombasa harbor was dredged in 1980-81 to permit the entrance of vessels of greater draft. This was financed by the Netherlands. Additional funding furnished by USAID resulted in further deepening of the channel in 1982, which allowed United States aircraft carriers to enter the harbor.

From 1975 through 1979 the port handled close to 6 million tons of cargo annually. Exports averaged about 1.9 million tons, of which dry cargo, including tea, coffee, and cement, was about 1.5 million tons; the remainder consisted of bulk petroleum products and some edible oils. Imports averaged about 4 million tons a year. Bulk petroleum imports varied between two-thirds and three-quarters of the total. In 1980 and 1981 the cargo throughput rose substantially to 7.5 million tons and 8.9 million tons, respectively, mainly owing to increased imports of dry cargo and petroleum; the proportion of the latter remained at about two-thirds to three-quarters of total imports, however. A notable feature in the period 1975-81 was the growing container traffic; measured in 20-foot equivalent units, the number rose from 1,298 in 1975 to 44,036 in 1981; it increased to 56,638 in 1982. The number of steamships entering Mombasa Harbor varied annually during this time but was about 1,600, ranging in total gross registered tonnage between roughly 5.6 and 6.3 million tons.

Since the breakup of the EAC in 1977, operation of the port has been under the Kenya Ports Authority (KPA), a parastatal body that was given legal status in February 1978. KPA also was responsible for the historic port of Mombasa located on the other side of Mombasa Island, which in 1983 was used by dhows, coastal vessels, and small bulk cement carriers. Additionally, KPA operated a number of minor ports, including Kilifi, Malindi, and Lamu along the coast north of Mombasa and Shimoni to the south. These ports were used by small fishing boats, ships involved in coastal trade, and pleasure craft.

Civil Aviation

In mid-1983 Kenya had two major air facilities: Jomo Kenyatta International Airport at Nairobi and Moi International Airport at Mombasa; medium-sized airports had been developed at Kisumu and Malindi. A fifth airfield, Wilson Airport at Nairobi, was used mainly by air charter operations but also serviced private company flights, the Kenya Police air wing, the government wildlife conservation service, and miscellaneous other activities. Widely dispersed throughout the country were more than 200 landing strips. Many were reportedly unusable, and few had paved runways. Usable strips, however, provided aerial access to many towns, tourist spots, isolated farming areas (for instance, along the Tana River), and other points. Scheduled domestic service between the four regular airports was furnished by the government-owned Kenya Airways, using a complement of two Fokker 27 Friendships and one DC-9. The airline first began operations in February 1977 after East African Airways (EAA), the common air service of the EAC, ceased operations because of financial difficulties. Air service to other parts of Kenya, some on regular schedules, was furnished by private charter operators.

International service was furnished also by Kenya Airways and by nearly 30 international airlines,including most of the major carriers. In early 1983 Kenya Airways flew daily to London. Other destinations in Europe were Athens, Copenhagen (the latter in conjunction with Scandinavian Airlines System), Frankfurt, Paris, Rome, and Zurich. It also flew to Bombay and Karachi in Asia and to Jeddah in the Middle East. Its African services included Addis Ababa, Cairo, Entebbe, Harare, Khartoum, Lusaka, Mahé in Seychelles, and Mogadishu. Aircraft used for the international and regional services included three Boeing 707s, one Boeing 727 and, during the main tourist season from about December to February, a leased wide-body Boeing 747.

Jomo Kenyatta International Airport is one of Africa's major air hubs. In the early 1980s over 1.4 million passengers annually landed at, embarked from, or transited the airport. Mombasa handled roughly 370,000 additional passengers. Of the approximately 1.3 million international passengers who began or ended flights at Nairobi and Mombasa, Kenya Airways served almost 234,000 in 1980 and 298,500 in 1981. A substantial amount of outgoing air freight, largely fresh vegetables and flowers, also originated from both airports—an average of over 20,000 tons annually from Nairobi and more than 9,000 tons from Mombasa in the late 1970s and early 1980s. Kenya Airways handled an average of about 4,500 tons of freight and mail annually during the same period.

Kenya Airways has experienced financial problems since its establishment. It started operations at a time when fuel prices, already high, continued to climb. Its fleet has been fuel inefficient, and the airline has faced intense competition from major United States and European carriers. Losses were regularly experienced, and by March 1980 the accumulated total had reached over KSh300 million. Restructuring of operations occurred in late 1981, including cutbacks of personnel and hiring of several expatriate professional staffs, but in late 1982 total losses were reported to have risen to about KSh600 million. Operating shortfalls were covered through government subsidies. The government appeared determined, however, to maintain a national flag carrier, approaching the situation from a long-range operational viewpoint that included approval in 1981 of a 15-year development plan providing eventual purchase of several more modern aircraft.

Employment, Wages, and Prices

The country's labor force, defined to include individuals between the ages of 15 and 64 years, totaled over 7.3 million at the time of the 1979 census. Of that total, more than 3.7 million were females. There were additionally more than 2 million young people in the 10- to 14-

year age bracket. Most resided in the rural areas, where many were in fact part of the economically active work force. A survey in 1977 and 1978 found that over 43 percent of males and almost 38 percent of females aged 10 to 14 were working. Over 41 percent of boys and 38 percent of girls aged 8 and 9 were also at work. Wage employment in the modern sector (in both urban and rural areas) included over 1 million people in 1981, approximately four times greater than in 1964. More than 80 percent were wage employees, about 5 percent were self-employed and unpaid family members, and the remainder (12.6 percent in 1981) were in the so-called urban areas informal sector. The latter in 1981 was estimated to consist of over 157,000 individuals engaged in a variety of small-scale occupations, such as shoe repairing, tailoring, hawking, peddling, operation of unlicensed taxis, and the like; by definition of the Central Bureau of Statistics, they conducted business in temporary structures or in open spaces. Operations were small-scale, labor intensive, and catered mainly to people of low incomes; a large number of these operations were in the squatter sections of the towns. Licensing regulations tended to discriminate against the group, and individual activities were often illegal. In the wage employee group, there was a steady rise during the 1970s in the number of public sector employees, which increased from 287,000 in 1972 to 424,800 in 1979; the total continued to rise in the early 1980s and reached 484,100 in 1981. Proportionately, public sector employees increased during the 1972-81 period from 40 percent to more than 47 percent of all wage employees.

By industry, the largest number of wage employees in the private sector was in agriculture and forestry. The sector has shown a gradual decline in the number of reported workers. This has been largely due to division of the large estates into small holdings, the owners of which have become self-employed instead of being wage employees. (The very sizable smallholder sector was not included in statistics on wage employment.) The decline in the reported number of agricultural wageworkers largely accounted for an apparently low growth rate in total wage employment. The number of employees in manufacturing has grown steadily except in 1980 when drought-caused shortages of commodities reduced plant operations, resulting in worker layoffs and a cutback in new hirings. Community, social, and personal services employment constituted the largest category in the public sector. Educational services, the major component, accounted for about 45 percent of all public employees at the beginning of the 1980s (see table 5, Appendix).

Statutory minimum-wage scales have been in force since national independence. Wages above the minimum were agreed on, either through collective bargaining or by wage councils that were appointed by the minister of labor to fix wages and conditions of employment for specific industries, trades, or occupations. In both cases, any new wage agreement had to be approved by the Industrial Court, consisting of members appointed by the president of Kenya and his minister of labor. The court's determinations had to conform with guidelines established by the government relative to the sizes of increases and the like. Minimum-wage increases have been made from time to time, and pressures for upward revisions increased as inflation mounted in the 1970s. Minimums were raised in late 1973 and again in late 1974. But in May 1975, as inflation soared and under the threat of a major strike, the government again raised the minimum wage of workers in the private sector to KSh300 a month in Nairobi and Mombasa and to KSh275 for those in other urban centers. In July the minimum was also raised for civil servants to KSh350 a month (up from KSh240) in the two cities and to KSh300 elsewhere. Pay raises were also given to civil servants whose wages were above the minimum. In May the minimum for agricultural wage employees had been more than doubled from KSh70 to KSh150 a month.

In 1975 the government also decreed restrictions on cost-of-living increases, the new guidelines permitting full increases only for workers receiving KSh250 a month or less. A gradually diminishing scale was set for wages above that to KSh1,000, beyond which no increases were allowed. Subsequently, increases were limited to 75 percent of the rise in the cost of living as a measure not only to combat inflation but also to encourage job expansion. In 1977 a wage increase was granted civil servants. In 1980 the minimum wage was raised from KSh350 to KSh456 a month; for agricultural workers the minimum was set at KSh215. An analysis of government employee salaries during the period from 1973 to 1980 has shown that their average real wage—after taking into account the increase in inflation—was roughly 10 percent lower in 1980 than in 1972. However, in 1981, in line with recommendations of the Waruhiu Commission, established in 1979 to examine the question of public sector earnings, substantial wage increases were given to civil servants.

The rate of inflation, as measured by the Nairobi consumer price indexes for lower, middle-, and upper income groups, was extremely moderate from independence until the early 1970s. For households in the lower income index, that is, then earning under KSh350 a month, the annual average price rise (in 1964 prices) through 1969 was only slightly over 2 percent. Based on a revised index in 1969 prices and a new top earning level of KSh399, the lower income group through 1972 then experienced an annual inflation rate averaging 4 percent a year. From 1973, however, external factors (mainly the increase in oil import costs) introduced new inflationary pressures. Adding to the inflation were a liberal credit policy, the effects of erratic weather on food production, and official price increases for the main staples. These forces were reflected in steep rises in the inflation rate to 15 percent in 1973, almost 16.1 percent in 1974, and 20.3 percent in 1975. In 1976 a new base (January-June 1975 equaled 100) was introduced, and the lower income earning limit was set at KSh699 a month. From this higher base, in the four years from 1975 to 1979, the lower income index rose almost 64 percent. From January 1980 through March 1983 a further increase of 57 percent was recorded, and the annual rate from 1982 was over 20 percent. Price rises for the middle- and upper income groups (from 1975 classified as earning between KSh700 and KSh2,499 and KSh2,500 or more, respectively) varied somewhat from that of the lower group and each other. Until the late 1970s they had tended to be lower but in the early 1980s experienced roughly comparable inflation rates.

Foreign Trade and Balance of Payments

At independence 60 percent of Kenya's exports went to two main areas: Tanganyika and Uganda received well over 30 percent, and an additional some 29 percent was absorbed by Britain and the European Economic Community (EEC—also known as the Common Market). Britain then accounted for 21 percent of the exports destined for areas outside East Africa, and West Germany for some 23 or 24 percent (see table 6, Appendix). Exports to the EEC and Britain consisted mainly of coffee (the larger share went to West Germany), tea (the major item purchased by Britain), sisal fibers, and pyrethrum extract. Britain also received a substantial quantity of meat and meat products. A variety of consumer manufactures made up half of the exports to Tanganyika and Uganda; the remainder consisted largely of foodstuffs, beverages, and tobacco. At the time, including its major trading partners, Kenya was exporting to more than 70 countries in Africa and worldwide. Other important purchasers of Kenyan commodities were the United States, which received about 6 to 7 percent of total Kenyan exports (mainly coffee and pyrethrum extract), Canada, India, Japan, and South Africa. Exports to Eastern Europe were relatively negligible. After independence, trade with South Africa, both exports and imports, was discontinued as a sign of Kenya's opposition to apartheid.

Throughout the 1970s and in the early 1980s, the EEC (enlarged in 1973 by the inclusion of Britain, Denmark, and Ireland) continued to be the principal destination for exports. It accounted usually for about 30 percent of the total in the early 1970s, but during the coffee and tea booms of 1977-79, heavy purchases of those commodities—the former especially by West Germany and the Netherlands, and the latter by Britain—raised the EEC's share of the total to an average of almost 45 percent. In the early 1980s the EEC's share declined to about 30 percent. Britain and West Germany varied between first and second positions as principal buyers. Between them they accounted for about two-thirds of the EEC total.

Regionally, Africa continued in second place as consumer of Kenyan exports. However, a change in markets had occurred as a result of severe restrictions placed on certain Kenyan exports in 1977 by Tanzania, associated with the collapse of the EAC. Uganda remained the single largest importer of Kenyan exports; manufactured goods and refined petroleum products constituted the main items. Zambia and Zaïre remained important purchasers, but by the early 1980s Burundi and Rwanda had surpassed them, and exports to Sudan had also increased significantly. Kenya's market in Africa was largely concentrated in those nearby countries to which exports were able to move by road, rail, and the inland lakes of the region. Sales of fuel to foreign airlines and ships' stores had grown in importance from the mid-1970s and in the early 1980s accounted for 11 to 12 percent of export values. Increased earning from these sources, however, were largely the result of increases in the prices of petroleum products rather than any significant increase in quantities.

At independence the industrialized West, Japan, and India were the source of more than 60 percent of Kenyan imports. Tanganyika and Uganda accounted for only about 11 percent. With the exception of the Middle East, which supplied oil for the Mombasa refinery and refined petroleum products, other areas and countries provided relatively small amounts of imports. Britain was the largest source, a position it retained from the colonial period until 1980, when the value of oil imports propelled Saudi Arabia into first place. Britain's relative share had declined, however, from almost 27 percent of total imports in 1964 to 20 percent in 1975 and in the early 1980s to about 17 percent, as Kenya's share of expenditures for oil increased proportionately. For most of the postindependence period, imports from Japan were in second place, and those from West Germany third in value, but in the late 1970s West Germany replaced Japan (see table 7, Appendix).

The largest imports from the West and other areas outside the EAC, by economic categories, had been industrial materials and supplies, machinery, other capital equipment, and transport items. Until the mid-1970s petroleum fuels and lubricants, although imported in large quantities, constituted in value only a comparatively small part of total import values. The oil price increases during the rest of the decade and in the early 1980s, however, expanded the share of oils and lubricants from under 11 percent in 1973—compared with almost 39 percent for industrial supplies and 30 percent for machinery, other capital goods, and transport equipment—to almost 39 percent in 1981 as against 25 percent and 26.5 percent for the other categories, respectively.

Imports from Tanzania and Uganda consisted of foodstuffs, basic supplies (vegetable oil, electric power, and others), and some manufactured goods. After Kenyan independence the amounts imported increased, and in 1976, the year before the breakup of the EAC, Tanzania supplied 3 percent of Kenya's imports. After Tanzania closed its border in early 1977, however, the import trade declined rapidly and through mid-1983 remained negligible. Imports from Uganda, which included important quantities of cotton piece goods and of electric power, had been high through 1972, at which time they constituted 4 percent of total imports. In 1973 they began to decline, the result largely of deteriorating economic conditions in Uganda associated with the regime of Idi Amin Dada. By 1976 they were minor; subsequent imports through 1982 consisted mainly of electric power. There were reports in the early 1980s of unrecorded trade across the Kenya-Uganda border, and similar reports existed with respect to Tanzania, but there was little information on the amounts.

Kenya has experienced a consistently favorable balance in its trade with the former EAC area and with other countries in Africa. With the remainder of the world, however, there has been an overall deficit that grew substantially from 1974, except for the coffee and tea export boom year of 1977 when, excluding the cost of oil imports, there was a positive balance. Largely, but not entirely, responsible for the rising deficit were the increases in 1974 and 1979 in world oil prices. The inflationary impact on general prices worldwide of the oil increases also had an adverse effect on Kenya's terms of trade as prices of imports exceeded those for exports. However, an important factor in the growing deficit also was the generally expansionary domestic policy pursued with respect to credit and government overspending, which led to a much higher rate of growth in imports compared with exports. Merchandise trade deficits were only partially offset by the usually favorable net invisible receipts from freight and insurance, tourism (a major earner of foreign exchange in Kenya), and others. The result was a regular deficit in the current account component—which encompasses trade and invisible transactions—of the country's balance of payments statement, the summary in money terms of total transactions with the rest of the world (see table 10, Appendix).

During the 1970s the deficits in the current account were covered about half the time by capital inflows. In the period 1972-77 net private long-term capital inflows and public long-term capital from external sources were about equal in size. In 1978-80 the amounts in both sectors rose substantially but at a much higher rate in the public sector. Until 1978 capital inflows (external loans and grants) to the public sector had been largely used for development projects. But beginning in 1978, external borrowings were also made to cover balance of payments shortfalls, as foreign exchange reserves declined to the equivalent of about two and one-half months' import costs against a desirable minimum covering four months. The deterioration of the balance of payments continued, foreign reserves dropped to one and one-half months' import coverage, and the government resorted to large foreign borrowing in the Eurodollar market at high interest rates. The external debt repayable in foreign exchange or goods rose sharply from US$917 million in 1977 to over US$2.2 billion at the end of 1981.

Kenya has been the recipient of very substantial aid in the form of bilateral and multilateral official loans and grants. A large part of the loans were made on concessional terms, i.e., having lower than standard interest rates and long-term repayment periods. But from the late 1970s the government began securing loans from commercial sources on terms considerably less favorable (see table 8, Appendix). The increase in the total debt, as well as the more onerous terms, added significantly to the size of the foreign exchange required to meet regular payments on outstanding loans. In 1975 debt servicing costs had been equivalent to 3.1 percent in terms of goods and services but were 11.5

percent of merchandise export receipts. By 1982 the latter ratio had risen to 19 percent. The seriousness of the situation was emphasized by the parallel growing deficit in the trade balance; in 1975 export earnings had met 74 percent of import costs but in 1981 covered only 46 percent.

Government Finance

Since fiscal year (FY—see Glossary) 1967/68 the government's current revenues have exceeded expenditures, resulting in various-sized surpluses applicable toward implementation of the national development plans. Such surpluses have ranged from 5 percent to almost 40 percent of development and government investment expenditures. Immediately after independence, direct taxes, of which income taxes constituted over 90 percent, made up 37 to 38 percent of total tax revenues. Income tax receipts rose rapidly thereafter, and by FY 1972/73 direct taxes accounted for 47 percent of all tax receipts. Import duties and excise taxes (revenue from the latter came mainly from beer, cigarettes, and sugar) constituted almost all remaining tax receipts. Effective mainly beginning in calendar year 1973, a 10 percent sales tax (raised later to 15 percent) was introduced on manufactured goods; some exceptions included flour, sugar, medicines, and fertilizer. By FY 1974/75 sales taxes accounted for almost 40 percent of indirect tax receipts, and the share of the latter in total taxes rose to 61 percent. Subsequently, sales taxes were usually the largest item in indirect taxes, and by the early 1980s they provided the government with almost as much revenue as the income tax.

Expenditures (including recurrent and development) increased greatly from about the mid-1970s. After the collapse of the EAC, large expenditures were made in order to establish new national corporations, including Kenya Airways and Kenya Railways, and to build up Kenya's defense capabilities. The latter, which required major imports of equipment, were contributory in considerable part to the country's balance of payments problems (see Military Missions, Organization, and Strength, ch. 5). Expenditure on education, the largest single item in the budget, rose from some 10 percent of total expenditures in FY 1964/65 to 20 percent in FY 1975/76 as educational opportunities were expanded and school fees were gradually abolished. However, education's share declined in the late 1970s and early 1980s to about 17 or 18 percent. Despite the relative decline, the rate of increase in expenditure on education averaged well above the rate of inflation. Real growth also occurred in almost all other economic and social sectors (see table 9, Appendix).

A major budgetary problem that has caused concern in efforts to bring about economic recovery and to ease the balance of payments situation has been the growing gap between government overall expenditure and revenue. This was particularly noted by the minister of finance in presenting the budget for FY 1982/83, when he called attention to continuing unchecked government spending. Specifically, he pointed out that between 1976 and 1981 revenues available to the ministries had grown by 110 percent but that actual expenditures had increased by 129 percent. This had forced large borrowing from the domestic banking system, therby reducing significantly the funds available to the private sector for development. Overly large expenditures had also greatly reduced the potential surpluses from larger revenues that would help cut back on external loans. However, projected budget figures still indicated a shortfall in overall revenue and the need for further external financing.

* * *

There are few extensive analyses of the current Kenyan economy in published form. Although somewhat dated, a survey by Arthur Hazlewood, *The Economy of Kenya: The Kenyatta Era*, covers all economic sectors rather thoroughly. A thoughtful examination of Kenyan capitalism is presented by Nicola Swainson in *The Development of Corporate Capitalism in Kenya, 1918-77*. This work bears the imprint of intelligently critical Marxism without the jargon. Still of value is the 1972 International Labour Office report *Employment, Incomes, and Equality: A Strategy for Increasing Productive Employment in Kenya*. For regular sectoral statistical detail that also includes results of periodic rural and industrial surveys of varying comprehensiveness, the *Economic Survey* and the *Statistical Abstract*, prepared annually by Kenya's Central Bureau of Statistics, are invaluable. Important policy statements on the economy and development are found in the occasional Sessional Papers of the National Assembly. Current economic information is also available in the *Africa Research Bulletin* (Economic, Financial, and Technical Series). (For further information and complete citations, see Bibliography.)

Chapter 4. Government and Politics

Kenyatta statue in City Square, Nairobi

AFTER TWO DECADES of independence, it could plausibly be asserted that Kenya had established one of the most stable governments among the former colonial territories of Africa. Substantial changes in the political system have been effected by orderly processes. In 1964, one year after Kenya obtained full sovereignty, the form of government was converted from a federation under a British monarch to a republic under a president. The National Assembly, originally organized as two houses, became a unicameral body by constitutional amendment in 1966. Election of the president by the assembly was superseded by a system of direct popular election in 1969. The primacy of a single political party, the Kenya African National Union, was formalized in 1982 when Kenya became a de jure one-party state.

The pronounced democratic features of Kenya's original constitution have been generally respected, although important lapses have occurred. The rule of law has prevailed in daily life, and the judicial system has preserved its independence. Politics have been dominated by the overwhelmingly preponderant African segment of the population, but participation of European and Asian citizens has been accepted. Tolerance for dissenting views is not deeply entrenched, although public life is marked by animation and debate. The practice, during periods of tension, of prohibiting opposition figures against engaging in politics and detaining them for remarks or conduct judged to be subversive, has discouraged frankness and nonconformity.

The president of Kenya is the personification of the state and the preeminent source of national authority. He prescribes all laws, which are approved as presented, in most cases, by the National Assembly. Various political tendencies are represented to a certain extent within the monolithic single-party structure. The practice of approving several candidates to compete against one another in a single constituency offers the voters a democratic choice of who will best defend their interests in Nairobi. On one occasion an opposition movement, the Kenya People's Union, formed by defectors from the government party, banded together in the legislature to challenge the government. The government's repressive attitude toward this challenge from the political left culminated in the banning of the opposition group in 1969.

Jomo Kenyatta, a hero of the independence movement and Kenya's first president, died in 1978 and was succeeded through proper constitutional means by his vice president, Daniel arap Moi. The new president launched a highly popular program of economic relief and an easing of constraints in public life. However, concerned that relatively isolated acts of dissent could broaden and unleash serious demonstrations of discontent at a time when Kenya was facing unprecedented economic adversity, Moi gradually reversed his course. The air force coup attempt of August 1982, although quickly suppressed, revealed evidence of widespread social tension. The accepted scope of political debate was further narrowed as Moi sought to reinforce his authority over the governmental establishment. Amid allegations of plots and disloyalty in his own cabinet, Moi unexpectedly called an early election for September 1983. A new stage in Kenyan politics was expected to follow in which political notables of the 1970s would be supplanted by a group having closer personal identification with Moi. The opportunity seemed at hand to introduce a more cohesive and vigorous leadership style in the pursuit of Kenya's great promise as a nation.

Constitutional Development

Kenya became an independent member of the Commonwealth of Nations on December 12, 1963. The independence constitution had its origins in a conference held in London in early 1962. At that time, the country was still administered as a colony under a governor general appointed by the British monarch. Legislative and executive councils, chosen to represent Africans, Europeans, and Asians separately, had only advisory powers (see Development of the Independence Constitution, ch. 1).

An unusually detailed document of over 200 pages, the independence constitution conferred a system incorporating features of both a unitary and a federalist state. It called for retention of the queen of England as head of state, represented in Kenya by a governor general. The prime minister headed a cabinet that was collectively responsible to the National Assembly, a body composed of two chambers: the House of Representatives, where real power lay, and the Senate, which could delay legislation. Each of the regions had an elected assembly empowered to legislate over a range of matters, such as education, health, agriculture, part of the police forces, and local government.

The regional aspects of the independence constitution proved unworkable, however, because of the opposition of the civil service and the central government dominated by the Kenya African National Union (KANU). KANU contended that regional distribution of power was incompatible with efforts to ensure unity, efficient national planning, and adequate police protection. After less than a year, KANU introduced proposals to shift to a republican form of government, to abolish regional powers, and to unify the offices of the head of state and the head of government. The necessary constitutional amendments were initially blocked by the Kenya African Democratic Union (KADU), a minority party, but this obstacle was overcome when KADU merged with KANU. Thus, by the first anniversary of independence, Kenyatta and KANU had ushered in a constitutional and political party system conforming closely to their original objectives (see Party Politics in the 1960s, ch. 1).

The republican constitution, which was promulgated on December 12, 1964, was a much shortened document. An amendment in December 1966 combined the Senate and the House of Representatives in the unicameral National Assembly. In April 1969 the assembly adopted a revised constitution of 128 sections, incorporating several new provisions, although it did not bring about major changes. The 1969 Constitution remained substantially in force in 1983.

The Constitution may be amended by the passage of an act with not less than 65 percent of the vote of all members of parliament. A number of amendments have been brought into effect since 1969, including one permitting the use of the Swahili language in conducting assembly business, in addition to English. In 1982 the de facto status of Kenya as a one-party state was made mandatory by a series of amendments designating KANU as the only political party and requiring that every candidate for parliament be a member of KANU and nominated by KANU.

Thirteen sections of the Constitution, known as the bill of rights, provide a broad range of protections of fundamental rights and freedoms of the individual. Personal liberty is guaranteed, and inhuman or degrading punishment is prohibited. Arbitrary search of the person and entry of private premises are forbidden. Freedom of conscience, freedom of religion, and freedom of expression are affirmed, as are the freedoms of assembly and association, including the right to form labor unions. No one may be discriminated against on the grounds of ethnicity, place of origin or residence, political opinion, color, or creed. This provision does not, however, preclude legislation of a discriminatory nature being enacted with respect to noncitizens. Marriage, divorce, burial, inheritance, or other matters may also be exempt when covered by ethnic customary law.

Protection is extended against expropriation of private property, except in the public interest and subject to prompt payment of full compensation. Persons whose property is compulsorily acquired are granted access to the High Court to determine the legality of the sequestration and the compensation to be awarded. These safeguards were important in the postindependence period when large tracts of European-owned land were transferred to African smallholders and the government extended its direct involvement in business and industry.

The fundamental political freedoms of the bill of rights were breached by a constitutional change in 1966, making it possible for the president to invoke a preventive detention law. The Preservation of Public Security Act, passed the same year, extended sweeping powers to the government to detain persons without trial or to restrict their movements if it was satisfied that the action was necessary for the preservation of public security. Certain safeguards were included in the Constitution, but they have not proved to be a deterrent to the government in imposing detention on political opponents (see The Legal System, this ch.).

During the early years of Kenyan sovereignty, citizenship had been a subject of widespread attention because of the pivotal role played in the economy by British citizens of European and Asian origin living in the country. The Constitution bestows automatic citizenship upon anyone born within Kenya after independence, as well as on anyone born there before independence if either parent had also been born in Kenya. British citizens residing in Kenya at independence were entitled to become registered as citizens of the country.

Any woman married to a Kenyan citizen may also become one by a simple registration process. Anyone over the age of 21 who has resided in the country for five years may apply for naturalization. During the first two years of independence, the granting of citizenship to persons in this last category was automatic, but after December 12, 1965, citizenship was granted only if the applicants could satisfy the government that they were conversant in Swahili, were of good character, and were planning to make Kenya their permanent home. Voting is limited to citizens who have attained the age of 18 and who meet certain residence requirements in Kenya and in the constituency where they register.

The Governmental System

Under Kenya's Constitution, legislative power is vested in a parliament consisting of the president and the National Assembly. The British parliamentary model has been adopted in which the executive and legislative branches are linked; the ministers who form the cabinet are also members of the assembly. The governmental structure, however, has been modified in a number of ways to meet the needs of Kenyan society. As a matter of political reality, power is concentrated in the president, who can count on the support of the National Assembly in enacting his program.

Executive Branch

The offices of head of state, head of government, and commander in chief of the armed forces are combined in the president. By the terms of the Constitution, he enters office by gaining a simple plurality of votes in a direct popular election. If only one candidate is nominated for president, he is then declared to be elected without a ballot being taken. Kenyatta and Daniel arap Moi, Kenya's only presidents since independence, have invariably been the exclusive candidates, making election unnecessary after their nominations by KANU. As a consequence of the 1982 constitutional amendment, every presidential candidate must be a member of KANU and nominated by that party. Endorsement by KANU is accordingly tantamount to election.

The president must also be an elected member of the National Assembly. He is entitled to take part in its proceedings and to vote on any question before it. (In practice, the president rarely attends ordinary sessions.) To continue to hold office, he must command support by a majority in the assembly. If he loses a vote of confidence, he must either resign or dissolve the assembly and call for new elections. The Constitution provides that a presidential election be held whenever the legislature is dissolved. Thus, although the president's maximum term of office is five years, his length of tenure may vary.

If the presidency becomes vacant in midterm (through death, resignation, or medical incapacitation certified by the chief justice), a new presidential election must be held within 90 days. The vice president acts as chief executive in the interim, but there are limits on his authority. He cannot, for example, dissolve the assembly or dismiss cabinet members. After Kenyatta's death on August 22, 1978, Moi, his vice president, was sworn in as acting president. Unanimously elected president of KANU on October 6, he was proclaimed the second president of Kenya on October 10 as the only legal contender for the office. Earlier, in 1976, Moi's opponents in KANU had moved unsuccessfully to give presidential power to the Speaker of the National Assembly during the 90 days following vacancy of the presidential office (see The Question of Succession, ch. 1).

The vice president's duties are assigned by the president and may vary. When Moi served as vice president under Kenyatta, he was also designated minister of home affairs. Moi's vice president, Mwai Kibaki, has served concurrently as minister of finance but was shifted to the home affairs portfolio in 1981.

The cabinet, consisting of the president, vice president, and other ministers, serves as the policymaking body of the executive. Its decisions, if they do not require legislative approval, are carried out by the individual ministers and their ministries. They play a direct role in the legislative deliberations of the National Assembly and may represent the executive in its presentations to it. In addition, they are individually responsible to the president and must retain his goodwill if they are to keep their posts. Therefore, they nearly always support the position adopted by the president on important issues (see Table 11, Appendix).

The assistant ministers are not members of the cabinet, although they may be co-opted to serve on cabinet committees. They assist in guiding government measures through the legislature, but they are not normally allotted specific administrative areas of responsibility within their ministries. Two assistant ministers are designated for each ministry. Day-to-day operations of the ministry are entrusted to the permanent secretary, a senior civil servant. The permanent secretary is often a person of independent influence owing to his extensive knowledge and experience in the inner workings of his ministry.

The cabinet has tended to be large, consisting in 1983 of 27 ministers (including the vice president) and the president. With the addition of 53 assistant ministers, the government totaled 81 individuals. They thus comprised more than one-half of the 158 elected members of parliament.

The extent to which the president consults the cabinet on government policies and initiatives is not fully known inasmuch as proceedings of the cabinet are secret. Political observers consider, however, that the cabinet is rarely the focal point for major decision making. The

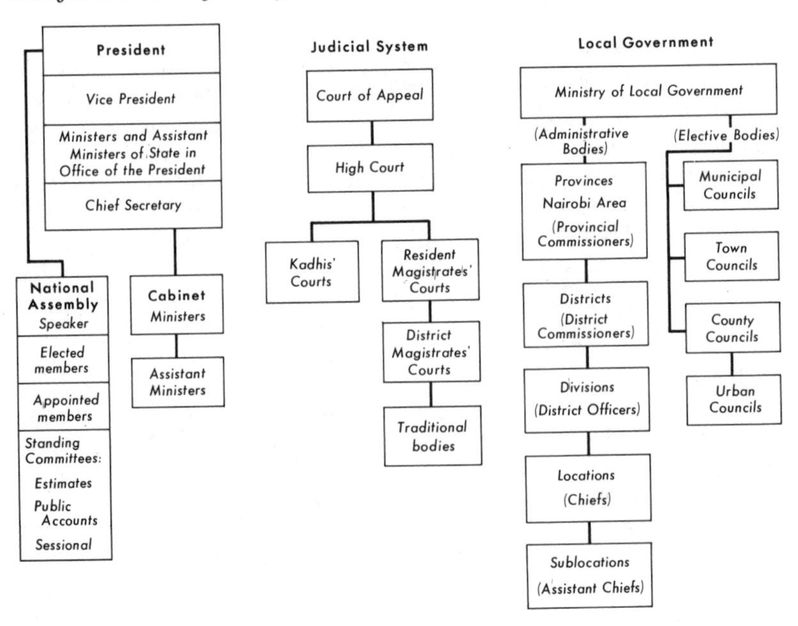

Figure 14. Organization of the Kenya Government, 1983

president, who appoints, shifts, and dismisses ministers at will, is not obligated to act on advice from the cabinet. Kenyatta was said to introduce important bills in the legislature and to make decisions affecting individual ministries without even consulting the minister concerned. Both Kenyatta and Moi have depended on a coterie of close advisers. Their precise identities have been a matter of speculation, but in the case of Moi they have been assumed to include, among others, ministers and assistant ministers assigned to the Office of the President. Another powerful office, that of chief secretary, was established by constitutional amendment to supervise the Office of the President and to coordinate all departments of government. The holder of this position in 1983, Jeremiah Kiereini, was also head of the civil service and chief secretary to the cabinet (see fig. 14).

Cabinet posts are reshuffled fairly frequently, although ministers who are out of favor are more likely to be shifted to less important portfolios than dismissed outright. Members of the government also risk loss of their offices through election defeat. In constituencies of the president, vice president, and a few senior ministers, KANU may refrain from approving rival candidates, thereby ensuring their unopposed reelection.

The only member of the cabinet not required to be selected from the National Assembly is the country's attorney general. Although he is granted ex officio membership in the assembly to take part in debates, he may not vote. The attorney general serves as both principal legal adviser to the government and chief prosecuting officer. The duties of his office include drafting all government legislation. He is empowered not only to order criminal prosecutions but also to halt cases, whether initiated by the government or not. Finally, he may direct the police to conduct criminal investigations. In carrying out his prosecutory and investigatory responsibilities, the attorney general is not subject to any higher governmental authority.

National Assembly

The National Assembly is empowered by the Constitution to legislate on any matter. It may delegate authority to the heads of ministries, who may promulgate subsidiary enactments in the form of ministerial orders, rules, and regulations. The assembly may not act upon any revenue or expenditure bill except at the recommendation of the government. In addition to its legislative duties, the assembly has the prerogative of reviewing government programs and the use of public funds. In practice, it is subservient to the president and usually exerts little influence over the content of legislation, although on a few occasions its determined opposition has persuaded the government to modify or withdraw hastily conceived measures.

The National Assembly has 170 voting members, of whom 158 are popularly elected from single-member constituencies and 12 are appointed by the president. As of 1981, four women were members of the assembly; one was an assistant minister. In addition to the attorney general, the Speaker is an ex officio member, although he plays a major role as neutral chairman, controlling debate and the transaction of business. He is elected by the assembly at the first meeting after a national election but need not be chosen from among sitting members.

Each government bill is guided through the assembly by a designated assistant minister. A bill is considered at three separate stages, or readings. The proposed bill must be published in the government's *Kenya Gazette* at least two weeks before the first reading in order to provide notice to interested parties. The major debate occurs at the second reading when members consider the measure's broad objectives. The assembly then converts itself into a committee of the whole house to examine the bill clause by clause and, if necessary, to entertain amendments. At the third reading a final vote is taken on the measure and, if favorable, is presented to the president for assent and becomes law.

Assembly sessions generally run from early March until early December of each year, averaging about 100 sitting days. The session is opened by a presidential address, reviewing recent developments and forecasting the government's legislative program. A general debate ensues in which members are not subject to a rule of relevance in introducing topics. Individual remarks are, however, confined to 10 minutes' duration, and the entire debate is concluded within seven sittings. The government's budget is generally introduced by the minister of finance in June for the fiscal year running from July 1 through

June 30. Final action is normally completed in late October, and provisional grants are made to keep government departments functioning.

Several standing select committees are appointed to facilitate the work of the assembly, but in practice they have not met regularly. Among them are the Estimates Committee, for dealing with departmental budgets in detail, and the Public Accounts Committee, intended to review the report of the auditor general on whether funds have been used in accordance with appropriations and drawing attention to waste, extravagance, or inefficiency. A sessional committee, usually consisting of 20 members, concerns itself with the ordering of business in the assembly. Ad hoc select committees may be appointed to study and report on special problems, but resort to such temporary investigative committees has been infrequent. A select committee on unemployment in 1970 did raise a number of issues that were addressed in the government's Development Plan 1974-78.

Debates in the National Assembly are often lively and, within imperfectly defined limits, the government tolerates a considerable measure of freedom to criticize. Economic shortcomings, evidences of official misconduct, and deficiencies in implementing government programs are acceptable issues to raise, whereas recriminations against cabinet ministers or disparagement of major government initiatives are viewed as unacceptable. Back-benchers (members who do not hold positions of authority in the government) are less hesitant in pleading the interests of their constituents, addressing demands for change, or producing evidence of inefficiency and inequity. They thus assume some of the functions of an opposition party. By interrogating ministers in the British style, back-benchers can in effect lobby on behalf of their districts or draw attention to local grievances.

The National Assembly has rarely been in a position to divert the government from carrying out its legislative objectives. Private bills that are doomed to failure are rarely introduced. Only when the government's position is clearly in conflict with popular opinion has the assembly been able to serve as a check on the executive branch. Although a reputation for aggressive advocacy of constituent interests is an asset in securing reelection, excessive criticism can lead to punishment of a member of the assembly by withholding resources from his district or blocking his path to a post as assistant minister or other senior appointment. Compliant members are more likely to be the beneficiaries of valuable business favors, such as government credits, licenses, and franchises.

Ensuring favorable dispatch of the government's business in the assembly is the large bloc of members—ministers, assistant ministers, and the 12 presidential appointees—who can usually be counted on to adhere to the government's position. A notable setback for the government occurred in 1975 when it attempted to suppress the conclusions of a legislative committee investigating the murder of a leading critic in the assembly, Josiah Mwangi Kariuki. A motion to block issuance of the committee's report implicating the government was de-

National Assembly buildings in Nairobi
Courtesy CNI News/Bill Chewning

feated by a vote of 62 to 59. In the next two years Kenyatta succeeded in intimidating the assembly by detaining three of its more outspoken members and bringing criminal charges against three others. Although Moi released all of Kenyatta's political detainees, prominent opposition figures have been banned from running for national office. Government pressure has resulted in assembly debates becoming increasingly noncontroversial, especially after the formal detention of a leftist member of the assembly in August 1982 and the arrest or flight of others charged with various financial offenses.

In spite of its circumscribed role in the legislative process and its decline as a forum for exposing official shortcomings, the National Assembly remained an important connecting link between the government and the *wananchi* (ordinary people—see Glossary). A member's performance was judged at election time to a great extent by success in contacts with officialdom at both national and local levels to ensure that governmental resources were allotted generously, or at least fairly, to the district. The assembly member was also expected to secure government backing for *harambee* (literally, let us all pull together) projects and to contribute personally if resources permitted, as they generally did.

Although citizens have had little opportunity to express themselves on major national issues at election time, the fact that a vote could be exercised among an assortment of candidates strengthened the sense of personal participation in the government process. This has been viewed as a contributing factor in the relative stability and the vitality of political life experienced by Kenya since independence.

Local Government

The country's major subdivisions in 1983 were its seven provinces and 40 districts. The Nairobi Area had separate status comparable to a province (see fig. 1; fig. 15). Under the independence constitution, a federal structure was imposed by creating seven regions, each having its own assembly and executive. The trend toward centralization of power soon led to a series of constitutional amendments that dismantled the regional system and reconstituted the provincial administrations as subordinate instrumentalities of the national government. At the provincial level the senior official was the provincial commissioner, who was responsible directly to the president. A district commissioner was the chief executive within each district and was responsible to the provincial commissioner.

Each district commissioner was assisted by a number of district officers, who were responsible for the next lower level of administration, the division. Divisional units numbered somewhat in excess of 200. At still lower tiers—the locations and sublocations—the central administration was represented by chiefs and assistant chiefs, respectively. In 1983 Kenya had more than 800 chiefs and 2,000 assistant chiefs, all of whom were salaried officials; in rural areas they might have also enjoyed authority as traditional leaders. The duties of chiefs were rooted in laws and ordinances dating back to the early part of the century. They were expected to represent small communities and be a focus of local development efforts. They had wide-ranging police powers and the right to mobilize males between the ages of 18 and 45 to work on public projects. Legal specialists have noted that with the evolution of other institutions and the extension of legal rights to all parts of the country, many of the chiefs' powers have become anachronistic and often could not be readily enforced. This was particularly true in urban areas, where chiefs performed mostly clerical functions.

The district commissioner coordinated the activities of various government agencies at the district level but had little formal power over them. This official's most important counterparts in providing services were the district education officer and the district medical officer of health. A third important function, road construction and maintenance, continued to be directed from the provincial level. There were formal consultative bodies, such as the District Development Committee, but ultimately decisions in the fields of health and education were taken by the respective ministries in Nairobi.

For purposes of administration and for determining location of infrastructural facilities, population centers have been classified as follows: 10 principal towns, consisting of communities with populations exceeding 19,000; 86 urban centers with populations over 2,000 (many of which were district administrative headquarters); 150 rural centers (which were also sometimes divisional headquarters); 420 market centers; and 1,018 local centers. Governmental guidelines typically assigned to principal towns the resident magistrates' courts, provincial police head-quarters, secondary-level technical schools, primary-level teachers' training colleges, and hospitals of provincial standard. Smaller urban centers had a district magistrates' court, divisional police headquarters, and a secondary school. Still smaller market and local centers had a police post, primary school, and dispensary. Certain recreational facilities—mobile library and film units, sports fields, and social halls—were located at the level of rural centers.

Distinct from the administrative apparatus accountable to the central authorities were the local governing units called councils. As of 1979 there were 11 municipal councils, of which seven provided the broadest range of services, including primary education, health, water, sewer services, and road construction and maintenance. The four smaller municipalities had fewer functions and were not responsible for primary education. In the next rank of 11 smaller communities, town councils were invested with a narrower range of responsibilities. Popular government of the 40 administrative districts fell under a system of county councils. (The boundaries for county councils were the same as those for administrative districts.) These councils served the entire area of the district except for those segments constituted under municipal or town councils. At a still lower level, urban councils, corresponding to urban centers, were to be established as subdivisions of county coun-

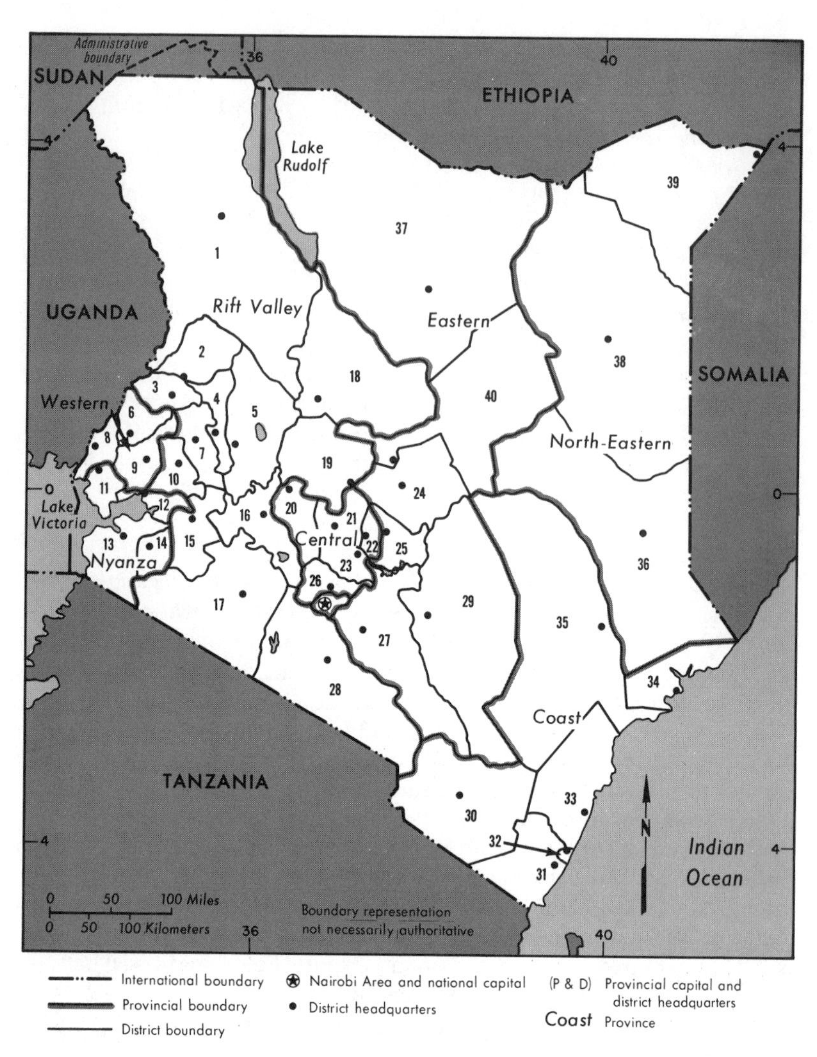

Figure 15. Principal Administrative Subdivisions, 1983

cils. Only incomplete information was available on the status of urban councils. The Murang'a county council had, for example, established urban councils in three communities in 1982 but had not yet provided for the election of councillors.

Councillors of the municipalities were elected directly by the citizens, and several additional members were appointed by the central government. All aspects of the electoral process were controlled at the national level. Accordingly, the minister of local government simply

	District	District Headquarters		District	District Headquarters
1	Turkana	Lodwar	21	Nyeri	Nyeri (P & D)
2	West Pokot	Kapenguria	22	Kirinyaga	Kerugoya
3	Trans Nzoia	Kitale	23	Murang'a	Murang'a
4	Elgeyo-Marakwet	Tambach	24	Meru	Meru
5	Baringo	Kabarnet	25	Embu	Embu (P & D)
6	Bungoma	Bungoma	26	Kiambu	Kiambu
7	Uasin Gishu	Eldoret	27	Machakos	Machakos
8	Busia	Busia	28	Kajiado	Kajiado
9	Kakamega	Kakamega (P & D)	29	Kitui	Kitui
10	Nandi	Kapsabet	30	Taita	Wundanyi
11	Siaya	Ukwala	31	Kwale	Kwale
12	Kisumu	Kisumu (P & D)	32	Mombasa	Mombasa (P & D)
13	South Nyanza	Homa Bay	33	Kilifi	Kilifi
14	Kisii	Kissi	34	Lamu	Lamu
15	Kericho	Kericho	35	Tana River	Galole
16	Nakuru	Nakuru (P & D)	36	Garissa	Garissa (P & D)
17	Karok	Narok	37	Marsabit	Marsabit
18	Samburu	Maralal	38	Wajir	Waijir
19	Laikipia	Nanyuki	39	Mandera	Mandera
20	Nyandarua	Nyahururu Falls	40	Isiolo	Isiolo

Figure 15. Continued.

dissolved all local authorities when the National Assembly was dissolved, and new council elections were held as a matter of convenience on the same day as the ensuing national elections.

The largest council, that of Nairobi, consisted in 1982 of 53 members, elected individually from the various subdivisions. Town councils had a maximum of 12 members. Although the normal term of the councils was four years, mayors were elected for two-year terms. The mayoral post was supposedly honorific, but intense political jockeying with ethnic overtones could precede an election in a city like Nairobi. The town clerk, a permanent official, was in charge of the administrative staff and wielded wide authority over day-to-day operations.

County council members are usually elected on the basis of one from each location. County councils played a significant role in the provision of services until 1969 when their influence declined with the shift of education, health, and the main road system from their jurisdiction to that of the respective ministries. Full council meetings are held periodically, e.g., monthly, to review and approve decisions taken by specialized committees of the council, such as those responsible for planning, public works, social services, and housing. The district commissioner and sometimes other government officials sit as ex officio members of the council. The highest titular authority is the council chairman, although the council clerk exercises broad powers as head of the county staff.

The operational budget for one county council in 1983 was KSh27 million (for value of the Kenya shilling—see Glossary), which was earmarked for activities such as nursery schools, youth centers, sports and community development, veterinary and forestry services, road grading and maintenance, and scholarships for needy students. The capital budget of KSh39 million provided funds for construction of five primary-school hostels and rural electrification programs in 28 market centers.

The Ministry of Local Government, which disburses central government grants and supervises the councils' accounts, is the primary conduit for the transmission of resources from the national level to the county councils. Links with other ministries, notably finance and economic planning and development, are, however, indispensable. These formal contacts are supplemented by networks of political patronage, through which the local officials may petition ministers, assistant ministers, and ordinary members of the National Assembly to lend their influence in securing benefits for their home constituencies.

Local authorities, especially the municipalities, rely on property taxes as their principal sources of revenue. Agricultural levies form the leading source of funds of the county councils. In urban areas the councils also assess charges for market stalls and water supplies and are in receipt of license fees for the operation of beer halls and other activities. Grants from the national government assist in meeting teachers' payrolls, and separate compensation has been paid since the withdrawal in 1969 of the right to assess a graduated personal tax that had been a major source of local revenue. This compensation grant has remained relatively static, aggravating the mounting financial stress of municipalities and towns.

High urban growth rates combined with the limited resources available to the cities and towns has meant that existing services, such as water, sewerage, housing, and public health, have deteriorated, and new facilities could not often be provided for newcomers. Shortages of qualified staffs have continued because the salary scales of local government bodies have not remained competitive with the private sector. Appointments and promotions are often subject to the influence of council members. Charges of financial mismanagement, nepotism, and irregularities in the issuance of business or housing permits have frequently been raised against councillors. The minister of local government has not hesitated to suspend councils or appoint entirely new councils when such shortcomings have become too flagrant to be ignored. In March 1983 the Nairobi city council was suspended after allegations were raised of improper granting of contracts and assignment of building plots, and trash collection and other services began to break down. Budgets of municipal councils must be submitted to the Ministry of Local Government for approval, but because of weak controls this procedure has failed to prevent severe deficits owing to excessive outlays. In Nairobi an investigative task force appointed by the ministry also drew attention to inefficiency in collecting real estate taxes and other revenues due the city.

The Legal System

The Judicature Act of 1967 provides the basic definitions of the country's legal system and establishes the court structure. It enumerates the sources of Kenyan law as the Constitution, legislative acts of the National Assembly, specific acts of the British Parliament before the establishment of the Republic of Kenya, English common law, and doctrines of equity in force at the beginning of colonial rule. African customary law, varying according to ethnic tradition, is required to be used as the guide in civil matters affecting persons of the same ethnic background as long as such custom is not in conflict with statutory law or modern morality. Islamic law has a role in some matters of personal law affecting Muslims.

The Judicature Act provides the country's courts a major role in creating legal precedent. Court decisions and interpretations have built up a body of national common law, a direct outgrowth of English common law but clearly Kenyan in scope. In 1982 the Law Reform Commission was appointed to undertake a broad view of the country's law, leading to reform, integration, codification, and removal of laws inherited from Britain that did not have relevance to independent Kenya's society.

Courts

Kenya has four levels of courts. The highest of these, the Court of Appeal, has final appellate jurisdiction in both criminal and civil matters, generally limited to hearing appeals from the High Court at the next level. The High Court has original jurisdiction for certain serious crimes and major property disputes and hears appeals from lower courts. In addition, it is empowered by the Constitution to judge the constitutionality of acts of parliament and all subsidiary legislation, as well as to enforce the provisions of the bill of rights. It has final authority on disputes arising from national elections.

The courts have often been resorted to in challenging election results, and the judiciary has acted impartially in cases where individuals have sought relief against violations of their constitutional rights. Judicial review of legislation and administrative action from the standpoint of constitutionality has, however, been rare. Observers have concluded that the pervasive control of public policy by the political authorities has discouraged the legal and judicial establishment from challenging the executive through court tests of the laws and their administration.

At the base of the judicial structure are the lower level resident and district magistrates' courts. Resident magistrates have nationwide jurisdiction and are empowered in criminal cases to render punishment of imprisonment for up to five years and fines of up to KSh10,000 and up to KSh3,000 in civil cases. Senior resident magistrates may try cases involving the death penalty and fines of any amount.

District magistrates' courts generally sit at district headquarters but may travel on circuit as well. Magistrates in these courts need not be lawyers but are civil servants who have completed a special course at the Kenya Institute of Administration. (Resident magistrates must be qualified lawyers with two years of court experience.) District magistrates' courts are divided into three classes, the major distinction being the severity of penalties they may impose. Courts of the third class may impose prison terms of up to six months and fines of not more than KSh1,000. Those of the second class have authority to inflict penalties twice as severe. Courts of the first class may impose sentences of up to five years and fines of up to KSh10,000. A similar distinction exists regarding civil matters. District magistrates' courts are competent to hear matters of customary law. These generally fall under headings of land disputes or personal and family matters, such as marriage, divorce, dowry, status of widows and children, guardianship, and estates. In rural areas, below the official courts, various traditional bodies are available to settle disputes. Groups of elders at the village level often consider matters of personal law, and legislation provides that on several subjects their decisions will be supported as final if taken to an official court.

Also at the level of the magistrates' courts are six kadhis' courts, which have jurisdiction over matters of personal Muslim law, such as marriage, divorce, or inheritance, when all the parties profess adherence to Islam. In 1981 a dispute arose over proposed legislation to enforce a single formula for division of estates in cases of intestacy. The Muslim community objected that this was in conflict with the Quran. The new law did not, however, prevent a Muslim from making a will declaring that his property was to be divided according to Islamic law.

The jury system does not exist in Kenya, but in cases involving murder, treason, or other crimes tried by the High Court, judges are assisted by assessors who are assumed to be of the same background as the accused and who are versed in the appropriate ethnic habits and customs. Opinions of assessors, however, are not binding on judges.

Kenya's chief justice is appointed by the president of the republic. Appointments to all other posts within the judiciary are controlled by the Judicial Service Commission. Although the president also appoints the judges of the Court of Appeal and the puisne (associate) judges of the High Court, he does so upon the advice of the commission. The commission selects, trains, assigns, and is responsible for the discipline of all the country's magistrates. Judicial appointments are permanent, but retirement is mandatory at age 68.

In early 1981 a white judge was dismissed by the president after 15 years on the bench on advice of the Judicial Service Commission. The judge had set free an American sailor who had confessed to the murder of a Mombasa prostitute. The verdict had provoked a major public outcry.

The Court of Appeal consists of the chief justice and three other members. The number of puisne judges is set by parliament at 11, giving the High Court a total membership of 12 justices, including the chief justice. Civil and criminal trials are heard by a single judge, as are most civil appeals. In criminal appeals there are usually two judges; specially referred constitutional questions must be heard by at least three judges. The High Court sits continuously at Nairobi, Mombasa, Nakuru, and Kisumu. Sessions are held regularly in other centers.

Civil Rights

In comparison with most countries of Africa, Kenya has maintained high standards of adherence to constitutional and legal safeguards of the individual. Persons accused of infringement of the law are assured of fair public trials, and their rights of counsel and appeal are respected. Due process is observed by the police, and other guarantees of English common law have with few exceptions been complied with. The Kenyatta regime sometimes had recourse to detentions without trial on security grounds that were authorized under the Preservation of Public Security Act. After Moi took office in 1978, he released about 20 political opponents who had been interned by Kenyatta and refrained from invoking the public security act himself until 1982, when nine persons were formally detained. The air force coup attempt of August 1982 resulted in the arrest of several thousand military personnel and some students. Trials of these individuals by courts-martial or in civil courts followed prescribed legal norms, and clemency was later extended to many of those who had been implicated (see Political Protest and the 1982 Coup Attempt, ch. 5).

The bill of rights in the Constitution promises Kenyan citizens a wide range of protections from arbitrary official actions. Police have ordinarily secured a magistrate's warrant before entering private homes although, in the aftermath of the aborted coup in 1982, lower class dwellings were searched without warrants, and large amounts of property that had allegedly been looted were confiscated. Censorship boards monitor movies and television; the press is not subject to censorship, but informal government guidelines ensure "correct" handling of sensitive issues. In July 1982 a leading editor was dismissed as a result of government pressure after he had criticized the renewed resort to detentions (see Newspapers and Periodicals, this ch.).

Constitutional rights governing association and assembly are in effect superseded by the Public Order and Police Act, which grants local authorities power to control public gatherings, and the Societies Act, under which the government can refuse to register any group whose activities it believes may be harmful to public security. For the most part, permits to hold meetings have not been denied unless it was claimed that the meeting might lead to a public disturbance. A former opposition political party, the Kenya People's Union (KPU), was proscribed under the Societies Act in 1969.

While Moi's initially conciliatory attitude resulted in the release of political detainees, 10 of his opponents (including several of the former detainees) were prevented from contesting the National Assembly elections of November 1979. The free exercise of political rights was seriously curtailed in 1982 in reaction to reports that former opponents of Moi were planning to resurrect a second political party. Detentions were ordered for George Anyona, a radical former member of parliament; Mwangi Muriithi, a former deputy director of intelligence in the police; the lawyer for both Anyona and Muriithi; and several university lecturers. As of mid-1983 most of these men, as well as a member of the National Assembly detained somewhat later, were still interned. In addition, several other academics and private individuals were arrested on charges of possession of seditious literature. Many of these victims of the government's crackdown were leftist in outlook and had stirred up feeling against the government among university students and faculty over such issues as the one-party constitutional amendment. However, the government's claims that the police had uncovered organized subversion were greeted with skepticism. No evidence of external support for those arrested was adduced.

Moi's detentions were authorized by the Preservation of Public Security Act as amended in 1978, an omnibus law empowering the state to take actions over a wide range of circumstances without recourse to the judiciary or other authority. Certain protections are embodied in the law. Detainees must be informed of the reasons for their arrest within five days. They have the right to have their cases reviewed by a special tribunal. The tribunal, which is appointed by the president, meets in camera, and the government is not bound by its findings. The detention of an attorney who had as clients two political detainees raised doubts concerning the adequacy of these safeguards and reportedly contributed to difficulties experienced by other political defendants in securing legal representation.

Political Setting

Kenyan political activity has been noteworthy for its liveliness and for the latitude, within the confines of a single-party system, that critics enjoy in voicing disapproval of official irregularities and inefficiency. The competition for political influence and status has been intense but, in the style of Kenyan politics, has been only partially reflected in parliamentary debates and electoral contests.

The road to effective power began in the home district, where the aspirant to office could be obliged to mount an expensive campaign against several others, all nominated by the local KANU branch. Without facing a strict test of loyalty to party principles, KANU candidates could embrace wide shades of opinion. Above all, candidates had to convince voters of their superior ability to keep patronage flowing to the home districts. Neglect of this objective could result in the rejection even of established figures in the government and the cabinet.

Successful political campaigns were invariably costly. Personal contributions to local self-help projects were among the generally unavoidable expenses. Politicians expected to be amply compensated for their efforts, either through benefits accruing to their own enterprises or through wealthy backers in the business world. The result was a tendency for political decisions to reflect the objectives of a dominant network of ambitious politicians and propertied elites, joined in a common interest in stable institutions and in a capitalist system hospitable to private initiative.

Because of the way districts and legislative constituencies have been drawn, ethnic factors have played a limited role in regional and local politics. At the national level ethnic forces have continued to operate, but in a manner largely screened from the public transaction of political business. Although far from united, the dynamic Kikuyu have seemed determined to recover the presidency, which they lost upon the death of Kenyatta. Coming from a smaller ethnic group (the Kalenjin), Moi could not hope to govern without building a broad inter-ethnic coalition. The Kikuyu have been allotted a strong presence in his government, but most other groups have been well represented. Moi has also sought to conciliate the important Luo faction, which had often ranged against the Nairobi leadership.

Although ethnic considerations have remained important in the struggle for national power, the rivalry has been conducted within the model of rule by a restricted circle of politicians in association with large business or agrarian interests. Stability of the system has depended on backing from a literate middle class, comprising bureaucrats, small entrepreneurs, educators, and small-scale farmers who have prospered in an expanding economy. By the early 1980s, however, the economic opportunities had contracted under conditions of recession, rural land shortage, and unemployment. The alliance of forces that had allowed Kenya to enjoy political stability and rapid economic growth had come under increasing strain. Although Moi had often spoken out against self-seeking and corrupt officeholders, little had been done to curb venal practices. In calling for early elections in September 1983, Moi denounced excessive ambitions and corruption, promising to "clean the system." Hope was expressed that, after receiving a new mandate from the electorate, Moi would be in a position to replace many of the entrenched politicians and officeholders who had put personal gain ahead of the nation's welfare.

The Kenya African National Union

At independence the majority party in the National Assembly was KANU, controlled by two of the leading ethnic groups, the Kikuyu and the Luo. The only other party, the Kenya African Democratic Union (KADU), was supported by smaller groups fearful of the concentration of ethnic political power exhibited by KANU. When KADU and KANU merged in 1964, the country became effectively a single-party state. Except for the defection of many of the Luo to the KPU between 1966 and 1969, KANU has remained an umbrella party under which Kenyan politics have been practiced (see Party Politics in the 1960s, ch. 1).

The justification for this one-party system as an amorphous, all-encompassing entity was rooted in Kenyatta's view that a multiparty system was extravagant, wasteful, and an obstacle to national unity. It was held to be alien to the Kenyan tradition that stresses decision through discussion and consensus rather than confrontation and majority rule. The comprehensive nature of KANU has permitted it to accept within its fold virtually all the country's political viewpoints and politicians, even former KPU leaders released from detention. It was feared that the alternative to a monolithic party system in which all groups could find legitimate expression was the evolution of opposition parties along ethnic lines.

The threat of a possible attempt to form a new socialist party prompted the quick passage of the one-party constitutional amendment in 1982. Although the official reaction seemed exaggerated, the government was evidently disturbed by the prospect of a coalescence of opposition forces along socioeconomic lines.

KANU has remained a loosely organized body without a pronounced ideological orientation. During the Kenyatta era, national conferences to hold party elections were repeatedly postponed on flimsy grounds, notwithstanding a party decision in 1971 to hold elections every two years. It was only when Moi became president that, after a delay of 12 years, party elections were held in October 1978 as a preliminary to the National Assembly elections of 1979. If the rule of biennial elections had been respected, new party officers would have again been chosen in 1980 and 1982. The KANU national conference was, however, further postponed ostensibly because Moi was preoccupied with his duties as chairman of the Organization of African Unity (OAU). The primary item of interest in the party conference was the election of the KANU vice president, who would then be in line for appointment as national vice president, thus revealing the president's preference for his own successor.

By early 1983 preparations were under way for another national conference, launched by a national recruiting drive for new KANU members. In April it was announced that the party had enrolled nearly 1.7 million members, or 22 percent of the eligible voters. This campaign, which had been regarded as a preliminary to national elections in 1984, was cut short when Moi unexpectedly announced that the elections would be moved up to September 1983.

A major purpose of the national conference is the filling of eight senior party posts, constituting the National Executive Council. In addition to the KANU presidency, which is by custom reserved for the president of the country, these positions include a vice president, a national chairman, and a secretary general. Except for the party secretary general, who in 1983 was Minister of Cooperative Development Robert Matano, national party officers had few responsibilities.

Nevertheless, candidates for senior party posts may engage in vigorous and expensive campaigning as a means of achieving national recognition and later appointment to high office.

Although all eight party posts below that of KANU president were contested at the 1978 conference, the earlier successes of Moi supporters in the branch and subbranch party elections ensured victory for his slate. A formula for geographic balance was adopted in which the party seats were distributed on the basis of one to each of the provinces.

In addition to the National Executive Council, the KANU party machinery embraces the National Executive Committee, which includes among others two members elected from each provincial conference, and a larger National Governing Council (129 members in 1983). Two members of the latter body are elected by each of the 40 district executive committees; among the others are representatives of the KANU parliamentary group from each province. The KANU Youth Group and KANU Women's Group are major affiliates of the party.

In spite of the elaborate party structure, there has been little evidence of sustained activity at the grass-roots level, other than the convening of lower echelon groups for the purpose of electing representatives to higher levels. Although KANU did publish a manifesto (or party platform) before the 1979 elections, its content was not a subject of open debate. The manifesto largely reiterated existing government policies and objectives in broad and noncontroversial form. It proclaimed support for a mixed economy, African solidarity, nonalignment, and rejection of rigid ideologies. Particular development strategies were heralded: labor-intensive cash cropping for small farmers, a shift from import substitution to export production in industry, more rural access roads, a policy of destocking in arid areas, conservation measures, and increased emphasis on family planning.

The all-embracing nature of KANU has been both a strength and a weakness in maintaining the viability of Kenyan politics. In the absence of structured and disciplined party machinery or a fixed ideology, KANU has been lenient in approving candidates to run for office under its banner. Although a screening of would-be nominees takes place, clearance is generally granted unless the candidate lacks the KSh1,000 life membership fee (a requirement subsequently rescinded), is of bad character, or cannot prove Kenyan citizenship. The relative liberality of KANU in approving candidates (an average of nearly five candidates contested each of the 158 constituencies in 1979, while 6,000 ran for local office) contributes to the resiliency of the political system. A number of critics of the government have been able to take their seats in the National Assembly and obtain a national audience for their views. Even the most powerful cabinet ministers and other national-level politicians have been forced to justify their records to the ordinary voters in their districts, and many of them have been turned out of office. Some leaders of KANU have suggested stricter screening of candidates, but the thousands of aspirants to office in 1982 were merely required to indicate that they remained loyal to the president, the party manifesto, the Constitution, and policies of the KANU government. To illustrate the freedom of the nominating process, Moi asserted that in a single constituency 19 candidates had been approved by KANU and in others even known thieves had been allowed to run.

Politics and Ethnicity

Political alignments among the various ethnic groups have been important factors at the national level since before independence. KANU was originally made up primarily of the Kikuyu, Luo, and Kamba groups. KADU, which merged with KANU in 1964, was a coalition of smaller ethnic groups preeminently from the pastoral and coastal regions, seeking to combine their strengths against domination by the Kikuyu and the Luo. Kenya's only other postindependence party, the socialist-oriented KPU, was essentially a Luo-based cleavage from KANU during its brief existence between 1966 and 1969.

At regional and local levels, ethnic factors are far less meaningful owing to the homogeneity of most districts and even provinces. In three of the seven provinces, between 88 and 96 percent of the population belong to a single ethnic group. In two others, over 93 percent belong to one of two groups. Only Rift Valley and Coast provinces lack such uniformity, but even within these, most districts contain a single ethnic group. This regularity results from conscious efforts during the colonial period to adjust political boundaries to coincide with ethnic divisions. Those few changes in boundary lines since independence have served to reinforce the pattern—nearly all resulted from efforts to give smaller ethnic groups their own political units. In major towns where intermingling is pronounced, ethnic solidarity constitutes an important ingredient in political life.

The pattern of Kikuyu dominance over Kenyan politics was altered in 1978 when Moi, a member of the Kalenjin minority, became president. He has made determined efforts to reduce manifestations of ethnic politics at the national level. A complex of wealthy businessmen, large landholders, and high government officials formed a community of interests that largely transcended ethnic factors. Popular discontent and demands emanating from the educated middle class, the unemployed, and the rural poor have not been perceived as ethnic issues. In any event, many of the ethnic categories lack cultural homogeneity, and some are largely artificial combinations of smaller groups (see Ethnic Groups, ch. 2). An analysis by M. Tamarkin, "The Roots of Political Stability in Kenya," has pointed out that the distribution of political rewards and the solving of grievances are managed through vertical patron-client networks, based on kinship, clan, or other subethnic relationships rather than on broad ethnic ties.

The preponderance of Kikuyu involvement in Kenyan politics is traceable to the Kikuyu role in the national independence movement. Always a hardworking and competitive people, the Kikuyu were also the group most affected by colonial rule. They had long occupied attractive areas of the country to which European settlers were drawn. The British government allowed Europeans to appropriate land that the Kikuyu, along with several other peoples, regarded as their own. The country's capital was established in the Kikuyu heartland, and the Kikuyu were among the first to demand a political voice for Africans. The Mau Mau violence of the 1950s was largely a Kikuyu uprising against the injustices of colonial rule, although other groups participated.

The forcible removal of Kikuyu from urban centers and the prohibition of Kikuyu leaders from political activity during the conflict enabled other groups to obtain government and political posts that the Kikuyu would otherwise have filled. After the decline of Europeans and Asians, however, the better educated Kikuyu were soon able to become strongly established in the state apparatus and the universities and to control the government-owned corporations. Kikuyu domination of the upper civil service ranks was very pronounced. Kikuyu also filled the majority of middle-level posts in the modern business sector, but in those parastatals and other firms over which the government had some control, efforts were made to ensure an ethnic mix on their boards of directors.

Comparing the ethnic distribution of Kenya's cabinets at several intervals, political scientist Vincent B. Khapoya has found a consistent bias in favor of the Kikuyu. Since independence the Kikuyu members have usually composed slightly over 30 percent of the cabinets, although their proportion of the population was slightly over 20 percent.

Having enlarged the cabinet and named additional assistant ministers, Moi was able to announce in 1980 that each of the 40 districts was represented in the central government, either at the ministerial or subministerial level. By 1983 Kikuyu representation had been reduced to less than 25 percent (seven of 27 ministers). The Luo and the Kamba each had three ministers; the Luhya, the second largest ethnic group, was underrepresented with two ministers. The fragmented Luhya were not regarded as being an influential factor at national political echelons. Moi's Kalenjin group had four portfolios, including the presidency. This constituted a doubling of the number of Kalenjin seats from the Kenyatta cabinet of 1974. The smaller ethnic groups held eight portfolios, including two by Kisii and two by Maasai.

Soon after taking office, Moi paid a well-publicized visit to Luo areas in western Kenya as part of an effort to reduce the political estrangement of the Luo people. A primary political issue among the Luo has been the status of the group's traditional leader, Oginga Odinga. Prevented from resuming his political career by Moi because of his intemperate utterances, Odinga's cause has served as a rallying point for the Luo people whether or not they agreed with his leftist orientation. His chief rival among the Luo, former minister Isaac Omolo Okero, was defeated at the polls in 1979 as a form of retribution for the banning of Odinga from the election. This left William Odongo Omamo, minister of environment and natural resources, as the leading member of the anti-Odinga faction in the central government. Another prominent Luo was the minister of foreign affairs, Robert J. Ouko.

The small Maasai group was prominently represented in the cabinet in 1983 by two members regarded as close to Moi—Minister of Culture and Social Services Stanley Oloitipitip and Minister of State in the Office of the President Justus ole Tipis. John Keen, another prominent Maasai politician and rival of Oloitipitip, was assistant minister in the Office of the President. The leading Kamba politician was Paul Ngei, minister of livestock development.

The southern Kikuyu who are concentrated in Kiambu District near Nairobi include many of Kenyatta's former collaborators and kin. The most powerful cabinet ministers under Kenyatta were from Kiambu, and they were disproportionately represented in higher civil service and government corporate posts. The northern group of Kikuyu of Nyeri District, as well as of the neighboring districts of Kirinyaga and Nyandarua, did not enjoy the patronage available to those having close access to Kenyatta. Relations between the northern and southern Kikuyu were further disrupted by the assassination in 1975 of Josiah Mwangi Kariuki, a charismatic figure among the Nyeri group. Although his murder was never solved, the Kiambu were widely suspected because of Kariuki's stinging attacks on high-level corruption and favoritism (see Government and Opposition in the 1970s, ch. 1). After their failure to prevent Moi's election, the Kiambu reconciled themselves to seeing the presidency pass at least temporarily out of their control. Collaborating with Moi in consolidating his authority were Vice President Kibaki of the Nyeri Kikuyu and Charles Njonjo who, although from Kiambu, had been instrumental as attorney general in deflecting the constitutional amendment movement aimed at denying Moi the presidency.

Through deaths and election defeats the principals were gradually replaced in Moi's cabinet. The leader of the Kiambu faction and Kenyatta's close confidant, Mbiyu Koinange, was not reelected in 1979. Njoroge Mungai, Kenyatta's nephew, who was pitted against Moi for the post of KANU president in 1978, was returned to the assembly in 1979 but remained a back-bencher. Thus, Njonjo was the major surviving Kiambu political figure until his fall from grace in 1983, although his unconventional style set him apart from the once-powerful circle around Kenyatta.

Upon the initiative of Moi, the disbandment of ethnic associations was ordered in 1980. These included the Luo Association (East Africa), the New Akamba Union, and the unions of the Kalenjin and Luhya peoples. Most of these groups were concerned with promoting the business interests and welfare of their members. Moi's real target was the more politically oriented Gikuyu [Kikuyu]-Embu-Meru Association (GEMA). Leading politicians of the anti-Moi faction among the Kiambu Kikuyu constituted GEMA's top officials. (The chairman of GEMA was a Kiambu business tycoon, James Njenga Karume. Elected to the legislature in 1974, Karume was serving in Moi's government in 1983 in the relatively modest post of assistant minister of energy.) Formed in 1971, later than the other associations, GEMA and its economic arm, GEMA Holdings, quickly became a powerful force of 2 to 3 million members, rivaling KANU itself. In addition to acting against these associations (although GEMA's business interests continued to be operated by a successor organization), Moi decreed an end to the practice of ethnic combinations forming caucuses within the National Assembly.

The president's efforts, together with the emergence of pressing economic and social issues transcending ethnic rivalries, contributed to a diminution of the ethnic factor in politics. As of mid-1983 it was difficult to assess to what extent the power struggle that induced Moi to call early elections represented a resurgence of Kikuyu ethnicity. It did appear, however, that Moi was finding his most trustworthy supporters among his own ethnic base or other minority groups.

Opposition Elements

During the first months of Moi's leadership, scarcely any resistance could be found to his conciliatory policies, reflected by the slogan "peace, love, and unity." By 1981, however, the underlying stresses of Kenyan political and social life had reemerged, and the government drifted increasingly toward more authoritarian measures to repress criticism. The relatively few "radicals" in the National Assembly and among university professors, students, and intellectuals were not a cohesive group, nor did they embrace a particular ideology, although many were socialist or Marxist in outlook. The government displayed considerable sensitivity because their charges of exploitation, favoritism, and misuse of political power struck a resonant chord among the public. The government's propensity to align itself with business and property interests exposed discontent that had previously been obscured by prosperity touching all classes. Inflation, consumer goods shortages, and unemployment accentuated the disparity between the mass of society and the fortunate few at the top.

A formal opposition party has not been sanctioned since 1969, when the KPU was banned on a charge that it had planned the overthrow of the government. It was formed in 1966 when 30 representatives and senators resigned from KANU. In the ensuing by-elections, KANU won overwhelmingly, only seven seats in the House of Representatives and two in the Senate going to the KPU. By 1967 the government had adopted a much harsher attitude toward the party after disclosures that it had been receiving funds from foreign communist sources. The leading figure in the KPU was Odinga who, until his resignation from the government in April 1966, had been Kenyatta's vice president. Most of those who lined up with Odinga were associated with the Luo ethnic group. Government suppression of the party and the detaining of Odinga and others intensified the feeling of persecution among the Luo. Their hostility was moderated, and political tensions in general were eased when Kenyatta introduced reforms for the December 1969 general election decreeing that candidates would be selected in primaries open to all KANU members. Inclusion of a significant number of Luo in the cabinet helped further to reduce the Luo sense of alienation (see The Kenyatta Era, ch. 1).

Although excluded from the 1979 elections in spite of having been allowed to rejoin KANU, Odinga seemed on the path to rehabilitation when Moi appointed him to head a major government marketing board. Odinga's outspokenness plunged him into new controversy, however, when he included the venerated Kenyatta in an attack on "landgrabbing politicians." In 1981 an assembly seat in a Luo area had been vacated to permit him to reenter the legislature after the formality of winning a by-election, but he was forbidden to run, and he also lost his post on the marketing board.

In early 1982 Odinga's rhetoric became even more inflammatory. He charged the government with inflicting on Kenya its economic reverses through corruption, misapplication of foreign exchange, continued import of luxury goods, misuse of foreign aid, and poor planning. Odinga condemned the military facilities agreement with the United States and the failure of the Kenyan government to obtain legislative approval for it. After mentioning the need for a second political party in Kenya while speaking in London, Odinga was expelled from KANU. Odinga was placed under house arrest after the August 1982 coup attempt, although suspicions that he was implicated were not corroborated.

In the absence of an opposition party, critical evaluation of government policies has been voiced mainly by a small group of younger members of the National Assembly. Labeled as radicals and springing for the most part from the political left, they have attracted popular support by their condemnation of corrupt behavior, favoritism in the redistribution of land, and social injustice. The most outspoken of the group, Koigi wa Wamwere, was subjected to detention in 1982; another, Waruru Kanja, was jailed for foreign exchange violations. Two others, Chelegat Mutai and James Orengo, fled the country to avoid arrest over purported discrepancies in their official accounts. The government's growing impatience with its critics apparently had a restraining effect on the six or seven radicals remaining in the assembly. None of them ventured to speak against the constitutional amendment for a one-party system, which passed unanimously in June 1982.

Apart from the assembly, the most persistent sources of opposition to the government have been found among the students and university faculties in Nairobi, a few writers, and some intellectuals. Student protests have been a frequent occurrence at the University of Nairobi and Kenyatta University College, induced for the most part by the government's inability to rid itself of corruption and its intolerance of dissent. In 1979 the debarring of former KPU leaders from contesting the election provoked a series of demonstrations. The University of Nairobi was closed for two months in 1981 as a result of unrest over a number of unpopular government actions and again in 1982 over student demands that the multiparty state be preserved. This precipitated a political screening of all faculty and students and the arrest of several lecturers on charges of possession of seditious literature. The government declared that "Marxist agents" were intent on bringing anarchy and totalitarianism, but no real evidence of conspiracy or foreign involvement was presented.

The government's purpose in acting against its critics seemed to be to deter professors having socialist or radical beliefs from indoctrinating their students with ideas deemed subversive. The direct threat to the established order from this source seemed limited. The politically active students were said to number no more than a few hundred, and many of these would soon be taking their places among the upper segments of the government and business community. Nevertheless, the recurrent student unrest was regarded by some observers as evidence of suppressed discontent among the important urbanized middle classes over shrinking economic opportunity and the diminished scope for political expression.

No combinations have emerged among the discontented students and disadvantaged groups in society, such as the poor peasants and urban unemployed. The potential for political action among these groups seemed low in view of their lack of organization and their tendency to respond on a basis of self-interest rather than in a wider spirit of dissatisfaction.

Kenya has a well-developed trade union movement, but its members have constituted a privileged group within the work force. The government has dominated the labor scene, beginning with the authority to register trade unions. Collective bargaining has been permitted, but labor disputes had to be referred to the Ministry of Labour for conciliation or arbitration. Almost all strikes were illegal under threat of fine and imprisonment. The Kenya Union of Civil Servants, the largest union in the country, was formally deregistered in 1980 because of its alleged political activity.

The Moi Presidency

The transfer of leadership to Moi upon Kenyatta's death in 1978, effected according to constitutional form, was a major accomplishment of the Kenyan political order. Kenyatta had been a symbol of nationhood, a rallying point for all Kenyans, and at the same time leader of the prominent and aggressive Kikuyu ethnic group. Although an experienced and close collaborator of Kenyatta since independence and vice president since 1966, Moi had not built up a national following. The main source of opposition to him was found among the Kiambu branch of the Kikuyu who had accumulated wealth and power through proximity to Kenyatta. First conciliating this group by retaining its leaders in the government and by stressing the continuity of Kenyatta's policies, Moi later felt strong enough to assert his own ascendancy by dissolving the formal Kikuyu structure and by rejecting other forms of ethnic factionalism. His critics to the left, who regularly denounced the prevailing system for its indifference to the well-being of ordinary citizens, were temporarily mollified by the release of dissenters confined by Kenyatta, by Moi's populist program, and by his anticorruption rhetoric.

Kenya's economic successes of the 1960s and 1970s provided the essential underpinning for social stability, offsetting the pressures of population growth and the public's resentment over the conspicuous accrual of wealth by a privileged few. By 1980, however, economic adversity was at hand, brought about by the steep decline in coffee prices, the loss of regional markets after the collapse of the East African Community (EAC), a worldwide recession, and spiraling oil prices. Mismanagement contributed to domestic shortages, bringing the disparity between rich and poor into sharper focus. Amid mounting tension, Moi clamped down on the government's critics, resorting for the first time to political detentions and reacting to the perceived threat of an opposition socialist party by formalizing in the Constitution KANU's status as the only legal party.

The revolt of the Kenya Air Force in mid-1982, although quickly sealed off and crushed, exposed the growing strains afflicting Kenyan society. Moi showed leniency in dealing with the rebels and aligned himself with the widely felt need for reform. At least superficially, his personal situation remained secure in the uneasy calm of the post-coup phase. The army had demonstrated both its loyalty and its effectiveness in rounding up the insurgents. The pressures for political conformity intensified in the less tolerant atmosphere. Moi appeared to turn to a more dependable, if narrower, political base. The prominent Kikuyu figures who had helped him to become established as Kenyatta's rightful successor were no longer among his confidants.

Moi's surprise decision to hold elections in September 1983, accompanied by charges of disloyalty against unnamed members of his government, was interpreted as an effort to dissipate political stresses and reinforce his authority. The post-election period would give Moi an opportunity to shift his most capable and loyal deputies into key posts to assist him in overcoming the problems still facing Kenya in the mid-1980s. Above all, this meant resuming economic progress, but it also included relieving social unrest, fighting venality in political life, containing the ambitions of the strong Kikuyu element, and persuading the Luo to pursue their aspirations through lawful channels.

Post-Kenyatta Developments, 1978-79

Moi's peaceful and smooth accession to the permanent presidency, after his unanimous election by KANU as the sole nominee, concealed a series of maneuvers to bypass him attributed to the Kenyatta "family" (see Glossary) of personal followers and relatives from the Kiambu Kikuyu. In addition to Moi's strong constitutional position, however, he had influential backing from Kibaki, Kenyatta's minister of finance and planning, and Njonjo, his attorney general. During the interim presidency Njonjo saw to it that civil servants, the police, the army, and district and provincial commissioners formed delegations from all parts of Kenya to pledge their support for Moi, as did nearly all KANU branches. A resolution of the cabinet, apparently engineered by Kibaki, proclaimed its total allegiance and loyalty to Moi. When this was followed by an endorsement of his candidacy by his rival, Mungai, as chairman of the Nairobi branch of KANU, an unopposed nomination by KANU was virtually assured. The Kiambu faction was handicapped by the fact that Koinange was too old for presidential ambitions, and Mungai had lost his elective assembly seat in the 1974 elections, making him constitutionally ineligible to be president.

During the first months of his presidency, Moi undertook a number of actions that earned him a massive surge of popularity. The amnesty for political opponents of Kenyatta who had been under detention was one such step. Redistribution of land was suspended pending the introduction of new procedures to minimize abuses that had favored wealthy and influential applicants. A free primary-school milk program was announced. Moi proclaimed a new campaign against corruption, government-owned corporations being the principal targets. Private employers were persuaded to enlarge their wage-earning staffs by 10 percent, and a similar policy was adopted for the public sector.

At the same time, Moi stressed the continuity of his presidency by dedicating himself to pursuit of the policies of the Kenyatta era under the slogan of *nyayo* (Swahili for footprints or footsteps). The cabinet was reshuffled in October 1978 after Moi's confirmation in the presidency, but none of Kenyatta's appointees were dropped. Kibaki was named vice president while retaining the finance portfolio. Koinange was moved from his key post in the Office of the President to a lesser ministry. With Njonjo remaining as attorney general, Moi, Kibaki, and Njonjo were regarded as the ruling triumvirate.

Consolidation of Moi's Authority, 1979-82

New elections to the National Assembly, required under the Constitution by the end of 1979, were called by Moi for November 11, 1979. In an effort to control underhanded practices and the peddling of votes, Moi introduced a bill limiting election expenses by candidates to KSh20,000. As approved by the assembly, however, the limit was set at KSh40,000 and applied only for the three weeks between nomination and polling day. The Kenyan press reported, nevertheless, that quantities of free food and beer were lavishly dispensed, and large amounts of money changed hands.

Although only KANU members could be nominated, party branches were liberal in approving candidates, enabling over 740 individuals to contest the 158 elective assembly seats. Civil servants desirous of running for office were required to resign their posts six months in advance of the election. Many leading officials, wealthy businessmen, academics, and executives of government corporations decided to enter the campaign. The election was marked by heated contests in which personalities and local issues predominated. Moi campaigned on behalf of some candidates who had loyally backed him and withheld his support from several who were closely connected to the Kenyatta "family." Of the 10 candidates refused nomination by KANU branches, five were former members of the banned KPU, among them the veteran radical, Odinga. The other five were among the most uncompromising critics of KANU political control, notably George Anyona, who had been one of Kenyatta's detainees released by Moi.

Conforming to the pattern of earlier elections, a large number of sitting members, including holders of cabinet seats, were rebuffed by the electorate. Nearly half of the assembly (as well as seven ministers and 15 assistant ministers) was defeated. Of special note were the election victories of a European candidate, Philip Leakey, and Krishna Gautama, an Asian, in predominantly African constituencies.

The rejection of prominent politicians of the Kenyatta era by the voters presented Moi with the opportunity to reorganize the cabinet and consolidate his leadership by introducing younger, more energetic ministers indisputably loyal to him. To avoid alienating other factions and ethnic groups, former ministers who had succeeded in gaining reelection were reappointed, and the rough regional and ethnic balance was retained. Mungai won his seat but was not invited into the government.

The period after the assembly election was clouded by Kenya's economic misfortunes as its previously steady progress was curtailed and increasing strain in the balance of payments necessitated a series of currency devaluations. The country was forced to accept lower development rates and to impose import curbs affecting even staple foods. Moi's commitment to capitalist development buttressed by foreign investment did not waver. In spite of consumer shortages, unemployment, and the leveling off of per capita incomes, Kenya's economic problems were less severe and more manageable than those of most other countries of Africa.

Moi posted himself at the head of the anticorruption movement, striking out first against a popular target—Asian businessmen engaged in illegal currency transactions (often aimed at amassing capital abroad in case their positions in Kenya became untenable). The excesses of *harambee* projects, often promoted by ambitious politicians for their own advantage, brought a series of temporary bans on such campaigns.

Having established himself firmly in the presidency, Moi gradually established his own protégés in key positions while appearing to distance himself from the two leading Kikuyu politicians whose help had been indispensable in the early days of his administration. Kibaki was demoted from the key finance portfolio to minister of home affairs in February 1982. The press had charged mismanagement of the economy, reporting that grain reserves had been exported while the country was facing a food shortage. (Kibaki retained his vice-presidential office.) In 1980 Njonjo had resigned as attorney general to assume a vacated seat in the National Assembly for which no other KANU members were nominated to run. Because only an elected member of the assembly may become president, this step was widely attributed to Njonjo's higher political ambitions. He was then named to the lesser Ministry of Home and Constitutional Affairs by Moi, but his position was downgraded further when home affairs was split off and assigned to Kibaki.

Aftermath of the August 1982 Coup Attempt

The deteriorating economic conditions that awakened discontent among the middle class and the poor during 1981 led to strikes and civil protests. The causes of their restlessness were articulated by a few nonconforming members of the assembly and intellectuals, accompanied by periodic student demonstrations. The early promise of a more democratic and responsive government under Moi was not fully achieved, as the president became increasingly rigid and intolerant of criticism. His populist economic program was adrift while scandals involving high officials continued to be uncovered. In spite of gathering tension, dissent remained directionless and unorganized.

The insurrection came from a wholly unexpected quarter. It appeared to have originated among enlisted men and junior officers of the small Kenya Air Force. The perpetrators of the coup claimed to have formed a body known as the People's Redemption Council and, in their broadcasts during a brief occupation of the national radio station, justified their action by citing widespread corruption and nepotism, the government's crackdown on civil liberties, the country's economic straits, and ineffective leadership.

Although hundreds of university students joined in the rioting that ensued, the rebellion was a clumsy failure and soon degenerated into disorder and plundering in the center of Nairobi. Within a few hours the threat of the government's overthrow was turned aside by loyal army units (see Political Protest and the 1982 Coup Attempt, ch. 5). Public courts-martial of hundreds of lower ranking air force personnel followed. Virtually all ranking air force officers were dismissed or arrested for having failed to react to evidence of the plot. A private and a senior sergeant, both of Luo background, who escaped to Tanzania by airplane, were identified as among the ringleaders. The minister of information and broadcasting, a Luo, was replaced, and several other prominent Luo were arrested on treason charges. Others who were penalized for dereliction of duty, including the air force commander and the head of the police Special Branch, were Kikuyu. The air force, considered to be the elite service with a high proportion of well-educated middle-class personnel, was staffed predominantly by Kikuyu. There was evidence of an effort to target Luo dissenters as scapegoats, but Moi himself warned against evaluating the rebellion from an ethnic standpoint.

In the months immediately after the coup attempt, Moi undertook to shore up his popular backing by promising new efforts to curb corruption and inefficiency in government. He called for a reduction of government involvement in business and industry, noting that the public sector was larger than that of many African countries claiming to be more socialistic than Kenya. He also promised to deal with poverty in the countryside by giving priority to rural infrastructure over industry. To underscore his dedication to reform, he appointed a working party in October 1982 to draw up a code of conduct dealing with private business and other conflicts of interest by civil servants.

The hallmark of Moi's stewardship in the period preceding the national elections announced for September 1983 was the tense and coercive atmosphere that had spread through political life. In May the president had aroused the country by denouncing greed and selfishness among ministers and senior civil servants. He spoke of a conspiracy within the cabinet by individuals promoting their excessive ambitions with assistance from foreign sources. Moi did not elaborate on his sensational charge, but heated attacks were mounted in the National Assembly against Njonjo. An assistant minister gave details of purported transfers of large sums to Njonjo's account from banks in London and the United States and claimed there was evidence of Njonjo's ownership of a firm in South Africa. Njonjo strongly denied any disloyalty, but at the end of June he was suspended as minister of constitutional affairs and resigned from parliament. A high-level judicial inquiry was called to look into what were described as serious irregularities attributed to him.

It was not made clear whether a cabinet plot had actually taken shape or whether Moi's charges were part of a broader campaign to rid himself of unfaithful and ineffectual officeholders. Outwardly at least, the episode seemed to solidify the president's position. Leading political personalities vied with each other to reaffirm their personal loyalty to the chief executive, and the KANU National Governing Council gave him unanimous support in suspending Njonjo from the party.

The 1983 election was expected to give Moi a renewed public endorsement of his leadership. In a time of internal ferment, he could emerge with the necessary political strength to carry out a controlled process of change. The election mechanisms and the ensuing period of reforming his cabinet could facilitate a purge of those corrupt politicians accused by him as unfit to deal with the country's problems. If he succeeded, his second full term of office could instill new cohesion and a fresh sense of direction. But if the administration continued to be burdened by ethnic rivalries and indecision, a period of inconclusive drift could set in, and the ability of the existing political system to respond to the unsettled social and economic situation could be called into question.

Politics and the Information Media

The newspapers and periodic literature of Kenya have performed an important service in enlightening the literate and educated members of society on public issues, particularly in the two urban areas of Nairobi and Mombasa. Although the freedom to report frankly and comment on political events has been subject to definite constraints, the Kenyan press has been among the liveliest and most informative in Africa. It was also exceptional in that its three widely read dailies had been controlled by foreign-based private interests. Government ownership has heretofore been confined to radio and television broadcasting, although in 1983 KANU began publishing official party newspapers in both English and Swahili.

The focal point of journalistic activity and readership was in Nairobi. For the 85 percent of Kenyans who lived in rural areas and others who were not regular readers of the press, radio was the main source of information. Radio has been an effective instrument for the government in publicizing the policies and activities of the political leadership and in presenting favorable information on economic prospects.

Newspapers and Periodicals

Kenya's first newspaper, started during the early years of the twentieth century, was the *East African Standard* (initially known as the *African Standard*), founded by an Indian businessman but soon acquired by Europeans. The voice of the white settler group until independence, it continued to be published in 1983 as the *Standard*. Along with several other local publications, the popular tabloid was part of the London-based Lonrho conglomerate that has held mining and other interests in many countries of Africa. The other long-established English-language newspaper, the *Daily Nation*, as well as the Swahili *Taifa Leo*, was controlled by Prince Karim Aga Khan IV, spiritual head of the Khoja Ismaili Muslims. In addition to separate weekend editions of these dailies, *Weekly Review*, a highly regarded journal of political and economic events, was published by a domestic company (see table 12, Appendix).

The two English-language newspapers resembled in layout the popular British press, emphasizing local and national current events and also containing sections on African and world news. The format of *Weekly Review*, founded by its editor, Hilary Ng'weno, in 1975, resembled those of American newsmagazines. Ng'weno had also produced a quality weekly newspaper, the *Nairobi Times*. After an unsuccessful effort in 1982 to shift to daily publication, it was purchased by KANU to be converted to the party newspaper, *Kenya Times*, relieving Ng'weno of bank debts that threatened his entire enterprise. A companion newspaper in Swahili, *Kenya Leo*, was launched in May 1983, as was a weekly, the *Sunday Times*. KANU officials gave assurances that the new publications would compete with existing privately owned newspapers on a commercial basis. It was pointed out, however, that a party newspaper would be bound to attract advertising from government and parastatal agencies, as well as from private firms doing business with the government.

Although during the mid-1970s the two principal newspaper chains were still directed by British expatriates, by 1983 the editors and staffs had been wholly Africanized. The foreign owners have in most instances refrained from interfering with the editorial policies of their journals. Sensitive to the need for good relations with the government, however, they have not hesitated to dismiss editors who have been the object of official criticism. In 1976 George Githii, editor of the *Daily Nation*, was subjected to official harassment as a result of Arab complaints over the pro-Israeli content of his paper. His resignation the following year, however, was caused by the intervention of the Aga Khan on a number of matters, including demands that Githii adopt a pro-Arab slant.

Both the *Daily Nation* and the *Standard* have tended to present government policies in a positive light and to avoid investigative reporting. Political misconduct at local and regional levels could be reported, as well as charges aired in the assembly or the courts. Matters reflecting unfavorably on the national leadership have been rarely alluded to directly. The *Weekly Review* has ventured to probe more deeply into controversial political subjects and questionable official practices. With the upsurge of political tensions that preceded the 1983 election campaign, the daily press increasingly confined itself to straightforward reporting of public statements and official pronouncements.

The privately owned journals have been associated to only a limited degree with definite political viewpoints. In 1976 the *Standard* backed the change-the-Constitution movement of the Kiambu Kikuyu. Githii, who moved to the *Standard* after leaving the *Daily Nation*, was seen as favoring the political fortunes of Njonjo, while the *Daily Nation* was leaning toward Kibaki. In July 1982 Githii, a firm defender of civil liberties, was bitterly censured by the government for a blunt editorial in which he denounced the roundup of political and academic figures and called for an end to detentions and intimidation of the press. Githii was immediately dismissed by Lonrho, which printed an abject apology for its editor's indiscretion.

Much of the news outside urban areas was gathered by the Kenya News Agency (KNA), which was operated by the Ministry of Information and Broadcasting. KNA distributed international news from Agence France Press, Reuters, and Tass to the local press by subscription. Newspapers could use the services of other agencies but generally relied on the cheaper KNA subscriptions.

With help from the United Nations Educational, Scientific, and Cultural Organization (UNESCO) and the Federal Republic of Germany (West Germany), a rural publication program was under way in 1983. Six rural newspapers, three of them run by the government, were included in the project, and six new publications were scheduled to be launched.

Radio and Television

The autonomous Kenya Broadcasting Corporation, modeled after the British Broadcasting Corporation, was taken over by the government in 1964 after it experienced serious financial difficulties and was subjected to complaints for catering to the European and Asian populations. It was nationalized under the Ministry of Information and

Broadcasting as the Voice of Kenya (VOK). Most operating costs were met by the government, although advertising was accepted.

VOK radiobroadcasts emanated from the central station in the Nairobi area by mediumwave, shortwave, and frequency modulation and by mediumwave from transmitters in Mombasa and Kisumu. In 1981 three services were offered: the national service in Swahili (120 hours a week), the general service in English (90 hours a week), and a vernacular service offering programs in 15 African languages and in Hindustani for the Asian community. The number of radio receivers was estimated at 1.6 million in 1981. For the large rural population that had little access to print news or was illiterate, the radio served important objectives of disseminating information, presenting educational material, and reinforcing national cohesion. News items tended to stress development plans and achievements. Actions of government officials were portrayed in a favorable light, and news considered negative was downplayed or ignored.

Television broadcasting in Kenya began in 1962, originally covering only Nairobi but soon extending to the heavily European-populated section of the Rift Valley centered at Nakuru and to the Kisumu area. A regional station at Mombasa was connected with Nairobi by microwave in 1974. An estimated 100,000 television receivers were in operation in 1981. Over one-half of television broadcast time was devoted to domestically produced programs. The single channel broadcast programs in English, Swahili, and Hindustani for about six hours each evening.

Press Freedom

Freedom of expression and of communication is guaranteed by the Constitution. All newspapers must register and secure annual licenses to publish. No major newspaper has been confronted with the threat of revocation of its license. Newspaper offices and journalists are not exempt from police powers of search and detention.

Formal censorship has not been imposed, but it was well established that government guidelines were to be adhered to in handling politically sensitive subjects. Editors have been contacted by cabinet ministers seeking to ensure treatment of news in a manner perceived as constructive and as serving the process of nationbuilding. The bounds of journalistic prerogatives have been generally well understood, but infractions could bring severe retribution. In addition to the dismissal of Githii as editor of the *Standard* for editorializing against detentions, two editors and four reporters for the *Daily Nation* were detained briefly in 1981 for the newspaper's comments on the physicians' strike and the barring of Odinga from a by-election. The editor in chief subsequently resigned.

Within limits the press has been able to deal with official incompetence, inequities, and shortcomings in the economic system; with social and ethnic conflicts; and with corrupt political behavior. A report in the *Standard* describing grain shortages arising from the ill-advised export of grain reserves led to the transfer of the responsible minister, although not to his removal from the cabinet. Direct criticism of Moi or other government leaders or unvarnished criticism of policies advocated by the government or its major decisions was not acceptable. Neither of the English-language dailies considered it expedient to oppose the single-party constitutional amendment, although the *Daily Nation* discussed concerns that debate might be restricted on national issues and urged KANU to introduce some method of ensuring that individuals and interest groups remained part of the decisionmaking process.

In spite of such taboos and the need for circumspection, the Kenyan press has been remarkably free, by the standards of Third World journalism, to present major issues and problems to its readers and to recount evidence of political scandal or injustice. The press has remained a factor in mobilizing public opinion that must be taken into account by political leaders. The campaign unleashed by the government to secure the removal of a responsible editor like Githii and its intimidation of other journalists have raised concerns that the government's efforts to control dissent might be extended to the suppression of legitimate media reporting. As of mid-1983 the implications of the appearance of the new KANU newspapers in competition with the long-established independent private press were not yet clear.

Foreign Relations

Kenya's foreign policy since independence has been characterized by moderation, pragmatism, and continuing reliance on the Western world as the source of needed capital and technical collaboration in developing the modern sectors of its economy. Except for issues involving its immediate neighbors, Kenya's international transactions have generally been channeled through several groups of which it is a member—the Organization of African Unity (OAU), the Nonaligned Movement (see Glossary), the Commonwealth of Nations, and the United Nations (UN).

Kenya's nonalignment policy has not inhibited it from taking an unambiguous position against aggressive behavior by the Soviet Union. It condemned the Soviet invasion of Afghanistan in late 1979 and withdrew from the Moscow Olympics in the summer of 1980, in spite of the fact that its athletes were among the most talented in Africa. Although Kenya backed proposals to declare the Indian Ocean a zone of peace and resisted the establishment of foreign military bases there, the growing Soviet presence impelled the Moi government to authorize United States access to naval facilities at Mombasa and to certain Kenyan air bases.

Nairobi's status as a major African capital and the site of many international conferences contributed to the decision to locate two international agencies there, the United Nations Environmental Program (UNEP) and the United Nations Commission for Human Settlements (Habitat). Kenya has aligned itself with other member states of the

Since its opening in 1973, the Kenyatta Conference Center in downtown Nairobi has hosted many international meetings, including the Eighteenth Ordinary Summit of the Organization of African Unity in 1981.

OAU that have insisted on the elimination of white minority rule in South Africa and Namibia (South West Africa), as it had for Southern Rhodesia before that colony became independent Zimbabwe. Under Kenyatta, Kenya was less strident than some African countries in condemning continued white political domination in the southern tier of the continent, rejecting rhetorical excesses that were not seen as contributing to solutions there. Moi's pronouncements on South Africa, especially during the period of his chairmanship of the OAU, were more uncompromising. Urging stepped-up efforts to achieve majority rule, he declared that armed struggle might be the only way to realize political rights for blacks in South Africa. Like other OAU members, Kenya accepts the South West Africa People's Organization (SWAPO), the Angola-based guerrilla movement under Sam Nujoma, as the sole and legitimate representative of the Namibian people in their pursuit of self-determination.

In strict observance of its policy of noninterference, Kenya has declined to criticize the presence of Cuban forces in Africa. It defended

Angola's right to call upon Cuba for help in protecting itself against incursions by South African troops across the Namibian border. In like manner, while disquieted by massive Soviet and Cuban involvement in neighboring Ethiopia, Kenya publicly justified Ethiopia's course as a response to Somali aggression.

The Moi government has regarded the Commonwealth as an additional mechanism for cooperation in the social, economic, and political fields among states formerly under British rule. These Commonwealth connections have reinforced links with the second echelon of developed countries, such as Canada and Australia, which may provide Kenya aid, technical assistance, and political support. Kenya, in turn, extends technical aid to some smaller Commonwealth members in certain agricultural and forestry fields where it has special competence. In 1980 Kenya contributed a small military contingent to the Commonwealth force monitoring the cease-fire and election in Zimbabwe. It was the only African nation represented.

The Kenyan government has been presented with an abiding challenge to its foreign policy in its efforts to preserve harmony with the nearby states of Uganda, Tanzania, and Somalia. In spite of several efforts to repair the breach with Tanzania arising from the breakup in 1978 of the ill-fated East African Community (EAC), normal commercial and economic ties had not been restored as of mid-1983. Relations with Uganda have gradually reverted to a more orderly pattern since the turbulence that accompanied the ascendancy of Uganda's Idi Amin Dada in 1971 and his overthrow by Tanzanian troops in 1979. Although Kenya and Somalia have committed themselves to cooperation in combating lawlessness in the northeast border area, the government in Nairobi has continued to be apprehensive that Somalia might one day reassert its irredentist claims to Kenyan territory. In late 1981 Kenya joined eight other nations of eastern and southern Africa, including Uganda and Somalia, in a treaty aimed at establishing a preferential trade area. Tanzania's unwillingness to participate reduced the treaty's significance for Kenya, particularly because transit privileges are essential for its trade with two other signatories, Zambia and Malawi.

Kenyan leaders have remarked on the fact that all of the country's neighbors are committed to a socialist approach, contrasting with Kenya's free-ranging private and state enterprise system. They have asserted that this has not been a cause of anxiety, noting the good relations that have long prevailed with Ethiopia in spite of its revolutionary,. pro-Soviet leanings. Cordial relations have also been maintained with Sudan, whose socialism has largely been abandoned in practice and whose political outlook since the mid-1970s has been more compatible with that of Kenya. In the early 1980s it was expected that the two nations would develop closer mutual interests when an improved road linking southern Sudan with Nairobi was completed. A direct telecommunications link between the two countries was also to become operational in 1983.

Kenyan president Daniel arap Moi (right), en route from the United Nations in New York to a meeting of Commonwealth leaders in Melbourne, Australia, confers with United States president Ronald Reagan in Washington, D.C., in September 1981. Courtesy White House Photo/Karl Schumacher

During his extended presidency, Kenyatta had not aspired to become a conspicuous figure on the world stage. Thus, the conduct of Kenya's external affairs was left to his foreign ministers, who faithfully conformed to his predilection for caution and restraint. Kenyatta neither attended OAU summit meetings nor made it a practice to visit other heads of state.

Moi has demonstrated greater readiness to intervene personally in pursuit of his country's international interests. He made several visits to the capitals of Western and Arab countries after his election as president in 1978. In July 1981 he was projected into the forefront of African politics when elected as chairman of the OAU just as two controversies were emerging that threatened to cause a breakdown of the organization. The first of these involved a division over OAU recognition of competing factions in Chad, and the second involved a dispute over territorial claims of the North African guerrilla movement in Western Sahara and its recognition by the OAU as the Sahara Arab Democratic Republic. In keeping with Moi's role as chairman, Kenya remained neutral on the various claimants to OAU recognition, but Moi worked unremittingly to find compromise solutions that would avoid a rupture of the organization. The OAU's inability to assemble a quorum for a summit meeting scheduled to be held at Tripoli, Libya, in 1982, prevented the election of that country's chief of state, Muammar al Qadhaafi, as the new OAU chairman. Moi was thus obliged to remain in the post until mid-1983.

Tanzania and Uganda

Tanzania and Uganda have occupied a distinctive place in Kenya's foreign relations since the colonial period, when the three countries were associated administratively under British rule. The common inter-territorial organs of the British administration that were combined in the East African High Commission were carried over after independence of the three territories under the East African Common Services Organization (EACSO). The growth of nationalism in the three states, differing domestic policies, and competing economies weakened the system. The decision to create separate currency boards in 1965 and the increasing barriers to free travel and the exchange of goods contributed to its disintegration (see Foreign Relations and Conflicts, ch. 1).

In an effort to reinvigorate the regional association, the heads of state of Kenya, Tanzania, and Uganda signed the Treaty for East African Cooperation in June 1967, creating the EAC, which was implemented in December of that year. Functionally, the EAC did not differ greatly from EACSO. The headquarters of the different services were dispersed to put one important staff headquarters in each capital city instead of combining them in Nairobi. The headquarters of the EAC itself was established in Arusha, Tanzania. Development of the community was disappointing, however, and no other states joined in spite of provisions for a broadened membership to include other countries of East Africa.

The EAC was greatly weakened by the military coup that brought Amin to power in January 1971, giving rise to hostility between Uganda and Tanzania. Julius Nyerere, the Tanzanian president, felt considerable affinity for Uganda's deposed president, Milton Obote, granting him asylum and support for his guerrilla followers.

Kenya sought to moderate the bitterness between its EAC partners. Amin's brutal and volatile course posed a threat to Kenya's own security and its profitable trade and transit links according landlocked Uganda access to the port of Mombasa. In spite of several incidents, among them the disappearance, kidnapping, and murdering of Kenyans, Amin found himself ultimately obliged to adopt a conciliatory attitude because of Kenya's control of Uganda's only outlet to the sea. A brief trade embargo by Kenya in 1976 led to OAU mediation followed by settlement of Uganda's debts and the return of a number of Kenyans held prisoner by Amin's forces.

Economic and trade differences springing in part from the ideological incompatibility between socialist Tanzania and the unfettered capitalism of Kenya were the main problems between the two countries until 1976. Underlying animosities broke into the open that year in the form of attacks by Tanzanian officials and the press on the business dealings of Kenyatta's "family," accompanied by accusations that Kenya was being manipulated by the United States. Kenyans in turn accused Tanzania of acting as China's African proxy. It was increasingly evident that Kenya, economically the most vigorous of the three EAC partners, was gaining disproportionately in spite of compensating transfer taxes. The public corporations in each state began to break down into independent national agencies, owing to mutual unwillingness to remit revenues or honor assessments. The final stage in the disintegration of the EAC occurred in early 1977 when Kenya suspended most operations of East African Airways and announced the formation of a national airline. Tanzania reacted by closing its border with Kenya.

Deeply suspicious of Tanzania's motives, Kenya nevertheless remained neutral after hostilities broke out between Uganda and Tanzania in late 1978. Nairobi viewed with relief Amin's overthrow a few months later but still regarded the attack as a violation of the OAU charter. It feared, moreover, that Tanzania was preparing for the reinstallation of Obote and a socialist state in the Tanzanian mold. Kenya adopted a friendly posture toward the new government in Kampala, extending some economic aid and repatriating Ugandan refugees and seized vehicles. Although Obote was elected president in the controversial Ugandan election of December 1980, he proved to be less doctrinaire than expected and cultivated good relations with Kenya.

In spite of the withdrawal of Tanzanian troops from Uganda, other matters under dispute contributed to continued coolness in relations between Nairobi and Dar es Salaam. Several meetings failed to untangle the issue of allocating the assets and liabilities of the defunct EAC, settlement of which, Tanzania insisted, had to precede reopening of the border. Some observers believed that the stark contrast between Tanzania's struggling socialism and Kenya's bustling free enterprise contributed to Nyerere's hesitancy over resuming economic contacts. Relations were further strained when Tanzania extended political asylum to two Kenyan airmen believed to have been ringleaders of the August 1982 coup attempt. The Kenyan government refrained, however, from bringing direct accusation that Tanzania was implicated in the plot.

Somalia and Ethiopia

Kenya shares extensive borders with Ethiopia to the north and Somalia to the northeast. Arid and thinly populated, these frontier regions have been weakly patrolled, offering refuge to bandits or guerrillas during periods of stress or conflict. Kenya has been periodically embroiled with Somalia over the latter's claim to sovereignty in Northern Frontier District, an area composed of present-day North-Eastern Province and part of Eastern Province. The Somali claim reflected its pan-Somali ambitions of extending its boundaries to include those adjacent areas of Kenya, Ethiopia, and Djibouti that were inhabited largely by ethnic Somali (see Foreign Relations and Conflicts, ch. 1).

Despite an expression of interest by Ethiopia in the late 1960s in formal economic ties with the EAC, little trade found its way over the single usable road linking sparsely populated areas remote from the primary centers of activity in both countries. A close personal friendship that developed between Kenyatta and Ethiopia's emperor Haile Selassie cemented an affinity based on shared anxieties over Somali irredentism.

The toppling of the emperor by a radical military junta in 1974 created an ideological gap with Kenya. Ethiopia turned to the Soviet Union for military aid and advisers and welcomed a large Cuban military contingent when faced with invasion by Somalia during the Ogaden war of 1977-78. Apprehensions Kenya might have felt about the large-scale introduction of communist arms and troops were subordinated to the Somali threat.

A 10-year treaty of friendship and cooperation negotiated by Kenya and Ethiopia in January 1979 was followed by a meeting between Moi and Ethiopia's chairman Mengistu Haile Mariam at Nairobi in December 1980, in which the two leaders joined in a harsh condemnation of Somalia. They demanded that Somalia renounce all territorial claims in Ethiopia, Kenya, and Djibouti and pay reparations for damages caused during the Ogaden war.

In a subsequent effort to appease Kenya, the government in Mogadishu declared that it had no claims against Kenyan territory and that it did not lend support to Somali insurgents in Northern Frontier District because, unlike Ethiopia, it did not regard Kenya as a predatory colonial power. Kenya remained distrustful of Somali intentions, but a thaw appeared to develop when, at the close of an OAU summit conference in Nairobi in 1981, Moi and Somali president Mohamed Siad Barre met to commit themselves to the promotion of better understanding and collaboration. Lower level officials have since been meeting to cooperate in maintaining law and order in the border area.

Arab Countries and Israel

Kenya has long maintained friendly relations with Israel based on trade and technical assistance. Under the threat of the loss of Arab goodwill during the world oil crisis, however, the government in Nairobi reluctantly joined other OAU members in severing diplomatic relations with Israel after the outbreak of the war in the Middle East in October 1973. Kenya rejected pressure to discontinue trade with Israel and to withdraw rights for the Israeli airline, El Al, to land at Nairobi on its route between Tel Aviv and Johannesburg, South Africa. The restoration of formal ties has been suggested periodically in the press and by individual members of parliament, particularly in light of the Egyptian peace treaty with Israel. The Moi government has remained unwilling to antagonize the Arab states by acting independently of the OAU on the recognition issue. In any event, the Israeli permanent representative to UNEP in Nairobi is said to serve as de facto ambassador to Kenya.

Strong pro-Israeli sentiment among the public was reinforced by bitterness over the economic burden of rapid increases in the price of crude oil. Arab backing for Somalia in its dispute with Ethiopia, underscored by Saudi Arabia's financing of the rearming of Somalia after its defeat in the Ogaden, contributed to cool relations with the Arab states. In an effort to refurbish ties with the leading oil suppliers, Moi visited Saudi Arabia in 1979 and Abu Dhabi and Iraq in 1980. Kenya also extended recognition to the Palestine Liberation Organization, which was permitted to open an office in Nairobi. Relations with the Arab world were thus placed on a more positive foundation, although this did not entail concessionary rates for crude oil, which Kenya was forced to buy at market prices largely from Saudi Arabia. Kenya was also disappointed that the strains of purchasing oil at inflated prices were not mitigated by substantial amounts of aid from Arab sources. In the early 1980s hopes of exploiting potential new markets in the Middle East had gone largely unfulfilled.

Western Europe

Kenya has been committed to continuing its long-standing economic involvement with Western Europe, viewing it as a valuable source of aid, investment, and trade. It has continued to look to Britain as its primary economic partner and has retained a high opinion of British social institutions and standards. The government in Nairobi has also engaged in substantial economic cooperation with West Germany, which surpassed Britain as the leading market for tourism in Kenya by the late 1970s. Under the Lomé Convention, Kenya is entitled to virtually duty-free access for its products to members of the European Economic Community (EEC) and to aid through the EEC's financing instrumentalities. London has been the largest donor of bilateral aid to Kenya, although in 1981 its disbursements, equaling US$75 million, were slightly below those of the United States. West German aid was also significant (the equivalent of US$42 million in 1981), as was that of the Netherlands (US$38 million in 1981).

Relatively minor points of discord that marred Kenya's generally harmonious relations with Britain diminished in importance during the 1970s. Britain retained its place as the leading supplier of goods. A significant share of Kenyan industry was owned by British firms, and two British banks, Barclays and Standard, were among Kenya's most prominent financial institutions.

Kenya, along with other African nations, held Britain responsible for failing to intervene in 1965 when the white settlers of Southern Rhodesia unilaterally declared independence and established an illegal, minority-ruled government. The issue became moot after British-led negotiations in 1979 brought agreement on a new constitution and the independence of Zimbabwe on the basis of black majority rule. Kenya has continued to urge more firmness on Britain's part on the issue of continued white political domination in South Africa and Namibia, but it has not been as insistent as the more militant African states that Britain and other Western nations impose punitive measures against South Africa.

West Germany has focused considerable attention on Kenya, particularly in the areas of economic development, cultural ties, and education. The Bonn government announced that, from independence through 1981, credits amounting to KSh2.6 billion had been supplied on extremely favorable terms, while grants amounting to KSh544 million had been provided in support of projects by private West German organizations. The Kenya program of the German Academic Exchange Service, which offered scholarships in Kenyan universities and in West Germany and supplied teaching staffs, was the largest sponsored by this body on the African continent. West Germany has become the largest importer of Kenyan products, slightly surpassing both Britain and Uganda; coffee has constituted the bulk of the West German purchases.

United States

Kenya and the United States have enjoyed close and cooperative relations at both official and private levels. A hospitable business climate has induced many American firms to invest in the country. Kenya has become one of the largest recipients of American aid in Africa. Pleasant living conditions and excellent international communications have persuaded many American organizations to select Nairobi as a regional center for banking, administrative, and marketing operations. The resident American population of over 6,000 includes about 1,400 missionaries and their families.

Kenya's moderate, conciliatory approach to the major problems of the African continent has accorded broadly with the policies being pursued by the United States on African issues. Kenya, along with the other African countries most concerned, has been consulted by the five Western nations (the United States, Britain, France, West Germany, and Canada) negotiating with South Africa over Namibian independence. Like other members of the African group, Kenya has opposed Washington's plan for linking UN-sponsored elections in Namibia to the withdrawal of Cuban troops from neighboring Angola. Moi persisted in this position after a meeting with United States vice president George Bush in Nairobi in November 1982, arguing that linkage would delay the eventual realization of Namibian independence.

After Kenyan independence the United States became an important source of development assistance. With its Western-oriented, open society and free market economic system, the East African country was regarded as an important growth model justifying American support. In recent years the United States aid program has been concentrated on rural production and employment, health services, and reduction of population growth. A Peace Corps contingent of 240 volunteers in 1982 was the largest in Africa and second in scope in the entire world.

The United States aid program for fiscal year (FY) 1983 earmarked US$25 million principally for agriculture and rural development, including programs such as rural access roads, on-farm grain storage, and research on fuelwood resources. A total of US$4.5 million was allocated to family planning. An additional US$30 million for balance of payments support was also keyed to agricultural productivity, including fertilizer imports. Food aid in the form of surplus grain under Title I of Public Law 480 (PL-480) amounted to US$15 million, and an additional US$3.5 million under Title II of the act was made available for nutrition programs administered by private American agencies. In the FY 1984 presentation to Congress by the United States Agency for International Development, a proposal was made to increase the aid program to US$80 million plus US$9 million for surplus food under PL-480.

Until 1976 United States-Kenyan cooperation did not have a military component. But that year rising Soviet military assistance to Kenya's volatile neighbors, Somalia and Uganda, caused Nairobi to embark on a program to modernize and expand Kenyan defensive capabilities. A squadron of F-5 aircraft and helicopters mounted with antitank missiles were the principal items of equipment procured from the United States (see Foreign Military Assistance, ch. 5).

Growing Soviet naval activity in the Indian Ocean, the Soviet invasion of Afghanistan, and the establishment of a radical Muslim regime in Iran had by early 1980 intensified American concerns over security in the strategic Persian Gulf and the Indian Ocean supply lines for Middle East oil. The United States felt impelled to expand its naval presence in the Indian Ocean and to create a domestically based rapid deployment force capable of being dispatched to trouble spots worldwide. In addition to the buildup centered on the British-owned island base of Diego Garcia, negotiations were opened with Oman, Somalia, and Kenya for access to certain support facilities.

The Facilities Access Agreement reached with Kenya on June 26, 1980, provided for overflights, landing rights at three airfields, and port of call rights at Mombasa, although the full terms of the agreement were not disclosed. At the same time, United States military assistance to Kenya increased from a level of US$20 million in FY 1980 to over US$30 million in FY 1982. The Moi government insisted that the agreement be implemented in an inconspicuous manner with a minimum number of United States personnel permanently stationed in the country and no plans for major new installations.

One objective of the new agreement was to permit increased calls at Mombasa by United States naval vessels stationed in the Indian

Ocean to provide relaxation for crews and to replenish supplies. In event of an emergency, airfield landing rights would facilitate the movement of rapid deployment forces based in the United States. An American-financed dredging project enabled United States aircraft carriers to dock at the port of Mombasa in all seasons. It was estimated that the crews of the 31 ships calling at Mombasa in 1982 gave a boost to the local economy amounting to more than US$9 million.

By 1981 the value of investments in Kenya made by the 200 private American firms amounted to more than US$315 million. Industrial production, food canning, hotel management, banking, insurance, and transportation were among the sectors represented. Major American companies operating in Kenya included Firestone, Colgate-Palmolive, Crown Cork, Del Monte, Union Carbide, General Motors, and Coca-Cola. A consortium of United States oil companies conducted drilling offshore in 1981-82 with inconclusive results. The more uncertain political climate since the 1982 coup attempt, as well as the worldwide recession, had served to discourage new investment plans in 1983.

Communist Countries

Although Kenyatta had studied for a year in the Soviet Union in the early 1930s, he exhibited as president a strong distrust of both communism and the communist nations. Moi has essentially followed the course plotted by his predecessor, maintaining distant but correct relations with the Soviet Union. He has cultivated improved relations with the new leaders in Beijing (Peking) after a mutual withdrawal of ambassadors between Kenya and China as a result of a series of discordant incidents during the Chinese Great Proletarian Cultural Revolution in the 1960s. Areas of collaboration between the two countries nevertheless have remained limited.

Any form of domestic political activity perceived by the Moi government as communist in inspiration has been quickly suppressed. In recent years no conclusive evidence has appeared establishing a connection between dissenters in Kenya and international communism. Moi has confined himself to the more general charge that some of the university activists were Marxist-inspired agents serving the interests of foreign countries with the ultimate aim of undermining political stability.

In the early years of Kenyan independence, the leading spokesman for warmer relations with the communist states was Odinga, first in his capacity as minister of home affairs and later as vice president. Aid agreements were signed by him with both Beijing and Moscow without cabinet approval. Odinga's actions were motivated in part by his radical leanings and in part as a means of countering private aid received from the United States by Tom Mboya, head of the Kenya Federation of Labour and later a key member of the independent government.

The controversial nature of the Soviet aid program, notably the sponsorship of an ideological school for KANU activists called the Lumumba Institute, resulted in a series of government moves to control the activities of Soviet representatives in Kenya. With the eclipse of Odinga's political fortunes, Soviet activities subsided correspondingly (see Foreign Relations and Conflicts, ch. 1).

Under Moi, diplomatic relations with the Soviet Union have been maintained on a fairly normal basis. Soviet economic aid to Kenya has been minimal, although a considerable number of scholarships have been granted for professional training in the Soviet Union. As of December 1981 it was reported that 805 Kenyan students were in the Soviet Union and Eastern Europe, while 35 Soviet and East European technicians were working in Kenya. Trade levels were very low, amounting to US$10 million in 1982 and consisting mostly of exports from Kenya of fluorspar and sisal.

Nairobi's sharp denunciation of the Soviet invasion of Afghanistan and its subsequent boycott of the summer Olympics at Moscow in 1980 were irritants to the Soviet Union. Equally unwelcome was the agreement with the United States on military facilities concluded in the same year. Although Moscow did not find it expedient to protest publicly or to engage in retaliation, the Soviet information media focused critical comments on the Kenyan economic system and the developing ties with the United States. Kenya's capitalist-oriented development and its openness to "penetration" by foreign private investors were blamed for a sharpened social conflict and the emergence of a new African landlord class.

In the postindependence period, relations with China were colored by doubts over the activism of the Chinese in neighboring Tanzania and elsewhere in Africa. Kenya reacted adversely to Zhou Enlai's tour through Africa in 1964 preaching armed revolution. Complaints of improper activity by the Chinese embassy in Nairobi contributed to mounting strains between the two countries. In 1967 further revelations of the embassy's assistance to Odinga led to a mutual recall of ambassadors. The Kenyan embassy in Beijing was closed after an attack on it by radicals of the Red Guard movement.

One of Moi's early diplomatic moves was to reopen the Kenyan diplomatic mission in Beijing (the Chinese embassy had continued to function in Nairobi). In September 1980 Moi paid the first visit to China by a Kenyan head of state. In addition to reestablishing harmonious relations with China, his actions were also interpreted as reproof to the Soviet Union for its growing political involvement in Africa.

During his stay in Beijing, Moi negotiated an interest-free loan of KSh350 million, the bulk of which was for construction of a modern sports complex in Nairobi, typical of the kind China has offered a number of African countries as a visible symbol of friendship. Chinese aid was also pledged in the sectors of cotton and rice production and in building a modern brick and tile industry.

* * *

The political era that followed the death of Kenyatta has not been the subject of comprehensive study, although *Modern Kenya* by Guy Arnold contains informative chapters on domestic politics and foreign affairs. Among surveys by knowledgeable specialists on Kenya are two articles by Patricia Stamp appearing in *Current History* in March 1982 and March 1983. Moi's political tactics and policies are assessed by David Goldsworthy in his article, "Kenyan Politics since Kenyatta," in the journal *Australian Outlook*. Earlier but still relevant is the examination of the component elements of the Kenyan political system by M. Tamarkin in his article, "The Roots of Political Stability in Kenya," in *African Affairs* of July 1978.

Two reference sources, the annual *Africa Contemporary Record* and the monthly *Africa Research Bulletin*, supplement the works cited previously with a systematic presentation of contemporary events. The Nairobi newsmagazine *Weekly Review* is an indispensable source of reporting on domestic developments in spite of the inhibitions on material produced within Kenya.

No recent comprehensive examination of Kenyan political institutions is available. Henry Bienen's *Kenya: The Politics of Participation and Control* and Cherry Gertzel's *The Politics of Independent Kenya* are important studies of the evolution of Kenya's political institutions and practices during the first decade of independence. H.B. Ndoria Gicheru's *Parliamentary Practice in Kenya* is a semiofficial discussion of the functioning of parliament. (For further information and complete citations, see Bibliography.)

Chapter 5. National Security

Ruins of Fort Jesus, sixteenth-century Portuguese defense installation near Mombasa harbor

SINCE ITS INDEPENDENCE IN 1963, Kenya has generally been characterized as one of the more stable countries of the Third World, but its stability has been threatened at times by neighboring states and by domestic social unrest and political dissent. During most of former president Jomo Kenyatta's strict but generally popular 15-year rule, the government had not encountered serious domestic challenges to its authority and had felt confident enough about its position in East Africa to spend relatively little on national defense. The country's stability was emphasized in 1978 when Kenyatta died and was succeeded by Daniel arap Moi, his vice president. Even before Kenyatta's death, however, hostile neighboring countries and Kenya's own social and economic problems had begun to be a source of concern.

In the 1970s Kenya found itself surrounded by countries that were increasingly well armed and demonstrably willing to use force to alter the status quo in the region. Somalia, which claimed a large section of northeastern Kenya populated by ethnic Somali, established an ominous precedent when it invaded Ethiopia in 1977 in an effort to annex Somali-populated territory. The Marxist government in Ethiopia remained friendly with capitalist Kenya because of their shared anxiety over Somalia's irredentist claims. But Ethiopia also concerned some Kenyans because it had achieved a semblance of regional military hegemony owing to massive Soviet assistance in rebuilding its armed forces during and after its war with Somalia. Uganda under Idi Amin Dada also had claimed Kenyan territory, but Amin was deposed by an invasion from Tanzania, another of Kenya's neighbors.

In response to the conflicts around its borders, Kenya built up its armed forces with Western assistance, primarily from the United States and Britain. In the early 1980s external threats to Kenyan security appeared to have eased, but the region's precarious stability and superpower competition for influence there could in the future re-ignite regional conflicts.

Kenya's domestic problems have become increasingly serious. In the late 1970s rising social tensions and an accelerating crime rate, which reflected the country's rapid economic growth and urbanization, were aggravated by an extremely high population growth rate. In the early 1980s the government's inability to solve these problems combined with a slackening economy, leading to increased popular criticism of Moi and his government. The government used its legal powers for the first time in 1982 to jail several of its most strident critics. A coup attempt that year launched by junior air force personnel, which led to widespread looting throughout Nairobi, demonstrated that the possibility of a military takeover in Kenya could no longer be dismissed out of hand.

For nearly two decades national leaders purposely limited the military establishment's size and strove to encourage its apolitical character. Even after the armed forces doubled in size between 1975 and 1982 and spending mushroomed, military influence in politics apparently remained negligible. The air force coup attempt demonstrated to political leaders, however, that the military could be a threat to their power. Conversely, army loyalists, by defeating the rebels, showed that the military could be a pillar of the government's support. After the abortive coup, the 2,000-man air force was disbanded and was placed temporarily under army command. In addition to the 13,000-man army, other security forces included the small 650-man navy, the 14,000-strong Kenya Police, and its 1,800-man paramilitary arm, the General Service Unit. These forces, particularly the armed forces and the General Service Unit, were well trained and equipped and, unit for unit, were considered by most observers to be as good as the best in Black Africa.

In 1983 the tumult of the previous year appeared to have quieted, and Kenya's political stability, although shaken, was intact. But the country's social strains and political problems remained a potential threat to the country's security.

External Security Concerns

Kenya's geopolitical position has changed since independence as political and security relations among countries in eastern Africa have grown more agitated and as the superpowers have displayed more interest in the region's affairs. In 1964, apart from Ethiopia, with which Kenya had excellent relations, the recently independent states in the region—Uganda, Tanzania, and Somalia—possessed only small, colonial-style military and police forces incapable of threatening their neighbors. Equally important, the leadership in most of the new states was hostile to the notion of using scarce resources to finance military expansion. After independence Kenya had not embarked on a major military buildup and continued to rely extensively upon the former colonial metropole, Britain, to train its forces and, if necessary, to defend the regime. By the late 1970s, however, all of Kenya's neighbors, with the exception of Sudan, had threatened Kenyan interests because of their internal instability, their hostility to Kenya, or both. Moreover, Sudan, Ethiopia, Somalia, and Tanzania had all been relatively well armed by the Soviet Union, which since the late 1960s had expanded its presence in the area while Kenya's British ally had withdrawn its forces from east of Suez. Nairobi sought to reduce the imbalance in part by reinforcing its small military establishment and strengthening its ties with Western nations, especially the United States, which sought to counter Soviet influence in the region. Although in the early 1980s Kenya had managed to avoid serious conflict, regional threats to its security had become a significant concern to Kenyan leaders.

Since before independence, Kenya's most consistently troubling external security problem has been its conflict with Somalia over that country's claims to northeastern Kenya, which is inhabited mostly by ethnic Somali. Although Somalia was incapable of threatening the central government in Nairobi at the time, for four years after Kenya's independence the Somali government had trained, equipped, and supported an insurgency designed to bring North-Eastern Province under the Somali flag. Despite the guerrillas' popularity among elements of the ethnic Somali population in the area, in the years after independence Kenya's small armed forces were able to control the situation and killed an estimated 3,000 rebels (generally referred to as *shifta*). By 1967 the Somali government agreed to end support for the insurgents, but in the 1970s the danger to Kenya posed by Somali irredentism increased owing to a massive buildup in Somalia's military capability. As a result of closer political and military cooperation with the Soviet Union, the Somali army by 1976 was equipped with some 250 tanks and 300 armored personnel carriers—the largest armored force in Sub-Saharan Africa at that time—and 24 supersonic MiG-21 fighter aircraft. Kenyan forces, by contrast, did not include tanks and supersonic fighters to match those of Somalia. As a result of this imbalance, some Kenyans and foreign observers feared the possibility of a quick Somali armored thrust to annex the Somali-populated sections of North-Eastern Province.

Fortunately for the Kenyans in 1977 Somalia directed its military force at Ethiopia. At the time, Ethiopia was in a state of internal upheaval: it was still reeling from a bloody political power play that had led to a Marxist-oriented military government taking control of the state, and its Somali-populated Ogaden region was struggling to secede. The Soviets refused to support the invasion, however, and cut off all military aid to Somalia. After the Somali occupied virtually the entire Ogaden, they were overrun in 1978 by the Ethiopians, who had been quickly equipped with vast quantities of Soviet equipment and were supported by 15,000 Cuban troops, as well as by Soviet and East European advisers. The war decimated the Somali armed forces and, without significant external support for Somali president Mohamed Siad Barre's regime, the conventional military threat posed by Somalia receded. A thaw in Kenya's relations with Somalia appeared to develop in 1981 when Moi met with the Somali president after the Organization of African Unity (OAU) summit in Nairobi and pledged closer relations. Kenya, however, continued to be wary of Somalia.

Although the overt military menace posed by Somalia declined after the Ogaden war, the *shifta* problem reemerged. In the latter part of 1980 armed gangs were involved in a series of robberies, the killing of a district officer, and an attack on a political headquarters in Garissa where five provincial officers were killed. After the latter incident the Kenyan police launched a sweep through Garissa that left many ethnic Somali dead, according to reports. Some Kenyan officials linked the upsurge in *shifta* activity that was continuing in 1983 to the Somali government, but other observers saw it as an ironic effect of the Somali defeat in the Ogaden war. According to this view, the war displaced Ogaden Somali herdsmen, and their livestock were killed; many moved into Kenya and, unable to pursue their traditional nomadic livelihood, some turned to banditry. Twenty years after independence it was not known whether Kenyan Somali, most of whom retained a strong ethnic identity, considered themselves to be Kenyans first or whether they identified themselves with Somalia's irredentism as they had during the *shifta* war. The Kenyan government's position has always been clear. Moi, speaking in Garissa in 1979, stated, "the soil on which we are standing is under my rule, it is my country and you are my people. I shall not allow anybody to take even an inch of it."

Because of their mutual concern over the Somali threat, Kenya and Ethiopia, despite their differences, continued the friendly relations that had previously existed between Ethiopian emperor Haile Selassie and Kenyan president Kenyatta. That their common national interests transcended their ideological differences was plainly to Kenya's benefit because after the Ogaden war, Ethiopia emerged as the preeminent military power in the region. In the early 1980s the Soviet-supplied 225,000-man Ethiopian army possessed over 800 tanks and a like number of armored personnel carriers, more than 10 times as many as in the Kenyan security forces. The Ethiopians were also aided by 12,000 to 13,000 Cuban troops and by 1,200 to 1,300 Soviet and East European advisers. Since the Ogaden war, Moi and Ethiopian head of state Mengistu Haile Mariam, as well as other high-ranking delegations, have exchanged state visits. At these meetings the two countries have regularly condemned Somali "expansionist activities" and urged countries that give Somalia military aid—including the United States—to stop arming their opponent. Ties between Kenya and Ethiopia continued to be harmonious in the early 1980s, but Kenyans remained wary of their northern neighbor's greater military strength.

Kenya also has had serious political problems with Tanzania and Uganda, which in the 1970s developed into significant national security concerns. Uganda, ruled between 1971 and 1979 by the despotic and mercurial Field Marshal Idi Amin Dada, was viewed as a potential threat to Kenya but one that could be controlled. In early 1976 relations deteriorated when Amin laid claim to virtually all of Kenya west of the Rift Valley (which in early colonial days had been part of Uganda); several Kenyans living in Uganda were also reported killed or disappeared at the time. Amin dropped his claims when Kenya demonstrated its control over Ugandan trade by briefly halting the shipment of Uganda-bound goods at Mombasa. The Kenyan government, however, remained apprehensive about the unpredictable Amin, whose military forces—on paper at least—were stronger at the time than were those of Kenya.

Despite their difficulties with Amin, Kenyan leaders' concerns were heightened after a Tanzanian invasion toppled the Ugandan dictator in 1979. As the invasion proceeded, the Kenyan government stated that it was in violation of the charter of the OAU and repeatedly called for a cease-fire. Kenya, realizing its own and Africa's vulnerability would be exacerbated if the OAU principle of noninterference in the internal affairs of member states was not adhered to, obviously did not wish to see a precedent set.

Acknowledging reality, however, Kenya quickly accepted the new Ugandan government, but the Kenyans were wary of the influence over Uganda of Tanzanian president Julius Nyerere, whose army had invaded with 10,000 troops. Relations with Tanzania had long been strained, and the Kenya-Tanzania border had been closed since 1977 because of the inability of the capitalist Kenyans and Nyerere's socialist government to coordinate their economic policies when Kenya, Tanzania, and Uganda had all belonged to the East African Community (see Foreign Relations and Conflicts, ch. 1; Tanzania and Uganda, ch. 4). The Kenyan political leadership and the press feared that under Tanzanian domination Uganda could develop into another hostile socialist neighbor. Although Tanzania's military presence in Uganda was gradually reduced (they were all removed by early 1982), Kenyan suspicions appeared to be confirmed when Milton Obote, the former Ugandan premier who had preceded Amin, was chosen president in controversial elections of December 1980. Obote was known to Kenyans as a socialist who was philosophically hostile to the Kenyan economic system and as a good friend of Nyerere, who had granted him a home in exile during the Amin era.

After assuming office, however, Obote took a conciliatory attitude toward Kenya, and the Moi government reciprocated. Relations between Kenya and its East African neighbors, although not close in the early 1980s, did not worsen, and the perceived possibility of armed hostilities declined. Uganda and Kenya, in particular, appeared to be willing to solve their differences peacefully. In 1982 the Ugandan government protested to the Kenyans about the activities of Ugandan refugees in Kenya attached to the anti-Obote Uganda Freedom Movement (UFM). The Kenyan government reacted by stating that it would not allow dissident refugees to use Kenya as a platform to attack their mother countries and quickly detained two prominent UFM leaders. Relations with Tanzania remained tense, and Tanzania's granting of asylum to rebels involved in the 1982 coup attempt against the Moi government further aggravated Kenyan suspicions. But fears of being militarily attacked or economically isolated by Uganda and Tanzania appeared to have subsided.

Kenyan vulnerabilities to military disruption from its neighbors were eased in part because of Kenya's own military buildup. Beginning in the mid-1970s in response to the country's uncertain relations with its militarily stronger neighbors and the increased Soviet military presence in the region, Kenya's armed forces had been expanded and modernized with considerable assistance from the United States and other Western countries (see Military Missions, Organization, and Strength, this ch.). Kenya's security against outside threats was also reinforced by the 1980 Facilities Access Agreement with the United States that allowed American forces to use certain Kenyan airfield and port facilities. Kenyan leaders have long realized, however, and the country's internal difficulties in the early 1980s further demonstrated, that national security was largely dependent on domestic peace and stability, goals to which military strength and foreign alliances would not necessarily contribute.

Domestic Security Issues

Since independence Kenyan leaders have focused their energies on maintaining Kenya's internal security and stability. Through a combination of rewards and sanctions, Kenyatta's tightly knit ruling circle was remarkably successful, and by the 1970s the country was widely known for its domestic peace and prosperity. The transition of power after Kenyatta's death appeared to confirm that Kenya's stability was built on a solid foundation. Moi, however, had to contend with establishing his control over a political system that was designed for his charismatic predecessor. Moreover, the political leadership began to feel the pressure of long-building social strains arising mainly from Kenya's 4 percent annual population growth rate, its income disparities, growing unemployment, and rapid urbanization.

Initially popular, Moi faced mounting criticism of his policies and resorted in 1982 to using the Preservation of Public Security Act to detain some of his critics. Within weeks an attempted coup by air force personnel appeared, at least temporarily, to shake the government's confidence. Although the long-term consequences of Kenya's situation could not be predicted with certainty, in 1983 it appeared that the Kenyan political leaders would find it increasingly difficult to preserve the high degree of political stability that had marked the country's first two decades of independence.

Kenyan Concepts of Internal Security

In order to understand Moi's domestic security concerns and policies, it is useful to examine the political security framework developed and practiced over the 15 years of Kenyatta's rule. During the Kenyatta era the security and political legitimacy of the small exclusive ruling group—the so-called Kenyatta family (see Glossary), most of whose members, like Kenyatta, came from the Kiambu branch of the Kikuyu ethnic group—were enhanced by Kenyatta's prestige gained during his imprisonment during the Mau Mau uprising against British rule in the 1950s (see The Mau Mau Emergency, ch. 1). Perhaps more important, the government's stability rested on its ability to prevent political rivals from building independent power bases. The size and influence of the armed forces were explicitly limited. Moreover, the leadership was able to provide economic incentives (often in the form of land grants) and political favors to encourage the integration of opponents and potential opponents into the system, and it encouraged important politicians and ministers to direct their energies to economic pursuits rather than political empire-building.

The Kenyatta government could also act harshly against real and suspected political opponents. Former vice president Oginga Odinga, a leader from the Luo ethnic group and a longtime government critic, saw his power undercut by a systematic government policy of questioning his motives, detaining him and his followers, and banning his political party (see Party Politics in the 1960s; Government and Opposition in the 1970s, ch. 1). Many Kenyans suspect, moreover, that during the Kenyatta era the government was involved in the murder of three politicians: Pio da Gama Pinto in 1965, Tom Mboya in 1969, and Josiah Mwangi Kariuki in 1975. All three were potential opponents of the regime and had established themselves as popular and trenchant critics of government policies in general and the ethnic favoritism shown toward the Kiambu-Kikuyu in particular. In the case of Kariuki, a parliamentary select committee, convened because of the political outcry, stated in June 1975 that it had found a "massive and determined cover-up" by the police who handled the case. The committee also raised questions of complicity in the murder by the commander of the General Service Unit (GSU) paramilitary police largely composed of Kikuyu (see The General Service Unit, this ch.).

During the Kenyatta era the government was given broad legal powers to deal with perceived security threats, and the Moi government has retained them. The police powers of the central government are based on a number of legal measures of potentially wide scope in matters involving political acts. The Preservation of Public Security Act (revised in 1978) conferred on the chief executive basic powers to issue special regulations, which are subject to certain constitutional limits and controls by the National Assembly, at any time "it appears to the President that it is necessary for the preservation of public security" and he so declares by notice in the *Kenya Gazette*, the official record of government acts. The act authorized the president to take special public security measures affecting virtually every aspect of national life and civil rights under a definition of the preservation of public security that included, but was not confined to, "the prevention and suppression of rebellion, mutiny, violence, intimidation, disorder, crime, and unlawful attempts and conspiracies to overthrow the Government or the Constitution."

A regulation that was put into effect under this act in June 1966 (and remained in effect in 1983) gave the president power to order the search or arrest of any person without stated reason and to hold people in indefinite preventive detention without trial or the right of habeas corpus. Even members of parliament did not have statutory immunity from this regulation. With these measures went a tendency over the years for authority to broaden the definition of sedition and subversion.

The Kenyatta regime was not gratuitously repressive, however. Parliamentary debates sometimes focused criticism on the government; a relatively free press existed; and student groups and labor unions were able to stage political demonstrations (although these were sometimes violently suppressed). But in this system, bolstered by a relatively efficient administrative system and a booming economy, a coherent political opposition was never allowed to develop to the point of mounting a serious challenge to the regime.

When Moi came to power in August 1978, his first challenge was to assume control over a political system that had been developed by and for the Kiambu-Kikuyu elite. Moi, a Kalenjin and a former leader in the defunct Kenya African Democratic Union (KADU) before it had been absorbed by Kenyatta's Kenya African National Union (KANU), had been named earlier to the position of vice president in large part to provide the government with ethnic and political balance. Several members of the "family" who preferred a Kiambu-Kikuyu as president had made an unsuccessful attempt to change the Constitution in 1976 so that the vice president would not automatically become acting president upon Kenyatta's death (see The Question of Succession, ch. 1). Nonetheless, the transition appeared to proceed smoothly, and Moi's erstwhile opponents pledged their allegiance to him. But two months after Kenyatta's death, Attorney General Charles Njonjo revealed in a speech that when Kenyatta died, the new leader had narrowly escaped assassination.

According to Njonjo, unnamed elements had financed the formation of a 200-man paramilitary structure, disguised as the police Anti-Stock Theft Unit, that was supposed to murder Moi, Vice President Mwai Kibaki, and Njonjo himself at the time of Kenyatta's death. Although Njonjo stated that he would locate and prosecute the plotters, no one was charged. Several weeks after a suspected police official was extradited to Kenya in December 1979, Njonjo announced that the official would receive a pardon. Moi and Njonjo then asked the country to forget the so-called *ngoroko* (literally, cattle rustler) affair and dismissed it as a "bad dream" in the country's history. The press soon ceased reporting on the matter, and the full story may never be known. At the time, however, most Kenyans viewed the alleged plot as the work of members of the Kenyatta "family" who were unwilling to relinquish power to Moi.

Moi's initially wide popularity served to reinforce his political position and limit the possibility that the Kikuyu elite, who had become politically unpopular during Kenyatta's last years, would seek his removal. Although he was equipped with the laws and the precedent to preserve domestic security through various measures of patronage and coercion, the new president initially appeared to eschew the tactics of his predecessor and substitute an all-encompassing populism. The Moi government released all political prisoners detained by the previous regime, allowing many to rejoin KANU and stand in the 1979 elections. Promised prosecutions of leading Kiambu-Kikuyu political figures—most for smuggling and other forms of corruption—were never pursued. Although the new president refused to campaign for certain "family" members in the 1979 parliamentary elections and banned ethnic associations, including the economically powerful and politically influential Kikuyu-dominated Gikuyu [Kikuyu]-Embu-Meru Association (GEMA) in 1980, the remnants of the Kenyatta "family" remained prominent in areas of government and business during Moi's first year in office. As his government began to encounter domestic opposition in the early 1980s, however, Moi, like Kenyatta, began to adopt tougher methods of social control and limited his circle of political intimates.

Political Protest and the 1982 Coup Attempt

After he assumed the presidency, Moi rapidly emerged as Kenya's most popular politician, but in 1982 the security of his regime was brought into question by a spectacular but unsuccessful coup attempt by the previously quiescent armed forces. Although overt opposition to the government remained basically political in scope, Kenya in the early 1980s was being confronted by a host of socioeconomic problems. The high annual population growth rate had more than doubled the number of Kenyans since independence, straining the government's and the economy's ability to employ them. Rapid economic growth in earlier years had created vast differences in wealth while rapid urbanization had disrupted traditional patterns of living and was, most observers believed, largely responsible for the country's growing crime problem. The slowing of economic growth in the early 1980s diminished the prospects for graduates from Kenyan secondary schools and universities; economic problems, limited arable land, and changing political attitudes reduced the ability of the government to placate its potential opponents and to gain supporters through patronage.

Antigovernment demonstrations by students, which often turned violent, increasingly became a source of concern to the Moi government. The president, who was the object of spontaneous progovernment student demonstrations in 1978, soon became the object of student complaints. Before Moi became president, conventional wisdom downplayed the significance of student demonstrations, citing the fact that most students looked forward to receiving government jobs after graduation. By 1981, however, Moi apparently began to regard the students as a threat to the state's stability and authority and closed the universities after violent demonstrations there. The government was particularly concerned because university protests had gradually taken on a more Marxist tone as demonstrators expressed their solidarity with workers and peasants and condemned the government's "neocolonial" relationship with the West. The attitudes and actions of the students were not seen by most observers as having potential to pose a significant threat to the government, but by 1982 it appeared that political criticism of the regime was shared by others beyond the university community.

Early in 1982 Moi was shaken by a surge of reaction to corruption from students, the press, and politicians at all levels. Despite his publicized calls to root out corruption, the president was widely perceived by students and other Kenyans to have merely shifted the source of government corruption from the Kiambu-Kikuyu to his own Kalenjin ethnic group. Apparently threatened by the increased criticism and by a concurrent political attempt by Odinga to establish a new left-oriented party, Moi within weeks detained some students and lecturers under the Preservation of Public Security Act (the first time the law was used since he took office), made Kenya a de jure one-party state by an act of parliament, and fired the editor of the progovernment *Standard* for criticizing his moves.

In this atmosphere of increased political tension, Nairobi was rocked by an abortive coup attempt. Early on the morning of August 1, 1982, young officers and enlisted men of the Kenya Air Force (KAF) seized control of the Voice of Kenya radio station in Nairobi as well as the air bases at Nanyuki, Eastleigh, and Embakasi. Radiobroadcasts indicated that a group calling itself the People's Redemption Council had seized power because of corruption and "ruthless repression" by "Moi's bandit gang." Before police, GSU, and army units finally overpowered the rebels, an officially estimated 150 Kenyans (and perhaps hundreds more) had been killed, and rioting and wild disorder had spread throughout Nairobi. Property damage was extensive, and it was feared that damage to Kenya's reputation for stability would cost the country much more if foreign investors' confidence in the government was shaken.

The abortive coup, although poorly planned and failing to demonstrate the existence of a coherent antigovernment organization, did illuminate sources of opposition to the president and his government. The operation was led and carried out mostly by radical junior officers of the KAF. As a result, the service was disbanded, and most of its 2,000 personnel were detained on suspicion of complicity in the coup. As of March 1983 some 900 servicemen had been court-martialed and had received sentences ranging from dismissal from the service to prison terms of up to 25 years. Several hundred were awarded presidential clemency, but six were sentenced to death for treason. Their appeals were pending in mid-1983.

The coup attempt, however, was not limited to a small group of KAF officers. Close ties existed between the airmen and university students, who were informed of the action in its early stages and broadcast their support for the "August 1 Revolution" over the seized Voice of Kenya radio station. About 50 students were killed in the rioting and in fighting between pro-coup and anti-coup forces. The radicalism of the air force officers was ascribed by most observers to the university's influence. Many air force personnel, who were generally better educated than their army and police counterparts because of the technical nature of their service, were recent graduates of the University of Nairobi or Kenyatta University College. Some maintained their links to the university community because the recently expanded KAF did not have the facilities to house all of its personnel in barracks, and many of the airmen lived in student areas in poor conditions (see Conditions of Service, this ch.). In the wake of the coup, the government arrested a large number of students for taking part in the looting or for supporting the rebels. Sixty-nine were charged with sedition, but 61 of these were later freed by an act of presidential clemency. The authorities also shut down the University of Nairobi and Kenyatta University College for seven months—the longest such closure in the school's history—and sent students to their home areas to report to their respective chiefs twice a week.

Apart from the KAF personnel and the students, the government moved against others who had performed unsatisfactorily during the attempted coup. Three weeks after order was restored, the commander of the KAF, Major General Peter K. Kariuki, was relieved of his command and placed in detention. He was later found guilty in a court-martial and sentenced to four years in prison for failing "to use [his] utmost endeavor" to prevent the coup or suppress it. The same day, Commissioner of Police Benjamin Gethi was dismissed by Moi "in the national interest" and was imprisoned for nine months. There also were persistent but unsubstantiated reports after the coup attempt that some cabinet ministers and other officials had been involved in planning separate coups at the time of the KAF rebels' action.

The government suspected that Odinga may have been involved in the KAF rebellion, and it banned him from traveling outside his hometown of Kisumu in western Kenya. The authorities also arrested his son, Raila Amolo Odinga, on charges of treason. Apart from the accusation of one of the plotters, the government apparently did not have any evidence that the Odingas had been involved. Nor could it be determined whether ethnic hostility had been a significant factor in the plot. The Kikuyu were suspected because the KAF had been largely composed of Kikuyu. The Luo were suspected because the Odingas were Luo and because two KAF enlisted men, who were Luo and claimed to be coup leaders, had hijacked an aircraft to Tanzania and were granted asylum. Although some Kenyan authorities suspected Tanzanian complicity, most outside observers believed that Tanzania did not know of the proposed coup in advance.

After the action an uneasy calm seemed to settle over Kenya as the government and its political opponents tallied the economic and human costs. The quiet was also reinforced by the government's demonstrated willingness to apply the Preservation of Public Security Act and by the closure of the Nairobi universities. Moi himself reiterated his earlier condemnations of Marxism as a "foreign ideology" and considered revamping the university curriculum and dismissing suspect lecturers. The president also continued to emphasize that he needed a loyal government and indicated that some ministers held over from the Kenyatta regime had "misinterpreted" this "goodwill gesture." Many observers noted that Moi appeared to be excluding Kikuyu from positions of influence in his government and throughout the bureaucracy and was relying increasingly on fellow Kalenjins for advice.

Crime

The most visible manifestation of the coup attempt was the complete breakdown of law and order in most sections of Nairobi for several hours on August 1. KAF men were joined by mobs of civilians and even a few policemen in a spree of looting and pillage. Preliminary estimates placed the damage at KSh500 million (for value of the Kenya shilling—see Glossary), most of which was directed at Asian shopkeepers.

The increase in criminal activity during the coup attempt was the most dramatic example of the lawlessness that has concerned officials since the mid-1970s. Crime rates had begun to rise even before that time, particularly in the urban areas. The increase was in part linked to the social and economic changes flowing from economic development and the growth of urban centers. In Kenya, as in other developing countries, forces at work in the mobile urban communities and in the new planned settlements have tended to loosen the hold of traditional norms and values, to weaken the social sanctions against deviant behavior, and to place increased value on material goods. These factors have been coupled with high unemployment, visible differences in wealth, and increased opportunity for certain kinds of criminal activity.

Nairobi has illustrated the urban crime problem in its sharpest form. The capital city's population increased by 62 percent to more than 800,000 people between the censuses of 1969 and 1979. Although it was thought that the urban growth rate may have slowed, the city's population continued to increase at an annual rate much higher than that of the national population as a whole. Nairobi's crime and delinquency rates were also by far the highest in the country, which were in accord with a tendency, noted in many areas of the world, for crime rates to vary directly with city size. Juvenile delinquency in particular was a distinctly urban phenomenon in Kenya, as in other countries of Sub-Saharan Africa.

Unemployment among Kenya's youth has been identified as an important underlying cause for the rising incidence of crime against property. Moreover, urbanization has consistently outpaced the jobs created through industrial and economic development. Kenya's ambitious program of educational expansion since independence has not been matched by an expansion of opportunities for the graduates of the school system. As a consequence, by the mid-1970s the rate of unemployment among secondary-school graduates was reaching crisis proportions. Moreover, the benefits of economic growth were unevenly distributed socially and geographically, which gave rise to growing discontent over the disparity of wealth between the mass of citizens and a small elite in Nairobi, not excluding national leaders. Kenya's Asian community was particularly resented by many Kenyans for its relative wealth, apparent dominance of the retail trade, aloofness from African society, and the alleged involvement of its members in illegal currency exchange practices.

In the late 1970s and early 1980s many Kenyans were blaming foreigners, particularly Ugandans, for the rising crime rate. Ugandans had begun to come to Kenya in large numbers in the mid-1970s after Amin seized power. The number of Ugandan refugees increased at the time of the Tanzanian invasion of Uganda in 1979, and there was little indication four years later that the Ugandans were returning to their homeland. The Kenyans in 1982 ended an agreement with Uganda that allowed their nationals to move freely between the two countries, and some expected that mass expulsions of Ugandans living illegally in Kenya might occur. The number of Ugandans in the country, many of them poor and disenfranchised, was not known but was estimated to be 10,000, concentrated mostly in urban areas. Kenyans also linked the upsurge in crime—especially stock theft—in the Somali-populated areas of the northeast to an influx of ethnic Somali who had left Ethiopia in the late 1970s.

Urban crime has become increasingly sophisticated, including highly organized gang operations, daylight bank holdups, the use of guns instead of the traditional *panga* (long-bladed bush knife) despite stringent gun control laws, and the use of automobiles for street robberies. Authorities also have noted increased sophistication in the most prevalent form of rural crime, the theft of livestock. Particularly in the regions bordering Somalia, Uganda, and Tanzania, where cross-border raids often marked by the killing of the victims have long been a serious problem, four-wheel-drive vehicles and automatic rifles have come into use. *Kondoism* (armed robbery by gangs, accompanied by murder or mayhem) has become a growing form of crime affecting individuals, homes, and stores in isolated locations.

Official statistics on crime reported to the police showed a steady progression from 38,702 in 1969 to 72,555 in 1980 (see fig. 16). Offenses against private and public property accounted for more than three-quarters of all reported offenses during this period. Such figures gave a reasonable indication of overall trends and of gross relationships among categories of crime. They were less reliable as a measure of the actual incidence of criminal activity, however, and did not provide regional or urban-rural breakdowns. Much crime undoubtedly has not been reported for reasons of inaccessibility of the police or inadequate communication. Traditional attitudes probably have stood in the way of reporting many offenses, particularly in rural areas. In some cases, formal legal procedures and sanctions have appeared alien or irrelevant to the victim or his family; in others, all concerned have preferred to deal with the matters through customary procedures. Some offenses, such as rape, have been largely unreported for reasons having to do with personal and family shame. When the law has been at variance with customary values—for instance, the penal code embodying a Western philosophy of punishment and the African emphasis on payment of compensation to the victims or their kin as the main sanction—the law itself has appeared less useful to the aggrieved individuals than some other recourse.

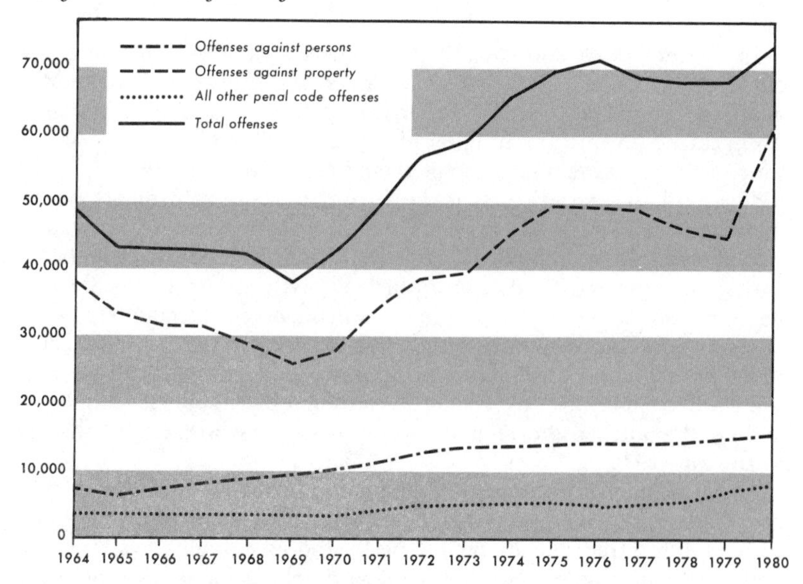

Source: Based on information from Kenya, Ministry of Finance and Planning, Central Bureau of Statistics, *Statistical Abstract, 1974*, Nairobi, 1974; and Kenya, Ministry of Economic Planning and Development, Central Bureau of Statistics, *Statistical Abstract, 1981*, Nairobi, 1981.

Figure 16. Crimes Reported to the Kenya Police, 1964–80

Armed Forces in the National Life

Throughout most of the period since independence, the armed forces have played a relatively minor role in society. Limited in size, the Kenyan military establishment neither cost very much nor was it considered to be a relevant political factor. In the late 1970s, however, increased spending to expand and modernize the military establishment began to burden the Kenyan economy. The military's overt role in politics remained negligible during this period, but its influence in politics may have increased in the wake of the abortive coup attempt of 1982.

Development of the Modern Military

Like those of most Sub-Saharan countries that achieved independence in the 1950s and 1960s, Kenya's military establishment was derived from the indigenous armed force maintained by the former colonial authority. First under the Imperial British East Africa Company and after 1895 under the direct control of the British government, indigenous armed forces under British officers were raised for keeping law and order. Designated in 1902 the King's African Rifles (KAR), these units comprised a total of six battalions of foot soldiers apportioned among the colonial territories of Kenya, Uganda and, after World War I, Tanganyika (present-day Tanzania). Assigned separately to the territories and recruiting from among the local populations, the KAR units each established a distinct territorial identity.

Beginning in World War I (and later in World War II), the KAR battalions were used in military operations outside their home areas. Wartime experience established the reliability and combat effectiveness of African colonial forces. At the beginning of World War I Africans had been employed chiefly as laborers attached to regular British forces; by the end of World War II KAR units had the status of regular combat units fully integrated into Commonwealth of Nations military operations in places as far-flung as Burma. As such, they had acquired a distinctive military tradition and a reputation as seasoned fighters. After the outbreak of the Mau Mau uprising in the 1950s, the KAR was employed for a time with the colonial police and British forces in suppressing the insurgency.

The British command in East Africa did little during the colonial era to advance Africans into the officer grades. The authorities made a start in 1956 when a new grade of *effendi* (warrant officer) was created for Africans. A special school for regular African officer candidates opened in Nairobi in 1958, about 10 years behind similar developments in British West Africa. The first East Africans were admitted to Britain's Royal Military Academy at Sandhurst only in 1959.

In December 1963 the three Kenya-based battalions of the KAR—the 3d, 5th, and 11th battalions—and their equipment were turned over to independent Kenya under the general transfer of powers and administration from the colonial authority. The approximately 2,500 men of the three battalions, renamed the Kenya Rifles, became the new country's army. At the same time, Britain provided additional grants equivalent to US$9.8 million in arms and equipment, US$23.8 million in installations and other assets, and US$3.6 million in assistance to establish a navy. Two militia units that were established during the colonial period—the white-dominated Kenya Regiment and the Kikuyu Guard—were disbanded at national independence, while naval and air force cadres were established shortly thereafter.

The three KAR battalions transferred to Kenya upon its independence were dependent in the middle and senior ranks almost entirely on regular British officers. By agreement of the two countries, these personnel were seconded to their former units. The desire of the civil leadership to retain the services of British officers appeared to stem in part from the belief that their retention would provide continuity and stability in the new army during the transition period and would give the government time to cope with the political and ethnic strains that Africanization would bring. There was also the pragmatic matter of a dearth of experienced African officers.

At independence the Kenyan army had 80 African commissioned officers, who constituted 48.5 percent of the total officer corps. The bulk of these were former *effendi*, most of whom had been given regular commissions after 1961; others were noncommissioned officers (NCOs) who had undergone a short officer training course. The new African officers were nearly all of junior rank, but one African lieutenant colonel commanded a battalion.

The disadvantages of British dominance of the officer corps were made clear in the first month of independence when a mutiny broke out among some men of the 11th Battalion on January 24, 1964. The immediate cause was disgruntlement over pay and the retention of expatriate British officers. The action may also have been sparked by a similar incident in the army of neighboring Tanzania. At the request of the Kenyan government, the mutiny was quickly quelled with the help of a contingent of British troops in the vicinity.

Kenyatta immediately reassured the army and the country of his general confidence in the military but moved decisively against those involved. Some 170 were court-martialed or summarily dismissed from the service; the leaders were sentenced to prison terms of up to 14 years; and the 11th Battalion was disbanded (but was reconstituted later as the 1st Battalion). Steps were also taken to remedy the grievances and to step up the professional training of the army. The January mutiny, although a transitory incident that posed no threat to national unity, pointed up the problems of ambivalent loyalty within the army and the urgent need for restructuring a still essentially mercenary colonial force into a national army.

Despite increased political pressure to "Kenyanize" the armed forces, the upsurge of guerrilla activity on the part of ethnic Somali in northeast Kenya dictated the retention of experienced British officers. The campaign against the *shifta*, which continued until late 1967, gave the army the opportunity to cast itself in the role of defender of the national honor and integrity against a threat that had some element of foreign instigation. The *shifta* challenge also heightened the civilian leadership's understanding of the need for an effective military force.

Although British officers were retained during the *shifta* conflict, the political fallout of the 1964 mutiny did accelerate the Kenyanization of the armed forces. The small elite officer contingent produced at Sandhurst, at Mons Officer Cadet School, and in other Commonwealth countries was inadequate to meet the army's revised staffing requirements in the 1960s. For a time in the mid-1960s, a number of young men received specialized officer training in other countries, such as Egypt, China, the Soviet Union, and Bulgaria, under private arrangements between these countries and political factions in Kenya. Many of these hopefuls, however, found upon their return to Kenya that their credentials for a commission were unacceptable to the Ministry of Defence, which regarded their officially unsanctioned foreign training as politically suspect. Israeli-trained personnel were accepted, but only after they retrained in Kenya. The great majority of new officers had to be commissioned from the ranks. A side effect of the rapid production of African officers was a lasting shortage, which became acute in several areas, of the experienced senior NCOs and technical personnel who had been the backbone of the colonial forces. It took much less time to turn NCOs into officers than to produce their replacements.

The British presence in Kenya's armed forces was only gradually reduced. A British army general continued to serve (on secondment) as army commander and as chief of the Defence Staff until 1969. The large British Army Training Team was withdrawn in 1970 and finally, in 1973, a Kenyan major took over command of the air force from a British officer to complete the Kenyanization process.

The Armed Forces and the Government

The Constitution provides that the president "shall be the Head of State and Commander-in-Chief of the armed forces of the republic." The president is prohibited from holding any office in the "naval, military, or air force." Over a period of nearly 20 years, the government pursued a variety of policies designed to ensure the loyal subordination of the military to political authority, and before the surprising coup attempt in August 1982 it appeared to have been successful.

In contrast to the situation in many other new nations where leaders quickly expanded their armed forces for reasons of security or prestige, the Kenyan government consciously limited the size of its armed forces and thus their potential to influence national politics and drain resources from the economy. The military did expand—manpower tripled in size in the decade after independence to 7,500 and doubled again in the six years after that because of the threats on Kenya's borders—but its growth and command structure were carefully controlled by the political authorities.

By retaining the British military in a major command, technical, and training role in the Kenyan armed forces into the 1970s, the apolitical traditions and standards of professionalism of the British army may have been reinforced among the Kenyans. Additionally, the British presence at all levels of the military represented a powerful force backing the Kenyan government and the status quo. Since the completion of Kenyanization the British, by mutual agreement with the Kenyan government, have maintained a military presence in Kenya, usually in the form of frequent battalion-size maneuvers (see Foreign Military Assistance, this ch.).

The government has moved to balance its desire for an effective military institution and its need to maintain control over the armed forces by modifying the high command. In 1966, during the period of the *shifta* conflict and after the establishment of the air force and the navy, a centralized high command was established to improve efficiency and coordination among the services. As chief of the Defence Staff, a British major general commanded the combined services and served as the country's ranking military officer until replaced in 1969 by a Kenyan, Major General J.M. Ndolo.

The disadvantages of the centralized military command were highlighted in 1971 when nine men having military connections pleaded guilty to being part of a plot to overthrow the government. Although not formally tried for participation in the affair, Ndolo was accused of involvement and was dismissed from the service. The government decided not to replace him with a new chief of the Defence Staff, apparently feeling that government security was enhanced when all interservice coordination was observed by civilians. As a result, during most of the 1970s the Ministry of Defence was an amorphous organization; the service commanders came under the direct operational control of the president. The army commander was the highest ranking officer and also acted as the senior military adviser to the president, but he did not have any operational responsibilities beyond his own service.

The practical limitations of this system became apparent, given the expansion of all three services in the 1970s, joint training, and the increased possibility of military conflict with neighboring states. Thus, after Moi assumed the presidency in 1978, the high command was again restructured.

In order to increase military efficiency while maintaining civilian control, Moi reestablished the centralized high command but abolished the Ministry of Defence and brought defense matters directly under the authority of the Office of the President. Long-serving Minister of Defence James S. Gichuru, an aging KANU veteran whose active role in military matters had long been circumscribed, became minister of state in the Office of the President and was responsible for defense until his death in 1982. Jeremiah Kiereini was promoted within the Office of the President, becoming the chief secretary and head of the civil service. In this position he supervised Archibald Githinji, who headed the new Department of Defence and dealt mostly with administrative and logistical matters. Responsibility for military operations was placed under the command of the newly formed General Staff, which reported directly to the president. The army's commander, Brigadier James K. "Jack" Mulinge, was named chief of the General Staff and by 1980 had attained the rank of general.

Observers also noted that after Moi became president, members of his Kalenjin ethnic group moved into prominence. Most notably, J.M. Sawe, a respected Kalenjin lieutenant colonel at the time of Kenyatta's death, had by 1980 become a major general and army commander. (He was a lieutenant general in 1983.) In addition, particularly after the 1982 coup attempt, Kikuyu personnel in the security forces lost influence. In 1983, after Moi dismissed the Kikuyu chiefs of the air force and the police in the wake of the coup attempt, none of the uniformed service chiefs were Kikuyu, and morale among Kikuyu servicemen was reported to be low.

The policy of basing important appointments on ethnic considerations was similar to the pattern followed by Kenyatta, which had favored the Kikuyu. Immediately after independence and the 1964 mutiny, the government sought to increase the loyalty of the armed forces by redressing the colonial legacy of ethnic imbalance that had virtually excluded the Kikuyu from military service. By 1967 about 23 percent of the officer corps was of Kikuyu origin, compared with the 28 percent that was Kamba. The increase in the Kikuyu ratio was attributed in part to their success in qualifying examinations for officer commissions because of the generally superior education system in areas of Kikuyu concentration. In addition, however, the influx was the effect of Kenyatta's Kikuyu-dominated government, which encouraged more Kikuyu influence in the armed forces, as well as in other parts of the state security apparatus. Because of the former dominance and seniority of the Kamba and the Kalenjin in the armed forces, the Kikuyu for political reasons were never able to dominate the top ranks of the armed services completely; for example, Kenyatta chose to appoint Ndolo, a Kamba, as the first Kenyan chief of the Defence Staff. Similarly, Moi relied heavily on Kamba military appointments to fill the top ranks, as Kalenjin personnel accounted for less than 10 percent of the military's manpower in the early 1980s. These Kamba appointees included Chief of General Staff General Mulinge and Chief of Defence Staff Brigadier J. Musombe.

Particularly after the British departure, the Kenyan government sought to ensure the loyalty of leading military officers by offering them economic incentives. This practice first became obvious in the early 1970s when it was discovered that Ndolo, shortly after having been unceremoniously removed from the post of chief of the Defence Staff, was living on a large, prosperous farm provided by the government. Later examples of this practice included several general officers—removed when Moi came to power—who were made head of important parastatal corporations. General Mulinge is known to have been given a large farm by the government, as was former air force commander Kariuki.

In the wake of the coup attempt the military had become more prominent in Kenyan public life. Mulinge appeared often on television, and the media showed more pictures of officers consulting with local leaders and performing ceremonial duties, such as opening schools or dedicating public projects. Foreign observers also noticed that changes in official protocol had made military officers more prominent at official functions than was previously the case. The air force move demonstrated that the military was both a threat to the regime and, because of the actions of the loyalist army personnel who defeated the rebels, a bulwark of Moi's government. While the air force was disbanded and purged of its militants, officers who demonstrated their loyalty have been rewarded. Army Major General Mohamoud Mohammed, an ethnic Somali who personally led a unit of soldiers to recapture the Voice of Kenya radio station from the KAF rebels, was given command of the air force and promoted to lieutenant general. Army officers and enlisted men were given a generous pay increase.

In 1983 it appeared that the role of the military vis-à-vis the government had been altered, at least in the short term. While few were confidently predicting an ever-growing military role in the government, it did not appear likely that the armed forces would retreat to their nearly invisible role of the 1960s and 1970s.

The Military and the Economy

The Kenyan government has always maintained tight control over military spending. After the 1978 reorganization of the high command, all budget decisions were jointly made by the government auditor and Permanent Secretary Githinji; the regular military was only marginally involved in an advisory capacity.

Budgetary expenditures for defense were well under 1 percent of total recurrent and development expenditures in the early 1960s. In 1963-64 the amount increased to 1.7 percent, and expenditures under the first independent government budget (1964-65) rose to 4.3 percent. However, British grant aid in weapons, equipment, and training had permitted the Kenyan government to establish its armed forces without a major impact on its financial resources, and through the rest of the decade defense costs remained relatively constant at under 5 percent of total expenditures. In the early 1970s outlays rose gradually, reaching 6.4 percent in 1973-74. In 1973, however, spending on education and health continued at over four times the level of defense expenditures. (In the late 1960s and at the beginning of the 1970s expenditures for the paramilitary and conventional police—the "law and order" component of the budget—were roughly double those for the armed forces.)

Defense costs mushroomed in the late 1970s when Kenya decided to expand and reequip its armed forces in view of the growing political tensions in East Africa. From a level of KSh429 million in fiscal year (FY) 1975/76, defense spending increased to KSh794 million the following year and to KSh817 million by FY 1979/80. Part of the increase was attributable to inflation, but during this period defense as a percentage of total central government outlays increased from 6.7 percent to 16.4 percent. Likewise, its share of the gross national product (GNP) was estimated by the United States Arms Control and Disarmament Agency to have grown from 1.5 percent in 1976 to 4.8 percent by 1979. Part of the reason the budget grew so quickly during the late 1970s was that the military equipment purchases and payments were made over a relatively short time. Thus, after payments for equipment were made, the defense budget in the early 1980s receded somewhat. There were indications after the 1982 coup attempt that the budget would increase in future years in order to cover increased personnel wages and salaries, training, and a new barrracks building program.

Although the military establishment in the late 1970s became a burden on Kenya's financial resources, it was never a significant drain on the country's manpower resources. In 1982 there were 16,500 Kenyans in the armed forces, or about 0.1 percent of the national population. With an estimated 3.5 million males between 15 and 49 years of age, 2.1 million of whom were considered fit for military service, conscription had never been necessary to fill the ranks of the armed forces. The officer corps was relatively well educated, but it was believed that military service had not significantly diverted educated manpower from more economically productive work because of the existence of high levels of unemployment among secondary-school graduates and even university graduates.

The government's Development Plan 1979-83, like earlier plans, emphasized the economic contribution of the military through "projects ranging from the construction of roads and bridges to disaster relief operations, desert locust control, crop harvesting, and transportation in inaccessible areas." First adopted after the conclusion of the *shifta* campaign in the 1960s, military construction and civic projects came to play a major role in the armed forces' mission, particularly for the two engineer battalions. Most military construction projects, rather than directly contributing to the civilian economy, were designed to improve military facilities, i.e., through the building of roads and barracks on bases, and so cut the economic costs of the military establishment. Hydrographic surveys by the navy and aerial photography by the air force were of assistance in national development schemes, fisheries, and agriculture. The armed forces by the late 1970s were also thought of as a training ground for the development of skilled manpower that could be used in other sectors (see Recruitment and Training, this ch.). Statistics were not available to suggest the aggregate extent or economic worth of such public works by the armed forces, but they were not thought to be insignificant.

Military Missions, Organization, and Strength

The Kenyan armed forces were organized to provide defense against external enemies; they could also be used in support of the police to contribute to the maintenance of internal security. In the late 1970s and early 1980s all the military services were expanded and reequipped so that their ability to defend the country against external attack was substantially enhanced. In 1983 the reequipment program was nearing completion, and the military was mainly concerned with reorganizing, recruiting, and retraining personnel in order to rebuild the air force, which had been disbanded after the 1982 coup attempt.

Under the overall command of the president, who served as commander in chief, and working in concert with Permanent Secretary for Defence Githinji and Chief Secretary Kiereini, the General Staff operated from the Armed Forces Headquarters Building in Nairobi. In addition to General Mulinge, who as chief of the General Staff served as operational commander of the armed forces, the General Staff included the service chiefs. In 1983 Army Commander Sawe served as deputy chief of the General Staff. A defense staff operated within the headquarters under the General Staff to coordinate the activities of the services and to administer the Women's Service Corps (WSC) and branches for joint operations and training, personnel, administration, and technical matters. Headed by an army brigadier, the defense staff was composed of officers from all three services. In 1983 the army was the only service that had its own chief of staff and staff organization.

The Army

The Kenya Army, largest of the three services, accounted for about 85 percent of military personnel before the air force was dissolved in 1982. Between the mid-1970s and 1982, the army doubled in size from 6,500 to 13,000 and was completely refitted with modern equipment. From a basic strength in the mid-1970s of four infantry battalions, the army's combat units by 1982 had increased to two armored battalions, one armored reconnaissance battalion, an air cavalry battalion, five infantry battalions, and two artillery battalions, in addition to engineer, transport, and communications units. The battalions and their component companies were mixed and matched according to operational needs and operated throughout the country under the command of two brigade headquarters: one at Gilgil near Nakuru and one at Nanyuki. The army expected eventually to expand to three brigade headquarters as funding became available.

In a few years the army had become a well-equipped modern force. Whereas in the mid-1970s it had no tanks and only 13 armored cars, in 1982 it was taking delivery of the last of 72 Vickers Mk3 main battle tanks from Britain. The tanks were supplemented by some 60 armored cars, most of which were equipped with 60mm and 90mm guns. For the most part, these operated in the armored reconnaissance companies. The army's artillery was also significantly expanded from a handful of light mortars and recoilless launchers to include 50 or more 105mm guns, as well as modern antitank guided missiles. The army was still basically an infantry force, but its mobility had been significantly improved by the addition of more than 50 armored personnel carriers (see Table 13, Appendix).

One of the most significant additions to the army was the 50th Air Cavalry Battalion, which took delivery of 32 Hughes Defender helicopters in 1980 and 1981. Approximately one-half of the battalion was equipped with helicopters armed with the modern rapid-fire 30mm Chain Gun, while the other half fielded tube-launched, optically tracked, wire-guided (TOW) antitank missiles, produced in the United States. The battalion was composed of three companies, each of which could operate autonomously to support ground forces operations. Some members of the unit, attached to Embakasi Air Base, participated in the coup attempt. But most of its personnel remained loyal, and a TOW missile launched from a Defender is credited with destroying the rebel communications center at the base.

After the coup attempt the army acquired from the KAF 10 Aérospatiale Puma helicopters, much larger craft than the Defenders, with accommodations for 15 to 17 passengers. It was not known whether these would serve with the air cavalry battalion or whether they would be used for other purposes. The air force's battalion-size Ground Air Defence Unit (GADU), most of whose personnel were involved in the attempted coup, was also placed under army command and renamed the 75th Battalion.

Members of the army's 50th Air Cavalry Battalion on parade
Courtesy Jon B. Crane

Concurrent with its arms acquisitions the army embarked on a large effort to train technicians to operate and maintain its equipment. The operational readiness rate was not known, but even before the coup attempt army equipment was rarely near a complete state of readiness. According to one report, the new tanks, tank transport vehicles, and army radar equipment were especially poorly maintained. The coup exacerbated problems because large numbers of army technicians and mechanics were transferred to the air force in order to make up for manpower shortages in that service. Despite these difficulties and the fact that it had not been tested in combat since the relatively minor *shifta* actions nearly two decades previously, the Kenya Army was regarded by outside observers as a well-trained force capable of defending the country against low-intensity external threats.

The Air Force

In 1983 the reorganized KAF was known as the 82 Air Force. Little information was available regarding the KAF's organizational structure, but before the coup attempt it was divided into the Flying Wing, the Technical Wing, and the Administrative Wing. The Technical Wing was responsible for the maintenance and servicing of aircraft and communications equipment, while personnel, supply, and housekeeping functions came under the Administrative Wing. Operations were centered in the Flying Wing, of which one fighter-bomber squadron, one light strike squadron, two transport squadrons, and one training squadron were the main operational units.

Army officers and technicians led by Lieutenant General Mohammed played a prominent role in the restructuring of the KAF, and it was expected that it would be rebuilt to its pre-1982 strength of 2,000 men. The force's 29 combat aircraft were based mainly at Laikipia Air Base (known as Nanyuki Air Base until after the coup attempt), and Moi Air Base near Nairobi (previously known as Eastleigh), but aircraft also had access to most of the more than 200 other airfields and landing strips scattered throughout the country. Air force headquarters was located at Moi Air Base.

Led by British officers and technicians and equipped with nine British-donated Chipmunk trainer aircraft, the KAF was officially inaugurated in June 1964. During the 1960s, African personnel steadily replaced the British (including pilots), and the force's equipment was gradually upgraded. Formation of the strike squadron was announced in 1970, and it was soon equipped with six BAC-167 Strikemaster jets operating in a training and ground attack role. The KAF also took delivery of six reconditioned Hawker Hunter fighter-bombers from Britain, which constituted the force's main combat strength in the 1970s.

The air force reequipment program began in 1976, when it was announced that the United States would sell Kenya a squadron of F-5E/F Tiger II supersonic fighter-bombers. The F-5s, which were equipped with Sidewinder air-to-air missiles, were delivered in 1978, replacing the Hunters and improving the KAF's combat potential. Two F-5Es were lost in operational accidents by 1983, but two more F-5Fs were delivered in 1982, which allowed the force to pursue a more efficient training program for F-5 pilots. The KAF also took delivery of 12 BAC Hawk T-52s in 1980-81 to supplement and eventually replace the Strikemasters in the light strike and training roles. Kenya's transport capability was also reinforced by the addition of De Havilland Caribou and, later, Buffalo twin-engine transports and Dornier Do 28D Skyservants (see table 14, Appendix). Further significant aircraft deliveries were not expected in 1983.

Most technical and flight training was performed inside the country with some assistance provided by British and American training teams and by representatives from companies involved in selling equipment to Kenya. Student pilots progressed from basic training in Scottish Aviation Bulldogs to advanced training in the Hawks and Strikemasters.

Before the abortive coup, the air force was regarded as one of the best in Black Africa, but the upheavals since then have, for the time being at least, undercut its quality. Although few pilots were implicated in the dissident action and no aircraft were damaged, most of the KAF's mechanics and specialists were dismissed from the service. To replace them, the military leadership recalled reservists and transferred mechanics and technicians from the army. Unfamiliar with air force equipment, they moved quickly into the service after intensive courses of one or two months, and maintenance suffered. Whereas before the attempted coup the KAF could sometimes achieve an aircraft operational rate of 85 percent (although it was usually much lower), reports indicated that in the months after the disorder the operational readiness rate had slipped to less than 50 percent. As a result, British and United States assistance in training new technicians had increased, but the process of rebuilding the force was expected to take years.

The Navy

Smallest and junior of the three services, the Kenya Navy in mid-1983 comprised some 650 men and officers and seven patrol vessels. Although established on December 12, 1964, the first anniversary of the republic, the navy became substantially operational only in 1967 when the first 10 Kenyan cadets reported for duty after graduation from the Royal Naval College in Dartmouth, England. Three new vessels were delivered from British shipyards that year (replacing a submarine chaser on loan from the Royal Navy). Command of the navy was assumed by a Kenyan naval officer, who replaced a seconded British officer on November 1, 1972. Service of the Royal Navy Training Team was terminated by the end of the year.

Under the command of Brigadier E.S. Mbilu, a Kamba who had been appointed to lead the force by Kenyatta in 1978, the navy has been primarily engaged in patrolling coastal waters to deter smuggling and poaching. Because of the small size of its vessels, however, the navy was not thought to be fully capable of patrolling to the limits of the new 200-nautical-mile limit, particularly during the monsoon season. Naval operations were also complicated by constant changes in charted waters caused by the growth of coral reefs and alteration of the coastal contours resulting from a gradual seaward intrusion of mangrove forests—as much as two kilometers in places. In 1983 the navy's inventory included the three Vosper 31.4-meter patrol craft built for Kenya in 1966 as well as four slightly larger Brooke Marine patrol craft delivered in the mid-1970s (see table 15, Appendix). The latter group of vessels was initially armed with light 30mm and 40mm guns, but in 1983 they were being reequipped to carry Israeli-made Gabriel surface-to-surface missiles.

Because of high costs and expansion and modernization of the other services, the navy did not take delivery of any new vessels between 1975 and 1982. Kenya was forced in 1981 to cancel a scheduled purchase of Vosper Thornycraft 56-meter missile-equipped patrol craft. Two years later, however, the navy was again engaged in discussions with Vosper Thornycraft and Lürssen to purchase new vessels.

The main naval base was located in Mombasa, one of the largest and finest ports in the Indian Ocean region. In 1978 indigenous repair capabilities were significantly enhanced upon completion of the 18,000-ton Mombasa dry dock.

A unit of the Kenya Navy in a ceremonial review
Courtesy Jon B. Crane

Recruitment and Training

Kenya's armed forces have never needed conscription to satisfy manpower needs. The basic technique for recruiting both officers and enlisted personnel has been the periodic recruitment safari in which military teams visit rural communities, schools, and universities throughout the country to accept applications from potential recruits. Publicity campaigns by press and radio have stimulated public interest in advance of the safari, whose arrival is a community affair. This recruitment method also has served the policy aim of enlisting a cross section of the nation's youth and maintaining an ethnic balance within the armed forces approximating the ethnic makeup of the population at large. According to observers, the army has strictly observed ethnic quotas. Although details of Kenya's preferred ethnic balance were not available in 1983, one report indicated that in the armed forces as a whole, Kikuyu personnel made up 19 percent of manpower levels, 12 percent were Kamba, and no other group had more than 10 percent of the total.

Limited manpower needs combined with high unemployment among civilians allow the armed services to be fairly selective in enlisted recruitment. The minimal initial term of enlistment ranged from two years for an infantryman to from seven to nine years for those who received technical training. Final acceptance was contingent upon applicants being able to meet specific height, weight, health, and education standards when they reported to the recruitment training center. The level of health and education of armed forces personnel was reported to be considerably higher than that of the population at large.

Educational requirements varied significantly among the services. Literacy was not a requirement for general enlistment in the army, although the service required that its men understand Swahili. Most soldiers came from the peasantry and were educated to no more than a primary level. The air force, on the other hand, obtained a majority of its recruits from technical and secondary schools. Most enlisted airmen had received their secondary-school certificates, some were university graduates, and all had passed tests measuring knowledge, learning potential, intelligence, and manual dexterity. The social differences between the two services also highlighted the fact that air force members were mostly Kikuyu. The army, although more ethnically balanced, had relatively high proportions of Kamba and Kalenjin personnel.

Regular officer candidate enrollment was open to persons between the ages of 18 and 22 who had at least secondary-school certificates and high class standing and to qualified NCOs. The services recruited aggressively at secondary schools and colleges to compete for a fair share of the educated and future leadership elite. Reserve officer training programs did not exist in the schools or elsewhere. Special inducements were given to university graduates, including direct entry commissions and, upon completion of training, the backdating of seniority to date of entry. Short-service commissions limited to five years were available to certain categories of officers.

Since 1970 all recruit and basic officer training, as well as most technical and in-service training for the army, air force, and navy, has been consolidated in the Armed Forces Training College at Lanet, near Nakuru. Army recruits undergo an intensive basic training course of about six months. Recruits of the other services and officer candidates take shorter periods of basic training, after which they continue in specialized instruction.

Officer training has been carried out by the Cadet Wing of the training college. Full-term cadet training, including flight officer training, has been provided for most army and air force officers within Kenya by an all-Kenyan training staff. Officer training, including specialized training, generally has taken two years to complete before officers are commissioned.

In the early 1980s the armed forces were seeking to train their own personnel within Kenya without foreign assistance. To this end, in 1981 the Kenya Armed Forces Technical College was established to train personnel from all three services as electronics, mechanical, and maintenance technicians. In 1982 approximately 200 students were enrolled, and it was expected that the school would eventually accommodate 650.

Conditions of Service

"A discontented soldier is a bad soldier," according to the Kenyan government in its Development Plan 1970-74. For this reason, Kenyan defense spending in the first decade of independence, especially after the end of the *shifta* war, was focused on improving the accommodations, food, pay, and medical care of service personnel. In the 1960s pay and allowances, for example, accounted for as much as two-thirds of the defense budget. In the late 1970s and early 1980s, however, conditions of service for most personnel became increasingly austere as the military establishment doubled manpower levels and shifted its spending priorities in order to procure more weapons.

In the early 1980s most of the army was housed on installations in rural areas where they lived in tents, self-built barracks lacking water or electricity, and old "temporary barracks," few of which could accommodate the married soldiers' families. In the air force, pilots and middle-grade officers were generally housed adequately, but enlisted personnel and technicians generally had to endure poor housing conditions. Some lived in tents on the air bases and, because they were not as a rule confined to barracks, many low-ranking members lived in the poorer sections of Nairobi without the benefit of a housing allowance.

Many observers linked the part played by well-educated, well-trained airmen in the 1982 coup attempt to their poor living conditions. As a result, although operating under severe financial constraints, the government moved quickly to devote resources to improving the standard of living of military personnel. In January 1983 two contracts equivalent to US$5 million were signed for constructing new barracks that had initially been planned in the mid-1970s but had been delayed because of higher priority needs.

Military pay was also increased. In November 1982 the government announced that army enlisted personnel and NCOs would receive a 15 percent pay raise, and officers would get increases up to a maximum of 30 percent. The pay raises had been recommended earlier by an armed forces review board appointed by Moi in December 1981 but had not been immediately put into effect. In 1983 data on military pay scales, or comparisons with wages in the civilian sector, were not available, but technically proficient enlisted airmen were paid significantly more than army infantrymen. It was expected that the FY 1983/84 defense budget would devote increased funding to service pay and to construction of military housing.

Morale among army personnel was higher than that among airmen, some believed, because army life provided more relative comforts for its personnel, who generally came from less prosperous backgrounds than did KAF members. Well-educated airmen, according to this view, were more inclined to have inflated expectations of their salaries and living conditions. Others noted that air force discipline was far more relaxed than in the army, which emphasized vigorous, regimented drill. Indeed, after taking command of the air force in 1982, General Mohammed quickly moved to make frequent drill mandatory in all air force units.

The rank structure of the Kenyan armed forces has been patterned on the British model. As part of the move to centralize administrative functions in the armed forces in 1968, the designation of officer grades and enlisted ranks of the three services was unified, adopting standard army titles with minor alterations (see fig. 17). In 1978 the highest officer grade was major general, held only by the army commander. The highest air force grade was colonel, while the highest in the navy was lieutenant colonel. By 1983, however, an army general served as chief of the General Staff, a lieutenant general commanded the air force (although he was an army officer), and a brigadier headed the navy.

Military benefits included a contributory retirement system with pay based on length of service and grade held, survivor benefits to dependents of servicemen disabled or killed while on active duty, and liberal leave policies. Retirement provisions in effect permitted voluntary retirement for officers after 20 years of service and for enlisted men after 21 years. Retirement was mandatory at ages that increased with rank up to 60 years. General Mulinge was more than 60 years of age in 1983, but Kenyan officials pointed out that there was no mandatory retirement age for officers above the grade of major general.

In-service civil education for military personnel was provided by the Armed Forces Education Services; courses ranged from basic instruction in literacy to adult education subjects. A secondary-school curriculum led to award of the Armed Forces Certificate of Education. Classes were conducted by instructors at the unit level, and correspondence courses were also available. Formal education centers existed at Moi School for the Armed Forces at Eastleigh (formerly the Armed Forces School of Higher Education) and at army and WSC headquarters. Considerable emphasis was given to in-service education throughout the three services; classes were usually conducted during duty hours. In 1982 the government reportedly was expanding the military education system to teach college-level classes and to accommodate the families of servicemen.

In keeping with the goal of establishing an indigenous national language, Swahili was in wide use in the army, particularly at the troop command level and in troop training. English, however, appeared to coexist with Swahili in many situations. Technical demands and training abroad undoubtedly placed a premium on a knowledge of English for officers and many enlisted specialists.

Uniforms of the three services were similar to those of the British forces with certain distinctive details to lend a national character. Rank and insignia were generally identical except for use of the Kenyan shield where the crown appears on British forces' insignia. Uniforms

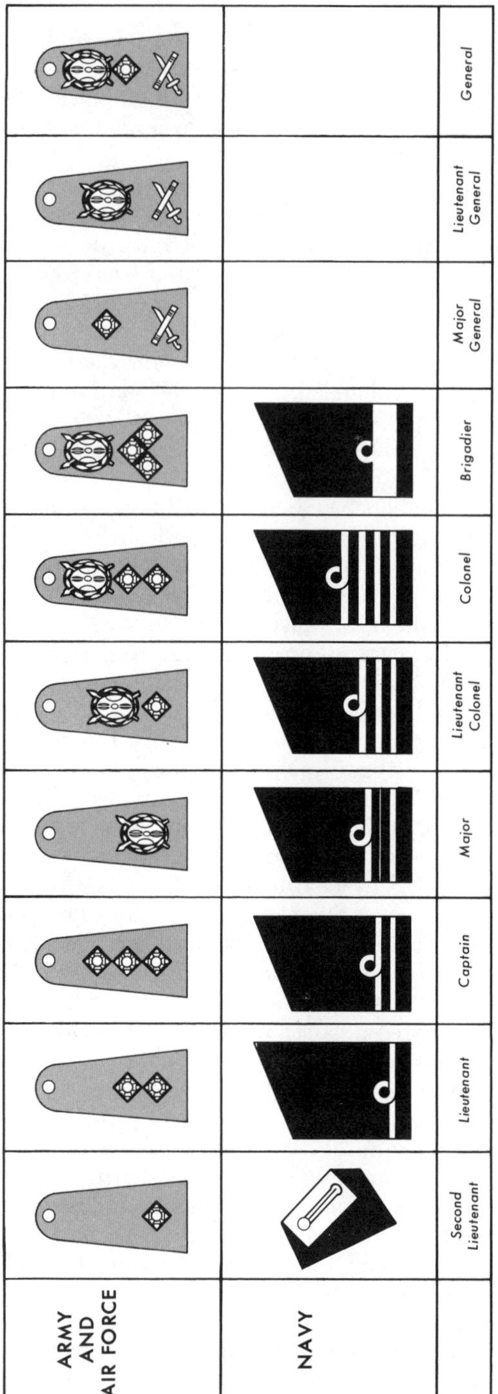

	Second Lieutenant	Lieutenant	Captain	Major	Lieutenant Colonel	Colonel	Brigadier	Major General	Lieutenant General	General
ARMY AND AIR FORCE										
NAVY										

NOTE—The services have used a uniform system of rank designation since 1968. After the air force was reshuffled in 1982, personnel were assigned army rank insignia.

Figure 17. Officer Grades and Insignia of the Kenyan Armed Forces, 1983

were of tropical-weight cotton; the standard army dress was of khaki-colored twill, and the navy uniform featured the standard navy white with British-style blue trim on the flat headgear and the square collar. After the 1982 coup attempt, air force uniforms were changed from the standard Royal Air Force blue to a lighter blue in the ceremonial uniforms and, in the service uniform, to a khaki color that some observers described as almost pink in tone.

Officers generally wore the same uniform as enlisted personnel but with certain distinctive features, such as the Sam Browne belt. For formal inspections or ceremonial occasions the standard army uniform was embellished with accessories such as white gloves and a field-green, visored service cap instead of the bush hat, beret, or helmet of the field uniform. On the anniversary of national independence in December 1980, thousands of Kenyans cheered wildly when Moi, for the first time in public, wore his dress uniform as commander in chief of the armed forces.

Foreign Military Assistance

Kenya has never had an arms industry and in 1983 did not appear to be seeking a capability to produce equipment that had exclusively military uses. As a result, since independence the country has been completely dependent on outside sources for military hardware. Although arms imports constituted a burden on the economy, figures supplied by the United States Arms Control and Disarmament Agency between 1971 and 1980 indicated that Kenyan arms imports never accounted for more than 2.9 percent of total imports, except for 1979 when the figure was 3.6 percent.

Britain has long been an important arms supplier, an outgrowth of the colonial past and continuing aid and trade ties. During the 1960s British advisers were instrumental in setting up all three of Kenya's armed services, and their presence, although reduced, continued through the 1970s and into the 1980s. Under a 1964 agreement between the two countries, British military units continued to undergo training in Kenya. Administered by the six-man British Army Training Liaison Staff, Kenya (BATLSK), four or five British army battalions of about 600 men each trained annually in Kenya, usually in 12-week shifts. Elements of Britain's elite commando unit, the Special Air Service (SAS), also practiced their tactics in Kenya's rugged equatorial terrain. Occasionally, British combat battalions would engage in maneuvers with their Kenyan counterparts and assist in training exercises. The Royal Engineers also sent sapper battalions to Kenya to assist in construction projects.

Britain continued to supply Kenya with arms, although it no longer monopolized the trade the way it had during the first years after independence. All Kenyan naval vessels were of British origin in the early 1980s. The KAF's Hawk, Strikemaster, and Bulldog aircraft were all produced by the British Aerospace Corporation. Britain was also the source of much of the army's equipment, most notably the Vickers tanks. Kenyan officers continued to train and be educated at British military academies, but most technical training had shifted to domestic facilities. A number of British military advisers and civilian technical representatives were active in 1983 in support of the tank and the Hawk programs.

By the early 1980s the United States had surpassed Britain as Kenya's largest arms supplier. American military assistance to Kenya was closely linked to United States security interests in the Indian Ocean-East Africa region and to concerns about what the Soviet Union was doing in the area. The United States and Kenya has no military supply ties before Washington offered to sell Kenya F-5 aircraft in 1975, months after Somalia and the Soviet Union signed a treaty of friendship and cooperation and the Soviet Union accelerated its arms deliveries to Somalia. Kenya initially turned down the offer of aircraft but the following year, amid signs of increased Somali belligerence, agreed to buy 12 F-5s, spare parts, and training for an initial payment of US$65 million.

The American role in Kenya's defense increased dramatically when the United States sought military ties with Kenya in order to counterbalance strategic losses incurred as a result of the Iranian revolution. In June 1980 the two countries signed the Facilities Access Agreement allowing United States access to certain Kenyan military facilities (see United States, ch. 4). Largely as a result of this agreement, United States naval ships in the Indian Ocean increasingly visited Mombasa for crew rest and relaxation. It was estimated that the 30,000 American sailors who visited Mombasa in 1982 spent more than US$9 million in the local economy and perhaps much more. But apart from the small staff of the Kenya-United States Liaison Office (KUSLO), which coordinated the arms deliveries and in-country assistance, the United States has not retained a permanent military presence in Kenya. Americans, however, were involved in a number of construction projects, particularly in the Mombasa area, that were designed to facilitate the military operations of the United States rapid deployment forces. Costing a total of US$57.9 million through FY 1983, these included dredging Mombasa port to accommodate American aircraft carriers, improving communications, constructing parallel taxiways and parking aprons at Mombasa's Moi International Airport, and various other improvements.

Kenya continued to purchase United States military equipment and training, notably the 32 Hughes Defender helicopters at a cost of US$43.4 million. Between FY 1976 and FY 1982, Kenya agreed to purchase US$149 million worth of United States military equipment and training. Over the same period it took out US$135 million in guaranteed foreign military assistance loans from the United States to ease the burden of expenditures. Beginning in FY 1982, the United States began to earmark military grants to Kenya under the Military Assistance Program (MAP). US$10 million was granted in FY 1982,

U.S. Air Force Photo

Courtesy Hughes Helicopters, Inc.

The United States has been Kenya's source of major military equipment, such as the Sidewinder-equipped F-5E Tiger II fighter-bomber (top) and the Defender helicopter.

US$17.5 million in FY 1983, and US$23 million was requested for FY 1984.

Between FY 1976 and FY 1983 Kenya also received US$5.8 million of grant assistance under the International Military Education and Training (IMET) program. Unlike the case with British and other military programs where virtually all technical training was done in Kenya, a large number of Kenyan military personnel were trained in the United States to operate the new equipment. In FY 1982 there were 72 Kenyans training in the United States under the IMET program. Most of these were pilots and technicians involved in the F-5 and Defender programs, but some were high-ranking officers undergoing instruction at command and staff colleges. In 1983 it was expected that an increased number of Kenyans would be trained under American programs to make up for the shortage of technically trained personnel exacerbated by the attempted coup.

Kenya also maintained a relatively close military relationship with Israel, but few details were generally available. The two countries began to cooperate militarily when Israel trained five Kenyans as air force pilots immediately after Kenya's independence and even before the KAF was established. Because their training was not officially sanctioned by the Kenyan government, the five were retrained by the British training mission before being admitted to the KAF. During the 1960s and early 1970s Israel was primarily involved in giving training and technical assistance to the GSU paramilitary police organization. Military cooperation declined when Kenya broke diplomatic relations with Israel after the October 1973 War in the Middle East, but the ties were apparently not severed entirely. In the early 1980s Israeli technical assistance increased when Kenya decided to reequip four of its naval patrol vessels with Gabriel surface-to-surface missiles. It was thought in 1983 that there were at least 20 Israelis in Kenya involved in the Gabriel program.

Kenya also maintained military ties with a number of other countries in the early 1980s. France, after nearly two decades of concentrating on its African military relations with former colonies, moved in 1980 to sell Kenya AML-60 and AML-90 armored cars, Panhard armored personnel carriers, and Aerospatiale Puma helicopters, as well as technical assistance. Canada supplied transport aircraft and in 1982 agreed to supply a further US$15 million worth of technical and educational military training to the Kenyans. India and other Commonwealth countries educated Kenyan officers at their military academies and staff schools.

The Police System

The Kenya Police, composed of nearly 16,000 regular personnel in 1983, was the country's sole legal internal security and law enforcement body. The force included a special semiautonomous paramilitary body (the GSU) and local units administered by ethnic communities in addition to the more usual police sections. Before 1978 the police were administered by Moi in his roles as vice president and minister of home affairs. After becoming head of state, he retained authority over the police by transferring control of most of its branches to the Office of the President. In early 1982 all police functions came under the control of that office, when in a governmental reshuffle the Criminal Investigation Directorate (CID) was transferred from the authority of the Ministry of Home and Constitutional Affairs. Within the Office of the President, the permanent secretary for provincial administration—J.S. Mathenge in 1983—was primarily responsible for formulating the budget and for giving general policy direction to the force. Commissioner of Police Bernard Njiinu was considered commander of the force and was responsible for all police operations. In FY 1980/81 the Kenyan government spent KSh327.4 million on internal security, about 6.1 percent of the national budget.

The Kenya Police traces its ancestry to various bodies of security guards that were first formed by British interests in East Africa and evolved during the colonial era to fit changing conditions and problems. The first organized security force was composed of armed guards called *askaris*, who were hired locally by the Imperial British East Africa Company beginning in 1887 for the protection of the stations along the caravan route from Mombasa to Uganda. In 1896, after the takeover of administration in British East Africa by the British Foreign Office, the beginning of a genuine police unit under a professional police superintendent was established in Mombasa, the coastal terminus of the trade route. A third independent force known as the Uganda Railways Police was organized the following year in connection with construction of the railroad.

The Mombasa police formed the nucleus of what became after 1902 a reorganized and consolidated British East Africa Police, whose headquarters was moved in 1905 to the rapidly growing city of Nairobi. The Kenya element of this force was renamed the Kenya Police on the formation of Kenya Colony and Protectorate in 1920. Expanded during the world wars by sizable levies of Indian and African recruits, the police took on border patrol duties and guarded installations. By the end of the 1940s the Kenya Police possessed a good communications system, a training school, a crime laboratory and a police-dog program.

Under the impact of the Mau Mau emergency from 1952 to 1960, in which it bore the primary operational responsibility, the Kenya Police underwent an unprecedented expansion and transformation. The regular police more than doubled in size to over 13,000 and were bolstered by the Kenya Police Reserve, which also doubled in size to over 8,000 men, and the adjunct Tribal Police. At least as important as numbers in the eventual ending of the emergency was the development under the impetus of the campaign of three important operational capabilities: a paramilitary strike force, the GSU; a first-rate police intelligence apparatus; and a police communications system whose base had been established during World War II. Upon national independence in 1963, the Kenya Police was transferred intact to the new Kenya government. A large contingent of British and Asian officers and other key personnel remained temporarily to ensure continuity and an orderly transition. The force was then a trained professional body of just under 12,000 men. The Kenya Police was established as a national force in 1964 (having been transferred from regional control by constitutional amendment).

The Kenya Police

Under the direction of the commissioner in 1983, Kenya Police headquarters in Nairobi established policy for the force throughout the country and supervised the operations of all subordinate units and elements. The commissioner was assisted by deputy commissioners in charge of operations and administration, respectively. Below the national headquarters in the chain of command were eight provincial commands, each headed by a senior assistant commissioner. Their jurisdictions were coterminous with the territory of each province and Nairobi Area. Under each provincial command were a number of divisions with headquarters usually in the capital city of the corresponding civil district. Under division headquarters were more than 200 police stations and posts in cities, towns, and other locations throughout the national territory. In practice, the outlying and provincial units enjoyed a good deal of operational autonomy under the general control of the provincial and district commissioners. An excellent communications system allowed the quick dispatch of mobile units or other special forces from higher headquarters to subordinate units.

Apart from the paramilitary GSU, major arms of the force were the general duty police, who performed the conventional policing and traffic functions, the Railways and Harbours police, the CID, the Intelligence Directorate (Special Branch), and the Police Air Wing. These units were commanded by assistant commissioners or senior assistant commissioners.

The CID was responsible for all matters relating to criminal investigation and maintained all criminal files. It served as Kenya's plainclothes police detective force. The Special Branch was concerned with domestic intelligence and subversive criminal activity. The CID, the Special Branch, and other specialized sections constituted distinct divisions in the various headquarters and had a functional chain of command to national headquarters.

The Railways and Harbours Police were charged with all functions relating to the prevention and detection of crimes committed on or against land and water transport lines and installations. A waterborne marine section had units at Mombasa and at Kisumu on Lake Victoria. Its independent criminal investigation division was popularly called the "formation crime branch." The commandant of the Railways and Harbours Police was an assistant commissioner of police.

The force's mobility was enhanced by the Police Air Wing, which performed reconnaissance, communications, supply, and evacuation services. Organized in 1959, the unit got its first operational experience in the campaign against the *shifta* insurgency in the mid-1960s. As of the early 1980s the air wing had seven Cessna light airplanes and three Bell-47 helicopters capable of operating from unimproved airstrips in remote areas.

An adjunct to the regular Kenya Police was the Administrative Police, earlier known as the Tribal Police, which served as the agent of law and order in the rural reaches of Kenya beyond the town-based stations and posts of the regular police. Members of the Administrative Police were recruited in the ethnic community where they served. Although they were under the administrative control of the district commissioner and were subject to the general direction of the provincial commissioner, members of the Administrative Police were under the day-to-day operational control of the local chief or subchief whose enforcement arm they were. It was principally through the chiefs, who had broad legal powers to prevent offenses, maintain public order, and arrest suspected wrongdoers (or those who fail to pay their taxes), that the district commissioner carried out his responsibility for law and order in his jurisdiction. Regular police were usually called in to handle serious crimes, such as murder, or in other matters beyond the capacity or authority of the Administrative Police.

Another auxiliary force, the Kenya Police Reserve, was formed in 1948 as a volunteer force to bolster the regular police in emergencies. It was used extensively for this purpose during the Mau Mau emergency, when it reached a strength of over 8,000 men. Its strength in the mid-1970s was believed to be about 3,000. Unlike the Administrative Police, which was a standing auxiliary force, police reservists served only when called for emergency or other duty, apart from scheduled training.

Volunteers were at least 18 years old and enlisted for at least two years. Police recruits were enlisted voluntarily on a nationwide basis by recruiting teams. The educational level of recruits has improved as recruiters have looked increasingly for applicants with secondary and higher education. National policy has called for achieving, as far as possible, an ethnically balanced force. No information was available, however, regarding the overall ethnic makeup of the police.

Training of police recruits and officers, as well as courses for reservists, were conducted at the Kiganjo Police College, which was established near Nyeri in 1948. Specialized training was provided at a number of institutions inside and outside the police establishment. The Criminal Investigation Directorate Training School in Nairobi conducted courses for that branch of the police. Located with the school was a training facility for Special Branch personnel. Communications personel received advanced training at Kenya Polytechnic and practical training at the directorate training school. Refresher and other kinds of training, including part-time literacy and continuing education courses for field personnel, were offered at provincial training centers. Six-week courses in weapons familiarization and basic refresher training were provided for Administrative Police, among others, on a space-available basis at the Armed Forces Training College at Lanet near Nakuru in the Rift Valley, as well as at the Administrative Police Training College at Embakasi, Nairobi. Supervisory and management training for senior police personnel were offered at the Kenya Institute of Administration in Kabete. Some police personnel are sent to Britain or other places abroad for special kinds of training.

Although they had long been regarded as a well-trained, effective, fully professional force, the reputation of the Kenya Police suffered during the 1970s. In part this perception was probably a result of the force's inability to control ever-increasing crime rates, but police corruption also became an issue for the first time. Public criticism focused on the force after several policemen were convicted of armed robbery in 1972. In 1978 Moi removed Commissioner Bernard Hinga—who had been appointed as the country's first African police commissioner in January 1965—partly because of controversy surrounding the *ngoroko* Anti-Stock Theft Unit that theoretically came under his command. In addition, however, he was perceived as unable to deal with the issue of police corruption generally.

By appointing Benjamin Gethi, the commandant of the efficient GSU, to head the force, Moi hoped to improve its reliability and its image. There were some indications that the reputation of the police improved over the next four years, yet there were still problems. The Kenyan press reported stories of citizens mistakenly being shot by policemen, in particular a 1981 incident involving Gethi. After the police commissioner was involved in a road accident with a truck in which his daughter was killed and Gethi was injured, a policeman who had appeared on the scene shot the owner of the other vehicle. In July 1982 two police officers were convicted in court for having tortured a prisoner to death and were sentenced to five years in prison. These incidents were by no means the norm, but they reflected poorly on the overall police performance and undoubtedly affected the public perception of the force.

In August 1982, shortly after the coup attempt, Moi relieved Gethi as police commissioner and ordered his arrest. Investigations indicated that the police—especially the Special Branch—had performed inadequately by either not knowing of the coup plans in advance or by knowing about the proposed action but not trying to squelch it or inform the president. Other reports indicated that Moi had grown to dislike Gethi personally and that the coup attempt provided a good excuse to change the police leadership.

After his appointment, Njiinu, who had previously been deputy commissioner for operations, announced that he would seek to restructure police operations in order to make them more efficient and would launch an effort to combat graft in the force. He did move to retire a number of Special Branch officers in late 1982 and spoke out against police bribery. Whether his efforts to reorganize the force or cleanse it of corruption would be successful could not be determined in early 1983.

The General Service Unit

In 1983 the GSU operated under the command of Erastus K. M'Mbijjiwe, a senior assistant commissioner who held the title of commandant of the GSU. The GSU was a mobile force having an organizational infrastructure separate from the rest of the Kenya Police. With headquarters at Embakasi, company-sized GSU units housed in their own barracks were situated strategically throughout the country. With the assistance of the Police Air Wing, the units (whose members were trained parachutists) could be rapidly deployed throughout the country to deal with demonstrations or other threats to public order. Because GSU companies and platoons had their own vehicles and communications equipment, they were able to operate in the field as self-contained units.

Formed in 1953 as a measure to deal with the outbreak of violence that later became known as the Mau Mau rebellion, the GSU was strengthened after independence and became the country's elite internal security force. Gethi, who became commandant in 1967, presided over the unit's expansion to 1,800 men (most of them Kikuyu) and its accumulation of equipment, including automatic rifles, submachine guns, mortars, and sophisticated communications gear. The GSU, which received substantial technical assistance and training from the Israelis before 1973, by the 1970s had established itself as a very competent force.

During the last few years of Kenyatta's rule, the GSU's reputation for discipline, incorruptibility, and ruthlessness contrasted with the apparent inefficiency and corruption of the regular police. The GSU was increasingly used by the government instead of the regular police to maintain public order in instances such as student demonstrations. The GSU's reputation (and that of the police) was clouded, however, by the fact that when opposition politician Josiah Mwangi Kariuki was murdered in 1975, he had last been seen alive in GSU commandant Gethi's company. Partly owing to what a select investigative committee of parliament called "a massive cover-up" by the police, no link was proved, and the controversy passed.

After Gethi was promoted to police commissioner, the force was led by his protégé, Commandant Peter N. Mbuthia, until he was, in turn, replaced in August 1982. In 1983, after four and one-half years of Moi's presidency, the autonomy of the Kikuyu-dominated GSU appeared to have lessened, particularly because Mbuthia's replacement, M'Mbijjiwe, had been appointed from outside the ranks of the GSU. Perhaps because the rivalry between the GSU and the regular police had lessened, the GSU appeared to have become less conspicuous and controversial than it had been during the Kenyatta era.

The Prison System

In mid-1983 management of the corrections system was the responsibility of the Kenya Prisons Service, which was under the Ministry of Home Affairs. The commissioner of prisons and the service's headquarters in Nairobi were in charge of the system. The headquarters staff included four senior assistant commissioners of prisons who headed the operations, administration, inspection, and industries sections, respectively. Each of the 70 institutions of the system was administered on a provincial basis by a provincial prisons command, headed by an assistant commissioner. Prisons Service personnel were part of the civil service system and had a grade and pay structure that closely paralleled that of the police. Most underwent training at the Prisons Training School, which in the early 1980s was in the process of being moved from Nairobi to Tutu in Kiambu District.

Prisons were classed by size and function. Principal institutions, headed by senior superintendents, were the largest prisons and were capable of handling long-term offenders and those accused of violent crimes. In 1979, according to Kenyan statistics, 27 of the 70 prisons housed prisoners serving sentences of seven years or longer, and it was believed that most of these facilities were principal institutions. In addition, there were smaller prisons serving particular districts, institutions for youthful offenders, and detention camps for what the courts called "persons of no fixed abode," usually vagrants or rural immigrants convicted of petty crimes.

Overcrowding has been a serious problem since the Mau Mau emergency; and facilities have been continuously burdened by a steady rise in the number of persons committed. The average daily prison population increased from 13,286 in 1964, to 19,670 in 1973, and to 24,581 in 1979. The latter figure was nearly three times the number of personnel in the entire Prisons Service and, according to authorities, severely strained their abilities to manage the institutions. In successive development plans from 1966 through 1978, the government proposed to solve the problem by expanding and improving correctional facilities. The Development Plan 1979-83, however, indicated that the government would reverse a long-standing trend to increase penalties for convicted offenders and would instead use probation extensively in the cases of those sentenced to six months or less (which in the late 1970s amounted to some 80 percent of the prison population).

According to the United States Department of State's *Country Reports on Human Rights Practices for 1982*, "prison conditions are generally poor and treatment of prisoners is often harsh." Official policy, however, emphasized inmate rehabilitation, and training programs to teach new skills were an important part of the prison program. The Prison Industries Section managed a program whereby prisoners engaged in carpentry, tailoring, metalwork, shoemaking, matmaking, and other crafts and trades. Prison industries provided a nominal source of income to the inmates as well as revenue for the government. The Farms Section managed 8,100 hectares of land used for agricultural instruction and the production of crops and livestock. The products were consumed by the prison population or sold to the general public.

At some institutions inmates could take courses to prepare them for Government Trade Tests or correspondence courses designed to prepare them for primary- or secondary-school certificates. Reportedly, increased privileges and improved living facilities were given to longer term prisoners as incentives to good conduct. These incentives included permission to have books and to attend cultural and other entertainment events, access to higher training and work opportunities, and authorization for more frequent correspondence and visits from friends and relatives.

Prisoners other than those under preventive detention or life sentences could have up to one-third of their sentence remitted for good behavior. The records of inmates serving sentences of seven years or more were periodically reviewed by a board of officials, who could recommend to the president that a prisoner be considered for a reduced sentence. In addition to remission of part of the sentence, the longer term prisoner with a good record could be released on parole, perhaps to a halfway house, three months early to aid his readjustment to civilian life.

* * *

There are few works available that deal expressly with Kenyan national security concerns, policies, or institutions, but much information is available in the press and in books and articles dealing with Kenyan politics. Among the more useful of these is *The Kenyatta Succession* by Joseph Karimi and Philip Ochieng, a controversial work that explores some of the personalities and institutions of Kenyatta's last years. M. Tamarkin, in his article, "The Roots of Political Stability in Kenya," gives an analysis of the Kenyan political security system, while Patricia Stamp's more recent articles, "Kenya: The Echoing Footsteps" and "Kenya's Year of Discontent," provide descriptions of the system's evolution into the 1980s.

Useful information on the military can be garnered from the International Institute for Strategic Studies' annual *The Military Balance*, as well as from the monthly magazine *Afrique défense*. Colin Legum's annual survey, *Africa Contemporary Record*, is also consistently useful. The monthly *Africa Research Bulletin* similarly contains worthwhile information distilled from the African and international press. The Kenyan press, particularly the Nairobi *Weekly Review*, contains numerous articles covering a variety of topics related to Kenyan security issues. (For further information and complete citations, see Bibliography.)

Appendix

Table

Table 1. Metric Conversion Coefficients

When you know	Multiply by	To find
Millimeters	0.04	inches
Centimeters	0.39	inches
Meters	3.3	feet
Kilometers	0.62	miles
Hectares (10,000 m^2)	2.47	acres
Square kilometers.....	0.39	square miles
Cubic meters..........	35.3	cubic feet
Liters....................	0.26	gallons
Kilograms	2.2	pounds
Metric tons	0.98	long tons
....	1.1	short tons
....	2,204	pounds
Degrees Celsius .... (Centigrade)	9 divide by 5 and add 32	degrees Fahrenheit

Table 2. Gross Domestic Product by Industrial Origin, in Current Prices, 1974–81
(in millions of Kenya pounds)[1]

	1974	1975	1976	1977	1978	1979	1980	1981[2]
Gross domestic product (at factor cost)								
Traditional economy								
Forestry	5.57	7.30	9.40	10.77	13.30	15.21	16.66	19.22
Fishing	0.18	0.20	0.29	0.29	0.43	0.46	0.55	0.73
Building and construction	14.79	19.35	21.86	25.99	31.01	37.19	41.57	47.67
Water	5.28	6.78	8.90	11.11	12.66	14.04	15.10	17.12
Ownership of dwellings	18.81	25.39	29.36	35.68	43.15	52.06	57.79	67.41
Total traditional economy	44.63	59.02	69.81	83.84	100.55	118.96	131.67	152.15
Monetary economy								
Enterprises and nonprofit institutions								
Agriculture	319.37	346.30	466.15	668.01	631.73	648.78	688.13	791.74
Forestry	5.42	5.93	6.24	6.89	8.52	10.70	13.96	18.88
Fishing	1.45	1.65	2.36	2.33	3.52	3.70	4.37	5.91
Mining and quarrying	3.20	3.42	3.41	4.17	4.41	5.04	5.73	5.16
Manufacturing	119.42	127.00	144.18	179.94	219.32	349.84	295.14	342.44
Electricity and water	10.43	13.20	14.20	19.96	23.05	82.26	96.33	100.56
Building and construction	41.23	44.30	45.22	53.94	66.88	27.57	32.48	40.86
Wholesale, retail trade, restaurants, and hotels	97.91	114.88	132.54	164.63	189.34	214.07	244.66	281.78
Transport, storage, and communications	53.73	60.25	69.15	78.62	100.84	114.65	127.81	143.39
Finance, insurance, real estate and business services	46.80	54.67	68.03	82.98	96.22	108.25	122.43	142.26
Ownership of dwellings	48.63	52.50	58.06	67.50	78.43	87.20	103.41	132.52
Other services	20.76	23.33	27.00	30.80	35.46	39.59	49.41	56.15

Table 2—Continued

	1974	1975	1976	1977	1978	1979	1980	1981[2]
Less imputed bank service charge	–18.12	–20.37	–23.88	–31.80	–37.31	–17.97	–47.64	–55.36
Total enterprises and nonprofit institutions	750.23	827.06	1,012.66	1,327.97	1,420.41	1,673.68	1,736.22	2,006.29
Private households (domestic services)	7.27	8.86	10.93	13.44	17.06	21.72	28.15	32.07
Producers of government services								
Public administration	33.15	38.30	43.08	48.52	56.91	61.44	71.30	84.54
Defense	7.21	8.51	9.63	11.73	13.49	14.19	14.90	15.26
Education	58.16	71.88	82.75	94.43	107.51	129.57	154.18	185.55
Health	13.33	15.24	17.43	21.90	27.40	31.24	36.16	36.19
Agricultural services	9.49	9.60	11.36	13.78	16.51	20.69	22.24	26.49
Other services	15.38	18.54	20.46	25.04	28.84	32.13	33.68	43.79
Total producers of government services	136.72	162.07	184.71	215.40	250.66	289.26	332.46	391.82
Total monetary economy	894.22	997.99	1,208.30	1,556.81	1,688.13	1,984.66	2,096.83	2,430.18
Total gross domestic product (at factor cost)	938.85	1,057.01	1,278.11	1,640.65	1,788.68	2,103.62	2,228.50	2,582.33
Gross domestic product per capita (in Kenya pounds)	72.71	78.90	92.30	114.43	120.38	129.16	140.08	156.37

[1] For value of the Kenya pound—see Glossary.
[2] Provisional.

Source: Based on information from Kenya, Ministry of Economic Planning and Development, Central Bureau of Statistics, *Statistical Abstract, 1980,* Nairobi, 1980, 37; and Kenya, Ministry of Economic Planning and Development, Central Bureau of Statistics, *Economic Survey, 1982,* Nairobi, June 1982, 16.

Table 3. Principal Crops: Production for Sale, Selected Years, 1965–81
(in thousands of tons)

Crop	1965	1973	1974	1975	1976	1977	1978	1979	1980	1981[1]
Wheat	172.2	124.6	159.5	145.5	186.8	169.9	165.9	201.0	204.6	192.0
Maize[2]	103.8	440.8	365.4	487.8	564.7	424.0	236.3	241.7	217.9	388.6[3]
Rice paddy	14.1	36.1	33.2	33.2	39.3	41.4	35.8	37.5	36.4	42.2
Pyrethrum extract	0.1	0.2	0.2	0.2	0.2	0.1	0.1	0.1	0.2	0.2
Sugarcane[4]	517.7	1,545.1	1,719.1	1,654.6	1,652.7	1,888.1	2,349.2	3,147.6	3,972.2	4,582.1
Seed cotton	12.4	16.2	15.0	16.1	15.8	16.3	27.2	27.6	38.1	21.4[3]
Clean coffee	39.3	71.2	70.1	66.2	80.3	97.1	84.3	75.1	91.3	90.4
Sisal	64.0	58.1	86.5	43.6	33.6	32.2	31.5	36.5	46.9	39.0
Tea	19.8	56.6	53.4	56.7	62.0	86.3	93.4	99.3	89.9	88.0

[1] Forecast.
[2] Deliveries to National Cereals and Produce Marketing Board.
[3] Actual: maize, approximately 473,000 tons; cotton, approximately 26,000 tons.
[4] Cane delivered to sugar mills for the production of white sugar.

Source: Based on information from Kenya, Ministry of Finance and Planning, Central Bureau of Statistics, *Statistical Abstract, 1974*, Nairobi, 1974, 119; and Kenya, Ministry of Economic Planning and Development, Central Bureau of Statistics, *Statistical Abstract, 1981*, Nairobi, 1981, 102.

Table 4. Value of Commercial Mineral Production, 1972–80
(in thousands of Kenya pounds)

Mineral	1972	1973	1974	1975	1976	1977	1978	1979	1980[2]
Aquamarines	3.7	0.8	n.a.	—	5.4	6.0	351.1	0.5	57.4
Barite	11.9	11.9	21.1	12.2	14.3	17.5	16.5	22.8	90.7
Carbon dioxide	109.5	162.5	193.9	193.7	204.0	116.9	234.3	—	314.9
Diatomite	37.2	27.3	39.8	46.7	69.4	63.5	37.8	62.0	—
Feldspar	11.4	10.2	32.0	44.0	26.6	41.6	25.6	0.3	13.4
Fluorspar ore	126.9	306.7	515.2	1,243.5	1,788.0	2,832.0	2,700.5	774.1	931.2
Garnets	3.1	41.2	70.6	21.6	204.3	438.1	361.2	96.3	48.6
Gold	1.3	4.1	11.0	6.2	160.0	6.5	10.7	14.5	9.1
Guano	15.4	41.4	11.0	11.9	10.0	4.0	1.9	0.6	—
Gypsum[3]	177.5	87.9	175.4	—	294.9	174.9	4.9	100.8	—
Kaolin	n.a.	1.0	1.3	—	1.0	12.5	202.2	134.4	45.8
Limestone and lime	184.2	227.4	295.4	382.1	432.7	523.4	296.0	1,717.8	470.4
Magnesite	6.5	12.5	0.7	1.0	—	39.3	0.1	—	—
Magnetite	57.5	123.4	98.9	73.2	114.3	178.0	120.1	136.6	109.3
Rubies	1.4	0.1	1,277.5	65.6	416.8	85.5	44.2	1.1	1.5
Salt (crude)	269.9	302.1	288.3	85.0	66.9	169.0	450.2	414.1	598.3
Salt (refined)	224.9	270.4	196.0	85.0	59.9	233.7	—	282.6	—
Sand	3.7	3.5	2.9	3.5	4.8	45.9	1,257.3	2.3	4.5
Sapphires	1.6	50.4	34.8	27.7	28.9	1.9	7.5	9.0	0.2

Table 4—Continued

Mineral	1972	1973	1974	1975	1976	1977	1978	1979	1980[2]
Soda ash	1,745.8	2,243.9	2,243.9	2,170.5	3,019.2	2,643.0	5,147.7	5,238.0	4,768.2
Soda (crushed, raw)	34.7	39.2	12.5	21.7	47.3	23.3	1.7	193.1	22.8
Tourmalines	0.4	1.8	3.8	37.9	55.5	33.6	33.6	1.8	57.0
Vermiculite	6.3	5.4	34.6	192.8	312.1	121.8	68.2	149.5	183.7
Wollastonite	—	1.1	1.0	2.4	4.4	3.5	1.5	5.0	—
TOTAL	3,034.8	3,976.2	5,561.6	4,728.2	7,196.7	7,815.4	11,374.8	9,357.2	7,727.0

— means none or negligible.
n.a.—not available.
[1] For value of the Kenya pound—see Glossary.
[2] Provisional
[3] Does not include gypsum used in the manufacture of cement.

Source: Based on information from Kenya, Ministry of Economic Planning and Development, Central Bureau of Statistics, *Statistical Abstract, 1981*, Nairobi, 1981, 161.

Table 5. Wage Employees by Industry in the Private and Public Sectors, 1976–81[1]
(in thousands)

Sector	1976	1977	1978	1979	1980	1981[2]
Private sector						
Agriculture and forestry	197.7	206.4	189.0	193.9	172.5	173.7
Mining and quarrying	3.1	2.4	1.9	2.0	1.7	1.5
Manufacturing	88.1	94.7	105.3	112.0	111.4	116.7
Electricity and water	—	—	—	0.1	0.1	0.2
Construction	30.1	29.6	28.6	32.5	31.7	32.6
Wholesale and retail trade, restaurants, and hotels	57.9	60.3	59.6	64.4	66.0	67.7
Transport and communications	18.0	19.7	20.6	23.3[3]	23.0[3]	18.9
Finance, insurance, real estate, and business services	20.9	24.2	25.9	28.1	31.9	31.1
Community, social, and personal services	85.4	89.2	90.6	91.3	95.9	97.9
Total private sector	501.1	526.5	521.6	547.6	534.3	540.2
Public sector						
Agriculture and forestry	45.3	53.9	54.1	60.7	58.9	61.9
Mining and quarrying	0.8	1.0	0.6	0.6	0.6	0.7
Manufacturing	20.7	23.3	24.8	26.4	29.9	29.7
Electricity and water	8.5	4.6	9.3	9.8	10.0	10.0
Construction	17.0	19.3	26.7	28.8	31.5	28.7
Wholesale and retail trade, restaurants, and hotels	2.3	2.3	3.0	4.3	4.5	4.9
Transport and communications	29.7	28.4	30.3	31.5	32.2	36.5
Finance, insurance, real estate, and business services	4.6	5.5	6.1	7.5	7.8	8.4
Community, social, and personal services	227.4	233.3	235.2	255.1	296.2	303.4
Total public sector	356.4	376.4	390.0	424.8	471.5	484.1
TOTAL	857.5	902.9	911.6	972.4	1,005.8	1,024.3

— means fewer than 50 employees.
[1] Figures may not add to totals because of rounding.
[2] Provisional.
[3] Believed to be overstated.

Source: Based on information from Kenya, Ministry of Economic Planning and Development, Central Bureau of Statistics, *Statistical Abstract, 1981*, Nairobi, 1981, 240–44; and Kenya, Ministry of Economic Planning and Development, Central Bureau of Statistics, *Economic Survey, 1982*, Nairobi, June 1982, 39.

Table 6. Destinations of Exports, Selected Years, 1964–80[1]
(in thousands of Kenya pounds)[2]

Country	1964[3]	1971	1973	1977	1978	1979	1980
Western Europe							
EEC[4]							
Britain[5]	11,272	15,471	20,622	63,594	57,197	58,791	58,846
West Germany	7,282	7,047	13,571	85,951	56,813	60,836	56,017
Netherlands	2,091	3,435	8,096	51,345	24,351	17,702	17,692
France	1,000	537	1,460	6,074	5,685	5,119	6,349
Ireland[5]	n.a.	456	620	2,687	2,537	3,795	4,140
Italy	1,147	1,543	3,687	13,442	18,891	23,804	23,733
Denmark[5]	514	187	553	2,841	1,146	1,190	870
Belgium and Luxembourg	618	556	3,207	6,233	5,565	6,326	7,459
Total EEC	23,924	29,232	51,816	232,167	172,185	177,563	175,106
Norway	191	88	198	381	487	202	563
Sweden	1,466	2,972	4,904	11,091	8,148	6,931	7,710
Spain	n.a.	647	945	1,672	1,088	1,485	2,808
Greece	n.a.	122	1,203	1,210	2,365	2,924	2,020
Other	n.a.	1,251	3,860	11,919	9,506	10,115	10,450
Total Western Europe	n.a.	34,312	62,926	258,440	193,779	199,220	198,657
Eastern Europe							
Soviet Union	—	393	1	896	710	1,096	1,658
East Germany	—	64	—	43	17	88	4
Yugoslavia	—	450	1,025	6,546	4,004	1,873	2,462
Czechoslovakia	310	214	589	285	189	9	54
Other	1,230	1,329	641	7,121	2,010	1,735	764
Total Eastern Europe	1,540	2,450	2,256	14,891	6,930	4,801	4,942

Table 6—Continued

Country	1964[3]	1971	1973	1977	1978	1979	1980
North and South America							
United States	4,870	5,625	7,532	27,593	18,519	16,737	16,929
Central and South America	—	690	2,220	271	380	2,561	225
Canada	1,894	1,119	2,706	8,458	5,336	5,715	5,070
Total North and South America	6,764	7,434	12,458	36,322	24,235	25,013	22,224
Africa							
Uganda	12,581	19,150	21,898	51,992	38,443	37,747	66,378
Tanzania	13,299	14,743	16,854	9,822	2,756	4,075	5,216
Zaïre	207	1,149	909	3,445	2,535	3,142	3,909
Rwanda	152	881	1,579	6,241	7,998	8,550	12,638
Burundi	228	412	513	1,855	3,412	4,552	7,329
Somalia	967	775	1,290	2,397	3,574	2,678	4,738
Sudan	1,393	488	1,046	5,035	7,027	7,665	9,949
Zambia	n.a.	5,529	7,283	6,897	5,702	5,846	4,948
Malawi	n.a.	238	317	377	407	348	285
Mauritius	692	557	1,376	3,287	3,067	4,832	3,605
Other	n.a.	3,594	6,025	18,913	19,063	19,521	22,010
Total Africa	n.a.	47,516	59,090	110,261	93,984	98,956	141,005
Middle East							
Yemen (Aden)	885	499	426	4,152	2,491	3,811	1,503
Kuwait	163	738	542	1,013	333	761	333
Iran	117	353	603	2,065	1,769	—	1,191
Saudi Arabia	152	75	433	1,128	1,292	725	2,509

Table 6—Continued

Table 6. (Continued)

Country	1964[3]	1971	1973	1977	1978	1979	1980
Bahrain	277	110	160	525	254	236	258
Israel	n.a.	256	465	1,302	1,431	1,603	1,716
Other	n.a.	1,030	1,012	2,441	3,084	7,711	11,840
Total Middle East	n.a.	3,061	3,641	12,626	10,654	14,847	19,350
Far East and Australasia							
Australia	978	817	670	1,848	1,450	1,238	1,621
Hong Kong	303	621	1,956	426	427	395	1,488
Japan	1,648	2,648	5,031	5,233	3,806	5,100	3,828
India	1,570	2,046	1,587	1,623	1,559	2,197	4,077
Malaysia	804	183	451	537	326	396	1,212
New Zealand	339	100	361	959	661	583	494
Pakistan	234	511	2,091	7,214	7,844	8,922	7,985
China	394	876	3,070	1,463	2,702	1,959	1,956
Other	n.a.	717	1,997	7,476	7,692	10,747	45,319
Total Far East and Australasia	n.a.	8,519	17,214	26,779	26,467	31,537	67,980
All other countries	n.a.	1,595	3,050	11,561	10,471	5,890	3,324
Ships' stores	2,247	7,354	7,047	30,939	29,201	32,523	58,221
Parcel post and special transactions	—	—	—	—	—	—	—
TOTAL	79,428	112,241	167,682	501,819	395,721	412,787	515,703

— means none or negligible.
n.a. —not available.
[1] Totals include reexports.
[2] For value of the Kenya pound—see Glossary.
[3] Totals not available for certain geographic areas.
[4] European Economic Community (also known as the Common Market).
[5] Britain, Ireland, and Denmark became members of the EEC in 1973.

Table 7. Sources of Imports, Selected Years, 1964–80
(in thousands of Kenya pounds)[1]

Country	1964	1971	1973	1977	1978	1979	1980
Western Europe							
EEC[2]							
Britain[3]	23,551	56,249	50,743	95,218	145,933	141,311	162,558
West Germany	6,989	16,104	20,312	57,851	87,755	68,809	77,661
Netherlands	2,143	5,176	7,926	10,901	15,096	14,111	22,879
France	2,028	6,771	6,583	26,316	30,831	17,627	32,690
Ireland[3]	n.a.	64	266	299	437	469	676
Italy	1,851	6,951	8,165	22,007	33,490	23,745	37,693
Denmark[3]	480	1,308	1,775	4,780	3,136	5,318	4,506
Belgium and Luxembourg	1,286	2,805	3,491	11,767	21,004	12,883	15,870
Total EEC	38,328	95,428	99,261	229,139	337,682	284,273	354,533
Norway	629	990	1,223	2,120	1,979	1,526	1,400
Sweden	1,216	2,759	4,679	6,400	8,904	13,375	13,405
Spain	n.a.	399	441	981	2,703	1,776	3,547
Greece	n.a.	62	127	1,361	2,254	569	993
Other	1,166	4,720	4,959	17,470	13,714	18,131	19,725
Total Western Europe	41,339	104,358	110,690	257,471	367,236	319,650	393,603
Eastern Europe							
Soviet Union	n.a.	720	134	140	236	533	878
East Germany	n.a.	269	513	65	204	85	298
Yugoslavia	n.a.	238	1,508	476	370	336	623
Czechoslovakia	542	2,166	1,061	2,045	1,939	1,736	2,374
Other	1,208	1,896	2,163	1,520	2,592	2,047	2,433
Total Eastern Europe	1,750	5,289	5,379	4,246	5,341	4,737	6,606

Table 7—Continued

Country	1964	1971	1973	1977	1978	1979	1980
North and South America							
United States	4,837	16,321	16,762	30,482	41,096	34,925	60,998
Central and South America	89	2,142	2,205	1,411	1,096	2,877	2,010
Canada	228	960	1,964	5,276	3,877	5,589	5,117
Total North and South America	5,154	19,423	20,931	37,169	46,069	43,391	68,125
Africa							
Uganda	7,244	8,026	4,668	581	1,977	803	1,206
Tanzania	4,110	7,932	7,627	1,622	353	102	309
Zaïre	725	731	534	606	467	533	157
Rwanda	—	353	—	1,259	2,333	3,289	2,623
Burundi	—	1	—	—	—	1,158	115
Somalia	9	56	69	105	20	71	44
Sudan	9	7	1	1,161	23	210	8
Zambia	n.a.	208	569	1,030	1,575	1,243	1,518
Malawi	n.a.	56	5	104	228	211	544
Mauritius	9	1	1	11	135	9	137
Other	1,347	1,262	1,110	1,678	2,064	4,324	22,776
Total Africa	13,453	18,633	14,584	8,156	9,175	11,953	29,447
Middle East							
Yemen (Aden)	113	37	211	9	68	1,458	2,187
Kuwait	5,043	569	—	—	320	7,245	29,166
Iran	2,052	9,991	15,648	45,506	44,815	26,289	20,577
Saudi Arabia	14	3,217	3,079	38,723	16,645	52,059	168,139
Bahrain	219	164	—	2,599	7,061	6,803	5,527

Table 7—Continued

Country	1964	1971	1973	1977	1978	1979	1980
Israel	n.a.	1,378	1,322	2,650	4,388	7,174	7,068
Other	1,437	338	713	879	363	35,193	69,506
Total Middle East	8,878	15,695	20,973	90,366	73,660	136,221	302,170
Far East and Australasia							
Australia	910	3,143	2,218	5,291	10,291	8,078	6,130
Hong Kong	876	2,141	2,951	6,454	4,707	3,512	5,442
Japan	7,122	19,330	25,998	65,603	67,912	49,927	88,409
India	2,367	3,649	4,032	11,720	15,818	10,154	13,007
Malaysia	461	2,173	2,210	5,295	2,909	3,565	6,245
New Zealand	47	357	175	847	1,099	447	1,117
Pakistan	764	1,429	415	377	509	237	317
China	696	1,435	1,613	5,814	5,103	4,804	7,608
Other	187	2,417	3,219	12,216	14,608	17,822	23,666
Total Far East and Australasia	13,430	36,074	42,831	113,617	122,956	98,546	151,941
All other countries	236	71	2,019	19,861	36,138	5,658	8,233
Ships' stores	—	—	—	—	—	—	—
Parcel post and special transactions	3,659	595	684	559	551	—	2
TOTAL	87,899	200,138	218,091	531,445	661,126	620,156	960,127

—means none or negligible.
n.a.—not available; figure included in "Other."
[1] For value of the Kenya pound—see Glossary.
[2] European Economic Community (also known as the Common Market).
[3] Britain, Ireland, and Denmark became members of the EEC in 1973.

Table 8. External Public Debt by Kind and Source, December 31, 1981[1]
(in thousands of United States dollars)

Credit Kind and Source	Disbursed	Undisbursed	Total
Concessional			
Bilateral loans			
Western countries and Japan			
Belgium	4,691	507	5,198
Canada	35,801	45,695	81,496
Denmark	19,814	6,513	26,327
France	15,774	11,243	27,017
West Germany	137,796	52,829	190,625
Italy	1,398	—	1,398
Japan	67,454	27,479	94,933
Netherlands	55,489	45,133	100,622
Sweden	598	—	598
Switzerland	2,227	3,341	5,568
Britain	19,256	—	19,256
United States	86,374	41,522	127,896
EEC[2]	15,152	—	15,152
Total Western countries and Japan	461,824	234,262	696,086
Soviet Union	31	—	31
China	2,807	37,193	40,000
OPEC[3]			
Iraq	—	30,000	30,000
Saudi Arabia	9,816	35,089	44,905
Total OPEC	9,816	65,089	74,905
Total bilateral loans	474,478	336,544	811,022
Multilateral loans			
African Development Bank	7,233		7,233
African Development Fund	4,656	4,655	9,311
BADEA[4]	2,395	2,500	4,895
European Development Fund	30,521	9,583	40,104
European Investment Bank	9,726	3,382	13,108
IBRD[5]	7,323	24,677	32,000
International Development Association	234,132	219,098	453,230
International Monetary Fund Trust Fund	59,614	207	59,821
OPEC Special Fund	9,155	8,145	17,300
Special Arab Fund for Africa	3,600	—	3,600
Total multilateral loans	368,355	272,247	640,602
Total concessional	842,833	608,791	1,451,624
Nonconcessional			
Bilateral loans			
Canada	11,471	—	11,471
Denmark	114	—	114
West Germany	3,620	—	3,620

Table 8—Continued

Credit Kind and Source	Disbursed	Undisbursed	Total
India	1,241	2,088	3,329
Japan	3,161	—	3,161
Netherlands	867	—	867
Britain	67,166	33,740	100,906
United States	21,964	65	22,029
Total bilateral loans	109,604	35,893	145,497
Multilateral loans			
BADEA	4,782	199	4,981
African Development Bank	19,634	29,070	48,704
European Investment Bank	19,607	9,380	28,987
IBRD	344,056	422,476	766,532
Total multilateral loans	388,079	461,125	849,204
Total nonconcessional	497,683	497,018	994,701
Private financial institutions			
Austria	23,107	1,976	25,083
Bahamas	23	—	23
France	107,403	23,186	130,656
West Germany	31,656	—	31,656
Japan	27,874	—	27,874
Pakistan	11,852	—	11,852
Switzerland	60,593	3,341	63,934
Britain	232,539	12,619	245,158
United States	122,103	13,846	135,949
Multiple lenders	270,667	15,000	285,667
Total private financial institutions	887,817	69,968	957,785
Total external public debt	2,228,333	1,175,777	3,404,110
Kenya share of EAC debt[6]	132,026	2,205	134,231
TOTAL	2,360,359	1,177,982	3,538,341

— means none.

[1] Debts repayable in foreign currencies or in goods and having a maturity of more than one year.

[2] European Economic Community (also known as the Common Market).

[3] Organization of Petroleum Exporting Countries.

[4] Banque Arabe pour le Développement Economique en Afrique (Arab Bank for Economic Development in Africa).

[5] International Bank for Reconstruction and Development.

[6] EAC—East African Community.

Table 9. Central Government Expenditures, Fiscal Years (FY) 1978/79–1981/82
(in millions of Kenya pounds)[1]

Purpose	1978/79 Recurrent Account	1978/79 Development Account	1978/79 Total	Recurrent Account
General public administration				
General administration	39.81	17.30	57.11	44.94
External affairs	6.00	0.63	6.63	6.83
Public order and safety	32.96	2.57	35.53	34.99
Total general public administration	78.77	20.50	99.27	86.78
Defense	96.81	8.85	105.66	104.61
Education	101.51	7.60	109.11	122.57
Health	35.38	7.75	43.13	43.72
Housing and community welfare	1.73	6.62	8.35	2.17
Social welfare	9.46	4.16	13.62	10.64
Economic services				
General administration	6.11	10.30	16.41	7.61
Agriculture, forestry, and fishing	25.12	39.65	64.77	27.53
Mining, manufacturing, and construction	10.17	5.02	15.19	10.81
Electricity, gas, steam, and water	7.14	30.43	37.57	8.97
Roads	10.83	32.28	43.11	14.74
Transport and communications	5.33	36.60	41.93	4.88
Other economic services	10.48	4.21	14.69	10.47
Total economic services	75.18	158.49	233.67	85.01
Other services, including public debt	76.68	6.12	84.80	93.76
TOTAL	477.52	220.09	697.61	549.26

—means none or negligible.
[1] For value of the Kenya pound—see Glossary
[2] Provisional.

Source: Based on information from Kenya, Ministry of Economic Planning and Development, Central Bureau of Statistics, *Economic Survey, 1982*, Nairobi, June 1982, 30.

1979/80		1980/81			1981/82[2]		
Development Account	Total	Recurrent Account	Development Account	Total	Recurrent Account	Development Account	Total
34.76	79.70	51.34	45.04	96.38	61.99	48.37	110.36
0.83	7.68	8.75	0.12	8.87	11.29	0.10	11.39
4.60	39.59	50.80	7.64	58.44	49.13	12.85	61.98
40.19	126.97	110.89	52.80	163.69	122.41	61.32	183.73
7.23	111.84	81.93	7.81	89.74	124.35	10.23	134.58
14.47	137.04	162.35	12.44	174.79	179.61	20.03	199.64
10.75	54.47	52.57	12.68	65.25	46.75	12.12	58.89
8.92	11.09	2.64	12.12	14.76	2.45	5.36	7.81
6.38	17.02	13.88	7.76	21.64	15.61	13.67	29.28
10.32	17.93	14.80	11.63	26.43	22.22	17.20	39.42
40.05	67.58	51.42	57.46	108.88	38.62	56.63	96.25
9.52	20.33	12.75	11.33	24.08	13.96	28.15	42.11
24.56	33.53	13.20	27.90	41.10	10.75	32.72	43.47
41.74	56.48	17.41	40.60	58.01	16.95	57.94	74.89
4.28	9.16	6.18	2.94	9.12	7.41	5.71	13.12
2.43	12.90	13.33	3.77	17.10	16.70	4.87	21.57
132.90	217.91	129.09	155.63	284.72	126.61	204.22	330.83
11.22	104.98	137.83	9.69	147.52	169.67	—	169.67
232.06	781.32	691.18	270.93	062.11	787.46	326.95	1,114.41

Table 10. Summary of the Balance of Payments, Selected Years, 1974–81
(in millions of Kenya pounds unless otherwise indicated)[1]

	1974	1976	1977	1978	1979	1980	1981[2]
Merchandise trade							
Exports (f.o.b.)[3]	207.5	312.1	468.0	369.4	385.5	461.0	462.8
Imports (c.i.f.)[4]	366.4	389.4	529.3	724.9	684.9	976.8	995.3
Balance of trade	–158.9	–77.3	–61.3	–355.5	–299.4	–515.8	–532.5
Net services and transfers	32.9	13.0	46.6	71.3	83.0	142.4	198.9
Current account balance	–126.1	–64.3	–14.7	–284.2	–216.4	–373.4	–333.6
Net inflows of long-term capital[5]	82.9	103.1	111.0	196.9	219.6	257.3	182.0
Basic balance	–43.2	38.8	96.3	–87.3	3.2	–116.1	–151.6
Movements of short-term capital[6]	11.6	–3.2	16.4	9.7	67.4	43.9	52.5
Overall balance	–31.5	35.6	112.7	–77.6	70.6	–72.2	–99.1
Memorandum items							
International reserves, gross of liabilities (year-end)	68.5	114.0	208.6	133.3	234.5	187.0	126.4
Months of imports represented by reserves (months)[7]	3.1	4.1	6.5	2.9	4.4	2.8	1.7
Proportion of import bill covered by export earnings (in percentage)	57	80	88	51	56	47	46

[1] For value of the Kenya pound—see Glossary.
[2] Provisional.
[3] Free on board.
[4] Cost, insurance, and freight.
[5] Government transfers have been reallocated from current account to long-term capital account.
[6] Includes errors and omissions.
[7] Calculations based on three-year moving average for imports.

Source: Based on information from Kenya, Ministry of Economic Planning and Development, Central Bureau of Statistics, *Economic Survey, 1982*, Nairobi, June 1982, 30.

Table 11. The Kenya Cabinet, June 1983

Office	Incumbent
President	Daniel arap Moi
Vice President	Mwai Kibaki
Ministers;	
Agriculture	Munyua Waiyaki
Basic Education	Jonathan Ng'eno
Commerce	John H. Okwanyo
Constitutional Affairs	Charles Njonjo
Cooperative Development	Robert Matano
Culture and Social Services	Stanley Oloitipitip
Economic Planning and Development	Zachary Onyonka
Energy	Gilbert M'Mbijjewe
Environment and Natural Resources	William Odongo Omamo
Finance	Arthur K. Magugu
Foreign Affairs	Robert J. Ouko
Health	Appolling Mukasa Mango
Higher Education	Joshua Joseph Kamotho
Home Affairs	Mwai Kibaki
Industry	Andrew J. Omanga
Information and Broadcasting	Eliud T. Mwamunga
Labour	Titus Mbathi
Lands, Settlements, and Physical Planning	Godfrey Githai Kariuki
Livestock Development	Paul Ngei
Local Government	Moses B. Mudavadi
Regional Development, Science, and Technology	Kiprono Nicholas Biwott
Tourism	Elijah W. Mwangale
Transportation and Communications	Henry K. Kosgey
Water Development	Jeremiah Nyagah
Works and Housing	Charles Rubia
Minister of State in the Office of the President	Justus ole Tipis
Attorney General	Matthew Guy Muli

Table 12. Selected Newspapers and Periodicals, 1983[1]

Publication	Circulation[2]	Ownership
Dailies		
Daily Nation	111,000	Prince Karim Aga Khan IV
Taifa Leo	55,000	–do–
Standard	50,000	Lonrho conglomerate
Kenya Times[3]	n.a.	KANU[4]
Kenya Leo[3]	n.a.	–do–
Weeklies		
Sunday Nation	116,000	Prince Karim Aga Khan IV
Taifa Weekly	68,000	–do–
Sunday Standard	39,000	Lonrho conglomerate
Weekly Review	18,000–25,000[5]	Press Trust of Kenya (Hilary Ng'weno and associates)

n.a.—not available.
[1] All published in Nairobi.
[2] Based on Audit Bureau of Circulations, London, July-December 1982, as reported in *Daily Nation*, April 27, 1983 (except *Weekly Review*.).
[3] First published in spring of 1983.
[4] Kenya African National Union.
[5] Estimated.

Table 13. Major Army Weapons, 1982

Type	Country of Origin	Estimated in Inventory
Armored vehicles		
Vickers Mk3 main battle tank	Britain	60 (12 on order)
AML-90 armored car with 90mm main gun	France	40
AML-60 armored car with 60mm main gun	-do-	40
Fox armored car	Britain	12
Shorland armored car	-do-	8
UR-416 armored personnel carrier (APC)	West Germany	50
Panhard M-3 APC	France	4
Artillery		
105mm gun/howitzer	n.a.	56
120mm mortar	n.a.	10
81mm mortar	n.a.	20
120mm Wombat recoilless launcher	n.a.	50
84mm Carl Gustav recoilless launcher	n.a.	50
Milan antitank guided weapon	France	n.a.
Swingfire antitank guided weapon	Britain	8
Aircraft		
Hughes 500 MD Defender helicopter with TOW antitank guided weapon	United States	15
Hughes 500 MD Defender helicopter (for scouting)	-do-	15
Hughes 500 MD Defender trainer helicopter	-do-	2
Aérospatiale Puma transport helicopter	France	10

n.a. —not available.

Source: Based on information from *The Military Balance, 1982–83*, London, 1982, 67-68.

Table 14. Major Air Force Weapons, 1982

Type	Country of Origin	Estimated in Inventory
Combat aircraft		
Northrop F-5E Tiger II supersonic fighter-bomber	United States	8
Northrop F-5F Tiger II supersonic fighter-bomber/trainer	-do-	4
BAC-167 Strikemaster	Britain	5
BAC Hawk T-52	-do-	12
Transport aircraft		
De Havilland DHC-4 Caribou	Canada	5
De Havilland DHC-5D Buffalo	-do-	6
Dornier Do 28D Skyservant	West Germany	7
Miscellaneous aircraft		
BAC Bulldog 103	Britain	14
Rockwell Turbo Commander 690	United States	1
Piper Navajo	-do-	1

Source: Based on information from *The Military Balance, 1982–83*, London, 1982, 67–68.

Table 15. Major Naval Weapons, 1982

Type	Country of Origin	Estimated in Inventory	Commissioning Date
Brooke Marine-type large patrol craft (37.5 meters) equipped with Gabriel surface-to-surface missiles (SSMs)	Britain	1	1974
Brooke Marine-type large patrol craft (32.6 meters) equipped with Gabriel SSMs	-do-	3	1975
Vosper-type large patrol craft (31.4 meters)	-do-	3	1966

Source: Based on information from *Jane's Fighting Ships, 1982–83*, New York, 1982, 279; and *The Military Balance, 1982–83*, London, 1982, 67-68.

Bibliography

Chapter 1

Abour, Ojwando. *White Highlands No More*. Nairobi: Pan African Researchers, 1973.

Adamson, Joy. *The People of Kenya*. New York: Harcourt Brace, 1967.

Allen, James de Vere. "Swahili Culture and the Nature of East Coast Settlement," *International Journal of African Historical Studies*, 14, No. 2, 1981, 306–34.

Alpers, Edward A. "Eastern Africa." Pages 469–536 in Richard Gray (ed.), *The Cambridge History of Africa, IV (from c. 1600 to c. 1790)*. Cambridge: Cambridge University Press, 1975.

Amin, Mohamed. *Cradle of Mankind*. London: Chatto and Windus, 1981.

Barnett, Donald L., and Njama Karari. *Mau Mau from Within*. New York: Praeger, 1966.

Bennett, George. *Kenya: A Political History. The Colonial Period*. (The Students' Library, No. 1.) London: Oxford University Press, 1963.

Bienen, Henry. *Kenya: The Politics of Participation and Control*. Princeton: Princeton University Press, 1974.

Brett, E.A. *Colonialism and Underdevelopment in East Africa: The Politics of Economic Change, 1919–1939*. New York: NOK, 1973.

Buijtenhuis, Robert. *Mau Mau Twenty Years After: The Myth and the Survivors*. The Hague: Mouton, 1973.

Carrington, C.E. *The British Overseas: Exploits of a Nation of Shopkeepers*. Cambridge: Cambridge University Press, 1950.

Chittuck, Neville. "The East Coast, Madagascar, and the Indian Ocean." Pages 183–231 in Roland Oliver (ed.), *The Cambridge History of Africa, III (from c. 1050 to c. 1600)*. Cambridge: Cambridge University Press, 1977.

Clark, Desmond J. *The Prehistory of Africa*. New York: Praeger, 1970.

Cooper, Frederick. *From Slaves to Squatters: Plantation Labor and Agriculture in Zanzibar and Coastal Kenya, 1890–1925*. New Haven: Yale University Press, 1981.

———. *Plantation Slavery of the East Coast of Africa*. New Haven: Yale University Press, 1977.

Dinesen, Isak (Karen Blixen). *Out of Africa*. New York: Time, 1963.

Doro, Marion E. "Human Souvenirs of Another Era: Europeans in Post-Kenyatta Kenya," *Africa Today*, 26, No. 3, 1979, 55–58.

Fox, James. *White Mischief: The Murder of Lord Erroll. A True Story of Aristocracy, Alcohol, and Adultery*. New York: Random House, 1983.

Freeman-Grenville, G.S.P. *The East African Coast: Select Documents from the First to the Earlier Nineteenth Century*. Oxford: Clarendon Press, 1962.

Galbraith, John S. *Mackinnon and East Africa, 1878–1895: A Study in the New Imperialism*. Cambridge: Cambridge University Press, 1972.

Gertzel, Cherry. *The Politics of Independent Kenya, 1963–8*. Evanston: Northwestern University Press, 1970.

Gifford, Prosser, and William Roger Louis (eds.). *Britain and Germany in Africa: Imperial Rivalry and Colonial Rule*. New Haven: Yale University Press, 1967.

Gregory, Robert E. *India and East Africa: A History of Race Relations Within the British Empire, 1890–1939*. Oxford: Clarendon Press, 1971.

Harbeson, John W. *Nation Building in Kenya: The Role of Land Reform*. Evanston: Northwestern University Press, 1973.

Harlow, Vincent, E.M. Chilver, and Alison Smith (eds.). *History of East Africa,* II. Oxford: Clarendon Press, 1965.

Hazelwood, Arthur. *The Economy of Kenya: The Kenyatta Era*. Oxford: Oxford University Press, 1979.

Historical Association of Kenya. *Politics and Nationalism in Kenya*. Nairobi: East African Publishing House, 1972.

Hobley, C.W. *Kenya: From Chartered Company to Crown Colony*. (2d ed.) (Cass Library of African Studies. General Studies, No. 84.) London: Frank Cass, 1970.

von Hohnel, Ludwig. *Discovery of Lakes Rudolf and Stefanie*. London: Frank Cass, 1968 (reprint.).

Huxley, Elspeth. *A New Earth: An Experiment in Colonialism*. London: Chatto and Windus, 1960.

______. *White Man's Country: Lord Delamere and the Making of Kenya*. New York: Praeger, 1968.

Jones, David Keith. *Faces of Kenya*. London: Hamish Hamilton, 1977.

Kamoche, Jidlaph G. *Imperial Trusteeship and Political Evolution in Kenya, 1923–1963: A Study of the Official Views and the Road to Decolonization*. Washington: University Press of America, 1981.

Karimi, Joseph, and Philip Ochieng. *The Kenyatta Succession*. Nairobi: TransAfrica, 1980.

Kenyatta, Jomo. *Facing Mount Kenya: The Traditional Life of the Gikuyu*. (African Writers series, No. 219.) London: Heinemann, 1979.

______. *Suffering Without Bitterness: The Founding of the Kenya Nation*. New York: International Publications Service, 1969.

Khapoya, Vincent B. "The Politics of Succession in Africa: Kenya after Kenyatta," *Africa Today,* 26, No. 3, Third Quarter 1979, 7–20.

Kirkman, James S. *Fort Jesus: A Portuguese Fortress on the East African Coast*. Oxford: Clarendon Press, 1974.

Kitching, Gavin. *Class and Economic Change in Kenya: The Making of an African Petite Bourgeoisie 1905–1970*. New Haven: Yale University Press, 1980.

Knappert, Jan. *Myths and Legends of the Swahili*. New York: Humanities Press, 1970.

Lambert, E. *Kikuyu Social and Political Institutions*. London: International African Institute, 1956.
Lamphear, John. "The Kamba and the Northern Mrima Coast." Pages 75–101 in Richard Gray and David Birmingham (eds.), *Pre-Colonial African Trade: Essays on Trade in Central and East Africa Before 1900*. New York: Oxford University Press, 1970.
Leakey, Louis S.B. *Defeating Mau Mau*. London: Methuen, 1954.
______. *White African: An Early Autobiography*. Cambridge, Massachusetts: Schenkman, 1966.
Leakey, Richard, and Roger Lewin. *Peoples of the Lake*. New York: Doubleday, 1978.
Low, D.A., and Alison Smith (eds.). *History of East Africa,* III. Oxford: Clarendon Press, 1976.
Marsh, Zoë, and G.W. Kingsnorth. *A History of East Africa: An Introductory Survey*. (4th ed.) Cambridge: Cambridge University Press, 1972.
Martin, Esmond Bradley. *History of Malindi: A Geographical Analysis of an East Indian Coastal Town from the Portuguese Period to the Present*. Nairobi: East African Literature Bureau, 1973.
Meisler, Stanley, "Tribal Politics Harass Kenya," *Foreign Affairs*, 49, No. 1, October 1970, 111–21.
Middleton, John, and Greet Kershaw. *The Kikuyu and Kamba of Kenya*. (Ethnographic Survey of Africa series. Daryll Forde, ed., "East Central Africa," Pt. V.) London: International African Institute, 1965.
Miller, Charles. *The Lunatic Express: An Entertainment in Imperialism*. New York: Macmillan, 1971.
Mollison, Simon. *Kenya's Coast*. Nairobi: East African Publishing House, 1971.
Mungeam, G.H. *British Rule in Kenya 1895–1912: The Establishment of Administration in the East Africa Protectorate*. Oxford: Clarendon Press, 1966.
Muriuki, Godfrey. *A History of the Kikuyu, 1500–1900*. Nairobi: Oxford University Press, 1974.
Murray-Brown, Jeremy. *Kenyatta*. New York: Dutton, 1973.
Naipaul, Shiva. *North of South: An African Journey*. New York: Simon and Schuster, 1979.
Ndegwa, R.N. *Mau Mau: A Select Bibliography*. Nairobi: Kenyatta University College, 1977.
Ogot, Bethwell A. "British Administration in the Central Nyanza District of Kenya, 1900–1960," *Journal of African History* [London], 4, No. 2, 1963, 249–73.
______. *Historical Dictionary of Kenya*. (African Historical Dictionaries, No. 29.) Metuchen, New Jersey: Scarecrow Press, 1981.
______. "The Impact of the Nilotes." Pages 47-55 in Roland Oliver (ed.), *The Middle Age of African History*. New York: Oxford University Press, 1967.

Ogot, Bethwell, and J.A. Kieran (eds.). *Zamani: A Survey of East African History*. New York: Humanities Press for the Historical Association of Kenya, 1968.

Oliver, Roland. "The East African Interior." Pages 621–65 in Roland Oliver (ed.), *The Cambridge History of Africa, III (from c. 1050 to c. 1600)*. Cambridge: Cambridge University Press, 1977.

______. "The Emergence of Bantu Africa." Pages 342–409 in J.D. Fage (ed.), *The Cambridge History of Africa, II (from c. 500 B.C. to A.D. 1050)*. Cambridge: Cambridge University Press, 1978.

Oliver, Roland, and Brian M. Fagan. *Africa in the Iron Age (c. 500 B.C. to A.D. 1400)*. Cambridge: Cambridge University Press, 1975.

Oliver, Roland, and Gervase Mathew (eds.). *History of East Africa, I*. Oxford: Clarendon Press, 1963.

Prins, H.J. *The Swahili-speaking Peoples of Zanzibar and the East African Coast: Arabs, Shirazi, and Swahili*. London: International African Institute, 1967.

Rosberg, Carl G., and John Nottingham. *The Myth of "Mau Mau": Nationalism in Kenya*. New York: Praeger for The Hoover Institution, 1966.

Salim, A.I. *The Swahili-speaking Peoples of Kenya's Coast, 1895-1965*. (Peoples of East Africa, No. 4.) Nairobi: East African Publishing House, 1973.

Sandbrook, Richard. *Proletarians and African Capitalism: The Kenyan Case, 1960–1972*. (Perspectives on Development, No. 4.) New York: Cambridge University Press, 1975.

Singh, Makhan. *History of Kenya's Trade Union Movement to 1952*. Nairobi: East African Publishing House, 1969.

Spear, Thomas. *Kenya's Past: An Introduction to Historical Method in Africa*. London: Longman, 1981.

Spencer, Paul. *The Samburu*. London: Oxford University Press, 1964.

Strayer, Robert W., Edward I. Steinhart, and Robert Maxon. *Protest Movements in Colonial East Africa: Aspects of Early African Response to European Rule*. (East African Studies, No. 12.) Syracuse: Maxwell School of Citizenship and Public Affairs, Syracuse University, 1973.

Swainson, Nicola. *The Development of Corporate Capitalism in Kenya, 1918–77*. Berkeley and Los Angeles: University of California Press, 1980.

Tamarkin, M. "From Kenyatta to Moi—The Anatomy of a Peaceful Transition of Power," *Africa Today*, 26, No. 3, Third Quarter 1979, 21–37.

______. "The Roots of Political Stability in Kenya," *African Affairs* [London], 77, No. 308, July 1978, 297–320.

Trimingham, J. Spencer. *Islam in East Africa*. Oxford: Clarendon Press, 1964.

Turton, E.R. "Somali Resistance to Colonial Rule and the Development of Somali Political Activity in Kenya, 1893–1960," *Journal of African History* [London], 8, No. 1, 1972, 119–43.

Unomah, A.C., and J.B. Webster. "East Africa: The Expansion of Commerce." Pages 270–318 in John E. Flint (ed.), *The Cambridge History of Africa, V (from c. 1790 to c. 1870)*. Cambridge: Cambridge University Press, 1976.

Wa-Githumo, Mwangi. *Land and Nationalism*. Washington: University Press of America, 1981.

Walter, Bob J. *Territorial Expansion of the Nandi of Kenya, 1500–1905*. Athens: Center for International Studies, Ohio University, 1970.

Wasserman, Gary. "European Settlers and Kenya Colony: Thoughts on a Conflicted Affair," *African Studies Review*, 17, No. 2, September 1974, 425–34.

______. "The Independence Bargain: Kenya Europeans and the Land Issue, 1960–1962," *Journal of Commonwealth Political Studies* [Leicester, England], 11, No. 2, July 1973, 99-120.

______. *Politics of Decolonization: Kenya Europeans and the Land Issue, 1960-1965*. (African Studies series, No. 17.) New York: Cambridge University Press, 1976.

Wipper, Audrey. *Rural Rebels: A Study of Two Protest Movements in Kenya*. Nairobi: Oxford University Press, 1977.

Ylvisaker, Marguerite. *Lamu in the Nineteenth Century: Land, Trade, and Politics*. Boston: African Studies Center, Boston University, 1979.

Chapter 2

Allen, James de Vere. "Swahili Culture and the Nature of East Coast Settlement," *International Journal of African Historical Studies*, 14, No. 2, 1981, 306–34.

Amey, Alan B., and David K. Leonard. "Public Policy, Class, and Inequality in Kenya and Tanzania," *Africa Today*, 26, No. 4, October-December 1979, 3–41.

Amin, Mohamed. *Cradle of Mankind*. London: Chatto and Windus, 1981.

Brokensha, David, and Jack Glazier. "Land Reform among the Mbere *Study of Churches and Religions in the Modern World, AD 1900–2000*. New York: Oxford University Press, 1982.

Brokensha, David, and Jack Glazier. "Land Reform among the Mbeere of Central Kenya," *Africa* [London], 43, No. 3, July 1973, 182–206.

Brokensha, David, and John Nellis. "Administration in Kenya: A Study of the Rural Division of Mbere," (Pt. 1.), *Journal of Administration Overseas*, 13, No. 4, October 1974, 510–23.

______. "Administration in Kenya: A Study of the Rural Division of Mbere," (Pt. 2.), *Journal of Administration Overseas*, 14, No. 1, January 1975, 17–29.

Bunger, Robert L. *Islamization among the Upper Pokomo*. (Eastern African Studies, No. 11.) Syracuse: Syracuse University Press, April 1973.

Campbell, David J., and George H. Axinn. *Pastoralism in Kenya*. (American Universities Field Staff. Fieldstaff Reports. Africa, No. 30.) Hanover, New Hampshire: AUFS, 1980.

Collier, Paul, and Deepak Lal. *Poverty and Growth in Kenya*. (World Bank Staff Working Paper, No. 389.) Washington: World Bank, May 1980.

Cowell, Alan. "A Fearful Reminder Lingers for Asians in Kenya," *New York Times*, September 1, 1982, 2.

"Debate over the Role of Kenya Asians," *Weekly Review* [Nairobi], November 12, 1982, 3–16.

Dow, Thomas E., Jr., and Linda H. Werner. "Continuity and Change in Metropolitan and Rural Attitudes Toward Family Size and Family Planning in Kenya Between 1966/1967 and 1977/1978." Nairobi: Population Studies and Research Institute, University of Nairobi, February 1981.

———. "A Note on Modern Transitional and Traditional Demographic and Contraceptive Patterns among Kenyan Women: 1977-1978." Nairobi: Population Studies and Research Institute, University of Nairobi, January 1981.

Edari, Ronald. "Social Distance and Social Change among Four Ethnic Groups in Mombasa." Pages 197–203 in John N. Paden (ed.), *Values, Identities and National Integration: Empirical Research in Africa*. Evanston: Northwestern University Press, 1980.

Edgerton, Robert B. *The Individual in Cultural Adaptation*. Berkeley and Los Angeles: University of California Press, 1971.

Elkan, Walter. "Is a Proletariat Emerging in Nairobi?" *Economic Development and Cultural Change*, 24, No. 4, July 1976, 695–706.

"End of the Road for Over Half Std. 7 Pupils," *Weekly Review* [Nairobi], January 8, 1982, 28–30.

Faruqee, Rashid, et al. *Kenya: Population and Development*. (A World Bank Country Study.) Washington: World Bank, 1980.

Glickman, Maurice. "Patriliny among the Gusii and the Luo of Kenya," *American Anthropologist*, 76, No. 2, June 1974, 312–18.

Goldsworthy, David. "Kenyan Politics since Kenyatta," *Australian Outlook* [Canberra], 36, No. 1, April 1982, 27-31.

Heine, Bernd, and Wilhelm J.G. Möhlig. *Language and Dialect Atlas of Kenya*, I. Berlin: Reimer, 1980.

Henin, R.A. *Recent Demographic Trends in Kenya and Their Implication for Economic and Social Development*. Nairobi: Population Studies and Research Institute, University of Nairobi, 1979.

Indire, Filomina. "Education in Kenya." Pages 115–39 in A. Babs Fufunwa and J.U. Aisiku (eds.), *Education in Africa: A Comparative Survey*. London: Allen and Unwin, 1982.

International Yearbook of Education, 32. Paris: United Nations Educational, Scientific and Cultural Organization, 1980.

Itebete, P.A.N. "Language Standardization in Western Kenya: The Luluyia Experiment." Pages 87–114 in W.H. Whiteley (ed.), *Language in Kenya*. Nairobi: Oxford University Press, 1974.

Joint Publications Research Service—JPRS (Washington). *Translations on Africa*. "Family Planning Battle Yet to be Won," *Daily Nation*, Nairobi, July 30, 1982. (JPRS 81626, No. 2680, August 25, 1982, 21-23.)

Kabwegyere, T., and J. Mbula. *A Case of the Akamba of Eastern Kenya*. (Changing African Family Project series, Monograph No. 5.) Canberra: Australian National University, 1979.

Kaplan, Irving, et al. *Area Handbook for Kenya*. (DA Pam 550–56.) Washington: GPO for Foreign Area Studies, The American University, 1976.

Karimi, Joseph, and Philip Ochieng. *The Kenyatta Succession*. Nairobi: TransAfrica, 1980.

Keller, Edmond J. "Harambee! Educational Policy, Inequality, and the Political Economy of Rural Community Self-Help in Kenya," *Journal of African Studies*, 4, No. 1, Spring 1977, 86–106.

Kenny, Michael G. "A Mirror in the Forest: The Dorobo Hunter-Gatherers as an Image of the Other," *Africa* [London], 51, No. 1, 1981, 477–95.

Kenya. *The Constitution of Kenya*. (rev. ed.) Nairobi: Government Printer, 1979.

______. *Development Plan, 1979–1983: Part 1*. Nairobi: Government Printer, 1979.

Kenya. Ministry of Economic Planning and Development. Central Bureau of Statistics. *Economic Survey, 1982*. Nairobi: Government Printer, June 1982.

______. *Statistical Abstract, 1981*. Nairobi: Government Printer, 1981.

"Kenya's Turkana: The Tribe That Lost Its Soul," *New African* [London], September 1981, 27.

Kenyatta, Jomo. *Facing Mount Kenya: The Traditional Life of the Gikuyu*. (African Writers series, No. 219.) London: Heinemann, 1979.

Kitching, Gavin. *Class and Economic Change in Kenya: The Making of an African Petite Bourgeoisie 1905–1970*. New Haven: Yale University Press, 1980.

______. "Modes of Production and Kenyan Dependency," *Review of African Political Economy* [London], No. 8, 1977, 56–73.

Langley, Myrtle S. *The Nandi of Kenya: Life Crisis Rituals in a Period of Change*. New York: St. Martin's Press, 1979.

LeVine, Robert A. "Witchcraft and Co-Wife Proximity in Southwestern Kenya," *Ethnology*, 1, No. 1, 1962, 39–45.

______. "Witchcraft and Sorcery in a Gusii Community." Pages 221–55 in J. Middleton and E. Winter (eds.), *Witchcraft and Sorcery in East Africa*. New York: Praeger, 1963.

LeVine, Robert A., and Barbara B. LeVine. "Nyansongo: A Gusii Community in Kenya." Pages 15–202 in B. Whiting (ed.), *Six Cultures*. New York: Wiley, 1963.

LeVine, Sarah. *Mothers and Wives: Gusii Women of East Africa*. Chicago: University of Chicago Press, 1979.

Leys, Colin. "Capital Accumulation, Class Formation, and Dependency: The Significance of the Kenyan Case." Pages 241–66 in Ralph Milliband and John Saville (eds.), *The Socialist Register, 1978*. London: Merlin Press, 1978.

Memon, P.A. "Kenya." Pages 59-89 in Harm de Blij and Esmond Martin (eds.), *African Perspectives: An Exchange of Essays on the Economic Geography of Nine African States*. New York: Methuen, 1981.

Mott, Frank L., and Susan H. Mott. *Kenya's Record Population Growth: A Dilemma of Development*. (Population Bulletin 35, No. 3.) Washington: Population Reference Bureau, 1980.

Myers, Norman. "Kenya's Baby Boom," *New Scientist* [London], 87, No. 1219, September 18, 1980, 848–50.

Njonjo, Apollo. "The Kenyan Peasantry: A Re-assessment," *Review of African Political Economy* [Sheffield, England], No. 20, January-March 1981, 27–40.

Nyong'o, P. Anyang'. "The Development of a Middle Peasantry in Nyanza," *Review of African Political Economy* [Sheffield, England], No. 20, April 1981, 108–21.

Ojany, Francis F., and Reuben B. Ogendo. *Kenya: A Study in Physical and Human Geography*. Nairobi: Longman, 1973.

Ominde, Simeon H. (ed.). *Studies in East African Geography and Development*. Berkeley and Los Angeles: University of California Press, 1971.

Parkin, David J. "Congregational and Interpersonal Ideologies in Political Ethnicity." Pages 119–57 in Abner Cohen (ed.), *Urban Ethnicity*. London: Tavistock, 1974.

———. *The Cultural Definition of Political Response: Lineal Destiny among the Luo*. New York: Academic Press, 1978.

———. "Language Shift and Ethnicity in Nairobi: The Speech Community of Kaloleni." Pages 167–88 in W.H. Whiteley (ed.), *Language in Kenya*. Nairobi: Oxford University Press, 1974.

———. "Language Switching in Nairobi." Pages 189–216 in W.H. Whiteley (ed.), *Language in Kenya*. Nairobi: Oxford University Press, 1974.

———. *Palms, Wine and Witnesses*. San Francisco: Chandler, 1972.

———"Status Factors in Language Adding: Bahati Housing Estate in Nairobi." Pages 147–66 in W.H. Whiteley (ed.), *Language in Kenya*. Nairobi: Oxford University Press, 1974.

"Runaway Baby Boom in Kenya," *Africa* [London], No. 120, August 1981, 108–109.

Salim, A.I. *The Swahili-speaking Peoples of Kenya's Coast, 1895-1965*. (Peoples of East Africa, No. 4.) Nairobi: East African Publishing House, 1973.

Saltman, Michael. *The Kipsigis: A Case Study in Changing Customary Law*. Cambridge: Schenkman, 1977.

Segal, Aaron. "Kenya: Africa's Odd Man In," *Current History*, 80, No. 463, March 1981, 106–10.

Soja, Edward W. *The Geography of Modernization in Kenya*. (Geographical Series, No. 2.) Syracuse: Syracuse University Press, 1968.

Southall, Aidan W. *Lineage Formation among the Luo*. (Memoranda of the International African Institute.) [London], No. 26, 1952.

Spear, Thomas. *Kenya's Past: An Introduction to Historical Method in Kenya*. London: Longman, 1981.

Spencer, Paul. *Nomads in Alliance*. London: Oxford University Press, 1973.

______. "Opposing Streams and the Gerontocratic Ladder: Two Models of Age Organisation in East Africa," *Man* [London], 2, No. 2, June 1976, 153–75.

______. *The Samburu*. London: Oxford University Press, 1964.

Stamp, Patricia. "Kenya's Year of Discontent," *Current History*, 82, No. 482, March 1983, 102–105.

______. "Kenya: The Echoing Footsteps," *Current History*, 81, No. 473, March 1982, 115–18.

Staudt, Kathleen. "Sex, Ethnic, and Class Consciousness in Western Kenya," *Comparative Politics*, 14, No. 2, January 1982, 149–67.

Swainson, Nicola. *The Development of Corporate Capitalism in Kenya, 1918–77*. Berkeley and Los Angeles: University of California Press, 1980.

______. "The Rise of a National Bourgeoisie in Kenya," *Review of African Political Economy* [London], No. 8, 1977, 39–55.

Tablino, Paolo. *I Gabbra del Kenya*. Bologna: EMI, 1980.

Tamarkin, M. "The Roots of Political Stability in Kenya." *African Affairs* [London], 77, No. 308, July 1978, 297–320.

Thedani, Veena. *Social Relations and Geographic Mobility: Male and Female Migration in Kenya*. (Center for Policy Studies Working Papers, No. 85.) New York: Population Council, June 1982.

Van Slambrouck, Paul. "Nation with the Fastest Growing Population Tries to Alter Parent Attitudes," *Christian Science Monitor*, April 19, 1983, 7.

Vitale, Anthony J. "Kisetla: Linguistic and Sociolinguistic Aspects of a Pidgin Swahili of Kenya," *Anthropological Linguistics*, 22, No. 2, February 1980, 47–65.

Whiteley, W.H. "The Classification and Distribution of Kenya's African Languages." Pages 13–68 in W.H. Whiteley (ed.), *Language in Kenya*. Nairobi: Oxford University Press, 1974.

Whiteley, W.H. (ed.). *Language in Kenya*. Nairobi: Oxford University Press, 1974.

Chapter 3

Arnold, Guy. *Modern Kenya*. Longman Group, 1981.
Avidor, Abraham. "Kenya's Farm Problems Retard Economic Growth," *Foreign Agriculture*, 19, No. 3, March 1981, 19–20.
Burrows, John. *Kenya: Into the Second Decade*. Baltimore: Johns Hopkins University Press for the World Bank, 1975.
Business International. *Kenya: Foreign Investment in a Developing Economy*. n. pl.: April 1980.
Campbell, David J., and George H. Axinn. *Pastoralism in Kenya*. (American Universities Field Staff. Fieldstaff Reports. Africa, No. 30.) Hanover, New Hampshire: AUFS, 1980.
Caplan, Basil. "Kenya's Pragmatism Pays Off," *Banker* [London], 129, No. 3, March 1979, 29–32.
Carroll, Jane. "Kenya Struggles for a Balanced Economy," *Euromoney* [London], May 1982, 169, 171.
Central Bank of Kenya. *Sources and Uses of Foreign Exchange in Kenya, 1974–1979*. Nairobi: Government Printer, 1981.
Clayton, Eric S. "Kenya's Agriculture and the I.L.O. Employment Mission—Six Years After," *Journal of Modern African Studies* [Cambridge], 16, No. 2, June 1978, 311–18.
Coldham, Simon F.R. "Land-Tenure Reform in Kenya: The Limits of Law," *Journal of Modern African Studies* [Cambridge], 17, No. 4, December 1979, 615–27.
Collier, Paul, and Deepak Lal. *Poverty and Growth in Kenya*. (World Bank Staff Working Paper, No. 389.) Washington: World Bank, May 1980.
Curry, Robert L., Jr. "The Global Economy's Impact on Planning in Kenya and Sudan," *Journal of African Studies*, 9, Summer 1982, 76–82.
East African Power and Lighting Company. *Directors' Report and Accounts, 1979*. Nairobi: 1980.
Food and Agriculture Organization. *FAO Production Yearbook, 1981*. 35. Rome: 1982.
———. *Tropical Forest Resources Assessment Project. Forest Resources of Tropical Africa: Part II, Country Briefs*. Rome: 1981.
"Geothermal Energy Sources Tapped," *Standard Chartered Review* [London], November 1982, 2–4.
Goldsworthy, David. "Kenyan Politics since Kenyatta," *Australian Outlook* [Canberra], 36, No. 1, April 1982, 27–31.
Harrison, Charles. "New Town Arises as River Is Tamed," *Times* [London], September 26, 1980, 11.
———. "Transport Takes to the Road," *African Business* [London], No. 19, March 1980, 55.
Hazlewood, Arthur. *The Economy of Kenya: The Kenyatta Era*. Oxford: Oxford University Press, 1979.

International Labour Office. *Employment, Incomes, and Equality: A Strategy for Increasing Productive Employment in Kenya*. Geneva: 1972.

Jansen, Eirik G. *The Fishing Population in the Kenyan Part of Lake Victoria*. Bergen, Norway: 1973.

Kabwegyere, T.B. "Small Urban Centres and the Growth of Underdevelopment in Rural Kenya," *Africa* [London], 49, No. 3, 1979, 308–15.

Kaniaru, Benson Kamau. "Economic Survey of Kenya: Hard Times Coming," *Development Forum Business Edition* [Geneva], No. 78, May 16, 1981, 1–2.

Kaplinsky, Raphael. "Foreign Capital, Employment, and Accumulation in Kenya," *Development and Change* [London], 12, No. 3, July 1981, 441–58.

Kaplinsky, Raphael (ed.). *Readings on the Multinational Corporation in Kenya*. Nairobi: Oxford University Press, 1978.

Kenya. *The Constitution of Kenya*. (rev. ed.) Nairobi: Government Printer, 1979.

______. *Development Plan, 1970–1974*. Nairobi: Government Printer, n. d.

______. *Development Plan, 1974–1978: Part I*. Nairobi: Government Printer, 1974.

______. *Development Plan, 1979–1983: Part I*. Nairobi: Government Printer, 1979.

______. *Development Plan, 1979–1983: Part II*. Nairobi: Government Printer, 1979.

Kenya. Ministry of Economic Planning and Community Affairs. Central Bureau of Statistics. *Statistical Abstract, 1979*. Nairobi: Government Printer, 1979.

Kenya. Ministry of Economic Planning and Development. Central Bureau of Statistics. *Economic Survey, 1981*. Nairobi: Government Printer, May 1981.

______. *Economic Survey, 1982*. Nairobi: Government Printer, June 1982.

______. *Statistical Abstract, 1980*. Nairobi: Government Printer, 1980.

______. *Statistical Abstract, 1981*. Nairobi: Government Printer, 1981.

______. *Statistical Abstract, 1982*. Nairobi: Government Printer, 1982.

Kenya. Ministry of Finance and Planning. Central Bureau of Statistics. *Economic Survey, 1976*. Nairobi: Government Printer, June 1976.

______. *Statistical Abstract, 1974*. Nairobi: Government Printer, 1974.

Kenya. National Assembly. *Sessional Paper No. 10 of 1963/65: African Socialism and Its Application to Planning in Kenya*. Nairobi: Government Printer, 1965.

______. *Sessional Paper No. 1 of 1968: A Forest Policy for Kenya*. Nairobi: Government Printer, 1968.

______. *Sessional Paper No. 8 of 1970: Co-operative Development Policy for Kenya*. Nairobi: Government Printer, September 1970.

———. *Sessional Paper No. 10 of 1973: On Employment*. Nairobi: Government Printer, May 1973.

———. *Sessional Paper No. 4 of 1975: On Economic Prospects and Policies*. Nairobi: Government Printer, 1975.

———. *Sessional Paper No. 14 of 1975: Co-operative Development Policy in Kenya*. Nairobi: Government Printer, September 1975.

———. *Sessional Paper No. 4 of 1980: On Economic Prospects and Policies*. Nairobi: Government Printer, 1980.

———. *Sessional Paper No. 4 of 1981: On National Food Policy*. Nairobi: Government Printer, 1981.

Kenya. National Irrigation Board. *Annual Report and Accounts, 1978–1979*. Nairobi: 1980.

Kenya. Tea Development Authority. *1979/1980 Annual Report and Accounts*. n. pl.: 1980.

"Kenya," *Financial Times* [London], March 22, 1982, 29–32 (Survey.).

"Kenya '82," *African Business* [London], No. 42, February 1982, 57–90.

"Kenya Focus," *Africa: An International Business, Economic and Political Monthly* [London], No. 100, December 1979, 87–119.

"Kenya Focus," *Africa: An International Business, Economic and Political Monthly* [London], No. 112, December 1980, 117–51.

"Kenyan Shilling," *International Currency Review* [London], 14, No. 5, November 1982, 132–35.

"Kenya Special," *Africa: An International Business, Economic and Political Monthly* [London], No. 119, July 1981, 95–122.

"Kenya Survey," *African Business* [London], No. 19, March 1980, 39–63.

"Kenya: The Agrarian Question," *Review of African Political Economy* [Sheffield], No. 20, January-April 1981 (entire issue.).

"Kenya: What Future?" *African Business* [London], No. 84, February 1983, 21-68.

Langdon, Steven W. *Multinational Corporations in the Political Economy of Kenya*. New York: St. Martin's Press, 1981.

Leo, Christopher. "The Failure of the 'Progressive Farmer' in Kenya's Million-Acre Settlement Scheme," *Journal of Modern African Studies* [Cambridge], 16, No. 4, December 1978, 619–38.

———. "Who Benefited From the Million-Acre Scheme? Toward a Class Analysis of Kenya's Transition to Independence," *Canadian Journal of African Studies* [Montreal], 15, No. 2, 1981, 201–22.

Low, Patrick. "Export Subsidies and Trade Policy: The Experience of Kenya," *World Development* [Oxford], 10, No. 4, April 1982, 293–304.

"Magadi Soda Co. Celebrates 70th Year," *Weekly Review* [Nairobi], November 13, 1981, 30–32.

Mbithi, Philip M., and Carolyn Barnes. *The Spontaneous Settlement Problem in Kenya*. Nairobi: East African Literature Bureau, 1975.

Mitchell Cotts Kenya. *Port Information: Mombasa*. Mombasa: 1977.

Morgan, W.T.W. *East Africa*. London: Longman, 1973.

Mosley, Paul. "Kenya in the 1970s: A Review Article," *African Affairs* [London], 81, No. 323, April 1982, 271–77.

Muller, Maria S. "The National Policy of Kenyanization of Trade; Its Impact on a Town in Kenya," *Canadian Journal of African Studies* [Montreal], 15, No. 2, 1981, 293–333.

Ojiambo, J.A. *The Trees of Kenya*. Nairobi: Kenya Literature Bureau, 1978.

Okidi, C. Odidi, and Sydney Westley. *Management of Coastal and Offshore Resources in Eastern Africa*. (Occasional paper, No. 28.) Nairobi: Institute for Development Studies, University of Nairobi, 1978.

Okoth-Ogendo, H.W.O. *The Adjudication Process and the Special Rural Development Programme*. (Discussion paper, No. 227.) Nairobi: Institute for Development Studies, University of Nairobi, January 1976.

"Recession Hits World Aviation Industry," *Weekly Review* [Nairobi], July 9, 1982, 38, 40.

Rempel, Henry, and William J. House. *The Kenya Employment Problem: An Analysis of the Modern Sector Labour Market*. Nairobi: Oxford University Press, 1975.

Richardson, Harry W. "An Urban Development Strategy for Kenya," *Journal of Developing Areas*, 15, No. 1, October 1980, 97–118.

Roberts, John E., et al. *Kenya: Rural Roads—Project Impact Evaluation No. 26*. n. pl.: United States Agency for International Development, January 1982.

Ross, Jay. "Kenya's Economic Slide Tests Viability of African Capitalism," *Washington Post*, July 27, 1981, A15.

Saha, Suranjit K. "Irrigation Planning in the Tana Basin of Kenya," *Water Supply and Management* [Oxford], 6, No. 3, 1982, 261–79.

"Sudan Road," *Times* [London], September 2, 1981, 10.

Swainson, Nicola. *The Development of Corporate Capitalism in Kenya, 1918–77*. Berkeley and Los Angeles: University of California Press, 1980.

Toksoz, Sadik. *An Accelerated Irrigation and Land Reclamation Program for Kenya: Dimension and Issues*. (Development discussion paper, No. 114.) Cambridge: Harvard Institute for International Development, Harvard University, March 1981.

United States. Agency for International Development. *Congressional Presentation, Fiscal Year 1984. Annex I: Africa*. Washington: n. d.

United States. Congress. 96th, 2d Session. House of Representatives. Committee on Foreign Affairs. *U.S. Economic Assistance to Zaïre, Kenya, and Zimbabwe*. (Report of staff study mission.) Washington: GPO, 1981.

United States. Department of Commerce. International Trade Administration. *Foreign Economic Trends and Their Implications for the United States: Kenya*. (FET 83-013.) Washington: GPO, February 1983.

———. *Marketing in Kenya*. (Overseas Business Reports, OBR 82-09.) Washington: GPO, May 1982.
United States. Department of Labor, Bureau of International Labor Affairs. *Country Labor Profile: Kenya*. Washington: GPO, 1980.
United States. Department of the Interior, Bureau of Mines. *The Mineral Industry of Kenya*. (Preprint from the 1981 Bureau of Mines *Minerals Yearbook*.) Washington: GPO, n. d.
Van Slambrouck, Paul. "As Wildlife Rebounds, Farmers Complain about Losses, Urge Hunting," *Christian Science Monitor*, May 3, 1983, 12–13.
de Veen, J.J. *The Rural Access Roads Programme: Appropriate Technology in Kenya*. Geneva: International Labour Office, 1980.
Williams, Simon. "New Approaches to Agriculture and Rural Development: The Mumias Sugar Company—Kenya," *Agribusiness Worldwide*, 3, June 1982, 50-53.
World Bank. *World Development Indicators*. Washington: May 1983.

(Various issues of the following publications were also used in the preparation of this chapter: *African Business* [London], September 1978–July 1983; *Africa Research Bulletin* (Economic, Financial, and Technical Series) [Exeter, England], January 1970-June 1983; Joint Publications Research Service, *Sub-Saharan Africa Report*, January 1982–April 1983; *Standard* [Nairobi], March 12, 1983-June 30, 1983; *Standard Chartered Review* [London], February 1982-June 1983; and *Weekly Review* [Nairobi], November 13, 1981-April 1, 1983.)

Chapter 4

Arnold, Guy. *Modern Kenya*. London: Longman Group, 1981.
Barkan, Joel D. (ed.), with John J. Okumu. *Politics and Public Policy in Kenya and Tanzania*. New York: Praeger, 1979.
Bhushan, Kul (ed.). *Kenya 1980–1981*. Nairobi: Newspread International, 1980.
Bienen, Henry. *Kenya: The Politics of Participation and Control*. Princeton: Princeton University Press, 1974.
Colebatch, H.K. *Government Services at the District Level in Kenya*. (Institute of Development Studies, Discussion Paper, No. 38.) Brighton, England: University of Sussex, 1974.
Conboy, Kevin. "Detention Without Trial in Kenya," *Georgia Journal of International and Comparative Law*, 8, Spring 1978, 441–61.
Gertzel, Cherry. *The Politics of Independent Kenya*. Evanston: Northwestern University Press, 1970.
Gicheru, H.B. Ndoria. *Parliamentary Practice in Kenya*. Nairobi: TransAfrica, 1976.
Goldsworthy, David. "Kenyan Politics since Kenyatta," *Australian Outlook* [Canberra], 36, No. 1, April 1982, 27–31.

Goodstein, Laurie. "Trouble in Kenya," *Index on Censorship*, 11, No. 4, August 1982 (back cover.).

Gupta, Vijay. *Kenya: Politics of (In) Dependence*. New Delhi: People's Publishing House, 1981.

Hodder-Williams, Richard. "Kenya after Kenyatta," *World Today* [London], 36, No. 12, December 1980, 476–83.

Hopkins, Raymond F. *The Kenyan Legislature: Political Functions and Citizen Perceptions*. Bloomington, Indiana: International Development Research Center, 1973.

Jackson, Tudor. *The Law of Kenya: An Introduction*. New York: Rowman and Littlefield, 1971.

Karimi, Joseph, and Philip Ochieng. *The Kenyatta Succession*. Nairobi: TransAfrica, 1980.

Kenya. *The Constitution of Kenya*. (rev. ed.) Nairobi: Government Printer, 1979.

______. *Development Plan, 1979–1983: Part I*. Nairobi: Government Printer, 1979.

"Kenya," *Financial Times* [London], June 9, 1979, 23–24 (Survey.).

"Kenya: A Special Report," *Guardian* [Manchester], June 8, 1981, 11–18.

Khapoya, Vincent B. "Kenya under Moi: Continuity or Change?" *Africa Today*, 27, No. 1, First Quarter 1980, 17–32.

______. "The Politics of Succession in Africa: Kenya after Kenyatta," *Africa Today*, 26, No. 3, Third Quarter 1979, 7–20.

Legum, Colin (ed.). *Africa Contemporary Record: Annual Survey and Documents, 1976–77*. New York: Africana, 1977.

______. *Africa Contemporary Record: Annual Survey and Documents, 1977–78*. New York: Africana, 1978.

______. *Africa Contemporary Record: Annual Survey and Documents, 1978–79*. New York: Africana, 1980.

______. *Africa Contemporary Record: Annual Survey and Documents, 1979–80*. New York: Africana, 1981.

______. *Africa Contemporary Record: Annual Survey and Documents, 1980–81*. New York: Africana, 1981.

Mans, Rowland. *Kenyatta's Middle Road in a Changing Africa*. (Conflict Studies, No. 85.) London: Institute for the Study of Conflict, July 1977.

Miller, Norman N. *East Africa's New Decade of Doubt: Part I: Kenya and Tanzania*. (American Universities Field Staff. Fieldstaff Reports. Africa, No. 9.) Hanover, New Hampshire: AUFS, 1980.

"Moi Versus the 'Network'," *New African* [London], No. 158, November 1980, 11–17.

Morgan, W.T.W. "Kenya." Pages 518-50 in *Africa South of the Sahara, 1980-81*. London: Europa, 1980.

Muriuki, Godfrey. "Central Kenya in the Nyayo Era," *Africa Today*, 26, No. 3, Third Quarter 1979, 39-42.

Ndege, William. "Kenya: Who is Who," *Africa, An International Business, Economic and Political Monthly* [London], 108, August 1980, 31–32.

———. "Politics of Confrontation," *Africa: An International Business, Economic and Political Monthly* [London], 131, July 1982, 10-19.

Pfeiffer, Steven B. "The Role of the Judiciary in the Constitutional Systems of East Africa," *Journal of Modern African Studies* [London], 16, No. 1, March 1978, 33–66.

Potholm, Christian P., and Richard A. Fredland (eds.). *Integration and Disintegration in East Africa*. Washington: University Press of America, 1980.

Segal, Aaron. "Kenya: Africa's Odd Man In," *Current History*, 80, No. 463, March 1981, 106–10.

Sevareid, Peter. "The Work of Rural Primary Courts in Ghana and Kenya," *African Law Studies*, No. 13, 1976, 145–54.

Stamp, Patricia. "Kenya's Year of Discontent," *Current History*, 82, No. 482, March 1983, 102–105.

———. "Kenya: The Echoing Footsteps," *Current History*, 81, No. 473, March 1982, 115–18.

Tamarkin, M. "From Kenyatta to Moi—The Anatomy of a Peaceful Transition of Power," *Africa Today*, 26, No. 3, Third Quarter 1979, 21–37.

———. "The Roots of Political Stability in Kenya," *African Affairs* [London], 77, No. 308, July 1978, 297–320.

Ungar, Sanford J. "Kenya: Without Kenyatta," *Atlantic*, 243, June 1979, 8–10.

United States. Agency for International Development. *Congressional Presentation, Fiscal Year 1984. Annex I: Africa*. Washington: n. d.

United States. Congress. 96th, 2d Session. House of Representatives. Committee on Foreign Affairs. *U.S. Economic Assistance to Zaïre, Kenya, and Zimbabwe*. (Report of staff study mission.) Washington: GPO, 1981.

United States. Congress. 97th, 1st Session. House of Representatives. Committee on Foreign Affairs. *U.S. Security Interests in the Persian Gulf*. (Report of staff study mission to the Persian Gulf, Middle East, and the Horn of Africa, October 21–November 13, 1980.) Washington: GPO, 1981.

United States. Congress. 97th, 1st Session. Senate. Committee on Foreign Relations. House of Representatives. Committee on Foreign Affairs. *Country Reports on Human Rights Practices*. (Report submitted by the Department of State.) Washington: GPO, February 1981.

United States. Congress. 97th, 2d Session. House of Representatives. Committee on Foreign Affairs. *Africa: Observations on the Impact of American Foreign Policy and Development Programs in Six African Countries*. (Report of congressional study mission to Zimbabwe, South Africa, Kenya, Somalia, Angola, and Nigeria, August 4–22, 1981.) Washington, GPO, 1982.

United States. Congress. 97th, 2d Session. House of Representatives. Committee on Foreign Affairs. Senate. Committee on Foreign Relations. *Country Reports on Human Rights Practices for 1981*. (Report submitted by the Department of State.) Washington: GPO, February 1982.

United States. Congress. 98th, 1st Session. Senate, Committee on Foreign Relations. House of Representatives. Committee on Foreign Affairs. *Country Reports on Human Rights Practices for 1982*. (Report submitted by the Department of State.) Washington: GPO, February 1983.

United States. Department of Commerce. International Trade Administration. *Marketing in Kenya*. (Overseas Business Reports, OBR 82-09.) Washington: GPO, May 1982.

United States. Department of State. Bureau of Public Affairs. *Background Notes: Kenya*. (Department of State publication, No. 8024.) Washington: GPO, September 1982.

______. *Horn of Africa*. (Statement by Deputy Assistant Secretary for African Affairs William C. Harrop, Current Policy series, No. 141.) Washington: 1980.

Werlin, Herbert H. *Governing an African City: A Study of Nairobi*. New York: Africana, 1974.

Wilcox, Dennis L. "Kenya." Pages 569–77 in George Thomas Kurian (ed.), *World Press Encyclopedia*. New York: Facts on File, 1982.

(Various issues of the following publications were also used in the preparation of this chapter: *Africa* [London], January 1977–May 1983; *Africa Research Bulletin* [Exeter, England], August 1978–June 1983; *Amnesty International Newsletter*, January 1982–June 1983; *Christian Science Monitor*, January 1979–June 1983; *Daily Nation* [Nairobi], October 1979–June 1983; *Economist* [London], January 1979-June 1983; *Financial Times* [London], January 1979–June 1983; Foreign Broadcast Information Service, *Daily Report: Middle East and Africa*, January 1983–June 1983; Joint Publications Research Service, *Sub-Saharan Africa Report*, October 1978–June 1983; *Keesing's Contemporary Archives* [London], 1978-1983; *New African* [London], January 1979–June 1983; *New York Times*, January 1979–June 1983; *Times* [London], January 1979-June 1983; *Washington Post*, January 1979–June 1983; and *Weekly Review* [Nairobi], November 1981–June 1983.)

Chapter 5

Arnold, Guy. *Modern Kenya*. London: Longman Group, 1981.

Attwood, William. *The Reds and the Blacks*. New York: Harper and Row, 1967.

Bienen, Henry. "African Militaries as Foreign Policy Actors," *International Security*, 5, No. 2, Fall 1980, 168–86.

______. *Armies and Parties in Africa*. New York, Africana, 1978.

———. *Kenya: The Politics of Participation and Control*. Princeton: Princeton University Press, 1974.

———. *The Military and Modernization*. Chicago: Aldine, 1971.

Clayton, Anthony. *Counter-Insurgency in Kenya*. Nairobi: TransAfrica, 1976.

Conboy, Kevin. "Detention Without Trial in Kenya," *Georgia Journal of International and Comparative Law*, 8, Spring 1978, 441–61.

Crocker, Chester A. "External Military Assistance in Sub-Saharan Africa," *Africa Today*, 15, No. 2, April–May 1968, 15–20.

———. "Military Dependence: The Colonial Legacy in Africa," *Journal of Modern African Studies* [London], 12, No. 2, June 1974, 265–86.

DeCalo, Samuel. *Coups and Army Rule in Africa: Studies in Military Style*. New Haven: Yale University Press, 1976.

Elkan, Walter. "Is a Proletariat Emerging in Nairobi?" *Economic Development and Cultural Change*, 24, No. 4, July 1976, 695–706.

Evans, Emmit B., Jr. "Education, Unemployment and Crime in Kenya," *Journal of Modern African Studies* [London], 8, No. 1, March 1975, 55–66.

First, Ruth. *Power in Africa*. New York: Pantheon Books, 1970.

Goldsworthy, David. "Kenyan Politics since Kenyatta," *Australian Outlook* [Canberra], 36, No. 1, April 1982, 27–31.

Gupta, Vijay. *Kenya: Politics of (In) Dependence*. New Delhi: People's Publishing House, 1981.

Gutteridge, William Frank. *The Military in African Politics*. New York: Barnes and Noble, 1969.

———. "Opportunism and Military Interventions in Black Africa," *East Africa Journal* [Nairobi], 9, No. 9, September 1972, 8–18.

Hewish, Mark, et al. *Air Forces of the World*. New York: Simon and Schuster, 1980.

Hodder-Williams, Richard. "Kenya after Kenyatta," *World Today* [London], 36, No. 12, December 1980, 476–83.

Jane's Fighting Ships, 1982–83.(Ed., John Moore.) New York: Jane's, 1982.

Kaplan, Irving, et al. *Area Handbook for Kenya*. (DA Pam 550-56.) Washington: GPO for Foreign Area Studies, The American University, 1976.

Karimi, Joseph, and Philip Ochieng. *The Kenyatta Succession*. Nairobi: TransAfrica, 1980.

Kenya. *Development Plan, 1979–1983: Part I*. Nairobi: Government Printer, 1979.

Kenya. Ministry of Economic Planning and Development. Central Bureau of Statistics. *Statistical Abstract, 1981*. Nairobi: Government Printer, 1981.

Kenya. Ministry of Finance and Planning. Central Bureau of Statistics. *Statistical Abstract, 1974*. Nairobi: 1974.

"Kenya," *Financial Times* [London], June 9, 1979, 23–24 (Survey.).

"Kenya Army Tightens Grip," *Africa Now* [London], September 1982, 14–15.

"Kenya: A Special Report," *Guardian* [Manchester], June 8, 1981, 11–18.

Kercher, Leonard C. *The Kenyan Penal System*. Washington: University Press of America, 1981.

Khapoya, Vincent B. "Kenya under Moi: Continuity or Change?" *Africa Today*, 27, No. 1, First Quarter 1980, 17–32.

______. "The Politics of Succession in Africa: Kenya after Kenyatta," *Africa Today*, 26, No. 3, Third Quarter 1979, 7–20.

Kibwana, J.R. "The Military Balance in East Africa: A Kenyan View," *Naval War College Review*, 30, Fall 1977, 97–101.

Lee, John M. *African Armies and Civil Order*. New York: Praeger for Institute for Strategic Studies, 1969.

Legum, Colin, and John Drysdale (eds.). *Africa Contemporary Record: Annual Survey and Documents, 1968–69*. London: Africa Research, 1969.

______. *Africa Contemporary Record: Annual Survey and Documents, 1969–70*. Exeter, England: Africa Research, 1970.

Legum, Colin (ed.). *Africa Contemporary Record: Annual Survey and Documents, 1970–71*. New York: Africana, 1971.

______. *Africa Contemporary Record: Annual Survey and Documents, 1971–72*. New York: Africana, 1972.

______. *Africa Contemporary Record: Annual Survey and Documents, 1972–73*. New York: Africana, 1973.

______. *Africa Contemporary Record: Annual Survey and Documents, 1973–74*. New York: Africana, 1974.

______. *Africa Contemporary Record: Annual Survey and Documents, 1974–75*, New York: Africana, 1975.

______. *Africa Contemporary Record: Annual Survey and Documents, 1975–76*. New York: Africana, 1976.

______. *Africa Contemporary Record: Annual Survey and Documents, 1976–77*. New York: Africana, 1977.

______. *Africa Contemporary Record: Annual Survey and Documents, 1977–78*. New York: Africana, 1978.

______. *Africa Contemporary Record: Annual Survey and Documents, 1978–79*. New York: Africana, 1980.

______. *Africa Contemporary Record: Annual Survey and Documents, 1979–80*. New York: Africana, 1981.

______. *Africa Contemporary Record: Annual Survey and Documents, 1980–81*. New York: Africana, 1981.

Leys, Colin. *Underdevelopment in Kenya*. London: 1975.

Mans, Rowland. *Kenyatta's Middle Road in a Changing Africa*. (Conflict Studies, No. 85.) London: Institute for the Study of Conflict, July 1977.

Matthews, L.L. "Kenya." Pages 402–403 in John Keegan (ed.), *World Armies*. New York: Facts on File, 1979.

Mazrui, Ali A. "The Resurrection of the Warrior Tradition in African Political Culture," *Journal of Modern African Studies* [London], 13, No. 1, 1975, 67–84.
Meisler, Stanley. "Tribal Politics Harass Kenya," *Foreign Affairs*, 49, No. 1, October 1970, 111–21.
Meister, Ulrich. "Precarious Stability in Kenya," *Swiss Review of World Affairs* [Zurich], 31, No. 6, September 1981, 25.
The Military Balance, 1971–72. London: International Institute for Strategic Studies, 1971.
The Military Balance, 1972–73. London: International Institute for Strategic Studies, 1972.
The Military Balance, 1973-74. London: International Institute for Strategic Studies, 1973.
The Military Balance, 1974-75. London: International Institute for Strategic Studies, 1974.
The Military Balance, 1975-76. London: International Institute for Strategic Studies, 1975.
The Military Balance, 1976-77. London: International Institute for Strategic Studies, 1976.
The Military Balance, 1977-78. London: International Institute for Strategic Studies, 1977.
The Military Balance, 1978-79. London: International Institute for Strategic Studies, 1978.
The Military Balance, 1979-80. London: International Institute for Strategic Studies, 1979.
The Military Balance, 1980-81. London: International Institute for Strategic Studies, 1980.
The Military Balance, 1981-82. London: International Institute for Strategic Studies, 1981.
The Military Balance, 1982-83. London: International Institute for Strategic Studies, 1982.
Miller, Norman N. *East Africa's New Decade of Doubt: Part I: Kenya and Tanzania*. (American Universities Field Staff. Fieldstaff Reports. Africa, No. 9.) Hanover, New Hampshire: AUFS, 1980.
"Moi Tightens His Grip," *Africa News*, December 13, 1982, 9–11.
"Moi Versus the 'Network'," *New African* [London], No. 158, November 1980, 11–17.
Morgan, W.T.W. "Kenya." Pages 518–50 in *Africa South of the Sahara, 1980–81*. London: Europa, 1980.
Mosley, Paul. "Kenya in the 1970s: A Review Article," *African Affairs* [London], 81, No. 323, April 1982, 271–77.
Moyse-Bartlett, Hubert. *The King's African Rifles*. Aldershot, England: 1956.
"The Mungai Affair," *New African* [London], No. 137, February 1979, 12–14.
Naipaul, Shiva. *North of South: An African Journey*. New York: Simon and Schuster, 1979.
Ndege, William. "After Kenyatta," *Africa*, 86, October 1978, 17–21.

______. "Politics of Confrontation," *Africa* [London], 131, July 1982, 10–19.
"Not an Ethnic Affair," *Africa Now*, September 1982, 16-19.
Odinga, Oginga. *Not Yet Uhuru*. New York: Hill and Wang, 1967.
Segal, Aaron. "Kenya: Africa's Odd Man In," *Current History*, 80, No. 463, March 1981, 106–10.
Stamp, Patricia. "Kenya's Year of Discontent," *Current History*, 82, No. 482, March 1983, 102–105.
______. "Kenya: The Echoing Footsteps," *Current History*, 81, No. 473, March 1982, 115–18.
Starke, Mike. "BATLSK's Band Calls the Tune," *Soldier* [London], March 1980, 30–33.
______"From Buckingham Palace to the Bush," *Soldier* [London], February 1980, 26–31.
Tamarkin, M. "From Kenyatta to Moi—The Anatomy of a Peaceful Transition of Power," *Africa Today*, 26, No. 3, Third Quarter 1979, 21–37.
______. "The Roots of Political Stability in Kenya," *African Affairs* [London], 77, No. 308, July 1978, 297–320.
Ungar, Sanford J. "Kenya: Without Kenyatta," *Atlantic*, 243, June 1979, 8-10.
United States. Arms Control and Disarmament Agency. *World Military Expenditures and Arms Transfers, 1971–80*. Washington: 1983.
United States. Congress. 95th, 2d Session. House of Representatives. Committee on International Relations. Senate. Committee on Foreign Relations. *Country Reports on Human Rights Practices*. (Report submitted by the Department of State.) Washington: GPO, February 1978.
United States. Congress. 96th, 1st Session. Senate. Committee on Foreign Relations. House of Representatives. Committee on Foreign Affairs. *Report on Human Rights Practices in Countries Receiving U.S. Aid*. (Report submitted by the Department of State.) Washington: GPO, February 1979.
United States. Congress. 96th, 2d Session. House of Representatives. Committee on Foreign Affairs. Senate. Committee on Foreign Relations. *Country Reports on Human Rights Practices for 1979*. (Report submitted by the Department of State.) Washington: GPO, February 1980.
United States. Congress. 97th, 1st Session. Senate. Committee on Foreign Relations. House of Representatives. Committee on Foreign Affairs. *Country Reports on Human Rights Practices*. (Report submitted by the Department of State.) Washington: GPO, February 1981.
United States. Congress. 97th, 2d Session. House of Representatives. Committee on Foreign Affairs. Senate. Committee on Foreign Relations. *Country Reports on Human Rights Practices for 1981*. (Report submitted by the Department of State.) Washington: GPO, February 1982.

United States. Congress. 98th, 1st Session. Senate. Committee on Foreign Relations. House of Representatives. Committee on Foreign Affairs. *Country Reports on Human Rights Practices for 1982*. (Report submitted by the Department of State.) Washington: GPO, February 1983.

United States. Department of Defense. Security Assistance Agency. *Foreign Military Sales, Foreign Military Construction Sales, and Military Assistance Facts*. Washington: September 1982.

Versi, Anver. "Kenya: The Anatomy of a Failed Coup," *New African* [London], No. 181, September 1982, 25–27.

Welch, Claude E. *Soldier and State in Africa: A Comparative Analysis of Military Intervention and Political Change*. Evanston: Northwestern University Press, 1970.

Various issues of the following publications were also used in the preparation of this chapter: *Africa* [London], January 1977–May 1983; *Africa Research Bulletin* [Exeter, England], January 1964-June 1983; *Afrique défense* [Paris], June 1978–June 1983; *Christian Science Monitor*, January 1979-June 1983; *Daily Nation* [Nairobi], October 1979-May 1983; *Economist* [London], January 1979-June 1983; *Financial Times* [London], January 1979-June 1983; Foreign Broadcast Information Service, *Daily Report: Middle East and Africa*, January 1983-June 1983; Joint Publications Research Service, *Sub-Saharan Africa Report*, October 1978-June 1979; *Keesing's Contemporary Archives* [London], 1978-1983; *New African* [London], January 1979-June 1983; *New York Times*, January 1979-June 1983; *Times* [London], January 1979-June 1983; *Washington Post*, January 1979-June 1983; and *Weekly Review* [Nairobi], November 1981-June 1983.)

Glossary

age-grade—A stage through which an age-set (*q.v.*) traditionally passes; the limited number of age-grades once common in Kenya included those of youth (the initiated), warrior (junior and senior), elder (junior and senior), and retired elder. As an age-set moved through the age-grades, the rights and responsibilities of its members changed, often abruptly, as did the behavior expected of them.

age-set—A group of persons of the same sex and approximately the same age having definite duties and privileges in common and constituting a social division within an ethnic group; the elaborate institution known as the age-set system once was an all-important element of traditional social structures.

Asian—Term used in Kenya for an East African resident of Indian or Pakistani origin. The term succeeded the word *Indian* in East African usage after the partition of India in 1947.

clan—A descent group (*q.v.*), the members of which are putatively descended from a common ancestor; often comprises several subclans, which in turn consist of lineages (*q.v.*), or the clan may comprise lineages and lack subclans.

descent group—A unit whose members have descended from a common ancestor (or are assumed to have done so). Most Kenyan ethnic groups are organized into a number of such entities, and the relations among them have been significant for political, social, and economic life. Membership in a Kenyan descent group—lineage (*q.v.*) or clan (*q.v.*)—occurs by virtue of descent from a common male ancestor through males, i.e., both males and females are members of patrilineal descent groups.

European—Standard Kenyan term applied to whites regardless of their country of origin.

extended family—A kin group consisting of two or more related nuclear families (*q.v.*); for example, a man, his wife or wives, his unmarried children, his married sons, and their wives and children.

fiscal year (FY)—An annual period established for accounting purposes. The Kenyan fiscal year extends from July 1 through the following June 30; July 1, 1983, through June 30, 1984, is expressed as FY 1983/84.

gross domestic product (GDP)—The total value of goods and services produced within a country's borders during a fixed period, usually one year. Obtained by adding the value contributed by each sector of the economy in the form of compensation of employees, profits, and depreciation (consumption of capital). Subsistence production is included and consists of the imputed value of production by the farm family for its own use and the imputed rental value of owner-occupied dwellings.

gross national product (GNP)—GDP (*q.v.*) plus the income received from abroad by residents, less payments remitted abroad to non-residents.

harambee—Swahili word (pronounced hah-rahm-BAY) derived from a term used by a group of Africans engaged in heavy labor and meaning "let us all pull together." Motto of Kenya inscribed on its coat of arms and widely used by former president Jomo Kenyatta as a call to cooperation in building the nation. Schools and other projects cooperatively constructed by Kenyan communities are often referred to as *harambee* schools.

International Monetary Fund (IMF)—Established along with the World Bank (*q.v.*) in 1945, the IMF is a specialized agency affiliated with the United Nations and is responsible for stabilizing international exchange rates and payments. The main business of the IMF is the provision of loans to its members (including industrialized and developing countries) when they experience balance of payments difficulties. These loans frequently carry conditions that require substantial internal economic adjustments by the recipients, most of which are developing countries. In 1983 the IMF had 146 members.

Kenyanization—A term used by the Kenyan government and others to refer to the process whereby positions in government and in the economy are to be filled by Kenyan citizens, particularly Africans, rather than by noncitizens and expatriates.

Kenya pound (K£)—A monetary denomination often used in economic and financial data despite its absence in the Kenyan currency system; K£1 is equivalent to 20 Kenya shillings (*q.v.*).

Kenya shilling (KSh)—National currency unit since September 14, 1966, when it replaced the East African shilling, the common currency of Kenya, Tanganyika, and Uganda from 1920 to mid-1966. The Kenya shilling is a decimal currency consisting of 100 cents. Until June 30, 1973, the exchange rate was maintained at KSh7.14 to US$1 (KSh1 equaled US$0.14). Later in 1973 the Kenya shilling was revaluated, and KSh6.90 equaled US$1; the earlier rate was restored in January 1974. In October 1975 the Kenya shilling was pegged to the IMF's (*q.v.*) special drawing right (SDR), resulting in a new rate of KSh8.16 to US$1. Subsequently, the shilling appreciated along with the SDR against the dollar, and at the end of 1980 the rate was KSh7.57 to US$1. After two devaluations of the shilling during 1981, the rate at the end of the year had declined to KSh10.29 to US$1. Further devaluation resulted in the shilling's depreciation, and KSh12.73 equaled US$1 in December 1982. The decline continued, and on March 31, 1983, KSh13.06 equaled US$1.

Kenyatta "family"—An inner circle of presidential confidants and advisers during the Kenyatta era, drawn primarily from the Kiambu branch of the Kikuyu political element. Included were actual relatives, by blood or marriage, as well as political cronies and wealthy businessmen.

lineage—A descent group (*q.v.*), the members of which can, in principle, trace their descent from a common ancestor; lineages of great generational depth may include lineages of lesser depth. In Kenya, lineages of lesser depth, i.e., composed of persons descended from a common grandfather or great-grandfather, are more likely to be active in social and economic matters than lineages of greater depth.

mzee—Swahili word (pronounced muh-ZAY) translated as old man or elder; in the latter sense, a reference to respected status; as such, given to Kenyatta as a title.

Nonaligned Movement—A grouping of countries that have deliberately chosen not to be associated politically or militarily with either the West or the communist states. Member countries are expected to pursue independent foreign policies, support national liberation movements, and refrain from participating in multilateral or bilateral military alliances with the major powers. The movement's seventh summit meeting, held in New Delhi in March 1983, was attended by 97 nations.

nuclear family—A husband, his wife, and their unmarried children.

nyayo—Swahili word meaning footprints or footsteps; adopted as a slogan by President Daniel arap Moi to indicate his intention to follow in Kenyatta's footsteps after assuming the presidency in 1978; term has subsequently developed a wider connotation of personal loyalty to Moi and his policies of "peace, love, and unity."

parastatal—An autonomous, government-owned enterprise.

shifta—A term meaning bandit, applied by the Kenyan government to the Somali dissidents who sought to break away from Kenya and join Somalia in the mid- and late 1960s.

wananchi—Swahili word meaning children of the soil; widely used to signify ordinary citizens as distinguished from the wealthy and powerful members of the society.

World Bank—Informal name used to designate a group of three affiliated international institutions: the International Bank for Reconstruction and Development (IBRD), the International Development Association (IDA), and the International Finance Corporation (IFC). The IBRD, established in 1945, has the primary purpose of providing loans to developing countries for productive projects. The IDA, a legally separate loan fund but administered by the staff of the IBRD, was set up in 1960 to furnish credits to the poorest developing countries on much easier terms than those of conventional IBRD loans. The IFC, founded in 1956, supplements the activities of the IBRD through loans and assistance designed specifically to encourage the growth of productive private enterprises in the less developed countries. The president and certain senior officers of the IBRD hold the same positions in the IFC. The three institutions are owned by the governments of the countries that subscribe their capital. In 1983 the IBRD had over 140 members, the IDA had 130, and the IFC over 120. To participate in the World Bank group, member states must first belong to the International Monetary Fund (IMF—*q.v.*).

Index

PUBLISHED COUNTRY STUDIES

(Area Handbook Series)

550-65 Afghanistan
550-98 Albania
550-44 Algeria
550-59 Angola
550-73 Argentina

550-169 Australia
550-176 Austria
550-175 Bangladesh
550-170 Belgium
550-66 Bolivia

550-20 Brazil
550-168 Bulgaria
550-61 Burma
550-83 Burundi
550-50 Cambodia

550-166 Cameroon
550-159 Chad
550-77 Chile
550-60 China
550-63 China, Republic of

550-26 Colombia
550-91 Congo
550-90 Costa Rica
550-152 Cuba
550-22 Cyprus

550-158 Czechoslovakia
550-54 Dominican Republic
550-52 Ecuador
550-43 Egypt
550-150 El Salvador

550-28 Ethiopia
550-167 Finland
550-155 Germany, East
550-173 Germany, Federal Republic of
550-153 Ghana

550-87 Greece
550-78 Guatemala
550-174 Guinea
550-82 Guyana
550-164 Haiti

550-151 Honduras
550-165 Hungary
550-21 India
550-154 Indian Ocean
550-39 Indonesia

550-68 Iran
550-31 Iraq
550-25 Israel
550-182 Italy
550-69 Ivory Coast

550-177 Jamaica
550-30 Japan
550-34 Jordan
550-56 Kenya
550-81 Korea, North

550-41 Korea, South
550-58 Laos
550-24 Lebanon
550-38 Liberia
550-85 Libya

550-172 Malawi
550-45 Malaysia
550-161 Mauritania
550-79 Mexico
550-76 Mongolia

550-49 Morocco
550-64 Mozambique
550-35 Nepal, Bhutan and Sikkim
550-88 Nicaragua
550-157 Nigeria

550-94 Oceania
550-48 Pakistan
550-46 Panama
550-156 Paraguay
550-185 Persian Gulf States

550-42 Peru
550-72 Philippines
550-162 Poland
550-181 Portugal
550-160 Romania

550-84	Rwanda
550-51	Saudi Arabia
550-70	Senegal
550-180	Sierra Leone
550-184	Singapore
550-86	Somalia
550-93	South Africa
550-95	Soviet Union
550-179	Spain
550-96	Sri Lanka (Ceylon)
550-27	Sudan
550-47	Syria
550-62	Tanzania
550-53	Thailand
550-178	Trinidad and Tobago
550-89	Tunisia
550-80	Turkey
550-74	Uganda
550-97	Uruguay
550-71	Venezuela
550-57	Vietnam, North
550-55	Vietnam, South
550-183	Yemens, The
550-99	Yugoslavia
550-67	Zaire
550-75	Zambia
550-171	Zimbabwe

☆ U.S. GOVERNMENT PRINTING OFFICE : 1984 O - 447-887